The Old-House Journal

Restoration Manual No. 10

The 1985 Yearbook

Copyright © 1986 by The Old-House Journal Corporation, 69A Seventh Avenue, Brooklyn, NY 11217

This **Old-House Journal Yearbook** is a one-volume compilation of all the editorial pages printed in The Old-House Journal in 1985.

One-year subscriptions to The Old-House Journal are available for $18. Mail your check or money order to The Old-House Journal, Subscriptions, 69A Seventh Avenue, Brooklyn, NY 11217.

Contents

Restoration Vs. Renovation

An old house brings with it some responsibilities along with its joys. A house that has survived the ravages of years and previous owners is now part of our cultural history. The following guidelines are offered for the consideration of those who have just bought — or are about to buy — an old house.

First of all, you have to be clear on your purpose — do you intend to restore your house, or do you only want to renovate it? A restoration involves putting the house back into a state that resembles its condition in an earlier period. Renovation means just putting the house back into sound mechanical condition without regard to any particular style. Restoration vs. renovation is a basic design decision.

Whichever course you select, there's one rule to keep in mind: Don't destroy detail. Removal of architectural detail should be regarded as a cultural high crime. Detail represents labor and craftsmanship which, because of today's economics, is an irreplaceable resource. Detail, both interior and exterior, is what distinguishes most old houses from the cardboard boxes of modern builders. By preserving detail, you are not only conserving a cultural resource, but also insuring the long-term market value of the house. The restoration of damaged or neglected detail is well within the capabilities of most home craftspersons; the basic ingredients are time and patience.

Don't do anything that can't be undone. Nothing lasts forever — everything you do to a house today will have to be re-done by somebody (maybe you) at a later date. So each project should be undertaken with the idea, "How can this be renewed in the future?"

Be wary of period changes. There's no way to transform a big old Victorian into a cute little colonial. Learn as much as you can about the period in which your house was built, and then try to keep your modifications consistent with the concept of the builders.

Old houses are a fragile resource. They're a responsibility and a commitment — and a considerable amount of work. They're also one of the greatest sources of pride and satisfaction a homeowner can experience.

The Editors

Restoration and Maintenance Techniques
For The Pre-1939 House

Jan.-Feb. 1985 / Vol. XIII No. 1 / $2.

The Old-House Journal

Stripping Exterior Masonry

by Patricia Poore

ONE DAY, the phone rings and it's a reader asking how to get the clinging, flaking remnants of old white paint off his red brick. There's no easy answer. Another phone call, another day. This time somebody wants to know how to get the romantic, old-fashioned look of clinging, flaking remnants of white paint on red brick, without waiting a hundred years for paint to weather. There's no easy answer.

I THINK the first caller should let time do the job. I understand love of the pristine, the need to "finish" the job. But for one thing, I sympathize with the second caller. I enjoy the imperfection of old things. For another, I've become aware of how downright practical it is to do nothing if you can get away with it. Making things new again is expensive and awful mistakes are made in the name of restoration.

TO GET BACK to exterior stripping: This article will help you decide whether you have to or really want to, and tell you how to do it right if you must.

cont'd on p. 26

In the next issue. . .
STANDING SEAM ROOFS

Annie's Tea Room and B&B in Big Sandy, Texas — one of the many B&Bs operated by OHJ subscribers.

Tell Us About Your Favorite Inn

We're Compiling A Unique Inns Guide For Old-House Lovers.
And We Need Your Help.

THE BEST WAY to see old houses, we think, is from a bicycle saddle. And after a hard day of riding, our reward is to check into an old inn or bed-and-breakfast guest house. Invariably, these establishments are run by folks who've fallen in love with the old places--and who are delighted to entertain like-minded guests.

OUR FAVORITE is Mountain House. A stone's throw from the Appalachian Trail, it is a survival from the days when Victorian city dwellers fled to the mountains to escape summer heat. Time has pretty much passed by Mountain House. The bathtub is down the hall, and the oak and wicker furniture might be called Spartan. But oh how we love to be there! On summer nights, we'll sit in rocking chairs on the century-old porch with owners Frank and Yolanda Brown, as the cool night air comes tumbling down the mountain.

MOUNTAIN HOUSE doesn't turn up in most B&B books (not yet, anyway). But you can be sure it will be in our special new Inns Guide.

THERE HAVE to be lots of other secret places...places whose reputations are local. We want to include them. But we need your help. We've already found a few thousand old inns and guest houses. Most of them are showcase restorations, or are located in well-known resort towns. To find guest houses off the beaten path, we need testimonials from you.

PLEASE LET US KNOW about your favorite right away. It may be big or small, built in 1760 or 1920. Your only criterion for submitting should be, "Would I recommend this place to other Old-House Journal readers?"

OF COURSE, if you run an inn or bed-and-breakfast yourself, and you'd welcome other OHJ subscribers, we especially want to hear from you! (We've found that many B&B proprietors are OHJ readers.)

HERE'S WHAT we need to know:
(1) Name of inn or guest house;
(2) Complete address; (3) Owner's name (if you have it); (4) Most important, what you think is special about it.

WE'LL FOLLOW UP with a detailed questionnaire to the owner. Send your nominations to: Tricia Martin, OHJ, 69A Seventh Avenue, Brooklyn, NY 11217.

ALL OF US at OHJ look forward to owning copies of the new Guide ourselves -- and to sharing it with you!

— Patricia Poore & Clem Labine

The Old-House Journal®

Editor
Patricia Poore

Production Editor
Cole Gagne

Technical Editor
Larry Jones

Assistant Editor
Sarah J. McNamara

Contributing Editors
Walter Jowers
John Mark Garrison
Roland A. Labine Sr.

Architectural Consultant
Jonathan Poore

Circulation Supervisor
Barbara Bugg

Circulation Assistants
Jeanne Baldwin
Garth White

Special Sales
Joan O'Reilly

Assistant to the Publisher
Tricia A. Martin

Catalog Editor
Sarah J. McNamara

Publishing Consultant
Paul T. McLoughlin

Publisher
Clem Labine

Published by The Old-House Journal Corporation, 69A Seventh Avenue, Brooklyn, NY 11217. Telephone (718) 636-4514. Subscriptions $18 per year in U.S., $25 per year in Canada (payable in U.S. funds). Published ten times per year. Contents are fully protected by copyright and must not be reproduced in any manner whatsoever without specific permission in writing from the Editor.

We are happy to accept editorial contributions to The Old-House Journal. Query letters that include an outline of the proposed article are preferred. All manuscripts will be reviewed, and returned if unacceptable. However, we cannot be responsible for non-receipt or loss — please keep copies of all materials sent.

Printed at Photo Comp Press, New York City

ISSN: 0094-0178
NO PAID ADVERTISING

A Philadelphia Stencil Story

by Esther Wideman

WHEN WE FIRST MOVED to Philadelphia in 1969, we bought a house that had been divided into five apartments, then de-converted to a one-family house in the 1950s. We kept up the roof, worked in the garden, and painted the exterior to keep the wood from rotting. That was the extent of our interest in old houses. But, after getting acquainted with The Old-House Journal and reading about how others had restored old homes to their original splendor, we began to think about restoring our home.

IT ALL STARTED with the bathroom on the second floor. Over the course of two years, we took out the shower, installed a 6-foot bathtub, refinished the pine panelling, and added a marble sink to the room. It was quite beautiful and successful. But by the time we had finished we decided to sell this house and buy another one -- one with more original details that we could bring back to life.

WE SUCCESSFULLY BID for a corner house just two blocks away, here on Woodland Terrace. It is one of a set of twelve Italianate twins built in 1861. These buildings share a common wall and are mirror images of one another. Corner houses -- ours is the last one left in this group -- have grand porches. We didn't realize what a treasure we had until the family we purchased the house from turned over all the original documents,

The Wideman's home as it appeared in 1910.

including deeds and records of sales. Before they had moved in, the house had been occupied by a single family for over 50 years. Before that, during the 19th century, another family had occupied it for 50 years. We were only the fourth owners!

THE HOUSE WAS VERY DIRTY and dilapidated, but it had large rooms and lots of potential. Of course, we started with the major work -- new heating system (gas, hot water), new kitchen, floor sanding, and new plumbing and electricity. The house had once been lit with gas, but when we bought it, the dining room, kitchen, middle parlor, and the bedrooms were lit only by bare light bulbs. Over time, we replaced all the bulbs with gas chandeliers adapted for electricity. We were able to buy one large fixture from a neighboring house of the same period, and another from the French Embassy in Philadelphia.

BECAUSE THE HOUSE has two parlors, we decided to turn one into a music room that would accommodate my pipe organ and grand piano. We began by scraping off the layers of old wallpaper. Surprisingly enough, the walls had never been painted! Underneath the paper, the original stencil-ling, well over a hundred years old, was still visible! Although the stencilling was faded and scarred, the design and color sheme of the original frieze was still visible, enabling us to reproduce it.

Top left: Though faded, the frieze was visible enough to be copied. To the left is the outline of the original mirror. The Widemans were able to replace it with one that fit the outline perfectly. *Top right:* The stencil was traced, then cut from a sheet of Mylar. *Bottom left:* Esther puts the finishing touches on the painted ceiling medallion in the music room. The room is large enough to accommodate her grand piano, harpsichord, and 12-foot-tall pipe organ.

Above: The finished ceiling medallion. Esther, who opened an antique shop not long after she and her husband bought the house, has decorated the Italianate twin with period furnishings.

I T TOOK ME SEVERAL YEARS to decide to tackle the job, but after I studied several stencilling books and practiced on the back stairway and the hallway to the third floor, I felt competent enough to go to work on the music room. Although the original frieze had been painted in two shades of green, we decided to repaint it in shades of blue. To preserve the original stencil and colors for future owners, we dated a portion of the frieze and papered over it.

BY TRACING THE DESIGN and then cutting it out of a sheet of Mylar, I was able to reproduce the music room frieze. Once the frieze was completed, I decided to supplement the wall decoration with a ceiling medallion I designed from a combination of 15 different Victorian stencils adapted from the stencilling books I had read.

I PLANNED ONLY the central portion. I enlarged a classical-style motif resembling a plaster ceiling medallion and painted it in shades of brown. But by the time I completed this, I realized it was too small for the room. I enlarged it and tied in the blue from the frieze with a leaf motif. The small circular tile patterns were inspired by encaustic tiles from an entryway of another old house. The tracery patterns, my own design, were added to enlarge the medallion even further. In the end we had over an 80-inch spread across the center of the ceiling -- much more in scale with a 23-foot room than the medallion we had originally planned on!

Above: The stencilling in the entryway was reproduced from ghosts found under old wallpaper. *Right:* These two photographs, taken in 1922, show the gallery and iris garden that were once located off the middle parlor.

OF ALL THE FORMAL ROOMS, only the middle parlor had its original mirror. We looked for several years for a suitable mirror for the music room before finding one. Jim had to refinish the frame and buy new mirror glass for it, but it perfectly fit the lines of old paint left around the original mirror. Other interesting features in the parlor include an old pressed-tin ceiling, possibly installed in the late 1880s along with the Lincrusta wainscot in the hallway, which continues all the way to the third floor. The middle parlor also contains the only working fireplace.

ORIGINALLY, the front parlor and all the bedrooms above were centrally heated, through vents in the fireplace, by a coal furnace in the basement. All the mantels in this side of the house are different. The main parlor mantel is made of white marble. The bedroom above the parlor has a painted wooden mantel with an inset mirror. The bedroom above that on the third floor has an Eastlake mantel with inset mirrors and two beautiful tiles showing children at play. This room must have been a nursery. The other parts of the house were heated with coal stoves. The vents for these stoves are still in the fireplace walls.

NOW, RESTORING the finishing touches has become our main interest. We were recently able to buy a documented bedroom and dining room set made by Schindler, Roller and Company in 1869. This furniture was made for Andrew Campbell in Brooklyn, New York, and came to Philadelphia through his granddaughter, who lived in our neighborhood for many years. I had collected marble sinks, tiles, and tubs for several years (I opened a small antique shop around the same time we bought the house), so we now have two finished bathrooms with antique marble washstand sinks, one with a painted bowl. I found a carved cherry armoire with a marble sink in it and had our carpenter install it on a long wall in the dining room with shelving for storage. Although it's not original to the house, it's just the kind of thing that might have stood there originally.

FOR US, THE HIGH POINT came when our house was shown in the Philadelphia Inquirer magazine section last year. The color photograph showing the two of us relaxed in the music room reflects very little of what our lives have really been like the past few years! Now we don't just "keep up" with the roof or the outside paint job -- the house is a major part of our lives. We still have work to do -- Jim is currently restoring the original standing-seam metal roof with the help of a local roofer -- but we have begun to enjoy having guests for the first time since we bought it six years ago. The house was seen by over 500 people during the Philadelphia Open House last year, and we recently entertained the Philadelphia Chapter of the Victorian Society in America at a musicale. These events, and others that I hope to plan, are my dream come true for this old house.

Jim and Esther Wideman on the porch of their 1861 Italianate villa.

My Old-House Discovery: The Screw Gun

by Jonathan Poore

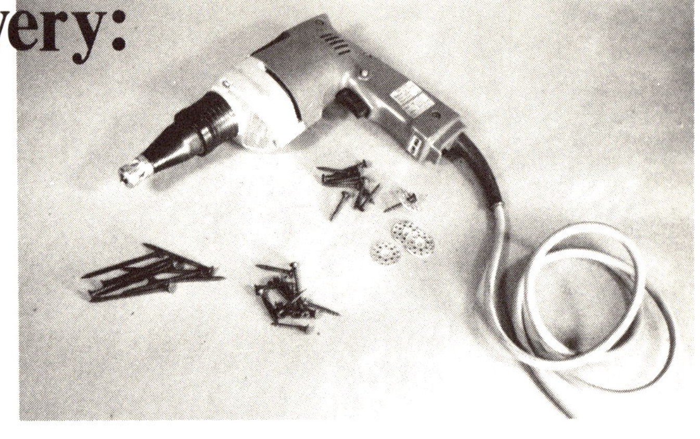

HAVE YOU EVER tried to nail a Sheetrock patch into a hole in an old plaster ceiling? Even if you've neatly cut back the loose plaster to the nearest joist, you end up with a face full of plaster dust and debris, because the hammering causes the surrounding plaster to crack, crumble, and fall. By the time you get the Sheetrock patch secured, you have a bigger hole than before, and the debris caught behind the Sheetrock keeps it from laying flat.

THE SOLUTION to this problem, I've recently discovered, is to use a screw gun. What a find! Contractors take this tool for granted, but a lot of homeowners haven't even heard of it. Some people assume it's like a nail gun, but the two tools are totally different. A nail gun literally shoots nails, and so can be very dangerous in an occupied building or in the hands of someone who doesn't know what he or she's doing; a screw gun drives screws in a completely safe and controlled manner.

BASICALLY, a screw gun is an electric-powered screwdriver. It resembles a common variable-speed electric drill, except for one important difference. At the business end of a screw gun, where the chuck for the drill bit would be, there's a magnetic screwdriver bit surrounded by a little sleeve. By adjusting the sleeve in or out, you control the depth to which the screw is driven. This screw bit turns only when pressure is applied to it. When the screw has been driven in the desired distance, the sleeve bottoms out, releasing the pressure on the bit. This allows the motor to spin free without driving in the screw any further.

BESIDES CONTROLLING the depth to which the screw is driven, the clutch mechanism spares the motor from being forced to a grinding halt whenever a screw has reached its proper depth. Because it can spin free, the screw gun motor isn't continually stalling, which would cause it to burn out prematurely. So even though it's possible to use an electric drill as a screw gun, you'd be letting yourself in for a lot of problems: You'd have to control depth by eye, and the continual stalling would be bad for the motor.

THERE'S YET ANOTHER advantage to a screw gun: It's reversible, so you can take the screw back out just as quickly and easily as it was put in.

SCREW GUNS were designed as a contractor's tool, intended for fastening Sheetrock to metal or wood studs. The depth adjustment allows the screw to countersink itself just barely below the surface of the Sheetrock without breaking the paper. The screw gun can rapidly and consistently drive many screws to the same depth without breaking through the paper face. And because its magnetic tip holds the screw in place, you can operate a screw gun with one hand. When you add

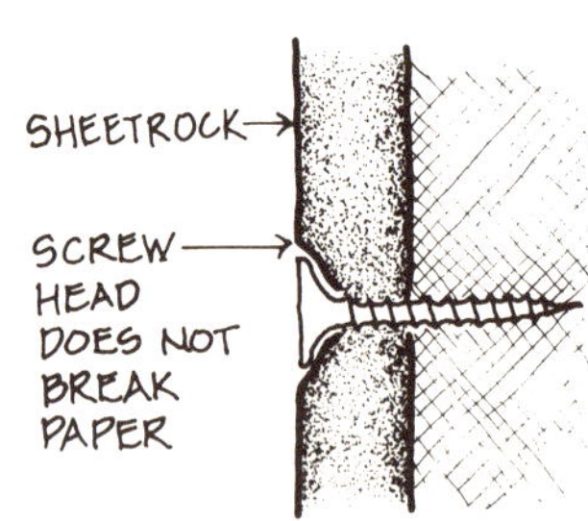

to its speed and convenience the fact that there's no hammer impact to jar or damage fragile plaster or woodwork, a screw gun becomes a real asset in working on an old house.

IT'S IMPOSSIBLE to name all the old-house applications of a screw gun, but here are just a few:

1) PLASTER TO WOOD LATH
Used in conjunction with plaster washers and Sheetrock-to-Sheetrock screws, a screw gun can refasten plaster that has separated from its wood lath. (The coarse threads of these screws hold very well, even to wood lath.)

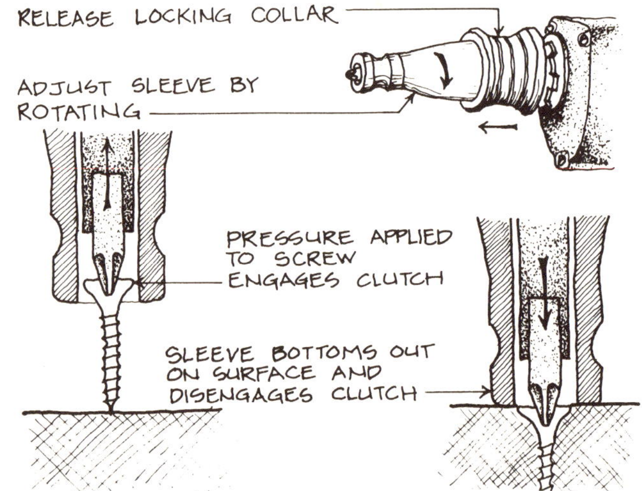

2) PLASTER AND WOOD LATH TO JOISTS OR STUDS
Plaster washers and slightly longer screws (generally available with conventional threads

only) can be used to rescue plaster and lath assemblies that have separated from joists or studs.

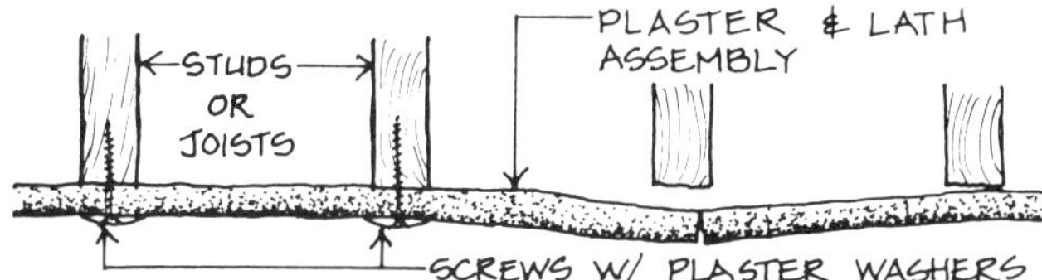

3) SHEETROCK PATCHES

The screw gun can be used with conventional Sheetrock screws to fasten Sheetrock patches. The surrounding (existing) plaster can be secured first, using the methods described above. The Sheetrock patch can then be fastened with the screw gun. There are several major advantages to using a screw gun for this process:

● No hammering is involved.
● You can fasten the Sheetrock to the lath in areas where there is no stud or joist.

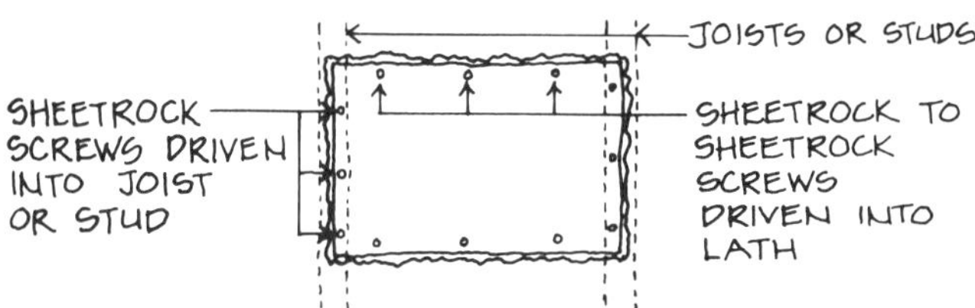

● If you misalign the level of the patch with the adjacent plaster, the screw can be backed out instantly, so the patch can be shimmed or trimmed to make it align properly. If the patch had been nailed in place, you'd have to tear out the Sheetrock (destroying it in the process) and start over.
● A screw gun enables you to do a major Sheetrock patching job quickly; the more extensive the work, the faster the screw gun pays for itself in time saved. It doesn't pay to buy a screw gun to put in one Sheetrock patch, but if you're rescuing plaster and installing Sheetrock patches in several rooms, a screw gun is a sensible investment.

4) FURRING OR LAMINATING OVER CRUMBLING PLASTER

Occasionally you may have to cover over a badly deteriorated plaster surface by installing Sheetrock, stamped metal ceiling panels, or the like. (It's usually better to remove the existing plaster first, but that can be a very messy demolition job.) Whether the new materials are to be applied over furring or laminated directly to the plaster, a screw gun is essential. It can fasten furring without causing the plaster to crumble any further. If Sheetrock is being installed, the screw gun makes for a fast, neat job, because the plaster won't be disturbed by any hammering. (A metal ceiling must be nailed to the furring, but the nails are so small they don't require heavy pounding to drive them.)

5) REPAIR OF OLD BUILT-IN-PLACE CABINETWORK

Built-in cabinets in old houses were most often actually built in place rather than fabricated somewhere else. This makes them subject to the movement and deterioration of the surrounding plaster and lath. Repairing an old cabinet with hammer and nails can often

knock the cabinet apart even more, as well as damage the surrounding plaster. Screws will hold much better than nails anyway, and a screw gun can make internal repairs in the cabinet and also resecure it to the wall. (Hardwoods often need to be pre-drilled to avoid splitting, but that's often the case with nailing as well.) Slender finishing screws with small heads can be used in areas which might show.

6) MISCELLANEOUS NEW WORK

A screw gun is good for installing nailers for new shelving and cabinetwork on existing plaster. It's also excellent, both for speed and strength, when assembling plywood cabinetry, such as kitchen cabinets.

THERE ARE many different screw sizes and types available for use with a screw gun.
A) The most common type of screw is a standard drywall screw with a sharp point (for puncturing the paper face on Sheetrock) and threads designed to go into wood. These screws are available from 1 to about 3 inches in length.
B) The self-tapping screw with a round head, sometimes called a 'teks' screw, is used for joining light-gauge metal studs together.
C) The self-tapping screw with a flat head is used for fastening Sheetrock to light-gauge metal studs.
D) A Sheetrock-to-Sheetrock screw is a fairly specialized variety of fastener, but it has many applications in an old house (as discussed above).
E) A finishing screw should be used only on woodwork, because the head is so small. If it were used on Sheetrock, the head would pull right through the paper face.

THE SCREWDRIVER TIP on the end of the screw gun is replaceable. Several tip sizes are available to match the screw being driven. For example, a finishing screw takes a smaller tip than a regular drywall screw. The tips also eventually wear out, and can be replaced easily by just pulling out the old one with a pair of pliers and slipping in the new one. It's usually a good idea to keep a few spare tips on hand in case one gets damaged or excessively worn.

IT TOOK ME A WHILE to decide to get a screw gun because, like any good power tool, it's expensive. But now I'd never be without one again! It's a tremendous time-saver.

CONSIDERED a contractor's tool, high-quality screw guns are not generally available at hardware stores. Therefore, we're offering our readers the screw gun chosen and tested by the author. See the inside back cover of this issue.

The Rumford Compromise

A Safe Modification For Victorian Fireplaces

by Jim Buckley

WHEN WE BOUGHT our 1880 house, its five coal-burning fireplaces were all in terrible shape -- and that's including the ones that hadn't been bricked up or used to vent gas space heaters in the bad old days when our home was a rooming house. Our insurance agent looked things over, shook his head, and wrote a special clause in our fire policy, one that voided it if we used the fireplaces.

THE NEXT FEW YEARS were very frustrating. Fireplaces dominated every room, and it offended us that they weren't functional. To make them safe and bring them up to modern building codes, they'd have to be made deeper, which meant obliterating the original hearths and plaster mouldings above the mantels.

THAT OPTION was unacceptable to us. There seemed to be no way out, until a friend of mine brought me <u>The Collected Works of Count Rumford</u>. I read it, and in a blinding flash I had the solution: Rumford fireplaces. They're tall, graceful, and above all <u>shallow</u>. They'd fit perfectly within my fireplace openings; all I'd have to do is change the insides of the fireboxes.

COUNT RUMFORD, an American, developed his fireplace in England around 1795. He understood that fireplaces produce radiant heat, and came up with a design to take advantage of that effect. His fireplaces were shallow, with widely angled covings and light-colored masonry materials. He experimented with the shape of the throat "to find out and remove those local hindrances which prevent the smoke from following its natural tendency to go up the chimney."

RUMFORD ROUNDED THE BREAST and reduced the size of the throat to a narrow slit. The throat is streamlined, measuring only about 1/20th the size of the fireplace opening. It forms a nozzle through which the smoke and air flow at an increased speed, and acts like a check valve against backdrafts.

"We live in an 1880 vintage Queen Anne Stick-style brick Victorian Italianate house, if you can imagine that."

THE ACCEPTED AUTHORITY for fireplace design today is the American Society of Heating, Refrigeration, and Airconditioning Engineers Handbook. This book states that a modern fireplace requires a flue at least 1/12th the size of the fireplace opening. If a damper is

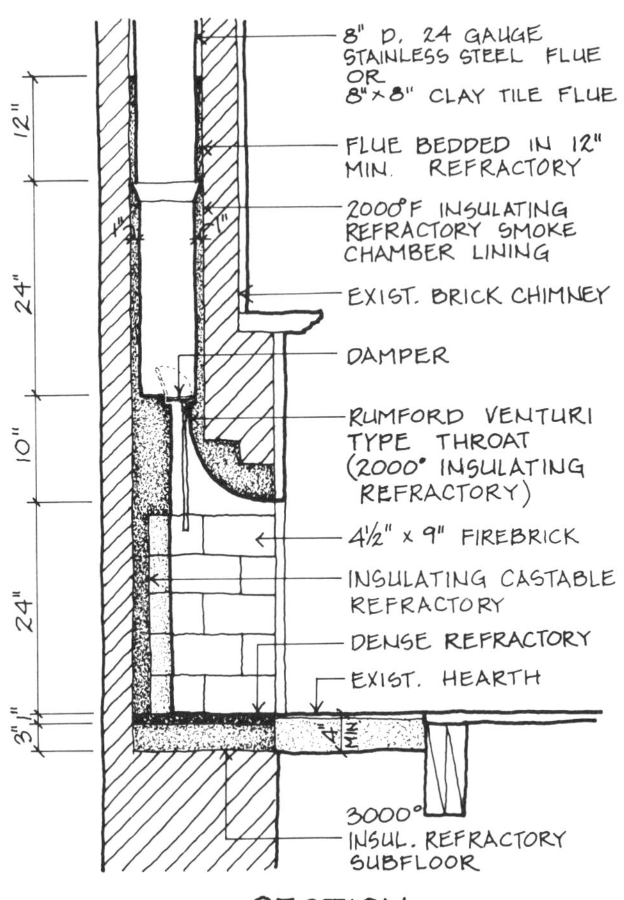

SECTION

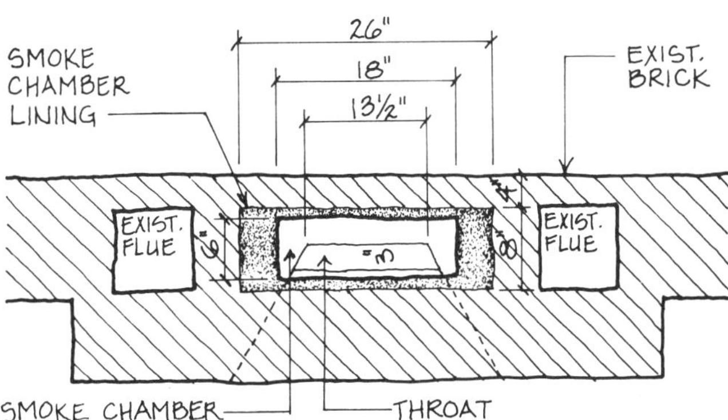

PLAN ABOVE DAMPER

used at the throat, the ASHRAE Handbook recommends it be twice as big as the flue -- that's about four times as big as a Rumford throat. No wonder modern fireplaces are inefficient: With their square lintels and sharp angles, they have to be deep and have gaping, oversized flues to keep them from smoking.

How To Rumford-ize A Fireplace

THE MORE I READ RUMFORD'S WORKS, the more convinced I became that they offered the definitive fireplace design. So I went ahead and built a Rumford in my house. I've since done many more, and want to share what I've learned with the readers of OHJ. Construction requires several refractory materials that are not commonly used by homeowners or home-improvement contractors, but they're generally available from firms such as Plibrico and A.P. Green. I use a 2000-degree, insulating castable refractory cement for casting the throat and smoke chamber, and 3000-degree refractory for some fireplace subfloors. I've found that I can mix refractories in a 5-gallon plastic bucket, using a 1/2-inch drill with a drywall mixer blade. It pours easily with the aid of a metal scoop.

I ALWAYS DIG OUT the firebox floor and replace it with 3000-degree castable refractory. Refractory cement is made in a wide range of insulating capacity and density -- the more insulating capacity the cement has, the softer it is. So, if there's any wood within 4 inches of the hearth extension, I pour a fireplace subfloor of softer 3000-degree refractory cement, then pour a denser refractory floor over that. The finish floor of the fireplace needs to be relatively hard, because it will be subjected to such abuses as pokers and falling embers.

Author Jim Buckley poses with the tools for the job. Left to right: half-inch drill with drywall mixing blade, bucket of refractory mortar, throat form with wooden blocks, firebrick and grate, smoke chamber form with bottom and legs, and 8-in. stainless steel flue pipe with metal-cutting saw.

POUR THE SMOKE CHAMBER NEXT, because you have to be able to get the form out the bottom. My plywood form is fitted to the inside of the firebox; it is about 18 inches wide at the base, 24 inches high, and 6 inches deep. It forms 1-inch-thick front and back walls in an 8-inch rough smoke-chamber opening (a standard size here in Columbus). A platform that just fits the rough opening (usually 8 inches by 24 inches) holds the form in place on wooden legs, 10 inches above the firebox lintel.

USING THE METAL SCOOP, pour the 2000-degree, insulating refractory through a hole in the wall, located just at the top of the form. The mixture has to be wet enough to fill voids, but not so wet as to compromise its

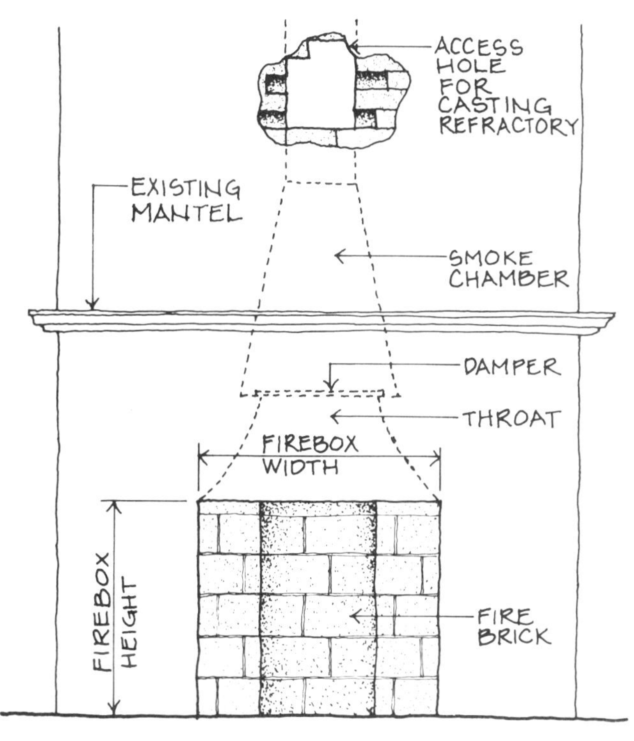

ELEVATION

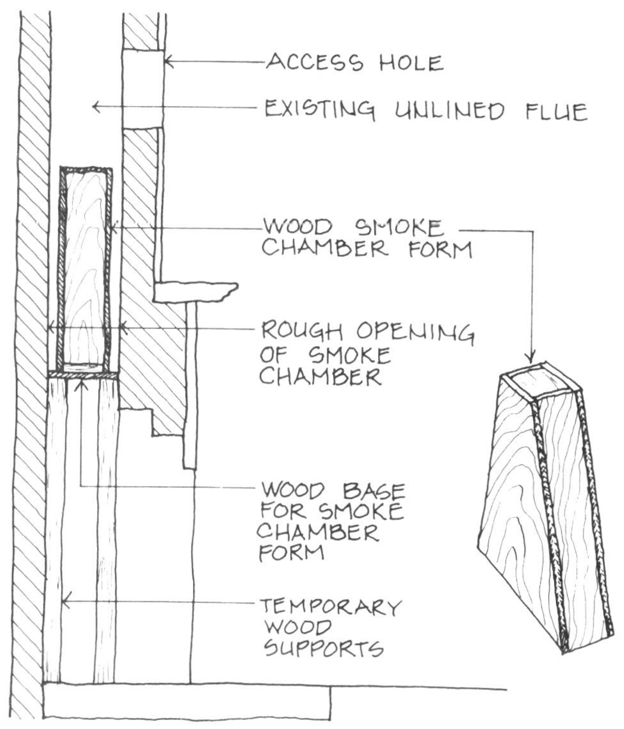

SETTING SMOKE CHAMBER FORM

Life With Rumfords

HAVING LIVED with Rumford fireplaces for a while, I feel compelled to tell you how wonderful they are. (Of course, I'm not biased!) Our brick Victorian house always felt cold when the outside temperature was low, even though the furnace kept the inside air temperature a constant 65 degrees. Brick is poor insulation, and so our wall temperature was usually about halfway between the 65-degree inside temperature and the cold outside temperature. When it got to be zero outside, the walls would be only about 35 degrees, and we'd feel cold.

RUMFORD first articulated the concept of radiant heat: "One must never forget that it is the room that heats the air, and not the air which heats the room." In other words the radiant heat from the fireplace heats people and surfaces such as the wall across the room. Supplementing our heat with fireplaces that warm us directly and keep our walls warmer,

we now can feel comfortable even at 60 degrees. It's like being in the sun on a 60-degree spring day. It feels warm, but step into the shade -- or in this case, the next room -- and 60 degrees feels cold.

PEOPLE OFTEN want to compare fireplaces with stoves. Stoves are basically air heaters, so you rely on convection to help heat adjoining rooms, or you can use fans to circulate the warm air much like a warm-air furnace does. Fireplaces, however, heat only what they 'see'; you can't pump 60-degree, warm air to help heat a 60-degree, cool adjoining room. On the other hand, you can't lose radiant heat through infiltration or convection.

SO IF YOU LIVE in a big, drafty brick house with high ceilings, and the kids and cats are going in and out all the time, a Rumford or two (or five) may be the secret to preserving your wintertime comfort.

---

strength; try making it just a little too wet to make a ball and hold in your hand. The material should be just barely pourable: If your mixture's too thick, it won't pour evenly; too thin, it pours too fast. (To be perfectly honest, I wasted a lot of expensive refractory in my experiments with mixing consistencies and setting times. I even had to burn out my first smoke-chamber form because I left it in too long and couldn't get it out.)

THE INSULATION VALUE of the refractory is necessary if your smoke-chamber walls are only 4 inches thick, so that the heat transfer through the casting and 4 inches of brick is equivalent to the 8-inch walls required by most codes. After about three and a half hours, pull the form. (You might have to use a hammer to get it down and out through the hole.) Do it too soon and the casting will fall apart; too late and you'll have to burn the form out. (Charcoal applied to the top of the form works best because it burns down.)

The Floor And The Throat

WITH A SHOP PENCIL OR CHALK, draw the firebox plan on the refractory floor. For fireboxes up to 28 inches wide, I use 1-1/2 standard firebricks per course for the back and both covings. (A standard firebrick measures 4-1/2 inches by 9 inches, which makes each course 13-1/2 inches long.) Using a level, lay the firebrick with fireclay mortar.

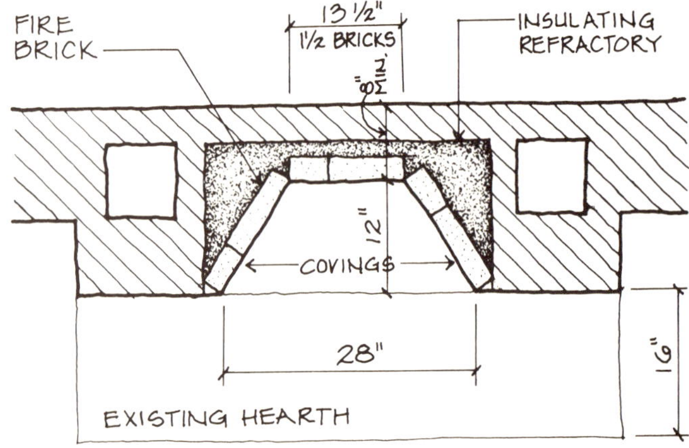

PLAN AT FLOOR

Keep your joints small, no wider than 1/16 inch. Fill the void between the firebrick and the common brick chimney wall with insulating castable refractory. Remember that firebox walls should be a minimum of 8 inches thick, and even then it's a good idea to place some insulating castable between the firebricks and the structural wall (especially if there's any wood on the back side of the fireplace). Excess fireclay mortar can be washed off the brick faces with water and a sponge.

THE FORM FOR THE THROAT uses 24-gauge sheet-metal for the curved part. (Construction of this form is time-consuming because of the

---

The firebox requires only 1½ firebricks for each course. Note the thinness of the joints; the excess fireclay mortar will be washed off after the firebox has been completed.

relatively complex geometry.) For the smallest part at the top, the throat must be 1/20th of the area of the fireplace opening. For a 20-inch-wide fireplace with a 13-1/2-inch back, the throat is 13-1/2 inches wide by about 2 inches deep. For a 28-inch-wide fireplace (still with a 13-1/2-inch-wide back), the throat is 13-1/2 inches by about 3 inches. The form must also be short enough so that when its supporting platform is taken away, it can be dropped down about a foot and removed.

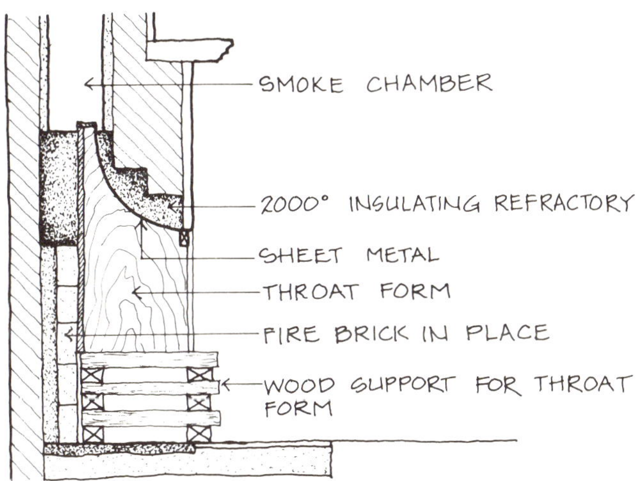

CASTING THROAT

INSERT THE THROAT FORM up into the firebox. (It will extend a bit into the smoke chamber -- see drawing.) Positioning it somewhat toward the front of the smoke chamber's opening will make it easier to get the damper in later. Make sure the form fits tightly against the firebox on all three sides, and that the the bottom of the form is lined up precisely with the bottom exterior edge of the fireplace. Pour the refractory to the top of the form so that the two castings overlap.

PULL THE FORM after about three and a half hours. Sometimes it's hard to get the refractory to fill the entire breast area, or it fails when the form is removed. But it usual-

ly can be patched with the same refractory, using a trowel. The casting may also need a little cutting and trimming with a trowel to make a smooth transition with the firebox and to make sure the throat is well formed.

MAKE A DAMPER out of a 3/16-inch-by-3-1/4-inch-by-16-inch steel plate; fasten a steel bar handle to it with a cotter pin. (You can also have a metal worker fabricate a conventional damper, one hinged to a metal frame). The damper can be inserted through the throat and a mortar ledge formed of refractory cement, so that the damper can open up and back, as if it were hinged at the back to the smoke shelf.

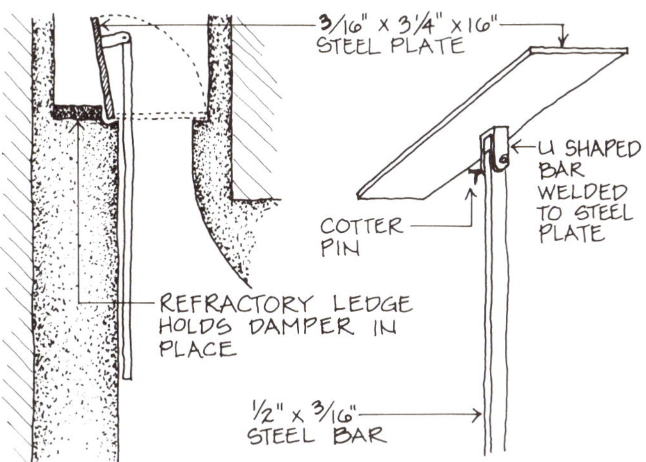

DAMPER DETAILS

Flue Facts

FOR THE FLUE, I use either modular, 8-inch-by-8-inch, clay-tile flue liners or 8-inch, rigid, 24-ga., stainless-steel flue pipe. With clay-tile liners, I like to fill voids between the tile and brickwork with insulating castable refractory; leaky butt joints and random air spaces scare me. Stain-

<hr>

Safety Considerations

THERE are three national model codes in the United States. Most state and local codes are based on them, and they're all pretty much the same when it comes to masonry fireplaces. They aren't written with Rumfords in mind (because they require deep fireboxes and large throats), but they should be followed in safety-related matters. The law, your insurance coverage, your house, and maybe even your life may depend on your building a safe fireplace that meets code and gets a building permit.

GET A COPY of your state or local code and become familiar with it. In old houses, wood framing generally isn't kept 2 inches away from chimneys, as is now required; smoke-chamber walls and sometimes the firebox walls and hearth aren't as thick as required. The original gas-burning fireplaces in some houses are totally unsafe for woodburning. (I have found wood joists running into the flue, tile hearths laid right on wooden floorboards in the firebox, and paper and wood trash behind the masonry.)

— Jim Buckley

<hr>

less steel makes an excellent flue because it's smooth and round, and has lapped joints. Just make sure you get the male ends down so that any creosote dripping down the pipe stays inside the flue. As an added precaution, because wood framing is often right up against old chimneys, I pour insulating castable refractory around the outside of the pipe, filling the voids.

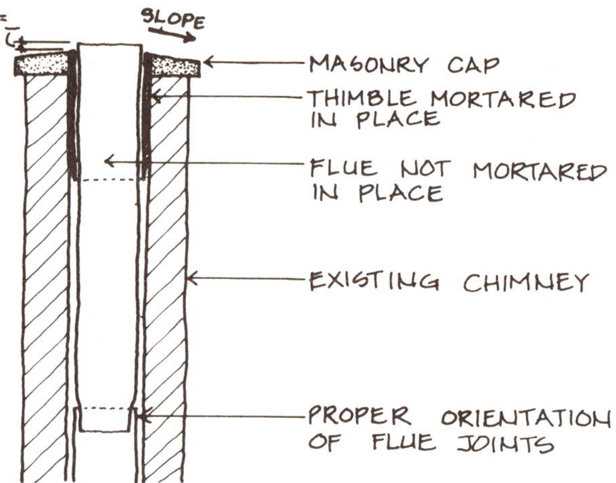

DETAIL AT TOP OF CHIMNEY

YOU SHOULD BE AWARE that all this hardened mortar inside your chimney makes this work irreversible; if your chimney needs rebuilding after you finish this job, the mortar will have to be chipped out by hand -- a nearly impossible job. Whichever liner you use, fit it to the top of the smoke-chamber casting through the pour hole, brick up the hole, and pour more refractory from the roof (or the upstairs fireplace, if available), seating the flue at least 1 foot deep in refractory.

I'M VERY FAMILIAR with insulating castable refractories, and I don't use the poured flues that are currently being franchised under various names. Most unlined chimneys here in Ohio are only one-brick-square (8 inches by 8 inches), and I need an 8-inch flue. A poured flue wouldn't have sufficient wall thickness to have structural integrity; besides, I'd have to pour the refractory overly wet to make sure I didn't have any voids in such a thin casting.

I ALSO DON'T USE flexible stainless steel because it's much thinner and more expensive than rigid pipe. Most bends in old chimneys occur so downstairs flues can go around upstairs fireplaces, but you can usually gain access to these bends through the upstairs fireplace opening by taking out part of the side of the firebox. Stainless-steel flues should be riveted together with stainless-steel rivets.

WE BROKE A FEW mortar caps because the stainless-steel flue pipe expands when it gets hot. So now we use a standard 8-inch thimble as a sleeve. Run the flue pipe through the sleeve and mortar the sleeve to the brickwork. Saw off the stainless-steel flue pipe about 1 inch above the masonry cap, so you don't see it from the street. Cut the stainless steel with an electric circular saw with a metal-cutting composition blade.

YOU CAN USE A CLAY CHIMNEY POT to finish off the chimney. Sometimes a 40-foot-high chimney that's 12 feet above a steep slate roof can be pretty scary. But the view's great! Figure out the type of scaffolding and safety harness arrangement that's safest for your situation, and use it.

Satisfying The Codes

AFTER I FINISHED my first fireplace, I named it the "Victorian Rumford Compromise." After all, it was somewhat anachronistic to put a 200-year-old fireplace in a 100-year-old house. And besides, I built it about 12 inches deep, rather than Rumford's recommended one third of the width, because it was only 20 inches wide.

DESPITE THE BENEFITS of Rumford's design, most building codes require fireplaces to be 20 in. deep. I did some research and learned that this requirement was adopted in the 1940s, more or less arbitrarily, as a guide for the builders who rarely had engineers or architects designing their fireplaces.

TO GET the required building permit, I had to appeal to the Columbus Building Regulation Commission. First I had to satisfy them that I understood the code and that my fireplace complied with all the safety-related issues. Then I argued the differences in the Rumford design, showing that the heat transfer through my insulating, refractory-lined smoke chamber and 4 inches of brick would be as safe as that of the 8-in. walls required by the code.

TO MAKE A LONG STORY SHORT, the entire Commission gathered early one July morning in 1982 for a "burn-in." They were well pleased with the demonstration, and I went into the business of building Victorian Rumford Compromises for other old-house owners.

Since writing this article, Jim has begun building modular components of the Rumford fireplace in his shop, to reduce the time and labor required for installation. Now these all-masonry Rumford components (firebox, throat with damper, & smoke chamber) can be custom built and shipped with detailed installation instructions to contractors and homeowners anywhere. Call or write Jim Buckley at Flue Works, Inc., 86 Warren St., Columbus, OH 43215. (614) 291-6918.

THE ART DECO HOUSE

by Walter Jowers

IN THE WELL-MANICURED neighborhoods of many cities, amidst the becolumned Neo-classical homes of the well-to-do, there is often one oddball house -- a house with a flat roof, curved glass walls, and, most obviously, no hint of classical architectural details like columns and pediments.

THOUGH MANY PEOPLE believe these houses were built around the time of the Apollo moon landings in the 1960s, they were actually built closer to the time of Buck Rogers' comic strip space travels. These are 1930s houses; examples of the style that was called, at that time, "modern" architecture. Today, we call the stark, unadorned (and usually white) ones International Style. We call the jazzy, whimsical ones Art Deco.

ART DECO GETS ITS NAME from an international exhibition of industrial design, the Exposition des Arts Decoratifs, held in Paris in 1925. This exposition focused attention on a new design aesthetic that featured elements of Egyptian, Aztec, and Mayan art, as well as stylized low-relief figures, and Cubist-influenced geometric designs. The idea was to combine these ideas in new ways, and use machine-age materials to create a fresh, eclectic, "moderne" look that had no historical antecedent. The moderne look caught on in a big way in the 1920s and 1930s, though the term "Art Deco" didn't catch on until the 1960s.

ART DECO ARCHITECTURE is a familiar part of the American cityscape; almost everyone is aware of the Empire State Building. And most of us have been in an Art Deco movie theater, or have passed an Art Deco roadside diner.

BUT HOW WAS the Art Deco style applied to residential architecture? First, in the shapes of the houses: Art Deco houses invariably have flat roofs. Visual emphasis in Deco residential architecture is most often horizontal, rather than vertical, as is the case with Art Deco skyscrapers. (This horizontal, streamlined look is typical of the Art Moderne subgenre of Art Deco architecture.) Many of the corners aren't square in a Deco house; the exterior and interior walls are often rounded into curves. Staircases usually curve, too.

MACHINE-AGE ENGINEERING brought new materials and new shapes to Art Deco houses, the same way the invention of the circular saw allowed changes in the shape of 19th-century buildings.

TWO NEWLY-MANUFACTURED MATERIALS, colored structural glass sheets (sold under the trade names Vitrolite and Carrara Glass), and translucent glass block (sold as Insulux) were very popular in Deco houses.

Many elements of the Art Deco skyscraper style are evident in this ca. 1930 house. The smooth facade, the narrow casement windows, and the flat roof are all characteristic of the style. The most striking Art Deco feature, though, is the repeating low-relief design on the bay window spandrels. This four-storey house displays much more vertical emphasis than later, streamlined Deco houses.

This rendering of a 1931 house shows some Art Deco design elements
-- a streamlined, horizontal visual emphasis, a large expanse of glass in
a curved exterior wall, and a fanciful spiral staircase.

Art Deco buildings often exhibit a strong visual emphasis on the
entryway. The curved walls flanking the entrance of this small apartment house guide the eye to the double doors. The large expanse of
glass block in a curved outside wall is another Deco feature.

LARGE EXPANSES of glass block were common;
these window-walls allowed light into the
house without sacrificing privacy. A favorite
placement was in the curve of an outside wall,
especially the wall adjacent to the staircase.
Operating sash were often factory-style
casement windows, and "porthole" windows were
common. The porthole windows, along with
tubular steel railings, combine to give some
of these streamlined houses a nautical look.

THE MODERN 1930s SURFACE FINISH was flat,
simple, and easy to keep clean. In keeping
with this, exterior walls were most often
stuccoed, though they were frequently a light-
colored brick or, in some instances, painted
brick. Interior walls were plaster, though
kitchen and bathroom walls were often over-
laid with ceramic tile or, in some instances,
structural Vitrolite or Carrara Glass.

THE ART DECO AESTHETIC of using new
machine-age materials in unprecedented
ways is most evident in the interior of
these houses. In a 1935 Architectural
Record article, J.E. Burchard stated: "Early
modern houses were created principally for a
well-to-do intelligentsia and gave rise
therefore to the impression that opulent
exotic woods and gleaming unusual metals were
the essence of modernism, were indeed
necessary to make otherwise simple designs
bearable." Interior appointments in Deco
houses range from grand to glitzy to kinky to
undeniably tacky.

STAIRCASES ARE THE VISUAL FOCUS in many of
these houses; many Deco design elements are
brought together here. The stair tower illustrated on this page is a monolith of reinforced black terrazzo, poured and polished in
place, with nonslip carborundum treads. The
rail is brush-finished aluminum. The stair is
incorporated into a curved, glass-block wall,
and the stairwell curtain is a yellow antique
satin. Quite an eclectic, "moderne" mix.

The quintessential Deco stair tower -- a sweeping curved staircase
surrounded by a wall of glass block. The stair is poured-in-place
black terrazzo, with carborundum treads and an aluminum rail
. . . very early high tech.

This period room, with its multi-colored tile floor and Cubist-inspired furniture and lighting fixtures, is a showplace of Art Deco design. The fireplace is typically simple and unadorned, but there is nothing understated about the multifaceted mirror overhead!

DECO FIREPLACES represent another departure from earlier traditional designs. Just as you won't see classical columns on a Deco house facade, you won't see columns on the fireplace surrounds. No triglyphs, gargoyles, or carved mouldings, either. Most Deco fireplaces are merely rectangles cut into the wall, with simple structural glass, marble, or metal hearths and surrounds; though there are some zippy designs with angular mirrors built into the surround. Most of these fireplaces have no mantel, or utilize the projection of the surround as a mantel.

IN ANY DECO HOUSE, one notices the unusual uses and arrangements of materials. The interior designers loved slick, shiny surfaces; and in some houses, the baseboards are glazed ceramic tile. Multi-colored marble or tile floors are common, as are two- and three-color tile or structural glass walls (especially in bathrooms). Some Deco houses have tile-floored rooftop sundecks, complete with rooftop fireplaces! The simple, angular geometry of the Art Deco style also found its way into garden and terrace designs of the period.

THOUGH ART DECO HOUSES are not as numerous or as obviously "old" as earlier types of houses, they do represent a definite architectural style, as well as a cultural phenomenon of the not-too-distant past.

ART DECO WAS THE LAST architectural style to encourage the use of ornamentation and decoration in buildings; some people say it was the last architectural style. By almost any measure, Art Deco was the last style to acknowledge the need for beauty, or at least the need for a sense of humor, in architectural design. These houses, which are so often egregiously altered due to their relative "newness" deserve the same attention, respect, and protection as our older (but no more historic) houses.

This Deco house has a central glass atrium -- you can look right through to the back yard! The long, low lines and the nautical look of the house give the impression of a submarine surfacing.

A house grown from crystals? This prismlike quality is often seen in Deco artifacts (graphic art, jewelry, glassware), but not so often in the houses of the period.

Special thanks to James Draeger (a true fountain of Deco knowledge), Amanda Gross, and Mark Sturtevant. Without their special insight and hysterical approach to historical research, this article might have been possible, but not nearly so much fun.

DECO MATERIALS

CARE OF PIGMENTED STRUCTURAL GLASS

(Vitrolite and Carrara Glass)

PIGMENTED STRUCTURAL GLASS was first manufactured in 1900, but it enjoyed its greatest popularity during the height of the Art Deco style period, the 1920s and thirties. This glass, sold under the trade names Vitrolite and Carrara Glass, has not been manufactured for several years.

WHAT DO YOU DO if the pigmented glass in your Deco house needs repair or replacement? The National Park Service's Preservation Brief 12 offers the following suggestions:

● REPAIR OF CEMENT JOINTS (the equivalent of grout joints): Re-"grout" with modern silicone joint cement, color-matched to the original by mixing the compound with tinted polyester resins.

● PATCHING CHIPS OR CRACKS IN THE GLASS: Use solvent (methyl ethyl ketone, methyl isobutyl ketone, or acetone) applied behind the glass with a syringe, then gently pry off the glass with a broad, flat tool (such as a nail-puller). Or, apply solvent, then use piano wire to saw the glass loose. CAUTION: THESE SOLVENTS ARE EXTREMELY FLAMMABLE, AND THEY IRRITATE THE SKIN. STORE THE SOLVENTS IN FIRE-SAFE CONTAINERS, AND WEAR RUBBER GLOVES AND GOGGLES WHEN YOU WORK WITH THE SOLVENT.

● REINSTALLATION OF GLASS PANELS: Clean the glass and the underlying substrate of dirt and old mastic, then reinstall the glass, using: (a) a modern silicone mastic, for small applications (large quantities of this mastic are quite expensive), or (b) hot-melt asphalt mastic (this is the material used to install structural glass in the '20s and '30s).

● REPLACEMENT OF MISSING OR DAMAGED GLASS PANELS: It's worth a try to call local "jobbers" to find out if they have any old structural glass in their inventories. If no one has any old glass, you must...

● SUBSTITUTE MATERIAL FOR MISSING OR DAMAGED GLASS PANELS: A new product, "spandrel glass," marketed under the trade names of Spandrelite and Vitrolux, is the closest thing to the genuine article. It is available in several colors. Other options: Paint the back side of a piece of plate glass to match the color of the existing glass; or try appropriately colored plastic.

MODERN GLASS BLOCK

GLASS BLOCK, in sizes and patterns matching most of the 1920s and thirties block, are still available from:

Pittsburgh Corning Corporation
800 Presque Isle Drive
Pittsburgh, Pennsylvania 15239

Write for a current brochure and installation specifications.

Thinline Series GlassBlock (Decora®, Delphi®, VUE® Patterns)

Argus® Pattern — Standard Block

Essex AA Pattern — Standard Block

Vistabrik® Solid Glass Block

These six glass block patterns are available from Pittsburgh Corning.

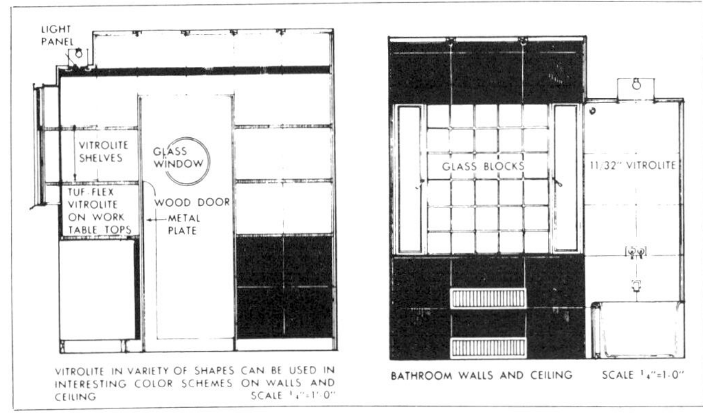

Kitchen and bathroom details from the 1937 Vitrolite catalog. Note the use of glass blocks in the bathroom wall.

OBJETS D'ART DECO

NEVER BEFORE in the history of American design had so many forces come together to create such an all-encompassing art form. The exuberance of the 1920s, the Paris Exposition des Arts Decoratifs, and machine-age, mass-production capabilities combined to make Art Deco the first real wave of industrial design. During the height of the Deco period, objets d'Art Deco could be found in every room, closet, and cabinet of an Art Deco house. In fact, the rooms, closets, and cabinets themselves might have been high-style Art Deco. The style touched everything from knick-knacks to floor wax, lipstick to locomotives.

DECO KITCHENS often look like they were designed in wind tunnels. The walls, the counters, the furniture, the appliances all appear to be built for speed. Raymond Loewy (the man who designed the Studebaker Avanti) designed refrigerators for Sears. General Electric made Art Deco waffle irons. The Saunders company marketed a two-tone solid Pyrex laundry iron, aptly named the "Silver Streak." Stoves, blenders, juicers, even tables and chairs looked like they were designed for aerodynamic efficiency.

This "wind tunnel" kitchen was entered in a 1935 design competition.

The triple-streamlined central bay of this 1930s trendy trailer shows how moderne design elements found their way into almost everything. (The two outer bays fold up for transport.)

A Vitrolite catalog kitchen with white walls, yellow ceiling and counters, and blue window trim.

Two hot irons of the period. Above is General Electric's Art Deco waffle iron. At right is Saunders Company's "Silver Streak."

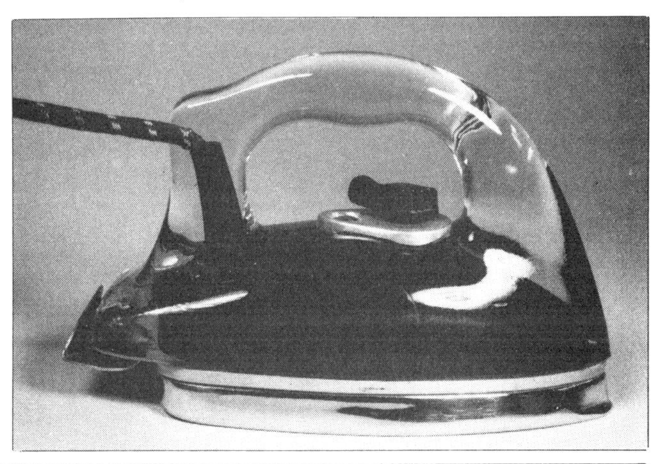

Above: The alternating horizontal bands of Vitrolite are pearl grey and Chinese red. The shower curtain is silver metallic cloth   Fixtures have red plastic handles. Below: A typical use of glass block in the bath.

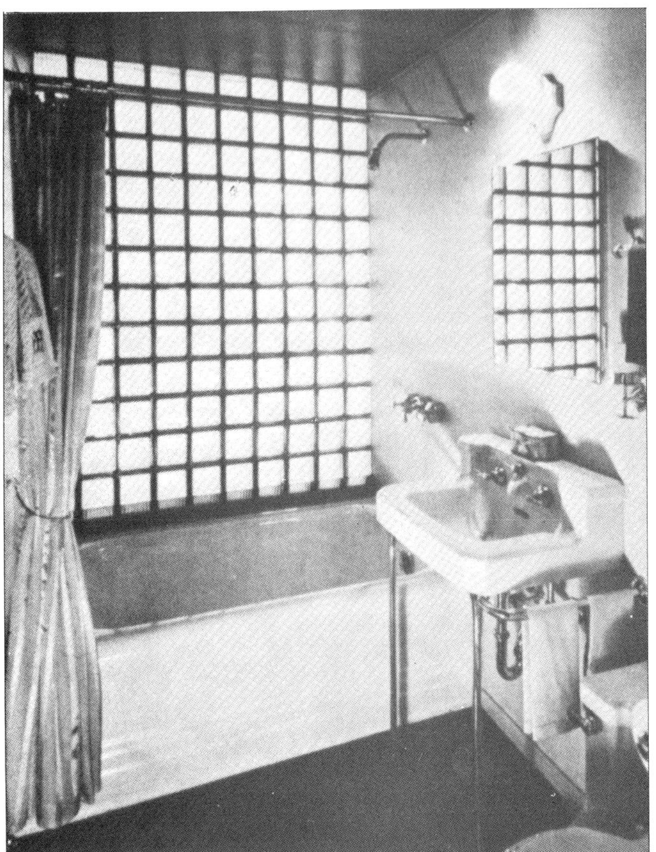

Though dining room decoration was usually restrained even in houses of the Art Deco period, some snazzy details slipped in. There is nothing traditional about this Formica-topped table, or the ''moderne'' chairs.

BATHROOMS WERE ANOTHER gleaming, slick, streamlined showcase for Art Deco residential architecture. In Libbey-Owens-Ford's 1937 Vitrolite catalog, the writer says of kitchens and baths: "Upon no other rooms in the modern home have architects and manufacturers of fixtures and equipment lavished more attention. Thus we have today kitchens and bathrooms furnished with fixtures, cabinets, utility equipment and accessories, all reflecting a high degree of beauty and mechanical perfection." High-contrast, multi-color patterns in Vitrolite and ceramic tile are characteristic of the Deco bath. Bullet-shaped faucet handles, angular shower heads, and mechanical-looking medicine cabinets are common. Robe hooks look like Klingon space cruisers.

A Vitrolite catalog bathroom. The tub surround is imitation marble Vitrolite; the walls are pale yellow.

The designers of this Art Deco recreation room went for the full effect: Vertical and horizontal tube lights, a stylized fountain on the bar, feline-skin upholstery. The cocktail-glass pattern set into the Formica floor exemplifies the fascination post-Prohibition designers had with cocktail paraphernalia.

DINING ROOMS were the most traditional room in the house, but some homeowners couldn't resist the urge to dine around a chrome-and-glass, or chrome-and-plastic, table like the one shown on the opposite page.

 THE DESIGNERS OF THE ERA were fascinated with cocktail and smoking paraphernalia. So what better room to make into a true Art Deco showcase than the recreation room? The rec room shown on this page is a fine high-style example: Tube lights! Leopard-skin upholstery! A stylized fountain painted on the bar! But the true Art Deco decadent indulgence is on the floor -- a varying cocktail-glass pattern set into the Formica! A 1935 Bakelite ad shows an entire rec room made out of Bakelite plastic products. Not the homely brown Bakelite that electrical plugs are made of -- but the swirly, marbled, iridescent Bakelite that was used to make the colorful, snazzy (and now quite valuable) radios shown on this page.

NO ROOM WAS UNTOUCHED by the Deco design influence. The bedroom suite shown at right is made of burl maple, with a white and brown enamel contrasting finish on the drawers and doors. The 1937 Vitrolite catalog shows some "modern furniture" made with Vitrolite.

ART DECO LAMPS, glassware, silverware, and clothing (cocktail dresses, of course) are fairly common sights in antique stores around the country. The furniture, and the architectural pieces are less common. If prices and availability are any indication, then Art Deco pieces of all types are enjoying a new popularity.

WE HOPE some of these pieces are being snapped up by owners of Art Deco houses who are decorating their houses in the original style.

Red and orange, yellow and brown, red-white-and-blue radios...These fanciful Bakelite numbers date from the late 1930s. Bright, high-contrast color schemes in the marbled plastic cases create a striking visual effect.

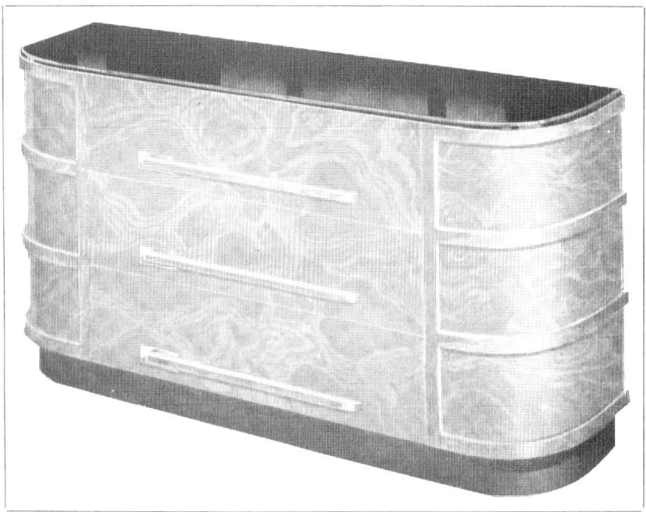

A buffet with a black Vitrolite top and base. The Vitrolite "resists burning from cigarettes and staining from alcohol."

A "modern" bedroom suite from 1935. The rounded corners and high-contrast finish are typical of period designs.

Restorer's Notebook

Two Helpful Products

THESE TWO PRODUCTS should be of interest to the OHJ readers. The first is called "Duro Tub 'N Sink Jelly." It removes stubborn rust stains on sinks and tubs with little or no elbow grease. Its active ingredient is phosphoric acid, so be careful to avoid any skin contact. Just wipe it on the tub or sink, let it sit for 5 to 10 minutes, and rinse it off. It's available from Loctite Corp., Automotive and Consumer Group, Dept. OHJ, 4450 Cranwood Court, Cleveland, OH 44128. (216) 475-3600.

THE SECOND product is called "Kilz," and it's designed to hold back stains on plaster walls prior to painting with a latex paint. It keeps crayon, lipstick, smoke and charring, ink, pencil, and grease stains from bleeding through the new paint job. "Kilz" won't raise the grain of the wood, and it dries quickly -- you're ready to recoat in 30 to 45 minutes. It's available from Masterchem Industries, Dept. OHJ, P.O. Box 2666, St. Louis, MO 63116. (314) 772-3979.

Michele M. Schiesser
Fredericksburg, Va.

Simplifying Staining

A CLEAN BLACK FELT chalkboard eraser and some tin pie plates are valuable tools for staining woodwork, doors, and other flat wooden surfaces. Pour the stain in the plate, dip the eraser in the stain, and rub it across the wood. (Remember not to stain more wood than you can wipe off with a dry cloth before the stain gets dry and dark.) We found that, as opposed to using a brush, this

method was much faster and wasted less stain.

Sheryl Connell
El Dorado, Kansas

Latex Priming

LATEX PAINT is excellent for color retention and for non-hardening over time. But its big drawback is weak bonding; it must be applied over a primer or itself (if clean). The primer you use must be alkyd or oil-based. "Latex Primer" is a contradiction in terms. A water-base "primer" will do very well on cardboard (i.e., drywall), but it simply won't penetrate wood or plaster surfaces sufficiently for a good bond.

THE SCIENTISTS at Forest Products Labs (USDA) in Madison, Wisconsin, suggest using a thick oil primer coating, one "heavy enough to cover the grain" on exterior wood, followed by two coats of latex. They say it'll give you a ten-year (or more) paint job.

Charles W. Wilson
Mechanicsburg, Penn.

A Soldering Shortcut

IN RENOVATING an old townhouse, I had to put a shutoff valve in a vertical waterpipe that ran from the basement. I shut off the water supply to the pipe, went to the top floor, and ran the fixture for this water line. Then I went back to the cellar and cut the half-inch copper water line. The remaining water in the line began dripping into a bucket I'd positioned below the pipe, and I decided to have a cup of coffee and wait for the drip to stop.

AFTER FINISHING my coffee and one-too-many doughnuts, I returned to the pipe and saw that it was still dripping. This was an old building with many branches of water lines running in the walls for all four floors -- a fixture somewhere was continuing to release water. I waited a few minutes, but the water kept on coming. Against my better judgment, I went ahead and soldered the shutoff valve into the moist water line. Needless to say, the slight dripping of water spoiled my soldering, and the joints leaked when I ran a test on it.

I DECIDED TO BACK OFF and give the problem some more thought. Regretting having ever started this "easy" project, I was having my third cup of coffee when my attention focussed on the partially eaten doughnut in my hand. Eureka! If the doughnut could soak up the coffee, why couldn't it soak up the drip?

INSTEAD OF WASTING A GOOD DOUGHNUT, I plugged the drip with rolled-up bread, using a pencil to force it into the vertical section of the pipe. Then I quickly assembled my soldering parts and sweated the valve onto the pipe. The bread absorbed the small amount of water for the time I needed to do the job. When I turned the water on again, there were no leaks -- and the water pressure blew the bread through the pipe and out the open faucet on the other end.

Joseph V. Scaduto
Lynnfield, Mass.

DO YOU NEED AN ENGINEER?

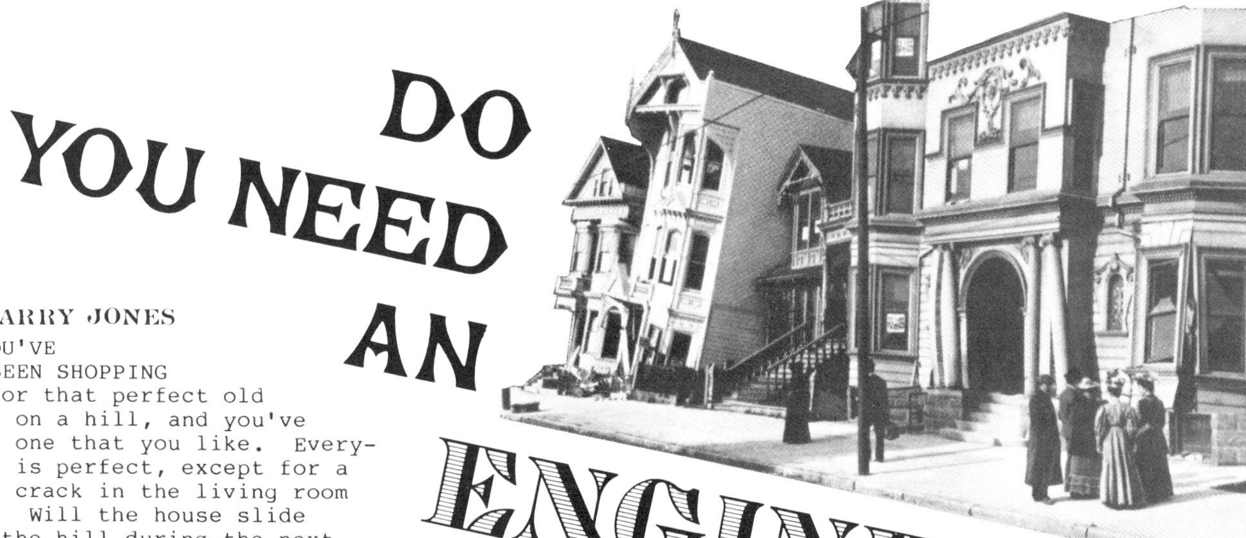

BY LARRY JONES

YOU'VE BEEN SHOPPING for that perfect old house on a hill, and you've found one that you like. Everything is perfect, except for a giant crack in the living room wall. Will the house slide down the hill during the next big rain?

OR CONSIDER THIS: You've been living in an old house for some time, and now you've decided to finish the basement. It would be easy, except for all those columns in the way. You don't know anything about forces and moments, clear spans and live loads. So, who you gonna call...?

YOUR FIRST THOUGHT might be to call a building contractor. There are some skilled tradespeople out there who seem to have almost magical abilities to fix things. But in cases like these, a contractor isn't the right person to evaluate the situation and make decisions. Generally, you hire a tradesperson when you already know what needs doing -- when there's an assignment.

IF THERE ARE DESIGN DECISIONS to be made -- decisions about the feasibility of a project, the planning of a project that involves the structure or aesthetics of your house, then you need a design professional. That means an architect or an engineer.

Which Design Professional?

IT'S HARD TO DRAW A LINE between what an engineer does and what an architect does. First and foremost, there are individual differences. Some architects understand structure and mechanical systems as well as many engineers. And some engineers are sensitive enough to offer sympathetic solutions to design probems, aside from being able to size a beam or a heating plant.

BUT GENERALLY, an architect is more concerned with the interrelationship of design and systems. An architect is concerned with aesthetic, structural, and mechanical considerations. An architect can make an overall evaluation if you want to know the feasibility, approximate cost, or aesthetic or structural implications of, say, an addition to, or the replacement of a mechanical system.

AN ENGINEER has specific technical knowledge, and can help with a particular problem or controversy regarding a structural or mechanical system. Generally, compared to an architect, an engineer is more of a specialist.

ARCHITECTS coordinate the aesthetic features and mechanical systems in a building. An engineer evaluates the appropriateness of each mechanical or structural system for a particular building, then specifies the items needed, and their proper installation.

LET'S USE AN EXAGGERATED (but true) example to make the differences between architects and engineers even more clear...

GIVEN: A 100-plus-year-old octagon house with a large domed roof that was added twenty years after the house was built. The domed roof is pulling itself apart, and the house needs new plumbing, heating and air-conditioning, and insulation.

IF YOU WANT the house ready to move into, you need an architect to evaluate the whole structure and design the interdependent additions of plumbing, heating plant, and insulation. He'll deal with the suitability of the materials and machines, the sequence of the job, and the aesthetic effect of the changes.

IF YOU JUST WANT to fix the dome, you need an engineer. He will specify materials and techniques necessary to stabilize the dome -- things like steel girdles and wire trusses.

IF YOU HAVE all of the above problems, you should hire an architect. When it comes down to specifying the answer to the dome problem, the architect can always engage the services of a consulting Structural Engineer. And, if the heating, electrical, and utility systems are complicated, the architect may call in a consulting Mechanical Engineer.

IF YOU OPEN THE PHONE BOOK to "Engineers," you'll find a bewildering array of titles and specialties. Here is a list of definitions, some of which overlap:

• STRUCTURAL ENGINEER: An engineer who specializes in the design or redesign of structures. Some states require special licensing for people who use the title Structural Engineer. These engineers usually act as consultants to architects, and provide designs, drawings, and specifications for structural items in the building plans. They also provide some supervision over parts of the project for which they have written specifications. Most of the same services offered to architects are available to contractors and homeowners.

● MECHANICAL ENGINEER: An engineer specializing in the invention, design, construction and adjustment of machinery. When they deal with buildings, Mechanical Engineers deal with the mechanical systems: heating, ventilation, air conditioning. Special training and licensing breaks this category down into specialties such as HVAC Engineer and Electrical Engineer.

● FOUNDATION ENGINEER: An engineer specializing in foundation problems. He may recommend suitable foundations for a proposed or existing building. For most projects involving residential-size structures, a Structural Engineer can handle foundation problems.

● CIVIL ENGINEER: An engineer involved in the design of fixed, often public, works such as highways, reclamation projects, harbors, water works, industrial facilities, and building design. (Prior to WW II there were two major designations for engineers: Military and Civil.) About 60% of all practicing engineers call themselves Civil Engineers. The remaining 40% claim a more specialized title; i.e., Electrical Engineer or Mechanical Engineer. Most Structural Engineers consider themselves as falling under the broad definition of Civil Engineer.

● CONSULTING ENGINEER: Any engineer can consult. When an engineer calls himself a Consulting Engineer, it generally means that he is in private practice and is available as a consultant in his specialized field. There are, of course, consulting engineering firms. Structural Engineers often call themselves Consulting Engineers.

● PROFESSIONAL ENGINEER (P.E.): A term used by many states to define an engineer in any branch of engineering who is licensed by the state.

A HOMEOWNER with residential-scale problems probably won't need the services of most engineering specialists. A homeowner is likely to need the advice of a Structural Engineer, if he or she needs an engineer at all.

What They Do

HOWEVER SERIOUS a structural problem may seem to you, most house-size problems are not very complex to an engineer. House problems that call for an engineer's advice almost always fall into one of two categories: natural settlement, or man-made damage.

SETTLEMENT PROBLEMS involve footings and foundations, shrinkage, and shifting caused by rotted structural members. Man-made damage can be caused by overloading structural components, or by a tradesperson randomly cutting through joists to make an installation. (Plumbers and electricians are infamous for this.)

FOR SETTLEMENT PROBLEMS, you may need an engineer to design a system and specify components for foundation underpinning, new footings, channelling groundwater away from a house, monitoring cracks in masonry, or leveling a building. To correct man-made damage, an engineer can inspect framing, specify the size of a new girder, or design a reinforcement system for a load-bearing wall.

WHAT IF A CONTRACTOR tells you that the only way to keep your basement dry is to completely excavate two sides of your foundation so the foundation walls can be waterproofed? You may want a consulting structural engineer to tell you if you need some temporary shoring around the foundation walls before excavation can begin. We know of cases where contractors undermined foundations, and the house dropped right into the hole.

OTHER FAIRLY COMMON old-house restoration jobs that might be best planned by an engineer: chimney stabilization and rebuilding, or adding onto a house when the soil conditions on the building site are particularly tricky (i.e., very sandy, very wet, or heavy clay).

BEFORE YOU HIRE AN ENGINEER, you should do a little homework. Connie Neuman of ACEC suggests that homeowners (or potential buyers) make an effort to understand the problems with the house as clearly as possible. Ideally, you should be able to call up an engineer and say something like, "Excuse me, but the southeast corner of my house seems to have settled about six inches. It's a nine-inch wide limestone foundation, and it's on a clay soil with poor drainage. This side of the house is heavily loaded because of a cantilevered turret, and I suspect that the builders of the house failed to use a proper footing. I'm prepared to spend whatever amount of money I must to correct the situation, and there's no hurry. When can I schedule an appointment?"

BUT IN THE REAL WORLD, most people are likely to say something like, "One corner of my house is lopsided, and there's a big crack. I don't have much money to spend because I just put on a new roof, but water is still coming in this crack. What should I do?"

YOU DON'T HAVE TO BE PARTICULARLY SAVVY about things structural to give an engineer some idea of what is wrong. (If something looks wrong, it usually is.) And during your preliminary discussions with an engineer, you should advise him of any special constraints on the project: Budget, time, the need to preserve the architectural details of the house. Once you've done this, the engineer will have some idea of what you need done, and whether or not he or she can do it.

Selecting An Engineer

PUT TOGETHER A SHORT LIST of engineers you might consider hiring for your project. You'll want the names of several; after all, prices and experience do vary. Check with your local preservation group, or call

your State Historic Preservation Office
(SHPO). Even if neither of these agencies
will recommend an engineer, they should be
able to give you the names of some engineers
who have worked on old-building restoration
projects. You can also write or call the
American Consulting Engineers Council in
Washington, D.C. They should be able to recommend an engineer in your area who has experience in old-house restoration. Above all,
before you hire any engineer, check his references! Try to find people who have recently
completed a project similar to your own.

ONCE YOU HAVE your short list, call a few
engineers and discuss your situation with
them. When you find someone with good
references who seems to understand the
project, schedule an appointment with that
person at your site. Some engineers will
charge to visit your site, others will charge
a low fee (or, if you're lucky, no fee) for
the initial consultation. If, after the
initial consultation, you are convinced that
you've found your engineer, hire him. If you
don't think you can work with this person, go
back to calling the people on your list.

WHAT IF YOU HAVE a large, complicated, or
unusual project? In such cases, you should
arrange for two or three engineers, or representatives from two or three engineering
firms, to make an on-site inspection of your
project. While you will be faced with considerably higher initial consultant's fees, it
might be worth the cost to hear different
opinions, and get several quotes for the
design work that needs to be done. When you
get quotes from engineers or engineering
firms, bear in mind that each of them will be
quoting a price for a design plan, and that
design plans are seldom alike. Don't be too
impressed by a low quote; make sure you choose
the plan best suited to your project.

SOME WORDS OF CAUTION: Don't hire inspectors,
planning people, and the like, who work for
the city, county, or utility company and
"moonlight" as consulting engineers. And
don't hire one of their relatives either!
Sometimes, there's a conflict of interest
here. ("Well, I can't approve that, but I've
got a brother-in-law who can bring it up to
code for you...") A lot of costly and
irreparable damage has been done to old
buildings by underqualified "para-engineers"
who aren't licensed, and don't carry liability
insurance.

IF YOU HIRE an engineer (or para-engineer) to
inspect a building, and he also happens to own
a construction company, it's always in his
best interest to find big problems with your
house.

How They Charge

"**A** BARGAIN is that which is excellent, not
that which is cheap." So says the
American Consulting Engineers Council
(ACEC). They continue: "You're not looking
for the cheapest design job. You're seeking
'design value,'" which comes when you engage
the most qualified firm at a fair price.
Remember that extra time (and cost) in the
design phase can save money in the long run by
reducing maintenance or replacement cost.

THE ACEC'S POINT IS WELL TAKEN: Engineers
design things, they don't build things, and
design is a creative process, not a commodity.
If you need an engineer, your first priority
should be to hire an engineer who is skilled
and experienced in projects like yours. If
you are restoring an old house, you want an
engineer with experience and expertise in
restoring old houses; you don't want a veteran
of several insensitive gut renovations. You
should expect the engineer's fee to be fair,
but this should not be your first priority.
Sort of like choosing a doctor.

AN IMPORTANT BIT OF PROTOCOL: For the reasons
cited above, engineers don't like the term
"bid." They really hate the term "low bid,"
so don't ask them to bid on your job. They
will respond to an "Invitation To Submit
Information".

HERE'S WHAT YOU GET CHARGED FOR: The engineer's visit to the site, his technical iden-
tification of the problem, an analysis of the
building and <u>written</u> recommendations. The inspection and <u>written</u> report will take several
hours of the engineer's time and may cost several hundred dollars. The cost for an engineer's services ranges from about $55 to $90
per hour. If the project is relatively simple
(an inspection, or specifying the size of a
load-bearing member), the engineer will probably charge you for about four hours' work.

YOU CAN SAVE yourself money doing some of the
prep work yourself. For instance, if you know
some basement panelling has to come out before
the engineer can inspect the foundation, go
ahead and pull it out before he gets there.

J UST BECAUSE you've hired a specialist to
come in and suggest the best course of
action doesn't mean you can't do some or
all of the repair work yourself. You can use
the engineer's report to guide you through
your project. In fact, Lowell Christy, of
Christy - Cobb Engineers in Birmingham,
Alabama, says that in three-quarters of the
residential projects she works on, the repairs
she recommends are done by the homeowner.

FOR MORE INFORMATION:

The American Consulting Engineers Council has
a book available for $5 ppd., entitled, <u>A
Guide to the Procurement of Architectural and
Engineering Services</u>. If you're considering
hiring an engineer or an architect, you should
get a copy. Its step-by-step approach is easy
to understand. Write to: ACEC, Dept. OHJ,
1015 Fifteenth St., N.W., Washington, D.C.
20005. (202) 347-7474.

Special thanks to Connie Neuman, Director of Information and
Communications for the American Consulting Engineers Council,
Washington, D.C.; Lowell Christy, of Christy-Cobb Engineering,
Inc., 1031 S. 21 St., Birmingham, Al.35205. (205) 251-0499; and to
David C. Fischetti, P.E., 109 Brady Court, Suite 200, P.O. Box 835,
Cary, NC 27511. (919) 467-3853. Both private firms specialize in
consulting work on historic buildings.

My Life With A Beehive Oven

by Barbara Hood
Hammondsport, New York

A follow-up to last month's article on building brick bake ovens

OUR LOCAL Landmark Society offered a very enjoyable and informative class on fireplace cooking, and I'd like to share what I learned with the OHJ readers. The first thing is the firing of the oven. It takes about one hour's worth of a good blazing fire to get the oven hot enough to bake bread (approximately 375 to 425 degrees). The smoke from the fire at first turns the oven bricks black, but as the temperature of the bricks increases, the smoke burns off and the bricks are clean again. By that point your oven is hot enough for baking. The next step is to clean out the oven. Do this as quickly as possible; the longer the door is open, the more heat you lose.

A LONG-HANDLED, shovel-like implement called an ash peel is used to clean out the ashes and any unburned wood. I prefer to shovel the hot ashes into the fireplace rather than the ash pit. This way, the smoke and gases can go up the chimney; that's better than having them infiltrate into the room, which is what happens if you shut up the ashes in a flueless ash pit. (Surprisingly, historians aren't quite sure how ash pits were used.) After cleaning out the oven with the ash peel, dip a fireplace broom in

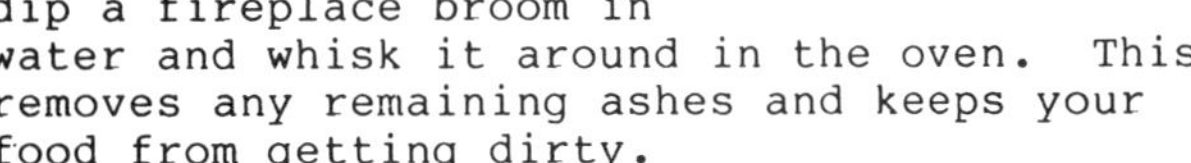

water and whisk it around in the oven. This removes any remaining ashes and keeps your food from getting dirty.

TO CHECK the temperature of the oven, put your arm straight into the oven as far as you can. Be careful not to touch anything! If you can leave your arm in for a count of seven, the oven should be around 400 degrees. If your arm gets too hot before you reach seven, leave the door off for a while and check again. The bricks hold a tremendous amount of heat; we've had our oven reach over 600 degrees. (You might want to add a modern touch by checking the temperature with a stove thermometer. Use one for high temperatures, at least over 600 degrees, with no liquid or mercury in it.) We've also found that the oven can retain a good deal of heat: 32 hours after one firing, the temperature was 125 degrees.

WHEN THE TEMPERATURE'S RIGHT, it's time to do some baking. Bread requires the hottest oven, so start baking that first. As the bread cooks you can then go on and bake cakes, quick breads, and puddings. Unfortunately, the brick oven isn't good for baking lots of cookies; you have to keep opening the oven, and that cools it down too quickly. While all those goodies are baking, you can also have a nice big pot of chowder or stew cooking on the crane over the open fire.

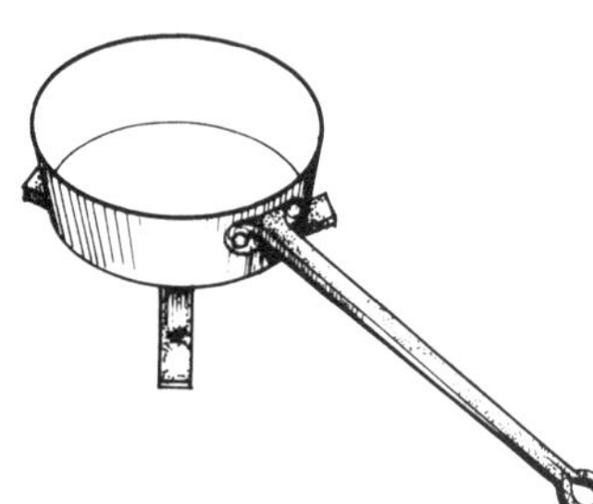

ANOTHER WAY to use your fireplace is to cook over hot coals on the hearth. When the fire in the fireplace is producing a nice bed of red coals, take the ash peel and shovel the coals onto the hearth. Set a dutch oven on the coals, put the cover on, and pile more coals on top of it. I particularly like the dutch oven for making small cakes and muffins. Another method of cooking on the hearth is with open pots or spiders. You set them up the same way, except you don't cover them with lids and coals. They're great for making sauteed dishes.

Design Ideas

I AM SURE each person's fireplace and oven are unique in some way. I know ours is because we built it ourselves, along with the entire house! When we decided to build an authentic Saltbox house, I began looking for old houses with intact fireplaces and ovens. I found quite a few, and in photographing and measuring them I learned that each one was different in some way. One variation in our construction, concerning the front edge of the fireplaces, I think will be of special interest to OHJ readers.

I DON'T LIKE the modern look of the square edge of the brick on the surface (illustration A at right). The old fireplaces used corner bricks (B). At the time we were building, corner bricks weren't available. Some masons tried slicing off part of the brick (C), but I didn't like the appearance of the cut surface: It was brighter in color and the circular saw marks were visible. Our solution was to cut angles on the ends of the bricks and mortar the edges together (D).

I'VE INCLUDED in this article some of the recipes I've used and liked. Oven owners should always try new things; experiment a little, it's usually worth it. One evening after baking I put some oatmeal in a bean crock and closed the door until morning. The oatmeal cooked slowly all night long. It was still warm in the morning, and delicious!

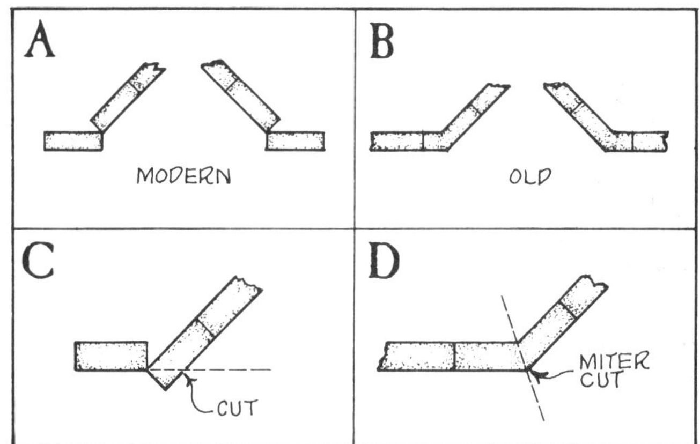

My Beehive~Oven Recipes

PIONEER MEAL BREAD

2 cups pioneer meal (equal parts corn meal, rye flour, & wheat flour)
2½ cups unbleached flour
1 cup whole wheat flour
1 pkg. or cake yeast
3 tbsp. butter
2 tbsp. honey

Dissolve yeast in ½ cup warm water with ½ tsp. sugar, and let set for 8 to 10 min. Mix pioneer meal with the unbleached flour and wheat flour in a large bowl. Mix 1-2/3 cups warm water with the butter & honey. Add yeast mixture to water mixture and add to flour. Beat together thoroughly. Add more unbleached flour; just enough to make the dough firm enough to handle. Turn out on floured board and knead about 10 min., until smooth. Shape into ball, put in buttered bowl, turn to butter top, cover, and let rise until double, 1 to 1½ hrs. Punch down, divide in half, and shape into 2 loves. Place in greased bread tins, cover, and let rise for 45 to 60 min., until almost double. Then bake at about 375 degrees for 40 to 60 mins.

CORN CHOWDER

4 to 6 strips of bacon, cut into small pieces
1 small onion, chopped
4 potatoes, cubed
2 cups corn cut from cobs & milk
4 cups milk
3 tbsp. butter
1 carrot, grated

Put bacon in iron kettle over open fire and cook slowly until crisp. Add onion & cook slowly another 5 min., stirring often. Add potatoes, corn and corn milk scraped from cobs, carrots, butter; salt & pepper to taste. Heat slowly to let flavor develop. If fresh corn is gone, use 1 cup kernels and 1 cup creamed corn. (I always double this recipe — it's even better the second day!)

Here's the best reason in the world for having a beehive oven: homemade cinnamon buns, just begging to be scarfed!

CINNAMON BUNS

1 pkg. or cake yeast
¾ cup scalded milk
½ cup butter, cut in small pieces
2 cups flour
¾ tsp. salt
2 eggs
1/3 cup sugar
2½ cups more flour
Cinnamon filling:
 ¼ cup soft butter
 ¼ cup white sugar
 ¼ cup brown sugar
 2 tsp. cinnamon
 nuts (optional)

Dissolve yeast in ½ cup warm water with ½ tsp. sugar. Let set for 8 to 10 min. In large bowl combine milk & butter. Cool to lukewarm. Add yeast mixture, 2 cups flour, 2 tbsp. sugar, and salt. Let stand covered in a warm place for ½ hr. or until mixture bubbles. Add eggs, beating after each. Add the 1/3 cup sugar & the remaining flour ½ cup at a time to make a soft dough. Knead on lightly floured board about 10 min. until smooth. Shape into a ball, put in greased bowl, turn to grease top, cover, and let rise until doubled, about 1½ hrs. Punch down and divide in half. Roll each half to about a 12-by-8-in. rectangle. Spread with butter, sprinkle with cinnamon filling. Roll from long side tightly. Slice each into 9 rolls and place in two 9-in. round pans or one 9-by-13-in. pan. Cover and let rise until almost doubled, about 45 min. Bake at about 350 degrees for 25 to 30 min., until browned.

DELICATE NUTMEG CAKE

¼ cup butter
¼ cup shortening
1 cup sugar
1 tsp. vanilla
3 eggs, beaten
2 cups sifted flour
2 tsp. nutmeg
1 tsp. soda
1 tsp. baking powder
¼ tsp. salt
1 cup buttermilk

Cream butter & shortening. Gradually add sugar, creaming until light. Add vanilla and eggs; beat well. Sift dry ingredients and add to creamed mixture alternately with buttermilk; beat well after each addition. Pour into one 9-by-13-in. or two round, greased pans. Bake at 350 degrees for 35 to 40 min. for 9-by-13-in. pan; 25 to 30 min. for two round pans. (This cake could be baked in the brick oven or the dutch oven.) May be finished by sifting powdered sugar on the cooled cake or a broiled frosting. Mix 3 tbs. melted butter, 3 tbs. brown sugar, 2 tsp. cream, and ½ cup chopped nuts or shredded coconut. Spread on warm cake & broil. To broil topping, heat the ash peel by laying it in the fireplace, right in the hot coals. When very hot, hold it over the topping, almost touching, until the topping starts to bubble.

To Strip Or Not

NOT STRIPPING MASONRY is cheaper, easier, and less risky than stripping it, so let's start with some good reasons not to strip. First of all, maybe the building was meant to be painted. Painted brick was quite popular in the 19th century, sometimes for a poly-chrome paint scheme, and sometimes to follow a European tradition of dark red paint with mortar joints "pencilled" in white.

OFTEN BUILDINGS were painted -- at the time of construction or soon after -- for more practi-cal reasons. Cheaper, less attractive, more permeable bricks may have been used by the mason on a budget who expected the building to be painted. Early in the life of the build-ing, water penetration may have been solved with a barrier of paint, which is less permeable than most brick. Or maybe the paint is later still, masking additions to the building. So, stripping may reveal ugly bricks, mismatched repairs or additions, or even architectural detail that turns out to be sandpainted wood, and not masonry at all.

ON THE OTHER HAND, there are some good reasons to strip masonry. The building may not have been painted until late in life, and then for a poor reason: It was dirty. Also, natural brick is, especially to our eyes, almost always prettier than a flat coat of paint. And once the paint is off, the long-term maintenance of the bulding is simplified: You no longer have to paint every few years.

YOU <u>MUST</u> STRIP failed paint from masonry before you can repaint. Depending on the degree of failure, you may have to completely strip the masonry. (There's no need to get every last bit off if you intend to repaint.) For practical rather than aesthetic reasons, you should strip masonry if:

(1) The paint is badly chalking, flaking, or loose. Find the cause! Flaking is most often due to moisture penetration and retention.

(2) The masonry has been "sealed" with an extra-heavy buildup of paint layers, or by gloss oil-based paint or aluminum/oil paint. In such a case, the masonry can't give up moisture and salts that accumulate in it.

The owner intended to repaint anyway, but look what stripping revealed: patches, bad pointing repairs, and wood trim.

Pressure will build up under the paint layers, and when the paint flakes, it will take some masonry with it. Look for signs of this happening. The masonry should be stripped with a commercial paint stripper, washed, repointed where necessary, and repainted with a high-quality latex masonry paint. Note: Paint will not stick to a powdering surface.

D-I-Y?

WHEN A BUILDING must be stripped, most owners hire a contractor. Exterior masonry stripping is difficult and hazardous. Besides needing specialized knowledge, the applicator works with strong chemicals, sometimes several storeys up. Professionals have experience and skill, a source of materials, and expensive extras such as scaffolding. The right masonry-stripping contractor should also know all about collect-ing and disposing of the effluent that comes off the building.

ONCE YOU'VE MADE the decision to strip, the contractor should do a test patch. This will settle the unique specifications for the job, as well as establish a "control" by which the rest of the job will be judged. Determine:

(1) The type of stripper to be used.
(2) The concentration to be used.
(3) The dwell time, or optimum time for the chemicals to sit on the masonry.
(4) The optimum pressure/volume of rinse water.

Disposing of Waste

WHAT'S COMING OFF the building is a chemical strong enough to strip paint, mixed with the softened paint itself. The paint sludge that comes off old houses contains lead (among other things) and is classified as a toxic waste. Flushing sludge into the soil will contaminate the ground around the house for many years to come. The sludge will contaminate well water. Flushing it down the sewers may contaminate water sources and is illegal — you will be fined if you're caught.

LEGALLY, it's the responsibility of the owner or architect to specify waste disposal procedures as part of the contract. Most contractors are not upfront about the disposal details, so press it: Make the final payment contingent upon your receiving a copy of the *hazardous waste manifest*. That way, you'll be heeding EPA regulations — and be-sides, it's the moral thing to do.

CATCHING the effluent is no big deal. Generally, it's contained in weighted tarps cov-ered with absorbent straw. Then it's put in 55-gal. drums and a waste hauler is paid to dispose of it properly. The cost to the customer is about $125 per drum — a propor-tionately small cost, as a residential-size job may generate only one drum.

SANDBLASTING

To THOSE OF US who have been dragged to see hundreds of awful sandblasting mistakes, it seems incredible that there should still be any need to warn against it. Yet we've prepared this article partly in response to the recent reader questions that have come by phone and in the mail, asking whether sandblasting is okay. People have been told by contractors (who have major investments in blasting rigs) that sandblasting "is the only method that will work." Others have heard that sandblasting causes problems, but don't know the alternatives.

SO ONCE MORE, let's review the case against sandblasting. In abrasive blasting, sand or another abrasive is shot against the building in a high-pressure jet of air or water. This quickly removes the paint, but as the abrasive doesn't know where the paint film stops and the masonry starts, it always removes some of the building, too. It is all too easy to lose control; in fact, with high pressures, it is impossible to keep control. Consider the variables:

1) type, condition, and hardness of masonry
2) density, hardness, size, and shape of the abrasive
3) the pressure
4) the constancy of the pressure used
5) the distance from nozzle to surface
6) the skill of the operator
7) visibility of the surface
8) the angle of "hit"

ALL of these factors significantly change the effect of the blasting on the surface. And there's no way sandblasters can control all of them. The machinery is heavy, the scaffold has to be moved; all workers become fatigued.

WHEN THE DUST clears, the masonry will be changed. Aggregate is exposed as the softer clay is blasted away. Depending on which material is harder, the relationship between the masonry units and the mortar will have changed, altering the character of the surface. The "skin" is removed, often exposing a more permeable core. Blasting increases the surface area of the wall, and so it will now get wetter than before, and it will become dirtier more quickly. With no crystalline planes to refract light, the surface reflectivity changes, sometimes even resulting in an apparent change of color.

IT CAN'T BE FIXED. Clear sealers (which the blaster will almost surely try to sell you) can't be recommended because they often make the problem much, much worse. Moisture _will_ get into porous masonry somehow; it always does. But sealed masonry won't be able let it back out anymore. Instead, the water will build up hydrostatic pressure behind the coating, and when it pops out, it will take some masonry with it. Also, clear sealers run from not effective at all to effective for only three to five years (you're back to a maintenance schedule worse than painting), and applicator error can leave streaks or variations in surface gloss across the facade.

NEED MORE REASONS not to sandblast? It's strictly prohibited by the Secretary of the Interior's Guidelines for Rehabilitation -- a condemnation from people who know, and you won't get your investment tax credit. Because of the environmental hazard of flying abrasive, it's now banned by many municipalities.

IF THE CONTRACTOR is smart, he or she doesn't call it sandblasting anymore. And in fact, sand may not be the abrasive used. The list of alternative grits has gotten ridiculous: ground slag, volcanic ash, almond and walnut shells, rice husks, corncobs, ground coconut shells, glass beads, crushed eggshells, microballoons, powdered limestone, chopped plastic. It doesn't matter; any grit blasted at high enough pressure to remove paint will harm the surface underneath. "Waterblasting" is popular; this is when the sand is carried by water instead of air. It has the advantage of letting the operator _see_ the surface, as opposed to being surrounded by a cloud of dust, but it doesn't soften the blow. We've heard the word "featherblasting," and silly things like, "don't worry, I put talcum powder in the sand."

THE WATER RINSE will introduce water into the masonry. You don't want to introduce it into the house, however, so be sure to inspect the pointing. If you are worried about water entry, at least do a temporary joint-filling job with caulk or soft mortar. It need not be a finished pointing job. In general, it's better to repoint after the stripping operation. You will be able to see better to match the mortar color, and the rinsing will have dislodged any loose mortar. Because of the water, finish up at least a month before the first potential frost. Water freezing in the masonry will damage it.

The Method Of Choice: Chemicals

CHEMICAL TECHNOLOGY for strippers is not as diverse or complex as that for masonry cleaners. Generally, masonry strippers are alkaline formulations, some quite basic, others close to pH neutral. In virtually all of the commerical preparations, sodium hydroxide (lye) is _not_ used, as it often causes efflorescence later. (Efflorescence is a whitish "bloom" on the masonry caused by water-borne salts coming to the surface.)

SOME CHEMICALS manufacturers recommend a dilute acid afterwash to neutralize the caustic stripping chemicals. This is done after the sludge has been rinsed away, and is followed again by a clear-water rinse. Other preparations don't need the neutralizing afterwash, especially if the masonry is not to be repainted.

HOWEVER, if you do intend to repaint, you must neutralize and rinse thoroughly, or the paint will not stay on. Do not repaint until the masonry is completely dry. If you have any doubts, hold off on painting for six months or a year, to allow the masonry to rid itself of residues (efflorescence can be simply brushed off the surface).

THE PROPRIETARY CHEMICAL strippers are much more expensive than lye-based strippers, but they are worth it in lowering the risk to the building. With lye, removing residue becomes all the more critical. And neutralizing with strong acid would probably damage the mortar. It virtually cannot be neutralized enough to allow repainting. Proprietary strippers contain additives which increase surface activity (where the paint is) while avoiding deep penetration into the masonry.

WHEN YOU CHOOSE a proprietary formulation, you are buying a company's experience, avoiding the labor and hazard of mixing your own ingredients, and lowering risk for your building.

THE MOST WELL KNOWN stripping products are from the Sure-Klean line, manufactured by ProSoCo. ProSoCo prefers to sell direct to the contractor; the company guarantees its chemicals and wants to know who is using them. They maintain four regional offices, not only for sales, but also to answer technical queries. A technician will even visit the site if a problem crops up. For product information or a list of qualified contractors near you, contact ProSoCo at 1040 Parallel Parkway, Dept. OHJ, Kansas City, KS 66104; (913) 281-2700.

ANOTHER manufacturer who distributes nationwide is Diedrich Chemicals--Restoration Technologies. Again, the products are guaranteed and he prefers to sell only to distributors, contractors, and architects. For a free brochure or to get the name of a local contractor using Diedrich products, write to 300A East Oak St., Dept. OHJ, Oak Creek, WI 53154; call (414) 764-0058.

SOLMICA Chemical Mfg. is a smaller company with a commendable track record. The company head, a chemist with experience in masonry restoration, sells only to fifteen or so trained applicators, who operate "franchises." Work is guaranteed, and each dealer is trained by the manufacturer. Contact Solmica Chemical Mfg. at 6240 Wiehe Rd., Dept. OHJ, Cincinnati, OH 45237; (513) 631-0076.

FOR THE WHOLE JOB contracted out, expect to pay about $1 to $1.50 per square foot for chemically stripping paint from brick; more if there is a lot of masking or an extra-heavy buildup of paint.

FOR EVERY masonry-stripping horror story that involves some rare and unforeseen variable, there are many jobs that go without a hitch. All we see in print are the exceptions, accompanied by explanations of the failure which are ever more technical and, sometimes, far-fetched. It seems only fair to give space to the other side — the straight-forward job.

I FIND IT hard to advocate the do-it-yourself application of lye under any circumstances: It's risky for the building and dangerous for the applicator. But "the proof is in the pudding." These people have successfully used the method on several brick buildings — and served their major concern of saving money.

MAYBE this is an alternative for the predictable job.

— P. Poore

Lye Stripping

by Adrian Lonnecker & David Miller

HISTORIC preservation publications are full of warnings about "improper" procedures on brick walls. They are short, however, on what's "proper," especially when it comes to stripping paint from brick.

SANDBLASTING is taboo, as are other abrasive methods. We stripped our building with chemicals and rinsed with cold water under high pressure. The latter <u>did</u> damage some of the mortar, which may have soon needed repointing anyway, but the bricks stood up very well. It cost us dearly to do this job, mostly because we lacked a methodology, even with the advice of professional paint chemists. If you are planning to strip bricks with chemicals, this article could save you thousands of dollars and help you avoid damage to your walls.

THE TYPE of paint stripper most of us are familiar with uses methylene chloride as an active ingredient. This isn't so suitable for outdoor work because of its quick evaporation. If you used an off-the-shelf solvent stripper, small areas would have to be power-rinsed about ten minutes after each application.

MOST OUTDOOR strippers are alkaline (pH basic). They work more slowly, and this is what we recommend. We further recommend that the stripper be mixed from raw chemicals, as opposed to buying ready-mixed concoctions. The only ready-mix we could find locally cost fifteen to twenty dollars per gallon. Our homemade stripper cost around fifty cents per gallon. Keep in mind that the mix should be applied in a layer at least 1/8-inch thick, so it doesn't cover nearly as much as paint does per gallon.

FOR US, homemade stripper has certain advantages over ready-mix:
1. It is much cheaper.
2. It can be mixed on a flat rooftop, reducing significantly the amount of weight to be carried up.
3. It can be left on a wall longer without forming a super-glaze.

HERE is a list of what you'll need to duplicate our method:
1 bag bentonite clay
one 100-lb. barrel caustic soda (lye)
a washtub on legs with drain spout
a 5/8-in. automotive heater hose, 50 ft. long
a drill-pump
a 1/2-in. vari-speed electric drill
1 gallon vinegar
a valve (see illustration)
AND:
respirator(s)
long rubber gloves
rubber or plastic suits
rubber boots
heavy-duty garden hose

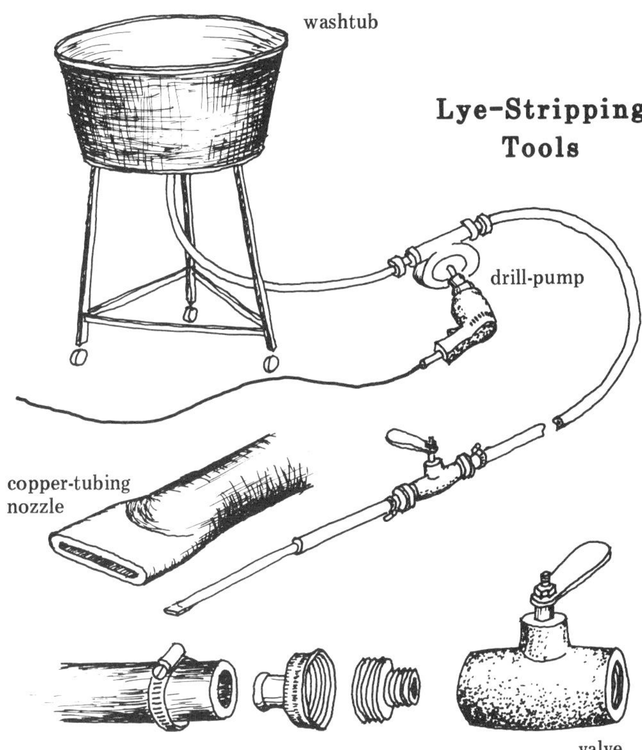

WE BASED our stripper on a formula from a
chemists' handbook:
33 lbs. water (lukewarm)
1.85 lbs. clay
6.11 lbs. sodium hydroxide crystals (lye)

SAFETY: Wear a respirator. The lye crystals
should be handled with rubber gloves, as a
speck will drill a hole in your skin. Like-
wise, the diluted mixture will eat your flesh
if not rinsed immediately. We experienced
burns on our arms. This was due to our early
ignorance, crude application techniques, and a
lack of rubber sleeves. (Ready-mix alkaline
strippers will burn you with equal vigor.)
And no joke -- ALWAYS wear eye protection.

TO MIX 5 GALLONS: Measure water and put in a
clean plastic 5 gal. pail. Sprinkle clay into
water while agitating with paint agitator pow-
ered by the 1/2-in. vari-speed drill. Mix as
furiously as possible for about five minutes,
as this will cause the clay to gel. The
mixture should start to thicken at this point.
Now carefully sprinkle in the crystals while
slowly mixing. (Never add water to crystals,
only crystals to water.) Before all of the
crystals are added, the mixture will turn to
"oatmeal," but don't be alarmed. Continue
agitating the stiff mix, for it will eventually get less thick as you add the rest of the
crystals. Beware: the mixture will self-heat
(like drain cleaner); it can be used in this
state. Now you should have a really thick
gel, perfect for vertical application. To mix
larger batches, we used the 15-gal. steel
drums that the crystals came in.

APPLICATION: We tried brushes, brooms, rollers, buckets, pitchers, and spray guns, but
found a pump works best. We used what is
called a "drill pump," designed for household

use. We went through four of them, so if you
have a big job, a good chemical-resistant pump
would be required. Just make sure the shaft
is 1/2 inch or smaller, so you can use the
drill to drive it. The caustic reacts with
aluminum, so don't use any aluminum fittings.

THE APPLICATOR should be suited up "to the
max," and the tub should be higher than the
wall if possible. All workers in the area
should wear goggles. It's alkaline, but post
"DANGER: ACID" signs to better warn people
below. Keep vinegar and a live hose ready for
first-aid.

MAKE NOZZLES by hammering the end of 5/8-in.
copper tubing, after inserting a piece of
thick sheet metal to maintain an opening of
sufficient size.

OUR RIG would throw the mixture two to four
inches and cover a wall thicker and quicker
than any other way. Once we perfected this
method, burns were drastically reduced.
Spills were drastically reduced, too. And it
really worked well on details.

BY THE WAY, protect your soil with plastic
sheets. The caustic and paint sludge will
kill grass and shrubs. Collect the sludge and
dispose of it properly.

THE RINSE: Test for the amount of time needed
for the chemical to work. We have left it on
overnight. When the mud gel is dry it stops
working, so it is imperative that it goes on
thick to stay wet. Rinse first with the
garden hose, so the high-pressure wash won't
blast chemical at you. We hired a water
blaster, and carefully supervised him so he
wouldn't blast out too much mortar. Catch
effluent in the plastic and pump it away if
necessary. If you do not get all the paint
off the first time, you're in trouble. The
paint on the brick has acted as a barrier so
that the bricks didn't soak up the chemicals.
But subsequent applications tend to leave un-
rinsable residues.

DRYING OUT: If you get it all in one pass,
there will be less residue. If you let paint
that has been through the process stay on the
wall, it can be extremely difficult to remove
later. A dilute acid rinse will help neutralize alkaline residues, but will eat the mortar. [Editor's note: Lye stripping makes more
sense for buildings that will remain unpainted. Residues will interfere with the adher-
ence of new paint.]

THIS STRIPPER will take paint off wooden
details, but will bleach and roughen the surface. [Editor's note: Wood will retain alkaline residues that cause new paint or varnish
to blister and fail. Lye is not recommended
for use on exterior wood.] It is obviously
not to be used on interior woodwork.

A QUESTION: Should you strip at all? Why not
just repaint? It certainly would have been
cheaper for us. Some random notes: Soft, permeable bricks are more difficult to work with.
Paving-quality or hard-fired bricks and high-
cement-content mortar would be ideal. Soft,
high-lime-content mortar can survive quite
well, provided the paint is softened sufficiently to be removed with one power rinsing.

Ask OHJ

Rust Stains in Clawfoot Tubs

LATELY, when cleaning my clawfoot tub, I seem to be bringing out rust-like stains. I've tried all kinds of products -- from bleach to rust remover -- to get rid of the stains, but they only seem to get worse. Can you help?

-- Cindy Wells Carrolton, Ga.

RUSTING IN CLAWFOOT BATHTUBS after long periods of disuse is a common problem. Unfortunately, there's not much you can do about it. Porcelain naturally wears thin, allowing moisture to penetrate it and cause the cast iron underneath to begin to rust.

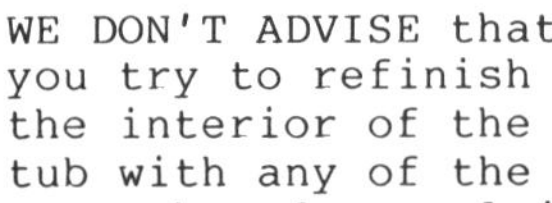

WE DON'T ADVISE that you try to refinish the interior of the tub with any of the epoxy-based porcelain repair products on the market. They wear through and chip easily.

ONE WAY YOU CAN PREVENT the wearing away of your porcelain is to use a nonabrasive cleaner -- we recommend Bon Ami. Bon Ami's old-fashioned Cleaning Powder scrubs with feldspar, so it won't scratch the porcelain like cleansers with silica.

Removing Carpet Mastic from Wood

WE JUST PURCHASED a 100-year-old house that has wall-to-wall carpeting. We're removing the carpet, but some of its backing is sticking to the wood floor. How can we remove this sticky backing from the floor?

-- Muriel Doll Northpoint, N.Y.

WE RECOMMEND that you remove the sticky, black carpet backing from your wood floor with a chemical solvent. Be sure to scrape off as much of the backing as possible with a sharp handscraper (the kind Sears sells with removable blades is good), so that the solvent won't soak the black stuff into the floor.

START WITH A MILD SOLVENT such as paint thinner. Be sure to try a test patch in an inconspicuous place first, especially if you are trying to save the original finish. Other solvents, from gentle to harsh, are naphtha, lacquer thinner, and acetone. Remember, all of these chemical solvents are flammable and should be handled with care. And don't forget to wear gloves!

Floor-Refinishing Kit

WE RECENTLY READ about a floor-refinishing kit that sounds too good to be true. It comes with fine steel wool, plastic gloves, and two liquids: one for cleaning the floor, the other for restoring the color and the finish. We would like to lighten the color of our floors, but we are anxious not to sand them. Is this kit indeed as good as it is advertised to be?

--Barbara and Bob Lewis New York, N.Y.

THERE'S NOTHING "too good to be true" about the floor finishing kit you saw advertised -- and there's probably nothing wrong with it either. Refinishing liquids are available from several companies and are sold in large hardware stores or building supply stores. The solvents in them clean the floors, remove wax, and reamalgamate the old finish to some extent. These people have turned it into a kit by including steel wool and gloves. If you do buy the kit, or use another type of refinisher, be sure to do a test patch in an out-of-the-way place.

Tar on an Old Copper Roof

I AM RENOVATING a 1930s house with a copper roof. The previous owner applied tar to most of the seams and other areas where he thought there might have been leaks. But the tar has not prevented leaking and at present needs to be removed in order for the roof to be repaired. Do you know of a preparation that can be used to remove tar from copper?

--James L. Wiegerink Los Angeles, Calif.

WE KNOW A CHEMIST who spent the better part of a year trying to find a way to remove tar from the copper roof of a major New York City landmark. He concluded that there was no cost-effective way. Solvents and dry ice (to embrittle the tar) were used with some success, but it was slow going.

YOUR ROOF MAY BE SALVAGED and repaired correctly, even with the tar patches. Perhaps some of the roofing can be replaced, while other areas are saved to keep the cost down. A competent roofer who specializes in metal roofing can tell you what's involved and what it will cost.

General interest questions from subscribers will be answered in print. The Editors can't promise to reply to all questions personally—but we try. Send your questions with sketches or photos to Questions Editor, The Old-House Journal, 69A Seventh Avenue, Brooklyn, NY 11217.

Woodwaiter–A Dumbwaiter for Firewood

Now here's an item that would have been a welcome gadget if it'd been around in the 19th century. If you seriously heat and cook with wood, you'll surely appreciate the Woodwaiter. Basically a small electric dumbwaiter, the Woodwaiter is an easy way of moving wood from the cellar to the hearth.

The Woodwaiter lifts 125 lbs. of standard 16-in. firewood. There are two designs; the Pop-up model has a trap door that opens as the woodbox comes up to floor level. The Permanent Woodbox model is grooved pine with an angled hinged top into which the Woodwaiter delivers a load of wood.

The units are designed for homeowner installation and can be installed in any house with sufficient clearance. The wood box sizes range from 18 in. to 26 in. square and are priced from $679.50 to $1,062 FOB Lennoxville.

For more information and a free brochure contact W.B. Fowler Industries Inc., 9 Haskell Hill Road, Lennoxville, Quebec, Canada J1M 2A3. (819) 562-8510.

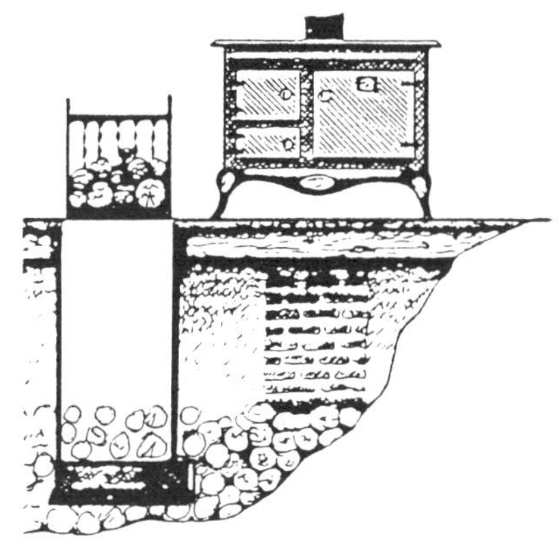

Weathertamers Catalog

Brookstone currently has a very good Fall and Winter catalog out entitled *Weathertamers ... For The Energy Conscious.* Here are a few items you and your old house might find useful: a small alarm that tells you when the basement is flooding; foam-insulating blankets for single-glazed windows; and attractive wool hearth rugs to protect your wood floors from hot coals.

For cooking on your wood or coal stove there is a Super Griddle and a cast-iron kettle. You can seal up leaky doors on your wood and coal stoves with a variety of woven fiberglass gaskets.

For a free copy of the Brookstone Weathertamers catalog, write to Weathertamers, Dept. OHJ, 630 Vose Farm Rd., Peterborough, New Hampshire 03458. (603) 924-7181.

New Thatch Roofing Comes To America

Thatched roofs are rare in this country, but Warwick Cottage Enterprises is changing all that with the introduction of their Warwickshire Thatched Roof Coverings. This is real water reed thatch, installed exactly as it's been for centuries by master thatchers (not some new product made from soda straws)!

Wes Warwick, general partner in the new firm, has done a quite impressive job in getting fire-retardant Class 'A' and treated Class 'C' rating certifications for the thatch, and in creating a very good thatching manual (available for $3). Even if you're not interested in having your Queen Anne thatched, you'll appreciate all of the intricacies of the craft, which are profusely illustrated in the manual.

From the late 1600s well into the 1800s, thatch roofing could be seen on buildings from Massachusetts to far-western territories such as Utah. Although there are few remaining structures here today that originally had such roofs, Wes is finding terrific interest for thatching on new commercial and residential structures as well as outdoor museum structures.

Far from being short-lived, water reed thatching can last as long as 70 years, will withstand 110 mph winds, is not affected by mildew and fungus, is waterproof, handles high heat and snow well, insulates to an R 11.8, and bugs don't like it.

John Cousins and Alan Lewis, master English thatchers, have been imported by the Warwick firm not only to apply the thatching in a traditional manner but also to train American apprentices in the craft. They dress the thatching to the roof, using a leggett tool, to a minimum thickness of 12 in. Ridge caps, a truly distinctive woven feature, are made from sedge, a type of reed similar to water reed. Thatching is applied over the battens and plywood sheathing on roofs having a minimum slope of 45 degrees (12:12). The cost of this type of roof is about $2500 per square (100 square feet).

To find out more contact Wes Warwick, Warwick Cottage Enterprises, Dept. OHJ, 2944 Greenhedge Ave., Anaheim, CA 92806. (714) 630-9251.

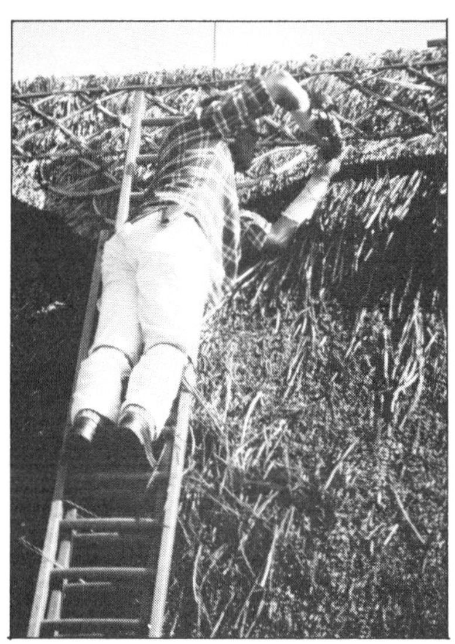

Finnish Fireplaces & Parts

Many of us have heard of Rumford fireplaces, but have you ever heard of Finnish style, wood-fired, masonry heaters? Albert and Cheryl Barden of Maine Wood Heat Co. are masters at designing and building this 200-year-old system of high-efficiency masonry heaters, bake ovens, cookstoves, and fireplaces since founding their firm in 1976.

You may recall that the Rumford fireplace and shallow firebox is designed to radiate heat out into a room, retaining little heat in its thermal mass. The Finnish design takes the opposite approach; a deep rectangular firebox radiates heat into itself for maximum temperature and combustion efficiency. Through a sophisticated downdraft technique, heat from the fire is absorbed and slowly radiated from the entire mass of the heater. All of this means that these masonry heaters, if carefully built and fueled twice a day for 1-1/2 hours for each burn, can serve as the primary heat source for a tight, well insulated, single-family home. The heaters are capable of generating as much as 50,000 BTUs per hour, an 80% efficiency rate. Once the burn is completed and dampers are closed, the entire mass of the heater will radiate heat for the next 12 to 24 hours.

You can build these heaters yourself, and if you want to find out more about the system and its requirements, send $2 for their catalog and price list. Their illustrated step-by-step construction manual contains technical drawings and a materials list and sells for $15.

Completed Finnish style fireplace with jack arch and cast iron doors.

The catalog contains one of the most extensive lines of cast-iron, masonry heater bake oven, and cookstove parts we've found. There is a cast-iron oven, numerous hinged access door designs, dampers, and even a complete stove cooktop. There are a number of fireplace, heater, and bake-oven plans ranging in price from $5 to $15.

Here's an interesting item: Did you know that some early fireplaces, beehive ovens, and chimneys were laid up with a clay rather than lime-based mortar? An early form of refractory mortar often consisted of 3 parts sand and 1 part clay. It was used for inner common brick exposed to high heat but not exposed to weather. Maine Wood Heat currently offers a high quality and hard-to-find Finnish clay-based heater mortar that is less brittle and rigid than cement-based mortars and is designed for use in inner heat-stressed walls of fireplaces. Also available is high-quality refractory mortar for use on firebrick.

Because Finnish Heaters are constructed differently from conventional fireplaces, Maine Wood Heat offers a complete assistance and training program.

For more information contact Maine Wood Heat Co., Inc., Dept. OHJ, P.O. Box 640, RFD 1, Norridgewock, Maine 04957. (207) 696-5442.

Remember Murphy Beds?

Even if you've never heard of a Murphy Bed, chances are you've seen the Marx Borthers or the Three Stooges fold themselves into one. This wonderfully American invention, technically known as the Murphy In-A-Door Bed, was invented by William L. Murphy at the turn of the century in San Francisco. He had a problem common to many old-house owners — not enough space. His bed took up most of the space in his one-room apartment, so he began experimenting with a folding bed to free up additional space.

In 1900, Murphy applied for his first patent and the Murphy Door Bed Co. was off and rolling. Eighty-four years later the company is still going strong, making it one of the oldest furniture firms in America. By 1918, Murphy had invented an ingenious pivot bed that swung out from a closet and lowered to a sleeping position. Shortly thereafter he created another space-saving devise, the first compact kitchen called the Murphy Cabrinette.

Today, Murphy Beds are available in standard sizes: twin, double, queen and king. All of the beds use standard-size bedding and go up fully made, no storing pillows or bedding during the day.

Murphy Beds can be mounted in custom-built cabinetry that suits your house, or fit into a wall behind doors.

The basic concept is a simple counter-balancing bed frame that attaches securely to the floor with screws. When not in use, the bed simply raises into a closet or cabinet wall that's from 16-1/2 in. to 23-1/2 in. deep (depending on the model). There's even a Murphy Sidebed that raises into an opening only 44-1/2 in. high.

Murphy beds have a number of features that make them attractive for use in older houses. First, the bed takes up very little space and can be designed into a wall, placed behind period-style doors that match the rest of the house, or with a little ingenuity, fitted into an old armoire. Secondly the bed itself uses conventional springs and mattressing, which make it comfortable to sleep on, unlike those folding beds and sleeper couches we've all gotten aching backs on.

Murphy Beds are priced from $332 to $803. You can order the Murphy Bed direct from the manufacturer and they will pay the freight. When you write for a free catalog be sure to check out their line of Cervitor Compact Kitchens, too. Murphy Door Bed Co., Inc., Dept. OHJ, 40 East 34th St., New York, NY 10016-4595. (212) 682-8936.

More On Vapor Barriers

I talked to a Vermonter named Bill Hults recently, a builder, inventor, and energy specialist who runs the Energy Conservation Equipment Company. We were discussing air infiltration problems, and he told me about a Canadian book entitled A Double Wall Retrofit Project, by I.H. Warkentin (available from Energy Conservation Equipment Co. for $5.95 ppd.). The book deals with the creation of a two-layer, insulating exterior wall structure on an existing 1906 Winnipeg (Manitoba, Canada) house. Particularly interesting was the unusual installation of a continuous polyethylene air/vapor barrier seal, and construction of a double-wall insulating structure (pioneered by the National Research Council of Canada). To over-simplify things, an old house was wrapped in plastic and new, insulated walls were built around it.

Now don't jump to conclusions! We're not suggesting that you try all of the energy-conserving measures that were carried out in this house. But there are a lot of very good techniques illustrated and backed up with facts and figures that could help you tighten up your old house. Here are some of the benefits you could expect: Elimination of drafts and cold spots, slower fluctuations in temperature, a healthier winter atmosphere with higher humidity, a cooler house in the summer, a quieter house that will retain heat longer, reduced heating and cooling costs, control of air quality and ventilation rates, and perhaps a higher resale value.

Air/vapor barrier film and boxes are shown sealed into place over insulation.

Not until the 1970s did we begin to fully appreciate the value of continuous air/vapor barriers.

Even though we stuff insulation into every nook and cranny, we're — at best — simply filtering the air as it comes in (infiltration) and goes out (exfiltration). And it comes and goes through an enormous number of little openings, which we hardly bothered to look for in the cheap-energy days.

The single biggest obstacle, of course, to installing an effective vapor barrier in an old house is that interior walls have to be removed. This simply isn't cost effective or desirable unless the original perimeter walls and ceilings are damaged beyond repair or missing altogether. If they are, you have an excellent opportunity not only to reduce infiltration but also to add additional insulation without increasing the overall project cost very much.

Installing an air/vapor barrier is relatively simple. Six-mil polyethylene is set into a bed of non-hardening caulk and stapled directly to the exposed studs of the interior walls around the perimeter of the house. Great care is taken to overlap and seal the poly sheets and to avoid punching holes in the plastic when finishing the wall installation.

Bill warns that electrical systems are one of the largest sources of air infiltration in most houses. Outlets and switches should be located on interior walls wherever possible, and ceiling-mounted light fixtures abandoned in favor of interior wall-mounted fixtures. The total elimination of recessed ceiling lighting and exhaust fans in exterior ceilings that are to have vapor barriers and insulation is also recommended. These units can't be sealed to the point where they won't leak air without over-heating and creating a fire danger.

Plastic vapor barrier is sealed around boxes and edges with non-hardening Tremco Sealant.

Where electrical boxes must penetrate vapor barriers, Energy Conservation Equipment Co. sells new patented air/vapor barrier boxes to be installed before the vapor barrier. The air-tight boxes are made in Canada and designed to enclose electrical boxes and be sealed to the vapor barrier. There is a type of air/vapor barrier box to fit all conventional electrical boxes. A box for a single outlet or switch sells for $1.10, and a ceiling box is $1.20 plus postage. For a complete listing of the available electrical boxes write for a free price sheet. Dealer inquiries are invited. Energy Conservation Equipment Co., Dept. OHJ, P.O. Box 161, Worcester, VT 05682. (802) 229-4236.

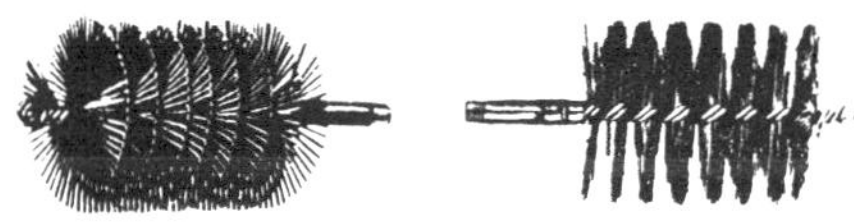

Chimney Sweep Brushes

Keeping chimneys and flues free of soot and dangerous creosote build-up is a job that many old-house owners are finding they can do themselves for less than the cost of hiring a chimney-sweep.

A firm here in Brooklyn that's been in business well over half a century makes a high-quality line of chimney cleaning brushes and accessories and sells them at reasonable prices.

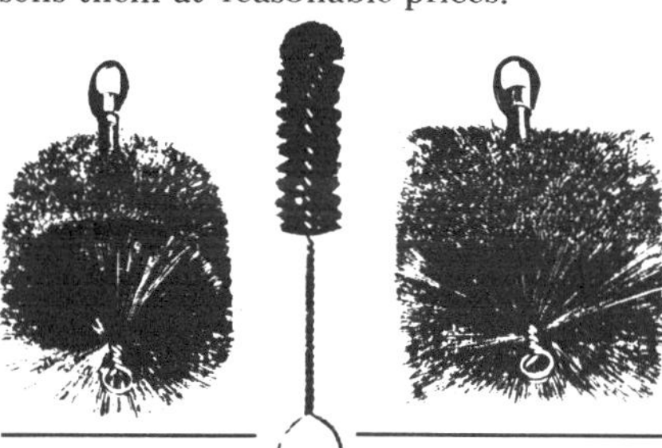

Round, square, and even rectangular brushes are available made from wire, fiber, or nylon. A 6-in. round chimney brush sells for $11, and the 6 in. x 6 in. square model is $16.50. Twisted flexible wire handles and fiberglass extension rods sell for $5.50 and $7 each for the 3-1/2 ft. length.

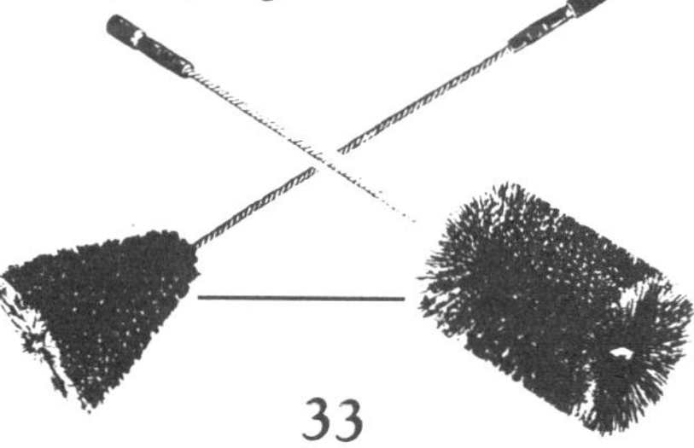

For a free brochure and a set of chimney cleaning instructions, write to Ace Wire Brush Co., Inc., Dept. OHJ, 30 Henry St., Brooklyn, NY 11201. (718) 624-8032.

MOST OF THE BUILDINGS featured on this page are residential, but a subscriber from Croton-on-Hudson, New York, submitted a non-residential remuddling we just couldn't refuse.

DEAR REMUDDLING EDITOR:

ENCLOSED IS MY CLAIM on your Remuddling bounty: An addition to one of God's old houses.

I CAME UPON THIS remarkable job at Clayton, in the extreme southwest corner of Massachusetts. The original church is, as you see, a very lovely little Shingle-style building -- a beautifully simple composition in a small rural center. Between the church and the road is an old burial ground with an iron picket fence, weathered stones, and fading flags.

THE ADDITION, I suppose, is also clean and simple -- notice how the three new front windows echo the original windows. And no doubt the new walls are going to be shingled to match, too. So there's an attempt at keeping in keeping. But look at the crude side windows, the bald new doors, the cement stairs, and the awkward vents and chimney. Where did these good people ever get the idea that one could, in any satisfactory way, hope to stick an immense addition onto the side of a small unified design, complete in itself? If I were God, I'd move.

YOURS TRULY,

David Roessler, Architect
Croton-on-Hudson, New York

The Old-House Journal®

**69A Seventh Avenue,
Brooklyn, New York 11217**

NO PAID ADVERTISING

Postmaster: Address Correction Requested

Restoration and Maintenance Techniques
For The Pre-1939 House

March 1985 / Vol. XIII No. 2 / $2.

The Old-House Journal

Standing Seam Roofs

by Walter Jowers
Illustrated by Larry Jones

A GENERATION AGO, sheet-metal workers built a lot of cornices, skylights, and roofs -- usually standing seam roofs. Since around 1940, though, few of these roofs have been installed on houses. The cost of the skilled labor required to install a handcrafted roof is out of reach for many homeowners, and a good roofer/metalworker is almost as hard to find as a good roof thatcher.

UNTIL RECENTLY, old-house owners who wanted to replace their worn-out standing seam roofs didn't have many good choices. Most roofing contractors won't go near the job, and the ones who will usually want to tear off the metal and install asphalt shingles or roll roofing. Or worse yet, they'll coat the metal with a horrid black ooze that will <u>not</u> stop leaks. Do not allow these people to darken your door. Or your roof. Anyone with time, gumption, and good native skill can install a standing seam roof using pre-formed panels and inexpensive rented tools.

cont'd on p. 44

A $1,000 OHJ grant is music to the ears of the Compton Heights Concert Band of St. Louis, seen here in front of their restored Victorian bandstand. Compton Heights is a historic neighborhood of 270 families, and the band (organized in 1976) has become a focal point of community pride. Band President Harry Swanger (upper right) spearheaded the fund-raising drive that sold 180 OHJ subscriptions. . .and added $2,080 to the band's treasury.

Six Groups Win $1,000 Grants

SIX PRESERVATION groups each have $1,000 more for their 1985 projects thanks to The Old-House Journal's Grant Program. The six winners became eligible for the grants by participating in OHJ's Revenue-Sharing Plan in 1984:

Arlington Historical Society — Arlington, Mass.
Sussex County Historical Society — Newton, N.J.
Compton Heights Concert Band — St. Louis, Mo.
Winchester Historical Society — Winchester, Mass.
Historic Albany Foundation — Albany, N.Y.
Preservation & Conservation Association of Champaign County — Champaign, Ill.

THE REVENUE-SHARING PLAN lets preservation organizations offer their members OHJ subscriptions at a discount. And each group keeps half of all the money it collects. Last year the 149 participating groups earned $22,000 for themselves.

THE FIRST $1,000 grant goes to the organization that sells the most subscriptions--this year,

the Compton Heights Concert Band. The other 5 grants were awarded by a drawing. Names were drawn by Mary Kay Gallagher, a resident of Brooklyn's much-admired Prospect Park South community since 1959. She has been a tireless advocate of Brooklyn's neighborhood revival through her work as a real estate broker specializing in historic houses, and as a Director of the Prospect Park South Assn.

WE STARTED the Revenue-Sharing Program to share money with preservation groups who help us sell OHJ subscriptions. Our alternative is to sell subs by direct mail. But instead of shoveling money into the Postal System, we'd rather give the money to preservation groups.

OVER $25,000 is available for the 1985 Revenue-Sharing and Grant Programs. If your group would like to participate, contact: Barbara Bugg, The Old-House Journal, 69A Seventh Ave., Brooklyn, NY 11217. (718) 636-4514.

The Old-House Journal®

Editor
Patricia Poore

Production Editor
Cole Gagne

Technical Editor
Larry Jones

Assistant Editor
Sarah J. McNamara

Contributing Editors
Walter Jowers
John Mark Garrison
Roland A. Labine Sr.

Architectural Consultant
Jonathan Poore

Circulation Supervisor
Barbara Bugg

Circulation Assistants
Jeanne Baldwin
Garth White

Special Sales
Joan O'Reilly

Assistant to the Publisher
Tricia A. Martin

Catalog Editor
Sarah J. McNamara

Publishing Consultant
Paul T. McLoughlin

Publisher
Clem Labine

Published by The Old-House Journal Corporation, 69A Seventh Avenue, Brooklyn, NY 11217. Telephone (718) 636-4514. Subscriptions $18 per year in U.S., $25 per year in Canada (payable in U.S. funds). Published ten times per year. Contents are fully protected by copyright and must not be reproduced in any manner whatsoever without specific permission in writing from the Editor.

We are happy to accept editorial contributions to The Old-House Journal. Query letters that include an outline of the proposed article are preferred. All manuscripts will be reviewed, and returned if unacceptable. However, we cannot be responsible for non-receipt or loss — please keep copies of all materials sent.

Printed at Photo Comp Press, New York City

ISSN: 0094-0178
NO PAID ADVERTISING

1984

1938

General Rochambeau Slept Here
The Story Of Breakneck Hill

by Lawrence M. Duryee

UNLIKE MOST OLD-HOUSE LIVING STORIES, this article focuses on a restoration completed over forty years ago. The Duryees bought the Josiah Bronson house in 1940 and still live there; they have spent years researching the history of their house. Although the restoration is long since completed, the Duryees' intimate knowledge of its past continues to make the house an important part of their lives. *—SJM*

MY WIFE ESTHER AND I first saw the old Josiah Bronson house one bright April day in 1940. We were galloping down an old logging road, paying attention to our mounts. Two friends riding with us slowed their horses and pointed. "That's the oldest house in Middlebury, Connecticut," they said. We couldn't believe it! The shingles were weatherbeaten and warped. The big central chimney needed repointing and rags were stuffed into holes in the door to keep the rain out. A rickety side porch didn't belong there. Piles of rusty farm machinery cluttered what was once a lawn. Under the old maple, a lopsided spring house once used for cooling milk was on its last legs. An old cowbarn leaned dangerously near the bend in the road, its roof caving in. Its south door, through which cows had been led for milking, was shattered.

DESPITE ITS WRETCHED condition, the Bronson house appealed to us in a way we couldn't define. We were very curious about its history. The next day we

The Duryees combed deeds, maps, land records, probated wills, and cemeteries for the history of their house on Breakneck Hill. They found Josiah Bronson's headstone in a local cemetery.

checked old land records and queried the town clerk. "Yep," he said in his Yankee drawl. "Oldest house in town. Maybe 1740, maybe earlier." We learned that Isaac Bronson, Josiah's father, began construction in 1738, but died before the house was completed. Isaac left the unfinished house to Josiah, "in building, with all the stone-work and the glass." A year or so later Josiah completed the house, moved in, and, with four wives and twelve children, lived until the age of ninety-two. We found his headstone in our local graveyard.

FOLLOWING HISTORIANS' LEADS, we tramped through the dense woods beyond Josiah's apple orchard and found the large stone monument that marks the spot where the famous French leader, General Rochambeau, had camped in 1781. Rochambeau led four thousand of his native troops, who had landed at Newport, Rhode Island, on the long march from Providence to the Hudson River where they joined forces with General Washington's Continental Army. (They went on to defeat Lord Cornwallis and the British Army.) The encampment at Breakneck oc-cured on a rainy night in June 1781. Rochambeau's mapmakers designated Breakneck Hill as Camp No. 9. It's reported that Bronson invited the French general to spend the night in his home. After the memorable battle at Yorktown, Rochambeau's victorious army came back through Connecticut and camped in the same spot they had earlier, labelled Camp No. 46 this time. Again, Josiah entertained his friend General Rochambeau.

Left: The basement vault hid the Bronsons' valuables during raids by the Algonquin Indians. (The skull is a recent addition to spook visitors.) *Center:* A neighboring farmer posed in front of the house in 1940, when the area was still quite rural. The Duryees removed the shutters, which were not original to the house. *Right:* Esther and her daughter Carol were proud enough of their thoroughbred to have him photographed in the living room. The colt, Crack O'Dawn, was raised in Josiah's south pasture and barn, which the Duryees also restored.

ON ANOTHER CLOUDLESS DAY two months after we first saw it, we mortgaged our future and bought the old Josiah Bronson place. With a picture in our minds of colonial charm, intimate gardens, and fields of hay and alfalfa for our horses, we dedicated ourselves to restoring the house. Two centuries of wind, snow, and summer storms had not changed its fundamental structure. What it needed most at this point was loving care.

MIRACULOUSLY, we discovered the original twelve-over-twelve windows in Josiah's neglected haymow. They'd been stored there for decades! The putty was gone, but the glass was still intact. Some of the glass had circular air bubbles, indicative of colonial glassblowers. When the fifty-year-old windows -- grotesquely out of place -- were finally replaced, we celebrated!

THE SOUTH DOOR -- called the "coffin" door because deceased family members made their final journey through it -- was in perfect shape. It was held in place by heavy hand-wrought iron hinges that we sanded, then burnished with 4-0 steel wool to bring back the glow of the old iron. The panelled front door, covered with layers of old pigment, needed scraping and refinishing.

THE POST-AND-BEAM CONSTRUCTION is the highlight of the house's interior. All of the posts and beams are visible and were never covered with plaster. All they needed was a thorough cleaning. We had to strip old paint from the wainscotting and panelling in the living and dining rooms and two bedrooms. We repainted all the surfaces, including the chair rails, in period colors.

A BATHROOM NOW TAKES the place of the Bronsons' "keeping room," where they once stored preserves. The plumbing was installed after we removed layers of old wallpaper and repaired the original horsehair-and-plaster walls. We painted the walls a dull white to simulate the whitewash the Bronsons had originally used.

THE PREVIOUS OWNER, a mechanical engineer, had started work on the interior and installed a unique invisible heating system (see OHJ, Dec. 1976) to supplement the three fireplaces. I made an eight-foot-long hinged trap door for the entry to the attic to prevent heat loss. After installing ventilators to let moisture out, I insulated the attic with six inches of glass wool.

THE CELLAR SENT US into ecstasy! When we inspected the oak beams, still covered with bark, each end was held in place with wooden pegs. We covered the dirt floor with gravel for easier walking and installed a pump to keep the basement dry during heavy rains.

OUR 90-YEAR-OLD NEIGHBOR took us aside and, as if telling us a great secret, insisted that we carefully examine the foundation stones of the central chimney. We finally found it -- a loose boulder two feet above the cellar floor. We removed the boulder by wedging pointed knives around the stone, being careful not to mar it. Behind this boulder was a cavern four feet wide and five feet high! Inside we could see the walls and the large smooth boulders that formed the domed ceiling. The vault floor, two feet above the cellar floor, was free of soot, so the cavern had not been used for cooking. Legend has it that the Bronson family used the vault as a hiding place for valuables during raids by the Algonquin Indians. After the Indians had gone, the treasures were removed. Silver, gold coins, and pieces of rare china brought from England were hidden there and then recovered -- all in complete secrecy.

A FEW YEARS AGO, Michel Rochambeau, the General's descendant, and his wife came to the United States from Paris. They not only traced the entire route their ancestor had followed in 1781, but spent the night in Josiah Bronson's house. Together, we were able to celebrate the continuation of a friendship that began on a rainy night in June more than two hundred years ago.

Lining Materials

by Stephen L. Wolf

OLD WALLS AND CEILINGS in need of repair ... bad cracks that keep coming back ... peeling and flaking paint ... tacky artificial wood panelling ... water-damaged plaster ... a cinder-block wall you'd like to make smooth. Frequently, the answer to these old-house problems is a lining material.

THE TERM "lining canvas" may be commonly used, but it's become a misnomer. Canvas or cotton is still the fabric of some lining materials, but today most are based on synthetics such as polyester or fiberglass. The lining material is coated with latex, usually an acrylic, which is pigmented white. This coating bodies the base fabric and acts as a primer.

DON'T CONFUSE lining <u>materials</u> with lining <u>paper</u>. Lining paper, as its name implies, is a paper product and is not primed. Unlike lining materials, it's intended for use only under wallcovering. To some extent, it will smooth out a not-too-rough wall, but basically it's used to provide good tooth and even porosity for the wallcovering adhesive. It also absorbs some of the moisture in the adhesive, thereby reducing the possibility of bubbles and wrinkles.

LINING MATERIALS, or fabrics, are available in several weights. The heavier ones, approximately 18 to 20 mils thick, are intended for use over such surfaces as cinder block, cement block, and brick. These fabrics are thick and stiff enough to bridge open areas, including mortar joints. They usually show a surface texture, and so are more frequently finished with wallcoverings that hide their texture, rather than with paint.

THE MORE LIGHTWEIGHT fabrics are recommended for walls that are relatively smooth, but have suffered minor damage such as flaking paint, cracking plaster, efflorescence due to past water damage, or less-than-perfect previous patching. Paint or wallcoverings can be applied over these liners.

WHEN SELECTING wallcovering designs and paint finishes, you should of course make your selection after your own decorative preferences. But bear in mind that certain designs and finishes will improve the overall appearance. If your walls are showing their age, avoid glossy finishes in either wallcovering or paint. The higher the gloss, the more light reflection will show up surface irregularities. Flat finishes are recommended (or at most an eggshell sheen). With wallcoverings, a fairly busy design will also help.

General Hanging Instructions

I. MASONRY
(Concrete, Cinder Block, Cement Block, Brick)

THE LINING MATERIALS recommended for masonry walls are heavier and stiffer than those used on smoother surfaces. But they won't conceal the bumps and protuberances of these rough surfaces; you'll have to smooth these irregularities by knocking or sanding them off. Extensive filling won't be required because the lining materials are strong enough to bridge pits and mortar joints. The only case where you should bother filling in crevices and

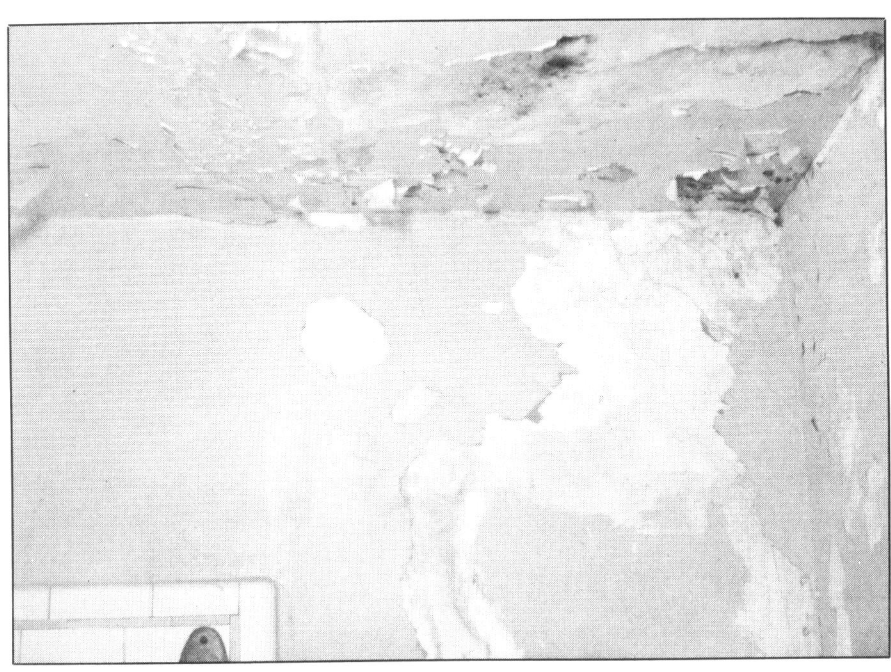

The best way to rescue a wall such as this one, with its water-damaged plaster and peeling paint, is by applying lining material.

joints is when you're covering cinder block. (If you're tackling that job, use a latex block-filler for a smoother surface.)

WHETHER OR NOT you use block-filler, be sure to size the wall. Use a mixture of 50% water and 50% ready-mixed vinyl adhesive; allow to dry at least two hours. If the wall was previously painted, replace the vinyl-adhesive size with an acrylic-emulsion primer (Roman's R-35, Zinsser's Shieldz, Insl-X's Aqualock, or any other product specifically designed to go under wallcovering).

CUT EACH STRIP of the lining material 2 to 3 inches more than the height of the wall. For the first strip measure from the corner approximately 1/2 inch less than the width of the material, so you can cover the corner. Paste the back of the strip, giving special attention to the edges. When you carry the strip to the wall, fold it over loosely, paste side to paste side.

That crumbling mess shown on the previous page has been brought back to life by the proper application of the appropriate lining material.

HANG EACH STRIP vertically, from the top down. Use a plumb line to make sure the hanging is exactly vertical. Smooth with a sponge or smoothing brush, one foot at a time. (Don't use too much pressure, or you'll force the lining into the joints and cracks.) Work from the center out to eliminate air bubbles. Butt the seams -- do not overlap. Trim the top and bottom with a razor blade.

ALLOW AT LEAST four or five days drying time -- even more if the area is poorly ventilated or if the weather has been humid. Afterwards, prime the lining with an acrylic-emulsion primer, and let it dry for several hours. These materials may then be painted or wall-covered. When hanging a wallcovering make sure its seams don't coincide with the seams of the liner.

II. PANELLING
(Wood, Composition Board, Plastic, Etc.)

HERE AGAIN you should apply heavier lining materials to bridge grooves, seams, and other irregularities. First roughen the surfaces with a coarse sandpaper (80 D production paper). You should also wash these surfaces thoroughly, as they've frequently been waxed or oiled. If you can stand the odor, ammonia makes a good wash; otherwise, a heavy-duty cleaner such as Ajax may be used. Rinse it off completely when you're finished.

THE PANELLING should then be primed with an acrylic-emulsion primer. Allow two or three hours drying time. Use a ready-mixed vinyl adhesive and hang the lining material horizontally. (This will give you the smoothest results.) If you find it easier, hang the material vertically, but be careful that the seams don't line up with the grooves in the panelling.

III. PAINTED WALLS

THE MOST FREQUENT USE of lining material is on walls that have been repeatedly painted over the years. It can create a new wall by removing all sorts of problems: peeling from water damage; cracks in the paint film (which sometimes extend to the plaster underneath); badly done spackling or other repairwork. The liners for these jobs are usually smoother in finish and more lightweight than those used on masonry. But heavier material may be best for badly damaged walls.

PREPARE THE WALL by sanding off all bumps and protrusions. Flaking and peeling paint must be rigorously scraped off. Wide cracks and depressions deeper than 1/4 inch should be filled with a paste spackling. Don't bother filling fine cracks -- the lining fabric will bridge them.

THE SMOOTHER THE SURFACE with which you start, the smoother your final result will be. Apply an acrylic-emulsion wallcovering primer before hanging the liner. Then hang the fabric vertically (although sometimes horizontal hanging is done), using a ready-mixed vinyl adhesive. Liners of synthetic fabrics are always butted at the seams; liners of cotton canvas can be overlapped and double-cut at the seams because cotton is subject to shrinkage. Air bubbles under the liner can be removed by slicing them open with a razor blade and pressing the material back into place.

ALLOW AT LEAST four to five days drying time before painting. Lining materials are factory-primed, so primer is usually unnecessary under a flat finish. For semi-gloss and high-gloss enamels, however, either an alkyd or latex enamel undercoater should be applied. If wallcovering is to be hung over the liner, always prime with an acrylic-emulsion wallcovering primer.

Product Name	Maker	Basic Uses	Composition	Thickness	Texture	Roll Size	Cost per sq.ft.
Wall Cover No. 9962	Imperial Wallcoverings a division of Collins & Aikmen	As a lining over cinder block, concrete block, & other irregular surfaces. Recommended particularly for use under flexible wall-coverings, but may also be painted. Heavier & stiffer than most liners.	25% cellulose 38% synthetic fibers 37% acrylic latex saturant	20 mils	slight surface texture	28 in. W by 15 ft. L; packed three single rolls per bolt, approx. 105 sq.ft. per bolt	29¢
						42 in. W by 150 linear yards, total 1,575 sq.ft.	27¢
Wall-Over No. 20950	Columbus Coated Fabric a division of Borden Chemical	A heavy, somewhat stiff lining fabric for use over masonry, painted surfaces, & drywall. It will bridge grooves & other deep imperfections, & result in a slightly textured surface that may be painted or wallcovered.	65% polyester 35% natural cellulose acrylic primed	18 mils	slight surface texture	27 in. W by 15 ft. L; approx. 34 sq.ft. per roll	30¢
No. 30950						54 in. W by 150 ft. L; approx. 675 sq.ft. per bolt	24¢
Wall-Tex Lining Canvas No. 20990	Columbus Coated Fabric a division of Borden Chemical	Lightweight, primed canvas for repair & restoration of damaged walls. Creates a new, smooth wall surface for painting or for hanging wallcovering. Not heavy enough to bridge deep or wide grooves & cracks unless filled.	80% cotton 20% polyester acrylic primed	12 to 14 mils	very slight texture	27 in. W by 15 ft. L; packed in double rolls, approx. 68 sq.ft. per double roll	30¢
No. 30990						54 in W. by 36 ft. L per bolt, approx. 162 sq.ft. per bolt. Also 54 in. W by 48 yards L (144 linear ft.) = 648 sq.ft.	25¢
Glid-Wall No. 70127	Glidden Coatings & Resins a division of SCM Corporation	Repairs cracked & damaged walls, ceilings, & woodwork. Can also be used on rough masonry & cement block. Creates a new, permanent surface that strengthens & smooths the substrate. Must be primed with Insul-Aid Primer Sealer.	Johns Manville Fiber Glass not primed	22 mils	smooth mat	48 in. W by 300 ft. L; 1,200 sq.ft. per roll	10¢*
No. 72659			*Additional cost of primer is approx. 15¢ per sq.ft.	30 mils	smooth mat		13¢*
No. 70884				22 mils	burlap finish	40 in. W by 300 ft. L; 1,000 sq.ft. per roll	14¢*

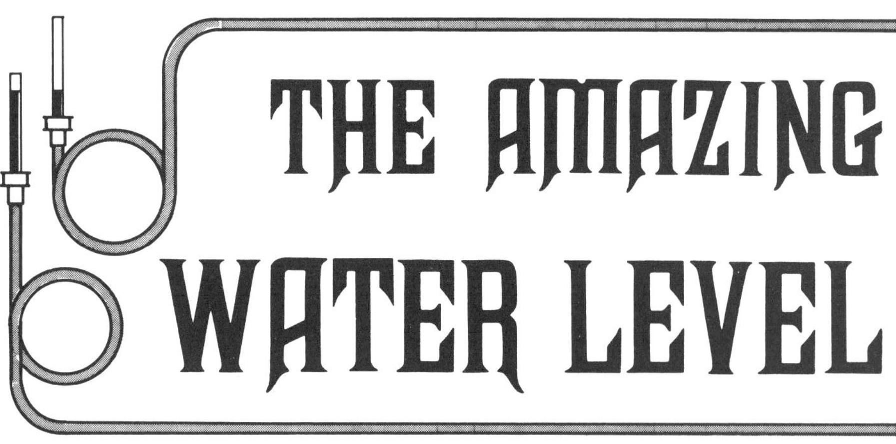

THE AMAZING WATER LEVEL

BY LARRY JONES

A WATER LEVEL IS A "LOW-TECH" GEM of a tool, quite useful for work around an old house, where nothing is level, but some things ought to be. I've used water levels to level porches, to translate the first-floor ceiling height to an outside wall, to set the tops of fence posts, and to establish a sloping grade for an underground foundation drain, among other things.

PLASTERERS USE THE WATER LEVEL for lots of jobs, including placing dots and screeds and running cornices. You may recall that John Garrison mentioned using a water level in his article on running plaster cornices in our Dec.'84 issue. The tool is so easy to handle that it even can be used from scaffolding and other tight areas on construction projects. (If you are doing any type of decorative plastering and want to find out more about how plasterers use this tool, see our new book Plastering Skills, available from the Old-House Bookshop.)

OF COURSE, A LOT OF LEVELING JOBS can be done with a bar level or a surveyor's transit. Most of us know know that a surveyor's transit is one of the best and most accurate leveling instruments available. But there are a few snags. First, you'll have to pay to rent one of these precision instruments. Second,

you'll need to know how to set up and use one. Assuming you need the extreme accuracy of a transit without all the bother you should try a water level. It can be of infinite length, and can go around walls or through windows. It's as accurate as any leveling tool, and it's real cheap.

TO MAKE A WATER LEVEL, all you need is:

● A garden hose 3/8 in. or 1/2 in. inside diameter, with a good rubber washer in the female end. You don't want your level to leak. The length depends on your needs; 25 feet is usually the shortest common length of garden hose you can buy.

● Clear plastic hose of the same inside diameter as your garden hose (get this at a hardware store). Buy two feet of this hose and cut it into two one-foot lengths. Rigid, clear acrylic tubing (available from plastics dealers) will also work, using hose clamps instead of couplings.

● One male and one female hose coupling; make sure the female coupling has its washer. (Get these at a hardware store, or cannibalize an old garden hose that's been chewed by the lawn mower or the dog.)

● Some hose clamps (hardware store or auto supply house) for connecting soft plastic hose to couplings.

Assemble the above parts as shown in the illustration.

THE EASIEST WAY TO FILL THE LEVEL is to funnel water from another garden hose or faucet into the level. If there's no running water on your jobsite, then you can fill the level by siphoning water from an uphill source (a big bucketful of water) into the hose. You may find it less messy, especially indoors, to have a second bucket downhill to catch the excess water. Once the level is full -- it's full when the water comes about halfway up in both clear plastic viewing tubes -- you should

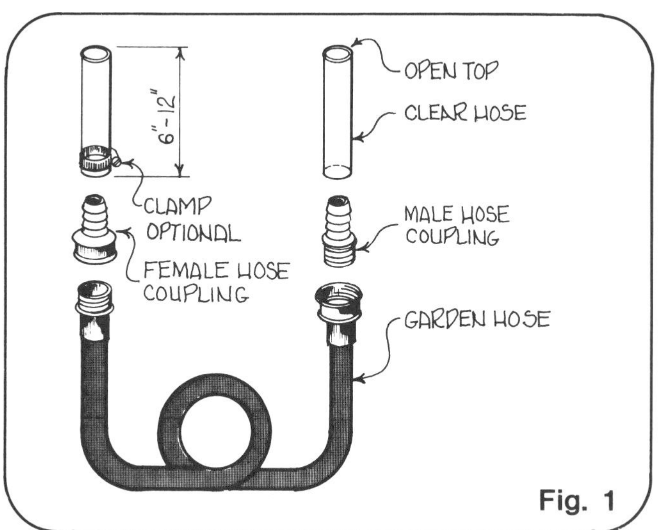

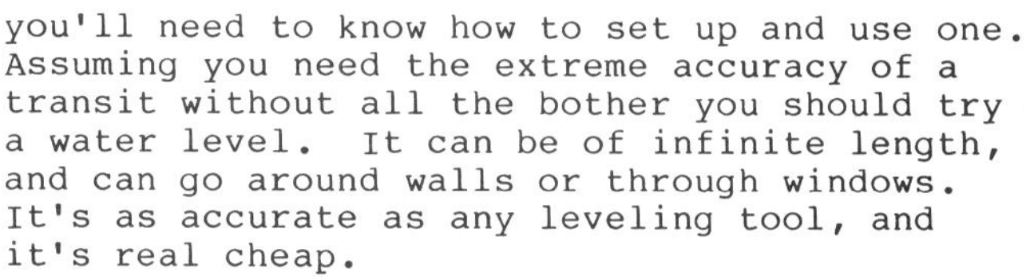

gently shake the level up and down (with the ends open) to dislodge any air bubbles in the hose. Errant bubbles will affect your readings.

TO CHECK THE LEVEL FOR PROPER FUNCTION, bring the ends of the level together as in Figure 2. The water line should be level. If it's not, there's something wrong (a kink in the hose, an air bubble, or a large bug in the line). You'll have to correct whatever is wrong so that water comes to the same level in both viewing tubes.

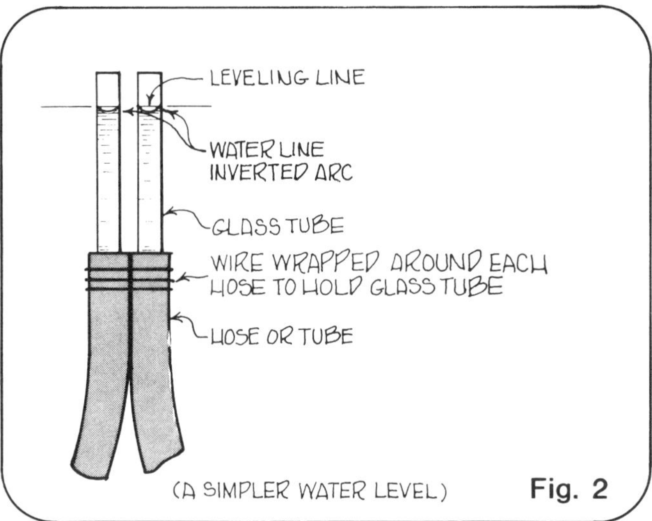

HERE'S AN EXAMPLE of how the water level works (see Figure 3): Let's say you have a wainscot that extends up the wall to point A, and you want to find the same height on the adjacent room wall (we'll call this point B). Hold the level so the water line comes to point A, and have a partner take the other end of the level into the other room. The water in the viewing tube at the other end will be at the same height, which is point B. It doesn't matter how far apart these points are; the only limit is the length of the hose.

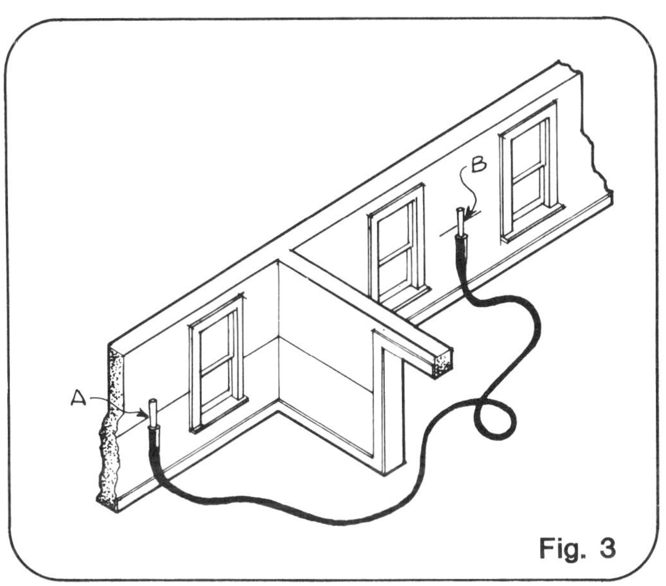

NOTE THAT THE WATER forms an inverted arc in the viewing tube (see Figure 2). You will get more reliable measurements by always reading the top line of this arc (make sure your partner reads this same line too). And when you sight or mark using the level, both of you should have your eyes level with the water to avoid distortion and inaccurate readings.

FIGURE 4 SHOWS how the water will move as you try to find the unknown point. As you hold the level with the water line at the known point, the water line will move as your partner looks for the unknown point. If the water line on your end goes up to X, your partner's end is too high, at x. If your end goes too low, to Y, then your partner's end is too low, at y. As you can tell from this illustration, if one end of the level gets much higher than the other one, water will slosh out the low end. To keep this from happening while you're moving the level, you and your partner should keep a finger over the end of the tubing. You have to take your fingers off when you are ready to read the level, though. Some plasterers simply stick corks in the ends of the tubes until they're ready to use the level.

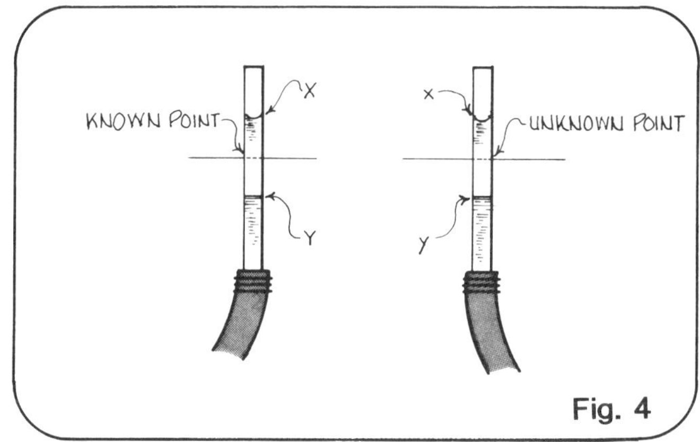

The first mention of a water level we've found was in a 1929 issue of Carpenter Magazine. The tool simply consisted of water-hose with a glass tube slipped into either end and filled with water.

IF YOU NEED TO MAKE SEVERAL MARKS, you should make all of them from the original mark. This reduces the possibility of cumulative errors as you progress. If the length of your hose requires you to move both ends, be sure to regularly measure back to previous points to check your work.

YOU CAN EVEN USE WATER LEVELS outdoors in cold weather. Just use a hose material that remains pliable (rubber is best), and put some anti-freeze in the water. If you do this, DON'T use the siphon method to fill the level -- you don't want to swallow any anti-freeze, because it's poisonous. The coloring in the anti-freeze will make the water line in the tubes easier to see.

IF YOU NEED A WATER LEVEL, but don't have the time or inclination to make one yourself, you can order one from U.S. General Tool Co., Dept. OHJ, 100 Commercial St., Plainview, NY, 11803. (800) 645-7077. Order the "Levelall," model #47001. Price: $24.99.

roof *cont'd from p. 35*

MOST OF THE OLDER standing seam roofs in this country are made of terne metal, though more than a few are galvanized iron or steel. Some are copper, and, in rare instances, black iron or black steel was used. There are even a few zinc roofs around. The old-house owner who wants to install a new standing seam roof need only consider these three materials:

● TERNE: This is a copper-bearing steel, coated on both sides with terne alloy, which is 80% lead, 20% tin. It has been used as a roofing material in this country since the 1700s. Monticello has a terne roof. The bad news about terne: You have to paint it, and keep it painted, or it will rust. The good news: You get to paint it any color you like; and, if it is kept painted, the roof should outlast the rest of the house. Material cost is about $75 per square (100 square feet), not much more than good asphalt/fiberglass shingles. Terne is available through distributors of Follansbee Steel Corporation, Follansbee, West Virginia, 26037.

● TERNE-COATED STAINLESS (TCS): This is stainless steel coated on both sides with terne alloy. The good news: You don't have to paint TCS. The bad news: It's silver, so you'll want to paint it. But if the family reprobate inherits your house and doesn't paint the roof for twenty years, the TCS won't rust. TCS costs about $150 per square; it is also available through Follansbee Steel distributors.

● COPPER: Copper and lead-coated copper roofing can be bought in sheets or rolls. You don't have to paint copper, but if you don't, it turns green. This green patina is a striking visual effect, designed into many buildings. You see a lot of copper roofs on domes and bay windows. Copper is seldom used on a large pitched roof because it is, and always has been, relatively expensive. Use copper to correct a known copper-removal remuddling, or to replace a worn-out copper roof. Copper costs $200 to $250 per square; the price is subject to fluctuation. You can buy copper at most sheet-metal supply houses.

ALUMINUM AND GALVANIZED STEEL are popular with contractors and homeowners. While some argument could be made for the use of these metals as low-cost flashings or gutters, it is not cost-effective to use less durable metals on such a labor-intensive (high labor cost) job as the application of a standing-seam roof.

IF THE ROOF you're working on is a simple shed or gable roof (most standing seam roofs are), the installation should not be too difficult. A hip roof is slightly harder to execute. A new standing seam roof full of hips, valleys, cross-gables, ells, etc., is a job for the rare experienced professional.

PRE-FORMED TERNE AND TCS PANS are available through Follansbee Steel distributors. The cost of the pre-formed pans is about ten dollars a square more than the cost of the unbent metal rolls. This is a bargain. A sheet-metal shop would be unlikely to bend the pans for anywhere near this price. If you use copper, buy the metal and have it formed locally.

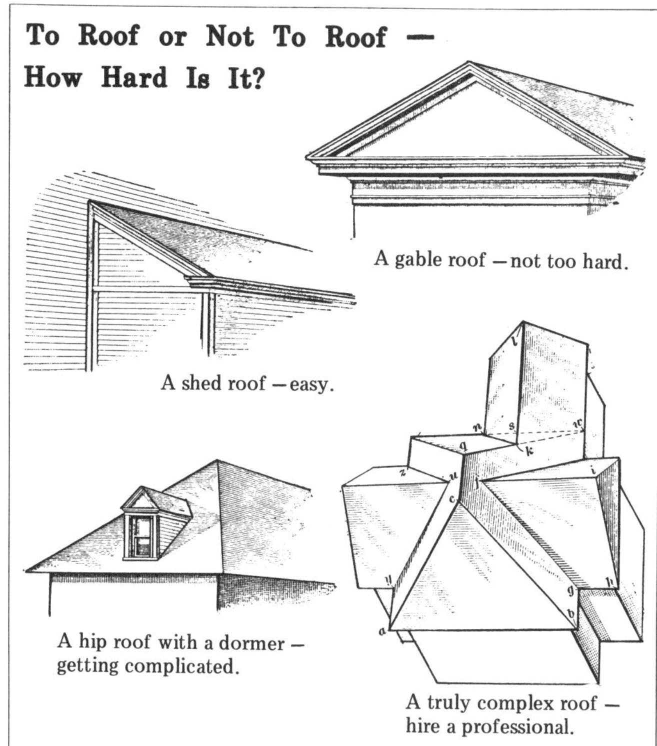

To Roof or Not To Roof — How Hard Is It?

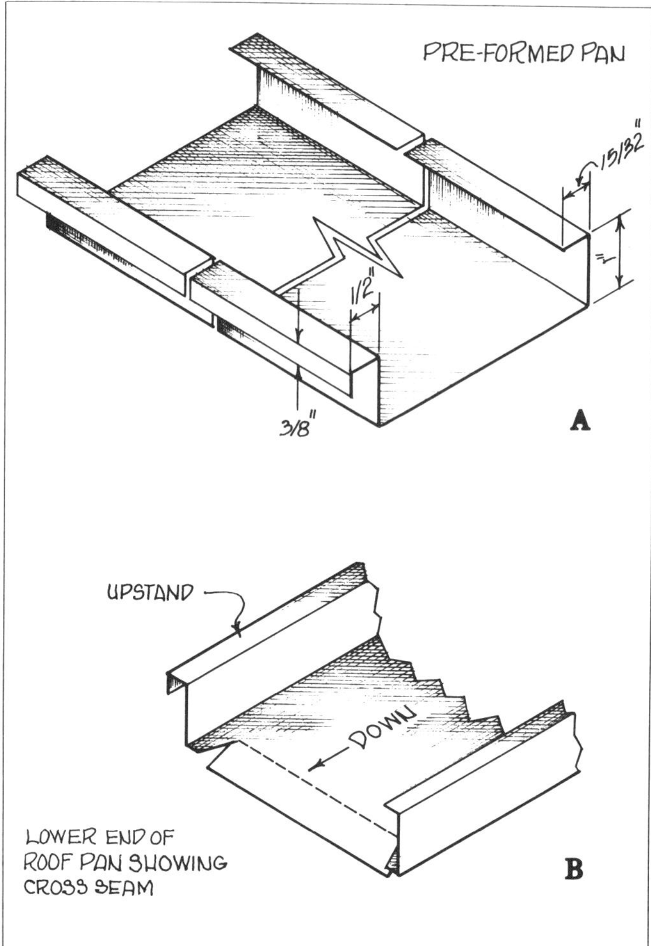

A: A pre-formed pan as it comes from Follansbee Steel. Available in terne or TCS, they come in 20- and 24-inch widths.
B: Pre-formed pans come without cross-seams cut or bent. You must form this seam yourself.

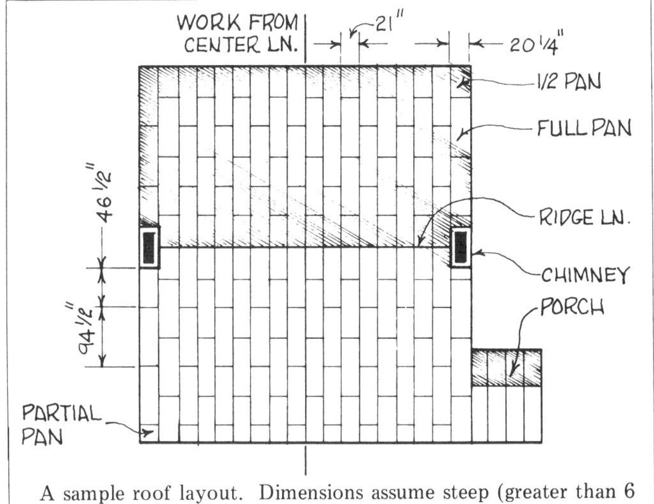

A sample roof layout. Dimensions assume steep (greater than 6 inches per foot) pitch and the use of 24-inch wide pans.

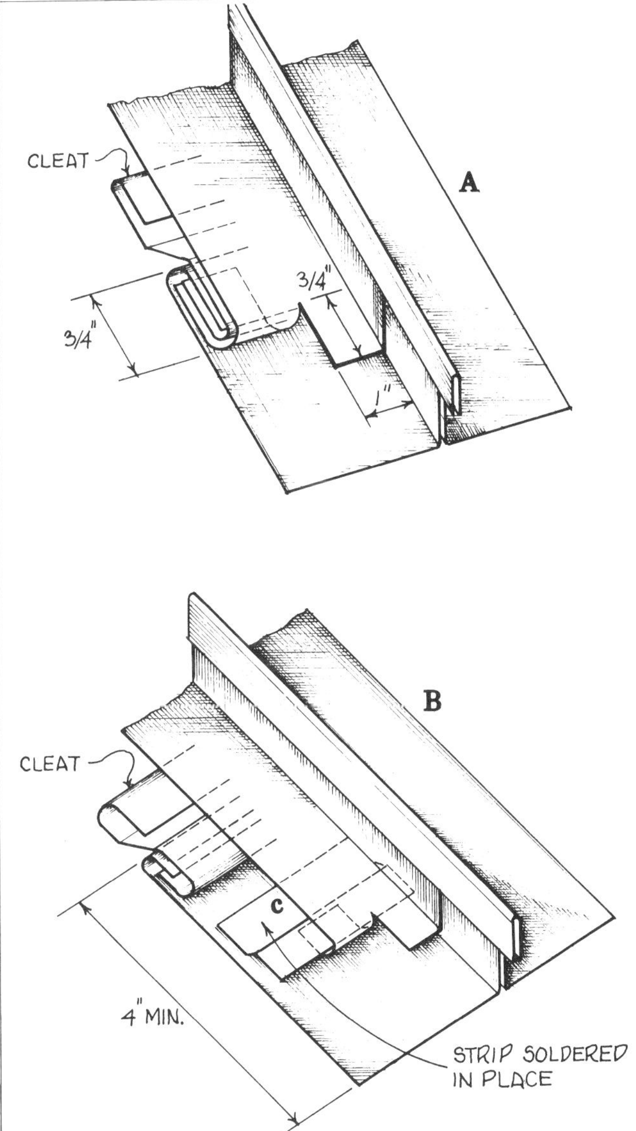

A: Steep pitch (greater than 6 inches per foot) cross-seam detail. B: Shallow pitch (less than 6 inches per foot) cross-seam detail. The soldered cross-seam connector (c) can be replaced with a solderless connector in terne or TCS.

MEASURE THE ROOF and figure for a standing seam at the centerline. Make a sketch showing the layout of the pans on the roof, and calculate the number of pans you'll need. If your sketch shows that the pans running along the gables (or at the corners, in the case of a hip roof) will be less than half-a-pan wide, shift the seams to allow one set of the edge pans to be full-width.

ALLOW 1-1/2" for cross-seams; that is, consider an 8' pan to be 94-1/2" long. For a shallow pitch roof (less than 6" per foot slope) consider an 8' pan to be 86-1/2" long, as the cross-seams are deeper on this type of roof, to allow for the installation of a cross-seam connector strip.

PRE-FORMED PANS come in 20" and 24" widths. As a general rule, use the 24" wide pan. Most of the work is in forming the seams, and wider pans mean fewer seams. You wouldn't want to use pans wider than 24 inches; wide pans buckle, or "oil-can," as they expand and contract. You might want to use pans narrower than 24" when the standing seams are used as a visual effect to echo existing architectural features, or on a small roof (for proportion). Standard lengths for pre-formed pans are 8, 10, and 12 feet. It's hard to handle a pan longer than 8' without wrinkling the metal; so, in most cases, you should use the 8' pans. (Exception: when a slightly longer pan would cover the whole roof, as on a small porch.)

FOR A ROOF made up of 24" wide pre-formed pans, allow 21" between seams; that is, consider a 24" pan to be 21" wide. For 20" wide pans, allow 17" between seams. Figure the gable end pans this way: When using pre-formed pans, you must cut off the upstand on the gable side, and allow 3/4" to fold over a drip edge. So, consider the pans that will run along the gables to be 20-1/4" wide (for 24" pans), or 16-1/4" (for 20" pans).

YOU'LL NEED a few specialized tools (see box on page 47). You can either rent these tools, or buy them at a sheet-metal supply house.

SOME OTHER things you'll need:

● Enough drip edge and/or gutter to run around the roof perimeter. (Gutters for the eaves, drip edge for the gable ends.)
● Enough 2" x 4" metal cleats to be spaced at 12" centers around every roof pan.
● Flashing, for chimneys or where the metal roof meets a wall.
● Optional: Valley flashing (necessary, of course, if your roof has valleys) and a ridge cap (more on this later).

ALL OF THESE MATERIALS should be the same material as the roof pans. Pre-formed drip edges, cleats, flashing, and ridge caps are available in terne or TCS. If you're using copper, you'll have to have these items made locally. Don't forget to allow for waste when you order materials; order 15% extra of everything, a greater percentage for a small roof.

IF YOU use terne, specify IX-40# terne. This indicates 28 gauge metal with a 40-pound terne coating. If you're using TCS, specify 28 gauge TCS. For copper (or lead-coated copper), specify 16-oz. material.

A METAL ROOF must be applied over a wood deck. Do not use treated wood for the deck. If your roof is covered with roll roofing, built-up roofing, shingles, or other roofing material, you must remove this covering before installing the metal roof. The decking must be clean, smooth, and dry. Lay rosin-sized paper over the deck -- just lay it, don't nail it. This paper serves as a slip sheet between the metal and the deck. Don't use roofing felt (tar paper) under a metal roof. The asphalt in the felt can cause the metal roof to corrode.

LOAD, TRANSPORT, AND WORK the metal carefully. Coated metals derive much of their durability from the coating. Nicks in the coating allow moisture and/or corrosive atmospheric pollutants to reach the underlying metal. Dimples in the metal act as little pools to collect moisture and corrosive agents.

DON'T LET loading dock workers or delivery people mishandle your future roof. And most importantly, when you (or your contractor) are on the roof, wear sneakers, crawl as often as possible, don't step on the seams, and don't store other materials on the roof.

IF YOU ARE using terne, it must be painted before it is installed on the roof. Paint the undersides of the pans with one coat of a good metal primer, suitable for ferrous metal. The exposed side of the metal must also be primed, so it's good to give the pans one coat of primer, top and bottom, before installation. Terne cleats, drip edges, and flashings must also be painted on both sides before they are installed. The paint must be brush applied. Do not spray or roll. You can use any compatible topcoat (from the same manufacturer as the primer) on the exposed side of the metal. With TCS or copper, painting is optional. (Remember, unpainted TCS is silver-grey.)

IF YOU'RE USING PRE-FORMED PANS, you'll have to cut some half-length pans. Use your straight or combination snips. You'll need one half-length pan for every row of pans on the roof. This allows for the cross-seams to be staggered, as is required for proper strength. If a local shop is forming your pans, simply order the correct quantity of half-pans. You'll probably need some pans of various lengths to fill out odd sections of the roof. You'll have to form these on-site.

IF YOU DON'T have access to a sheet-metal brake, you'll have to bend the cross-seams on-site. On all of the pans except those that will be installed at the roof peak and along the gable ends, make two 3/4" cuts into each end of the pan, one inch in from the standing seam upstands. Cut a 2 x 4 board to the length of the flap created by these cuts, and make a 3/4" deep saw cut the length of the 2 x 4. This board is your low-tech sheet-metal brake. Insert the flap of metal into the saw cut, and bend the bottom flap down 90 degrees; bend the top flap up 90 degrees. Then place these flaps against the 2 x 4, and bend them loosely over, roughly parallel to the pan. The pans that will reach the roof ridge will have this seam only on the bottom. Leave the tops of these pans uncut for now.

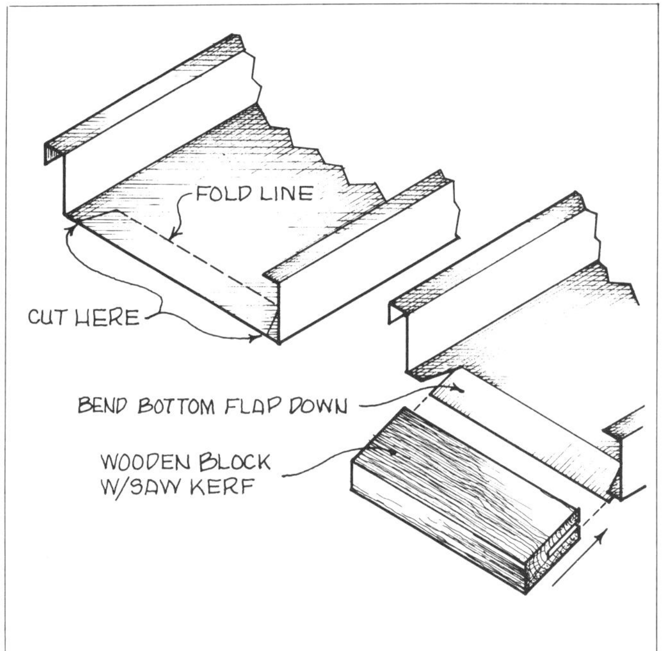

The low-tech way to form cross-seams. Use a kerfed 2 x 4 to get a clean bend.

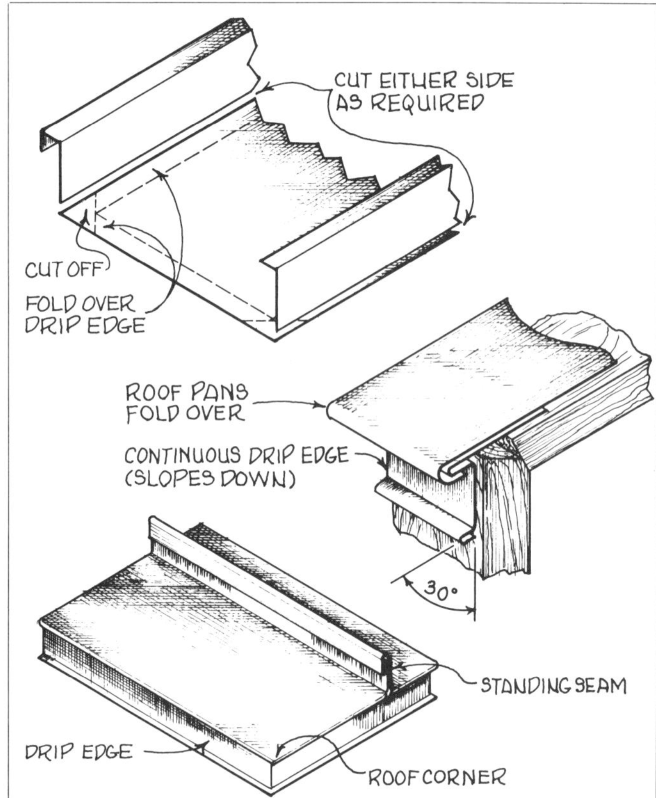

How to form the edges:
Make a 45-degree cut at the outside corner, fold the edges under 3/4 inch, and lock them into a drip edge or gutter.

USING A KERFED BOARD as described above, bend the seams that mate with the drip edges. With pre-formed pans, you must first cut off the upstand on the gable side of the pan.

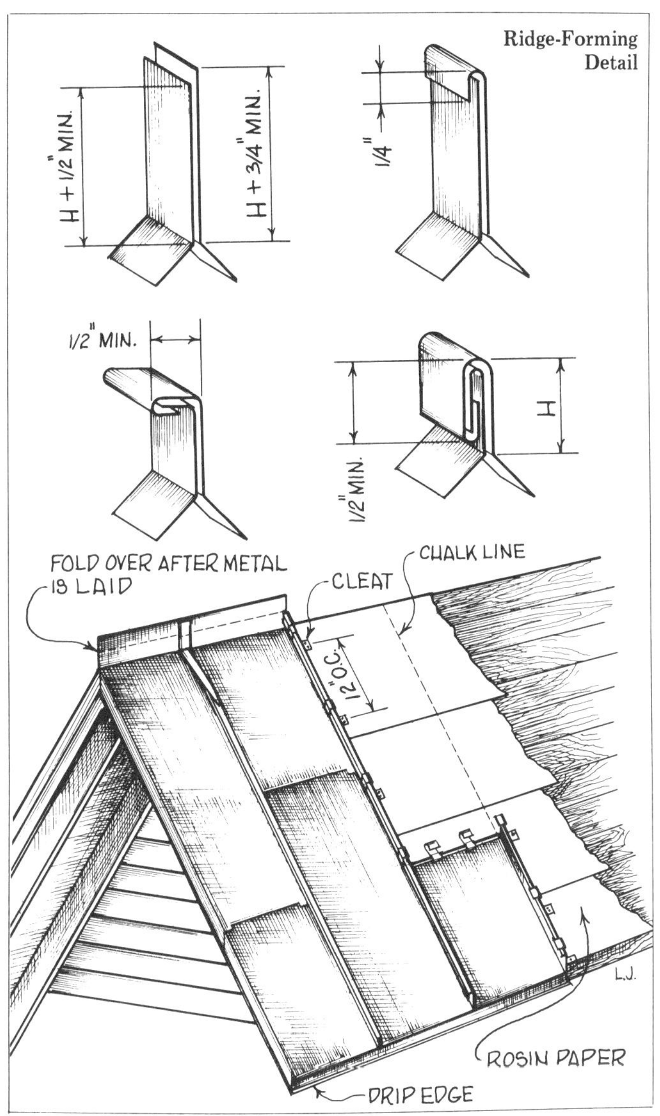

INSTALLATION

INSTALL THE DRIP EDGES (or gutter) according to the manufacturer's directions. (You can buy these pre-formed in terne or TCS, or have them formed locally.) To install the pans, start at the bottom left edge of the roof, and hook the first pan into the drip edges. Using a mallet and a block of hardwood, flatten the seams at the drip edges. Then, using Vise-Grip crimpers or roofing tongs, crimp the pan/drip edge seam tightly together. Install hold-down cleats at 12" spacing up the right side of the pan, and across the top edge of the pan. Fasten the cleats to the deck with two 1" roofing nails. For terne and TCS, use cleats the same material as the roof, fastened with galvanized nails. For copper, use copper cleats and copper nails. Fold the tail of the cleats over the nail heads.

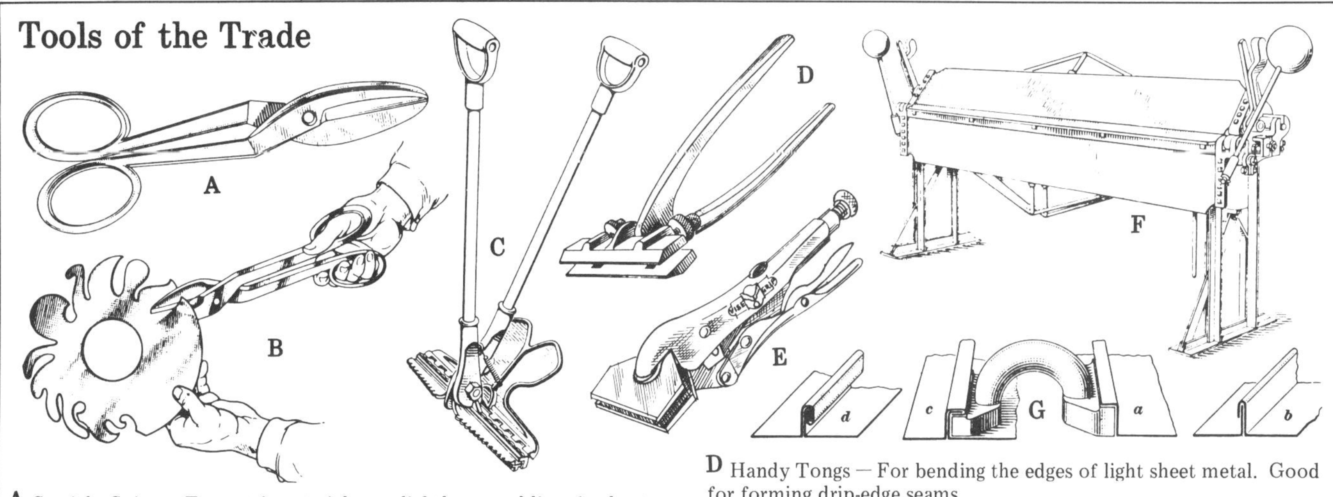

INSTALL THE SECOND PAN above the first pan by hooking it into the top of the first pan and into the drip edge. Close the seam at the drip edge as before. Flatten the cross seam between the two pans with your mallet and wood block. Be careful with this pan (and all subsequent pans) to keep the seams straight. Installing a standing seam roof is a lot like hanging wallpaper; small errors at the beginning of the run create impossible problems at the end. Anchor the second pan with cleats, then install the remainder of the first row of pans all the way to the ridge of the roof.

TO INSTALL the first pan of the second row, hook the triple bend over the double bend and slide the pan up until it hooks on the drip edge. Crimp the seam at the drip edge, and install cleats along the right edge and top edge of the pan.

Tools of the Trade

A Straight Snips — For cutting straight or slightly curved lines in sheet metal 24 gauge or lighter. They come in right-handed and left-handed versions.

B Combination Snips — Similar to straight snips, but will make highly irregular or scroll cuts.

C Roofing Double-Seamer — This hand-and-foot-operated tool closes the standing seams of pre-formed pans. This is the tool you can rent from Follansbee Steel.

D Handy Tongs — For bending the edges of light sheet metal. Good for forming drip-edge seams.

E Vise-Grip Crimpers — More commonly available than handy tongs, they do the same job, and stay clamped where you put them.

F Sheet-Metal Brake — This is a stationary shop tool, used to form sheet metal into roof panels (and cornices, gutters, etc.).

G Hand Roofing Double-Seamer — An ingenious antique tool. Used to form double-lock standing seams. Some very old roofs were formed with just this tool and a mallet.

NOW YOU ARE READY to close the first standing seam. Here are two ways to do this:

METHOD 1: Use roofing tongs or Vise-Grip crimpers to close the seam. First, crimp the small flange tight with the top of the horizontal flange on the adjacent sheet. Then, use your mallet and wood block to bend this seam down enough for the Vise-Grip crimpers to close the seam. This is the cheap, but labor-intensive way to do it.

METHOD 2: Rent a pair of seamers from Follansbee Steel. You have to pay a healthy deposit, but when you return the tools intact, they refund your deposit, less $50 a week for the use of the seamers. This method costs a little more, but it's a lot quicker.

INSTALL THE REST of the pans in the manner described above. Remember to stagger the cross seams, and keep the pans properly aligned -- a chalk line is recommended.

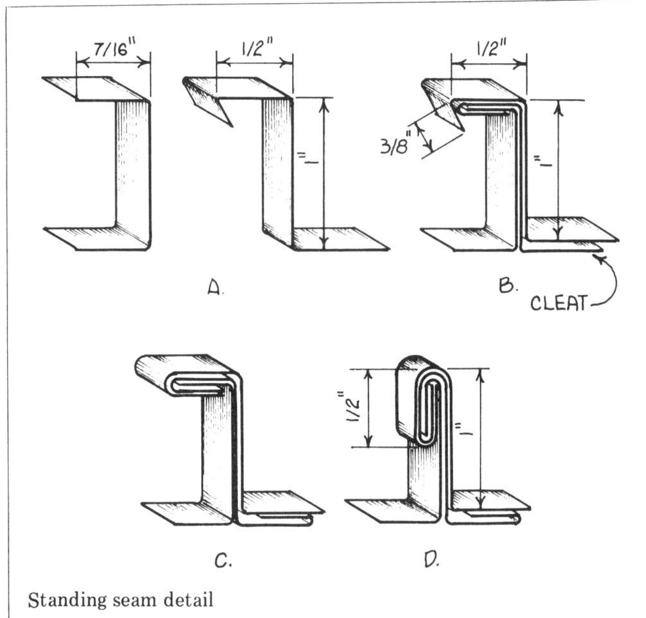

Standing seam detail

FINISHING TOUCHES

HERE ARE TWO WAYS to finish the ridge of a gable roof:

METHOD 1: Flatten the standing seams three inches from the ridge, loosely fold back the ends of the pans 180 degrees, and install a ridge cap. This is the modern way to do it. Ridge caps for this type of installation are available pre-formed in terne or TCS.

METHOD 2: Flatten the standing seams three inches from the ridge, and form one more standing seam along the ridge line. You might have to do this with your mallet and wood block, as neither light tongs nor the Follansbee seamers will easily bend this many thicknesses of metal. (See "Ridge-Forming Detail" on page 47.) This is the traditional method. There are roofing tongs large enough to form these seams, but they're very expensive and nearly impossible to rent. (This ridge finish also applies to a hip roof. The only difference is that the ridges of the hip roof are mitred together.)

IF THE ROOF abuts a vertical wall, flatten the standing seam just before the wall, bend the pans up the wall, and counter-flash over them, using the same material as the roof for the flashing.

TO FLASH A CHIMNEY, treat the roof pans as if they were base flashing. Use your mallet and wood block to bend the pans to conform to the vertical surfaces of the chimney, and counterflash.

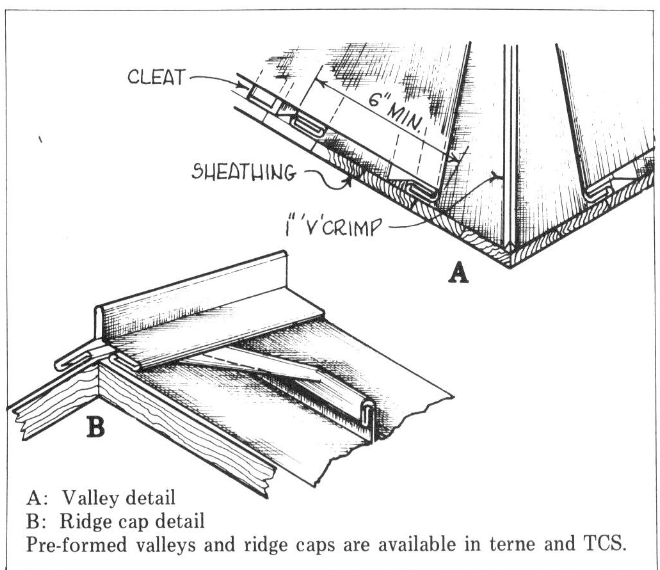

A: Valley detail
B: Ridge cap detail
Pre-formed valleys and ridge caps are available in terne and TCS.

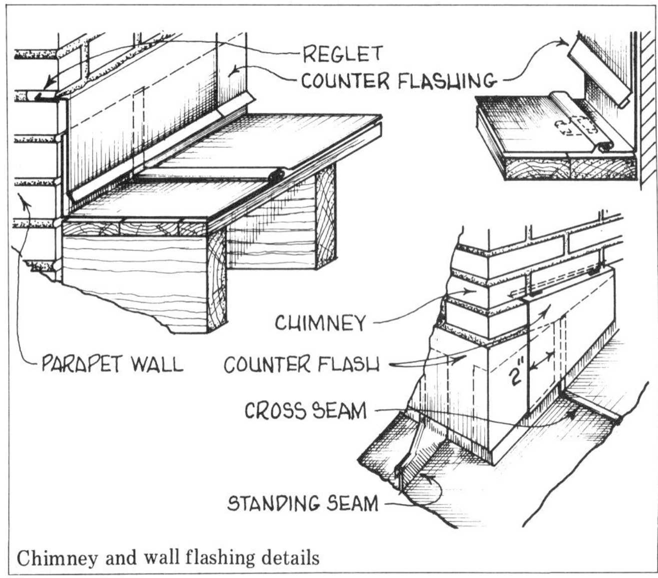

Chimney and wall flashing details

NEVER USE ANY BLACK GOOP (asphaltic roofing compound) or caulk to seal joints on a metal roof. Asphalt attacks metal roofing, and no caulk lasts long enough for this application.

OLD-HOUSE OWNERS are accustomed to learning "lost arts" such as plastering, slating, and wall glazing. Installing a standing-seam roof is another of these lost arts, and one of the most rewarding. Few things please an old-house lover more than knowing that the art relearned, the work redone, and the house repaired, will endure. And few things will ensure the endurance of an old house more than a handcrafted metal roof.

Yes, I still use
WHITEWASH

by
Gordon H. Bock

WHITEWASH has been used throughout the history of this country as an inexpensive, easily obtainable, white surface coating for both the outside and inside of buildings. During the last century, it was most commonly applied to the exteriors of cottages, barns, and outbuildings.

WHITEWASHING IS STILL a cheap, quick method to paint a building white, and it's especially appropriate for a building that has always been whitewashed. Such buildings usually have unplaned vertical-board siding -- just the type of rough finish that holds whitewash best. Whitewash was sometimes used on masonry buildings, but masonry was often left unpainted, so you don't see whitewashed masonry nearly as often as you see whitewashed wood.

AS WHITEWASH IS APPLIED, it builds up in cracks, knotholes, and joints between boards, acting as a filler for these imperfections. The result, if you work carefully, is a smooth, even finish. Because it's basically lime, whitewash also acts as a wood preservative; it's repugnant to most insects and has moderate water-repelling qualities.

MODERN OIL OR LATEX PAINTS do not adhere well to whitewashed surfaces, or to surfaces that held whitewash until recently. So there are two options for repainting a previously whitewashed building: Either completely remove the old whitewash by scraping, then repaint with modern paint; or, renew the whitewash coating. Renewing is by far the easier option.

Making It

WHITEWASH, LIKE ANY PAINT, will not adhere to an unsound surface. You must brush or scrape any dirt or loose lime scale off the surface before you re-whitewash. A quick brooming of the building is usually all that's necessary.

YOU CAN BUY all of these materials, except for the salt, at any good lumberyard.

● Hydrated masons lime (one 40-lb. bag covers approximately 160 square feet.)

● 1 pound kitchen salt per two or three bags of lime

● A 2- or 3-gallon plastic bucket

● A whitewash brush (6- or 8-inch hemp bristle type)

● Paint sticks (for stirring)

A WORD OF CAUTION: Lime is caustic and will burn you if it comes in contact with your skin. Be careful, especially during mixing, not to splash the powder near your eyes and nose. It's a good idea to wear goggles and gloves when you work with whitewash.

MIXING WHITEWASH is like mixing cocktails: It is done according to inexact formulae, largely to individual taste. The basic proportions are: Two parts lime to one part water, and 1/4 cup of salt per batch. The mixture is best prepared as needed in the bucket from which it will be dispensed. This way, it's ready for application as soon as it's mixed. The mix should be readily workable with a brush -- about the consistency of frozen custard or light cake icing.

PAINTING WITH WHITEWASH is easy and requires only the amount of care you want to put into the job. Simple, haphazard strokes in all directions produce a stucco-like effect that is fine for sheds and small buildings. Long, parallel strokes take time, but give a more finished appearance and improve the looks of the building.

A WHITEWASH JOB can last for many years. While sometimes prone to bleed-through from knots in new wood, or rain erosion at ground level, whitewash can be touched up invisibly at any time. A 40-pound bag of lime costs about $5.50, so whitewash is substantially cheaper than paint. And best of all, it never fades. A whitewashed building will stay whitewash white!

Neglected whitewash —
an outbuilding on the author's property.

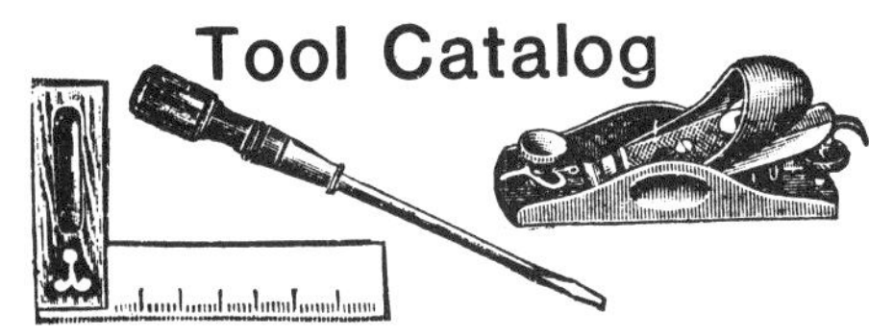

Tool Catalog

You may not know about Woodworkers Supply of New Mexico, but their free catalog of high-quality and often hard-to-find woodworking tools, finishing products, furniture hardware, and books is certainly worth ordering.

Almost anyone restoring an old house could use the Delta 14-in. bandsaw I spotted in their last catalog on sale at a $200 savings. Another really special find were two beautiful, rosewood-handled squares with brass blades. These handsome and highly functional tools were made by John Economaki at Bridge City Tool Works. The Master Try Square sells for $47 and the Joint-maker's Square is $32. The pair is $69.

The catalog is full of other fine tools that last a long time and don't cost a lot. To get your copy of the latest catalog, write to Woodworkers Supply of New Mexico, 5604 Alameda N.E., Albuquerque, NM 87113. (505) 821-0500.

Fireplace/Bake Oven Tools

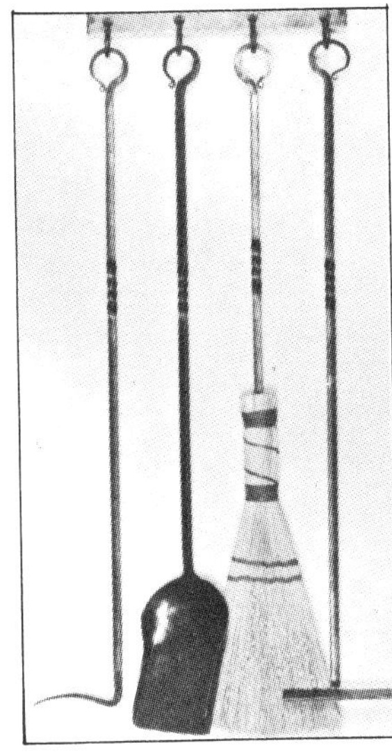

If you like to cook in a brick bake oven or fireplace, Ian Eddy the Blacksmith has a set of stove and fireplace tools that you need. Available individually or in a set of four, the tools come in 3/8-in. round or square steel stock and are 28-in. long.

I find the ash rake to be one of the most handy tools. It looks like a hoe and is great for cleaning ashes out of a bake oven. It sells for $18. Another useful tool is the $14 poker that also works well for pulling pies out of the oven. The shovel is conventional, but holds a lot. It sells for $26. The broom is not only good for ashes, but will also brush water into the brick-oven interior before baking.

For Rumford fireplaces or stoves, Ian has the same tools listed above in 3/8-in. round stock that are 25 in. long. Ash rake, $16; poker, $12; shovel, $25; and broom, $22. The sets can be ordered with a four-hook, matching wall rack and sell for $100 complete, $95 for the shorter set. A three-legged, four-hook, fireplace tool stand can be ordered in place of the wall rack for $140 complete or $135 for the shorter set. Shipping is extra.

To find out more, order the catalog ($2, refundable with order) from **Ian Eddy, Blacksmith, Dept. OHJ, RFD 1, Sandhill Rd., Putney, VT 05346. (802) 387-5991.**

good news good news good news good news good news good news good news good news goo

New Period-Style Fireplace Tile...At Last!

These days there aren't many old-house parts that can't be recreated by craftspeople, purchased new as reproductions, or eventually found at architectural antique shops. Original designs in fireplace mantel and hearth tiles seem to be the exception. Short of pirating them out of someone else's house, they just don't exist.

Well now there's one source, if Anglo-Japanese transfer tiles are to your liking. (Remember Bruce Bradbury's Anglo-Japanese article, Nov. '83?) The series consists of five outstanding period patterns, all hand-decorated in sepia and cream with a matte finish. Artist Steve Bauer, responsible for some of the sophisticated wallpaper designs of Bradbury & Bradbury, created the intricate patterns for these tiles. Both Bradbury & Bradbury and Designs In Tile, the Northern California art tile studio who produces the tiles, will be selling them.

The five new designs were expressly created for use around fireplaces, but their rich design and variety of sizes allows them to be used in bathrooms and kitchens for wainscot borders, splashes, and trim. Matching, undecorated tiles can be purchased nationwide and offer greater design possibilities at a reasonable cost.

6 in. x 6 in. tiles are available for $11 each, designed for use around the fireplace opening. 6 in. x 3 in. repeating borders, designed for use around fireplace openings and hearth perimeters, are $9. Hearths frequently had smaller corner blocks, such as the 3 in. x 3 in. tiles that sell for $8 each. Handling, shipping, and insurance is extra.

For more information on the tiles, send $.50 for a one-page flyer to: **Bradbury & Bradbury, Dept. OHJ, P.O. Box 155, Benicia, CA 94510, (707) 746-1900**, or **Designs In Tile, Dept. OHJ, P.O. Box 4983, Foster City, CA 94404, (415) 571-7122.**

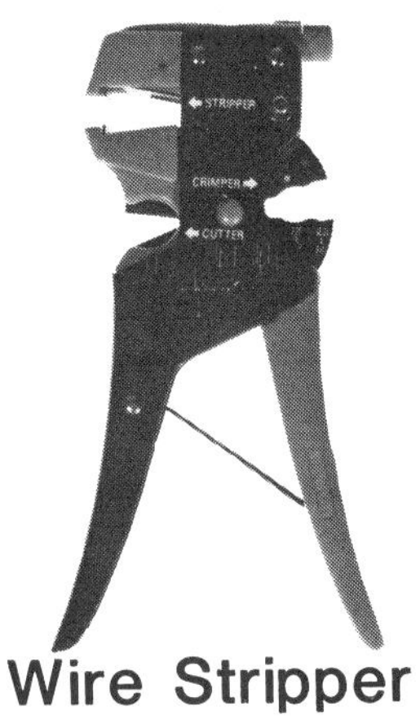

Wire Stripper

One of the handiest, most time-saving tools in my tool box is an automatic wire stripper. In the past they've only been available from electrical supply houses who cater to professionals. Snapit, however, has just introduced the Wire-Multi-Tool, which combines three useful functions into one tool.

The Multi-Tool has a set of double-action wire stripping jaws that grabs onto electrical wire and pulls off a pre-determined length of insulation in another. There's no tugging at the wire with this tool. A tension adjustment allows you to strip wire from 300 ohm t.v. up to 14 ga. A built-in cutter is designed to nip wire of all sizes. Open- and closed-ended wire terminals, contacts, and splices can be neatly crimped onto wire with an automatic crimper on the back of the tool.

The tool is built with high-grade steel cutters, and crimpers with glass-filled plastic and hardened steel grip handles. Available at hardware stores and home centers nationwide including True Value Hardware stores, the tool sells for $11.49 by itself or $13.49 in a kit with 28 wire terminals. If you can't find the Wire Multi-Tool in your area write to Cable Wire Products, Inc., Dept. OHJ, P.O. Box 6767, Providence, RI 02940 for the dealer nearest you.

Interior Storm Windows

Here's an inexpensive way to reduce air infiltration in your old house, which is reversible and requires little labor. The Jasmine Company of Denver has introduced what they call the Sensible Storm Window. For less than $2.50 per square foot, you can install this interior storm window system to almost any wall or window trim surface.

Basically what you are buying from the Jasmine Company are the instructions and enough foam weatherstripping and magnetic and steel tape to allow you to make a set of storm windows. You supply the acrylic glazing and labor. Does it work? Colonial Williamsburg uses a similar system to cut the air infiltration and heating costs on some of its buildings, and finds the approach to be cost effective and easily removable without leaving any holes or damage.

To find out more, send for the free brochure or enclose $3 for the Sensible Window Booklet which contains instructions and buying information: Jasmine Co., Dept. OHJ, 1929 Jasmine St., Denver, CO 80220. (303) 399-2150.

New Mouldings

Grinling Architectural Mouldings has a new line of hard polyurethane cornices, ceiling medallions, wall brackets, chair rails, and corbels. Designed for interior use, the mouldings closely resemble carved wood or cast plaster but are much easier to fit and install.

The ceiling medallion or rose comes in 9 styles and range, in price from $27 to $50. The medallions and wall brackets/corbels come with adhesive for mounting. Cornice mouldings and dado rails are attached with ceramic-tile adhesive (not supplied) and are held in place with small nails which are removed later and the holes filled.

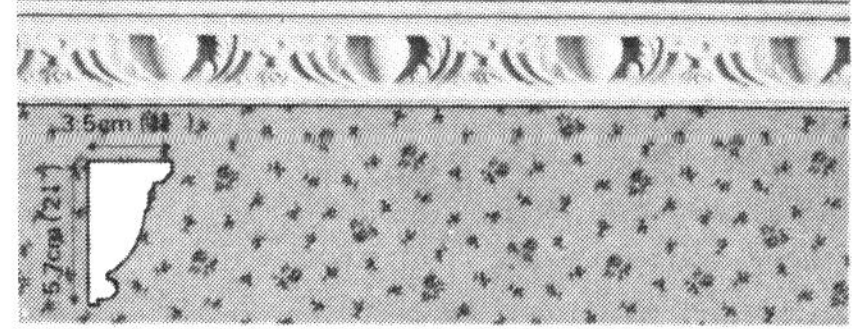

The cornice mouldings come in 7 styles ranging in price from $24 to $44 for each 6-ft. length. The single chair rail/dado comes in 6-ft. lengths and sells for $25. The wall brackets/corbels come in 2 styles and sell for $21 each.

For a free brochure write: Grinling Architectural Period Mouldings, Dept. OHJ, 192 Christopher Columbus Dr., Jersey City, NJ 07302. (201) 435-8682.

Sheet Metal Manual

If you're planning to do sheet metal work, don't make a move without first consulting the SMACNA Architectural Sheet Metal Manual! I've had a copy for the last six or seven years and have found it to be a gold mine of information on just about every sort of sheet metal you're likely to encounter.

The manual is designed to provide architects and specifiers with an up-to-date reference on the proper design and installation of sheet metal. But it is just as valuable to old-building owners who are either planning to do sheet metal work themselves or just want to better understand what their contractors are about to do. One of the real benefits of the manual is the abundance of very clear drawings and easy-to-understand recommendations. Often alternative design solutions and installations are presented for varying climatic conditions through the country.

As good as the manual is for helping you specify practically any architectural sheet-metal requirement, you should always consult reputable sheet metal contractors in your area. They can offer suggestions on choices of metals, the relative economics of different techniques, as well as local area practices and climatic concerns.

The Architectural Sheet Metal Manual, Third Ed., Vol. 1 sells for $50 ppd. (This spring, Vol. 2 is due out.) The 5th edition of the Architectural Sheet Metal Specifications, which sells for $10 ppd., is also useful. These prices will be discounted 40% to practicing architects and engineers, provided they are not in the contracting business; educational institutions (such as universities, high schools, trade schools, etc.), public libraries, bookstores; federal, state and local government agencies. Perhaps your State Historic Preservation Office or local library either has copies you can use or would be interested in purchasing them as reference material.

For a free catalog of publications write SMACNA, Inc., Dept. OHJ, P.O. Box 70, Merrifield, VA 22116. (703) 790-9890.

Remuddling of the month

DANIEL D. REIFF of Fredonia, New York, sent us these photos of two 19th-century farmhouses in northern New Jersey. The beauty and character of the house at right are intact. The house above has become a substitute-siding showcase. Vari-colored Permastone encases the ground floor; light-blue vertical aluminum siding covers the second floor. Fat strips of aluminum siding hide the seams between all the different coverings. The porch is gone (because it blocked the view of the sidings?), and the aluminum canopy replacement adds insult to injury. Should anyone find the house lacking in visual variety, the addition has white horizontal siding. --CG

The Old-House Journal®

**69A Seventh Avenue,
Brooklyn, New York 11217**

NO PAID ADVERTISING

Postmaster: Address Correction Requested

Restoration and Maintenance Techniques
For The Pre-1939 House

April 1985 / Vol. XIII No. 3 / $2.

The Old-House Journal

Carpet Bedding

Promiscuous Beds In The Victorian Landscape

by Scott G. Kunst

AS YOUR TRAIN PULLED INTO THE DEPOT in Ypsilanti, Michigan, circa 1890, you would have been treated to "the Liberty Bell, flanked by cannon and crossed muskets" or maybe "the cantilever bridge at Niagara Falls with a locomotive just starting across and the falls beneath" -- all worked out in colorful bedding plants.

YOU MIGHT HAVE BEEN IMPRESSED, but hardly surprised. Carpet bedding was very Victorian and very popular. Most railway stations had a rococo display, as did cemeteries, municipal buildings, public parks, and every stylish home.

TODAY NIAGARA FALLS or elaborate floral clocks may be beyond the resources and taste of most of us. But a small, easily managed carpet bed can add a Victorian flair to the smallest front yard. The principles are readily understood, the plants widely available, and the results are really a lot of fun.

cont'd on p. 61

Is **Remuddling** Snobby, Elitist, Mean, and Unhelpful?

NO...we don't think so and neither do the newspapers and magazines that pick it up, the organizations who ask us to lecture on it, nor the majority of subscribers who flip to the back page first.

FOR YEARS, the Mega-Buck Monopoly has spent millions --no, billions!--of dollars convincing homeowners that aluminum siding, vinyl soffits, metal doors, and plastic awnings are "home improvements," outward signs of success, maintenance-free substitutes for traditional materials. Their right to deliver that message is unquestioned, despite their being motivated by profit. As a

preservation publication, it's our duty to express a divergent opinion. Even with the admittedly sledgehammer approach of our Remuddling column, we are but a small voice up against Advertising Tyranny!

USING public views that must be endured by any passerby, we illustrate the two golden rules of sensitive rehabilitation: Don't Destroy Good Old Work, and To Thine Own Style Be True. The classic remuddling breaks both rules. It isn't right that a building which has stood as a recognizable product of its own time should be compromised by the whim of a single owner. Remuddling creates true ugliness: a building which has lost its character.

OHJ'S REMUDDLING of the month gets noticed. It's a whole philosophy of architecture in a single word. Try to explain sensitive rehabilitation/ original charm and character/ historical appropriateness, and you'll see the problem. It's too much to explain to a fast and busy world. But show them an ugly picture and give it a catchy name ... next thing you know, you've coined a word and invented a symbol.

BUT DO OUR readers need such basic instruction? Subscribers generally don't; we do it more for the others. We do it for the mailmen and the neighbors, and for the thousands of people who get a sample issue from us or from a preservation group. We do it for the dozens of house-and-home magazines that subscribe to OHJ for ideas, and for the newspapers that run items about remuddling because they know it makes good copy. And thus we prick the mass consciousness.

THERE'S HUMOR in it too. It helps to laugh in the face of adversity, and some of the

Remuddlings have been downright funny. That must be why so many subscribers love the back page; according to a recent reader survey (and our mail), Remuddling is the #1 favorite page in OHJ.

A FEW subscribers do object. I understand their misgivings. To those who dislike Remuddling, all I can say is, remember that our worthy if unsubtle message is getting to a fair number of the unenlightened, too.

Patricia Poore

The Old-House Journal®

Editor
Patricia Poore

Production Editor
Cole Gagne

Technical Editor
Larry Jones

Assistant Editor
Sarah J. McNamara

Contributing Editors
Walter Jowers
John Mark Garrison
Roland A. Labine Sr.

Architectural Consultant
Jonathan Poore

Circulation Supervisor
Barbara Bugg

Circulation Assistants
Jeanne Baldwin
Garth White

Special Sales
Joan O'Reilly

Assistant to the Publisher
Tricia A. Martin

Catalog Editor
Sarah J. McNamara

Publishing Consultant
Paul T. McLoughlin

Publisher
Clem Labine

Published by The Old-House Journal Corporation, 69A Seventh Avenue, Brooklyn, NY 11217. Telephone (718) 636-4514. Subscriptions $18 per year in U.S., $25 per year in Canada (payable in U.S. funds). Published ten times per year. Contents are fully protected by copyright and must not be reproduced in any manner whatsoever without specific permission in writing from the Editor.

We are happy to accept editorial contributions to The Old-House Journal. Query letters that include an outline of the proposed article are preferred. All manuscripts will be reviewed, and returned if unacceptable. However, we cannot be responsible for nonreceipt or loss — please keep copies of all materials sent.

Printed at Photo Comp Press, New York City

ISSN: 0094-0178
NO PAID ADVERTISING

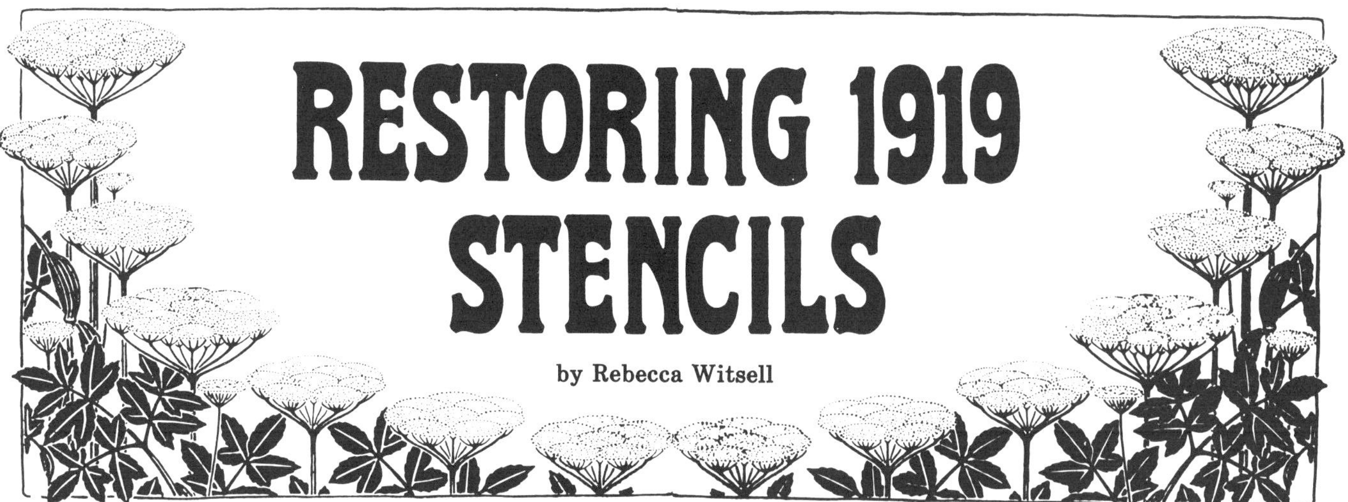

RESTORING 1919 STENCILS

by Rebecca Witsell

T HE CORNISH HOUSE in Little Rock, Arkansas, is a grand early-twentieth-century (1919) house designed by a local architect, Theodore Sanders, for a prosperous couple, Ed and Hilda Cornish. The house has an interesting, eclectic blend of period design elements, including Prairie School-inspired ribbon windows, Tudoresque gable treatments, and a massive rusticated stone entryway. But what brought me to the house were the fine Craftsman-inspired wall stencils.

QUITE UNLIKE THE WALL STENCILS of the Colonial and late Victorian periods, which range from folk artsy to florid and fussy, the stencils in the Cornish House were much more stylized, somewhat more angular in design. The patterns were reminiscent of the graphic art used in Gustav Stickley's turn-of-the-century art and architecture magazine, The Craftsman.

WHEN THE PRESENT OWNERS of the house, Nancy and Hampton Roy, asked my company to restore the original stencils, I knew we would be facing a difficult job. We had three old photographs showing stencils on the walls of the living room, the sun porch, and the smoking room. But years of "redecorating" had seen the stencils buried under thick coats of paint -- some oil-based, some latex, and some calcimine. Before we could restore the stencils, we would have to strip the walls down to their original finish.

WE DID MOST of the wall-stripping with a semi-paste methylene chloride-based paint remover. We made repeated light applications of the remover, then picked up the remover with coarse (#3) steel wool pads. We used this technique to keep sludge to a minimum. When we encountered a layer of calcimine paint, we switched to a powder-type paint remover -- Dry Strip. Dry Strip is dissolved in water, and water dissolves calcimine paint, so the Dry Strip cut through the calcimine as well as the paint underneath. (We could have used Dry-Strip for the whole job, but we prefer methylene chloride stripper.) When we saw a stencilled pattern start to emerge from beneath the paint, we washed off the paint residue with xylene.

The Cornish House.

Above: Stripping reveals the stencilling in the living room.
Below: A newly-exposed dining room stencil.

WE DECIDED that while we were stripping, we would look for stencils in rooms that we hadn't seen in photographs. It's a good thing we did. We found more stencils in the dining room, breakfast room, and entrance hall.

THE COLORS in the designs in the living room, dining room, and sun porch had been hand-painted in varnish glazes. This protected the stencilled patterns from the paint remover, so most of the original detail survived the ordeal of the paint stripping. The designs in the entrance hall, breakfast room, and smoking room were not originally done with glazes, however, so the paint remover obliterated much of the detail of these patterns along with the overlying paint. There was enough detail left to trace, though, so trace we did.

Duplicating The Stencils

WE TAPED 36" wide tracing paper (available from architectural supply houses) over the patterns, and traced the patterns in place on the walls. These tracings were our rough sketches. We took them back to our shop, and retraced them on our drawing boards, using straight-edges, triangles, and french curves. For designs that were bilaterally symmetrical, we drew one half of the pattern, then folded the tracing paper down the centerline of the pattern and made a mirror-image tracing for the other half of the pattern. This method cuts down on errors in duplicating the design.

WE MAKE STENCILS this way: We spray the back side of the tracing with 3-M Spray Mount artist's adhesive and stick the tracing to stencil paper. (Our favorite is heavy oiled stencil board made by Hunt-Bienfang.) Then we cut through the tracing and the stencil using a very sharp X-acto knife. (We change the blades frequently so we can cut sharp lines.) A tip on stencil-cutting: Always keep the knife blade perpendicular to the stencil paper. If you bevel the edge of the stencil, you'll never get a sharp line when you apply the paint. Use a straight edge when you can, and be particularly careful on curves. Some stencil-cutters hold the knife stationary, and move the paper when they cut curves.

ONCE THE STENCIL IS CUT, we peel off the tracing and throw it away, then clean any residual adhesive off the stencil with mineral spirits. Then we coat both sides of the stencil paper with orange shellac mixed 1-to-1 with denatured alcohol. This keeps the edges of the stencil sharp and enables us to clean the paint from the stencil with paint thinner after each application of paint. We recoat the stencil with the shellac mixture at the end of of each day's work. This freshens the stencil and ensures consistently sharp lines.

A HINT for first-time stencil reproducers: Remember to wipe <u>both</u> sides of your stencil with a dry rag after each repeat of the pattern. This will help you avoid smears when you place the stencil on the wall for the next repeat of the pattern.

T HE ENTRANCE HALL in the Cornish House is a large and complex space, cut up visually by mahogany beams and door trim. The only stencilling we found in this room was a two-inch classical band running beneath the picture moulding. The walls in this room were originally painted a tan-cream color; the stencils were a cool grey-green.

THE SMOKING ROOM was painted the same tan-cream color as the hall. The stencilling, executed in grey, pale orange, and dark brown, had an African look.

THE BREAKFAST ROOM was bolder in color and design. We found a simple triangle-and-square stencil at the ceiling below the picture moulding, and an intricate Egyptian-style pattern in pale blue and orange at wainscot height. The room was painted dark blue below the wainscot, light blue above, with a quarter-inch brown line separating the two colors.

TO RECREATE the unglazed stencilling in these rooms we used tube artist's oils. If you plan to use these paints to restore stencilling, you should know this: Art supply shops carry two types of artist's oils -- the traditional linseed-oil based paint and a modern alkyd paint. If you are working on a surface that

The living room of the Cornish House, with the original stencils.

An early photograph of the den.

is painted with oil-based paint, you can use
either type. But if you're stencilling over
latex paint, you should use the alkyd-based
paint, because the oils in the traditional
paints "halo" when applied over latex paint.
We always prefer to use traditional oil paints
over an oil-painted surface, because we
dislike the "stringy" quality of the faster-
drying alkyd paints. Another hint: Use as
little paint on your brush as possible, but be
careful not to use too little. When you are
trying to reproduce earlier stencilling, you
want to apply the paint to the same thickness
and achieve the same degree of opacity as did
the original painters.

THE STENCILS in the living room, dining room,
and sun porch were bold, high-style, "1919
modern" patterns. These were the intriguing
Craftsman designs, a style quite popular in
interior decoration, as well as in graphic
arts of the period. A particularly interesting period influence in these stencils is the
use of the broken line as a divider; one sees
this motif in some graphic art of the period,
poster art in particular. To make our stencils for these patterns, we had only to trace
and cut out the broken lines.

BEFORE WE COULD STENCIL in these rooms, the
walls had to be primed and painted in the
original colors with flat alkyd oil paint.
This is the best base coat for the glazed
patterns we had to reproduce.

ONCE THE WALLS WERE DRY, we applied paint in
the original brown color to the pattern delin-
eated by our broken-line stencils. After the
line pattern had dried completely, we applied
translucent glazes, in the original colors, to
fill in the rest of the stencil pattern. We
also duplicated original highlights in the
glaze by wiping parts of the pattern with a
finger or thumb wrapped in cheesecloth. After
the stencils were dry, we glazed the walls in
a "Tiffany" finish. (See OHJ December 1983
for more information on wall glazing.)

Rebecca Witsell is a partner in a company that does exhibit
and book design, as well as reproduction of period architectural graphics. For further information call: Designed Communications, 704 Boyle Building, 103 W. Capitol, Little Rock,
Arkansas, 72201, (501) 372-2056.

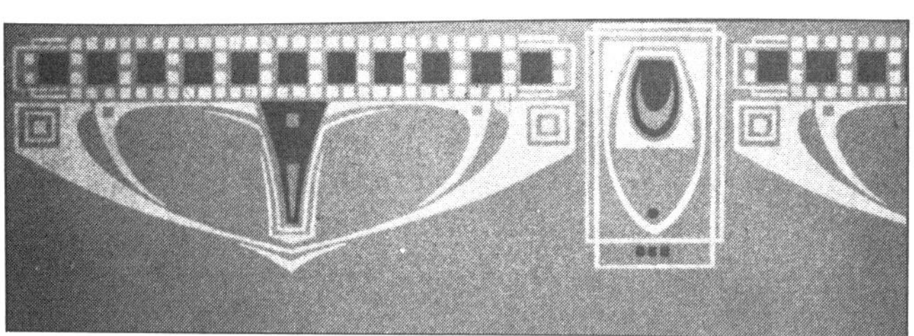

Above: Smoking room design, in grey, pale orange, and brown.
Top Right: Breakfast room design, in pale blue and orange.
Middle Right: Living room design, in grey-green, pale blue,
and ochre.
Bottom Right: Dining room design, in grey-green and ochre.

SEEING THROUGH OPAQUE STAINS

by Sarah J. McNamara

I'VE JUST SPENT four months scraping and sanding and melting paint off my house! I never want to go through that again. I hate paint! I'm going to use opaque stain instead." We've heard this understandable avowal from many readers. But do opaque stains really work? The theory is that opaque stains give you the best of both worlds: the color and coverage of paint without buildup and peeling problems. In actuality, opaque stains are only a compromise.

Is It Stain Or Thinned Paint?

OPAQUE STAINS are more like paint than transparent stains. They contain solids that remain on the surface of the wood after application. The U.S. Department of Agriculture's Forest Products Laboratory states: "Commercial finishes known as heavy-bodied or opaque stains are available, but these products are essentially similar to paint because of their film-forming characteristics. Such 'stains' do find wide success on textured surfaces and panel products such as hardboard."

LIKE ALL PAINTS AND STAINS, opaque stains can be latex or oil-based. Oil-based opaque stains may partially penetrate wood, although the solids remain on the surface. (Some manufacturers swear that oil-based opaque stains penetrate wood, others claim that's a myth.) Latex stains do not penetrate the surface of the wood at all; they adhere to it. They are porous and more flexible. The Forest Products Laboratory considers latex -- especially acrylic latex -- opaque stains superior to oil-based.

THE MOST COMMONLY-ASKED question regarding opaque stain is: "Can opaque stain be made simply by thinning paint?" Most of the manufacturers we spoke with said, hesitantly, that it is theoretically possible. They went on to say that making these stains is much more complicated than simply adding mineral spirits to oil-based paint, or water to latex paint. The proper percentage of pigment to vehicle determines the amount of coverage and protection an opaque stain can achieve. You may think you're getting more paint for your money if you thin it, but you may be getting less protection in the long run. The characteristics of thinned paint may be less predictable than those of opaque stain, and you'll void the manufacturer's guarantee by using unrecommended additives.

What Kind Of Surface Can Opaque Stains Cover?

OPAQUE STAINS CAN BE USED to cover many types of wood, as well as primed metal and well-cured masonry. Oil-based opaque stains are not recommended for previously-coated wood, even if it has been stripped. No matter how well the surface has been prepared, some of the old coating will remain and hamper penetration. It's also recommended that oil-based opaque stain not be used again after the initial application. It will build up and cause shiny splotches to appear on the surface. Latex stain, because it adheres to whatever surface it's applied to, can be used on previously-coated wood. Manufacturers recommend that latex opaque stain be used for all subsequent applications.

How Are Opaque Stains Applied?

OTHER THAN CLEANING, no preparation is required when applying opaque stain to new wood. All loose paint and wood fibers should be removed from previously painted or stained wood. Sandblasted or badly-weathered wood should be primecoated with a primer that's recommended for the stain you use. Remember, the stain will only be as stable as the surface it covers. If the paint underneath a stain peels, the stain will peel along with it. Proper preparation of the surface, as always, is necessary if the coating is to last. Dirt, grease, mildew, moisture, loose paint, and any chalky residue should be removed before application of stain.

This close-up of subscriber Fritz Klinke's house shows opaque stain peeling off oil-based primer and old paint giving way beneath opaque stain.

Fritz Klinke's house in Silverton, Colorado, at 9300 feet. Extreme temperatures (it was 39 degrees below zero the day this photo was taken) and harsh ultraviolet light cause opaque stain to deteriorate rapidly. After this bad experience with opaque stain, Klinke plans to paint the house with a good quality oil-based paint.

A BRUSH IS THE BEST TOOL for applying opaque stains, although rollers and sprayers may also be used. Stains should not be applied in direct sunlight (it accelerates drying) or in cold temperatures. Two coats of opaque stain are recommended for maximum coverage and durability. Opaque stains are not recommended for decks, railings, porches, and window sills. Because water tends to pool on horizontal surfaces, these areas require a more protective coating -- like paint.

The Pros And Cons

OPAQUE STAINS have been around for over fifty years, although they've been hailed only recently as the answer to chronic paint failure. One of the reasons they've gained this reputation is because they won't build up or peel as easily as paint does. They're often used on old houses without vapor barriers because, like transparent stains, they allow some moisture to exit the house. While opaque stains may relieve the symptoms of peeling paint resulting from excessive interior water vapor, this solution does not address the real problem. The solution rests in controlling the migration of excessive water vapor through the walls of the house. If you have a moisture problem, either install a continuous vapor barrier, or control the amount of moisture generated within the house with ventilating fans or a dehumidifier.

NO COATING is maintenance free. If you already have a severe buildup of paint or chronic paint failure, opaque stains will not help you avoid major preparation work. Because a coating is only as sound as the surface it covers, you're going to have to scrape or strip the old paint off your house to make the new coating as effective as possible. It will take time and effort no matter what kind of coating you choose to apply.

OPAQUE STAINS, with their promise of breathability, are a great temptation. In coastal areas where paint can fail within three years of application, opaque stains may save you future preparation work. But even though you won't be dealing with peeling paint anymore, your house is getting less protection from the elements. You'll have to reapply opaque stain as soon as it show signs of fading or weathering. These stains don't stand up well under the harsh light of day. Southern and western exposures, where ultraviolet radiation is the strongest, fade quickly and require touching up.

ALTHOUGH OPAQUE STAINS may be the industry's best answer to the problem thus far, they are not a miracle cure-all for chronic paint failure. Paint remains the best material for protecting wood from moisture and ultraviolet rays, as long as it forms a continuous film on the surface of the wood. If you decide to use opaque stain on your old house, consider all the factors. Is it possible to control your moisture problem from inside the house? Are you willing to trade the protection paint offers for the flexibility of opaque stain? Opaque stains may be the right choice for your house, but before you do anything, remember that another way to save paint buildup is with good preparation and good maintenance. Repaint only when absolutely necessary. If you think your house is beginning to look dingy, try washing it to improve its looks. And when you do paint or stain, use good quality materials on a well-prepared surface.

Sandstone To The Rescue

IF YOUR VICTORIAN HOUSE has an ashlar foundation like mine, you know that it's almost impossible to rid its rough-textured surface of oil-paint spills. I have found that a piece of sandstone rubbed on the spill will successfully remove it. It also works on old cement-block foundations.

> Birdie Bates
> Kellogg, Iowa

Hot-Dipped Nails

YOUR CARPENTER is sure to protest, but before he does any exterior work, buy him a box of 16d hot-dipped finishing nails. The coated or plated (galvanized) common nails he'll bring to the job will result in an unattractive appearance and eventually leave rust stains. Because the finishing nails are headless, they can be countersunk and then caulked over. Nails grip with their shanks, and so the rough surface of the hot-dipped nail will hold better than the smoother surface of your carpenter's cherished common.

> Charles W. Wilson
> Mechanicsburg, Pa.

Hypodermic Oiling

WHEN I WANTED to oil the pulleys for the sash cords of my windows, I discovered that no oil can had a spout small enough to get to the center of the pulley, which was where the oil was needed. So I purchased a 1-1/2-inch hypodermic needle and plastic disposable-type syringe from the veterinary-supply shelf of a local farm-supply store: total cost, 75¢. (Similar hypos are used for gluing and can be purchased at cabinetmaker-supply stores or through fine-tool catalogs; pictured below is a glue injector from Woodcraft Supply Corp.)

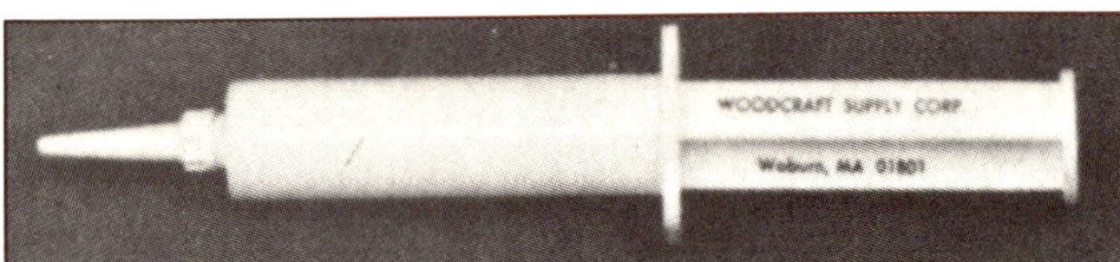

IT WORKS PERFECTLY FOR OILING with pinpoint accuracy in hard-to-get-at places. I bought a second one and learned that it will also work with powdered graphite.

> Leonard Hollman
> Eudora, Ks.

Handle-ing Plywood

THE JOB of lugging around sheets of plywood or drywall is a lot easier if you use a piece of cord or clothesline about 20 feet long. Tie it in a loop and slip the loop around the bottom corners of the sheets. Reaching over the top of the sheets, grab both sides of the loop and hold them together like a handle; then you can carry the sheets just like a big briefcase.

> James Dickey
> Iowa City, Iowa

Vinegar & Salt

AFTER MUCH EXPERIMENTATION I have found the following method to be the easiest and most successful way to restore solid brass hardware. Place the items to be cleaned in a stainless-steel or enameled pot. (Aluminum cookware will pit with this method.) Cover the hardware with white vinegar, then pour on a coating of regular table salt -- just sprinkle it over the hardware so all areas are touched. Simmer on a low heat for 10 to 15 minutes. Remove the hardware with tongs, and buff with 0000 steel wool. Rinse well, dry, and re-buff to a satiny luster. Hardware may then be spray lacquered if desired.

THIS METHOD will remove old lacquer, paint, and decades of built-up dirt. The process does smell (like strong vinegar), so you may want to do it outdoors. Try using the gas grill to maintain heat.

> John McPeak
> Pitman, N.J.

Removing Tar

HERE'S SOME GOOD ADVICE for anyone stuck using tar on their house: Baby oil is a very useful solvent for removing any of the stuff that you may get on your skin or in your hair. Apply some to exposed skin surfaces prior to working with the tar -- it can also prevent sticky problems from happening!

> Joe Longo
> New York, N.Y.

Tips To Share? Do you have any hints or short cuts that might help other old-house owners? We'll pay $15 for any short how-to items that are used in this "Restorer's Notebook" column. Write to Notebook Editor, The Old-House Journal, 69A Seventh Avenue, Brooklyn, NY 11217.

Carpet Bedding cont'd from p. 53

cont'd from p. 53

CARPET BEDDING reached its peak in America in the late 19th century, but its roots (so to speak) go back much earlier. In the "ancient" style of European landscaping -- as seen today in the gardens of Williamsburg -- elaborate formal designs called "parterres" or "knots" were common. Despite certain similarities, these were fundamentally different from the later carpet beds. They were less flowery and more "geometric," and generally clustered together and edged by paths. Most importantly, they were enclosed by walls or fences, not scattered about in an open lawn.

ORNAMENTAL LAWNS didn't really exist until the advent of the English landscape style in the 1700s. This "modern" style -- familiar to us in New York's Central Park and the grounds of numerous old estates -- emphasized naturalistic lakes and woods and broad expanses of velvety grass. At first, flowers were more or less banished from these elemental new landscapes. But by the time the style reached America, flowers were once again being included -- not in the ancient manner, however, but in simple beds cut here and there in the lawn: the earliest carpet beds.

"OPEN" OR "INFORMAL" BEDS are better names for these early lawn beds, because at first they contained a mixture of plants, rather than the ordered ranks of bright annuals which we usually associate with carpet bedding. In 1806 seedsman Bernard McMahon became one of the first Americans to write of open beds. He advocated "clumps" of flowers as well as shrubs and trees in "moderate concave and convex curves and projections," all in the open lawn.

IN 1841 ANDREW JACKSON DOWNING, Victorian America's most influential landscape designer, recommended irregular or "arabesque" beds filled with "a miscellaneous collection of perennial flowering plants" arranged "so that those of a few inches in height shall be near the front margin of the border, those of a larger size the next, and so gradually increasing in size" to the rear or center. By the 1880s Peter Henderson was describing these mixed beds as the old-fashioned, "promiscuous" style of bedding, but "mingled" seems to have been the more common term.

Alternanthera and lavender cotton (light-colored section) blend with fuchsia and geranium standards in this carpet bed.

ALL SORTS OF FLOWERING PLANTS were included in these mingled, promiscuous beds. In Cottage Residences (1842) Downing offers pages of appropriate perennials arranged by height and month of blooming. For those who want "a considerable effect" at "little or no cost," he especially recommends an even dozen that includes ragged robin, Chinese pinks, larkspur, white hosta, johnny-jump-ups, summer phlox, peonies, violets, and madonna lily.

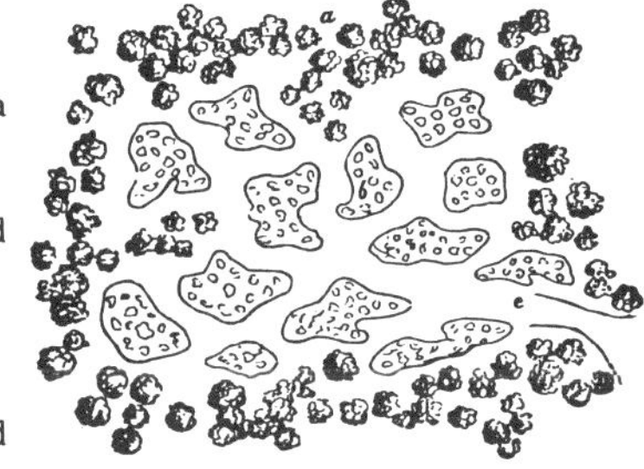

THE SIMPLEST mingled beds were wholly irregular (right). These best suited a "rustic" Victorian landscape, and could be scattered as well as clustered. Downing more often drew smoothly curving, "arabesque" beds (below). These dramatic shapes, frequently long and laid out as borders, would flatter most Gothic and Italianate houses.

This carpet bedding in Sarnia, Ontario, alternates ageratum with spider plant, in front of red begonias and red geraniums.

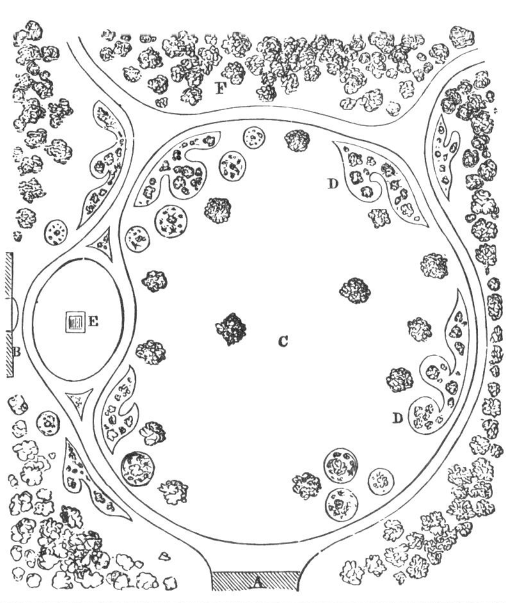

ANOTHER VERY POPULAR OPTION was to lay out promiscuous beds in a variety of "cookie-cutter" shapes: ovals, circles, crescents, teardrops, quatrefoils, pudgy stars, and numerous combinations and permutations of these (Figs. 1, 2, & 3). Dot these beds singly along a walk or cluster them to make a fancier design.

Single Beds

MIDWAY BETWEEN mingled beds and the ambitious designs of carpet bedding at its peak, a fashion for simple, single-species beds held sway. Following English landscape designers, Downing recommended this style in the early 1840s, arguing that promiscuous beds by midsummer present an unsightly, "lean and parched appearance," showing too much dirt and not enough color. He advised homeowners to plant single-species beds of everblooming annuals and enjoy "a mass of rich leaves and blossoms" all summer long.

A MEASURE of the new style's popularity is the twelve pages of "Further Hints" on bedding that Downing added to later editions of Cottage Residences. In the following decades, Downing's opinions on bedding were echoed by numerous writers. In 1856, for example, Cleaveland, Backus, and Backus counseled homeowners to lay out "small patches of ever-blooming flowers ... scattered here and there in the grass" and directed that "each bed must be planted with but one sort, which must fill and cover the entire spot."

"COOKIE-CUTTER" SHAPES were most favored for single-species beds. In 1851 seedsman Joseph Breck wrote that these "should be either round, oval, starry, or irregular; but never square, diamond shape, or triangular," apparently because the rectilinear shapes were considered old fashioned. Other writers were less fastidious, however, and as time went on rectilinear single-species beds were also admitted in fashionable gardens. Sometimes a bed was centered on a tall, flower-filled urn or vase (left). Basket-vases were also used in the same way (right). Today rustic versions can be made as easily as they were by the Victorians.

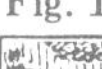

RECOMMENDED PLANTS were spring bulbs (crocus, hyacinths, tulips, etc.), followed mainly by annuals that were "striking and showy," of low height and continual bloom. Some of these had been around for years, while others were recent, exotic introductions such as verbena and petunias. Downing seems to have been especially taken with the latter two and recommended three dozen varieties with such evocative names as Defiance, Kermesina, Hebe, and Sir Seymour. Other flowers suggested for single-species beds were German asters, balsam, bedding dahlias, mignonette, Drummond phlox, portulaca, the modern "monthly" roses, and (a little later) lobelia, alyssum, California poppies, nasturtium, and geraniums.

SINGLE-SPECIES BEDS are easy to plan, plant, and maintain, and they are appropriate for most mid-19th-century houses. A teardrop of purple verbena in the lawn by the porch steps and a quatrefoil of Drummond phlox out by the sidewalk would suit a fashionable Gothic cottage. For an Italianate villa you might try something more formal: on either side of a sunny path, a curving panel of portulaca -- in a mix of brilliant oranges, corals, and reds -- around a small circle of low, yellow bedding dahlias. Single-species beds are still appropriate for later

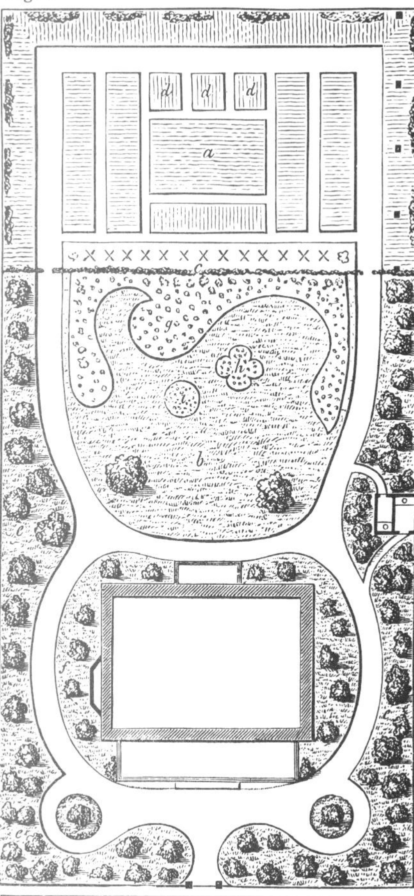

Fig. 1

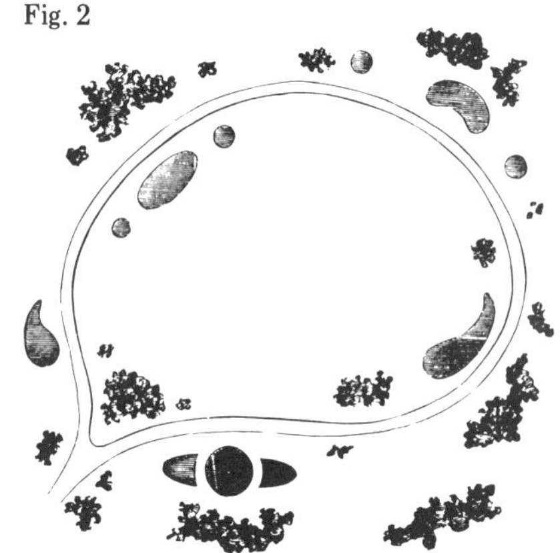

Fig. 2

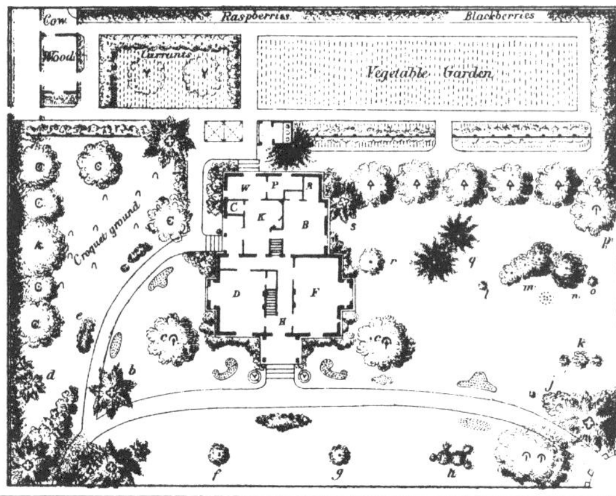

Fig. 3

Fig. 1, from A.J. Downing's *Cottage Residences* (1842): "As this cottage is decidedly ornamental in character, it may fairly be presumed that it would be required that a considerable portion of the limited ground near the house should be rendered ornamental also."

Fig. 2, from J. Weidenmann's *Beautifying Country Homes* (1870): "Smaller grounds are more suitably decorated by merely scattering the beds."

Fig. 3, from Frank Scott's *The Art Of Beautifying Suburban Home Grounds* (1870): "The shrubbery adjoining the house may be composed of a great variety of common species; but none that attain a height of more than 6 ft."

houses, and you have a wider range of authentic plants from which to choose. Highlight your Queen Anne tower, for example, with a fan of small beds planted in red salvia, blue ageratum, and golden coleus.

SINGLE-SPECIES BEDS, particularly in clustered designs, continued to be used throughout the century, but by 1870 more elaborate designs were coming into vogue. The new style was called ribbon bedding or carpet bedding because it usually involved contrasting rows, or "ribbons," of plants, arranged in (as Peter Henderson explained) "such patterns as would make a beautiful carpet." Sometimes these designs were representational -- a flag, the name of a town, or a basket of flowers -- but more frequently they were just patterns.

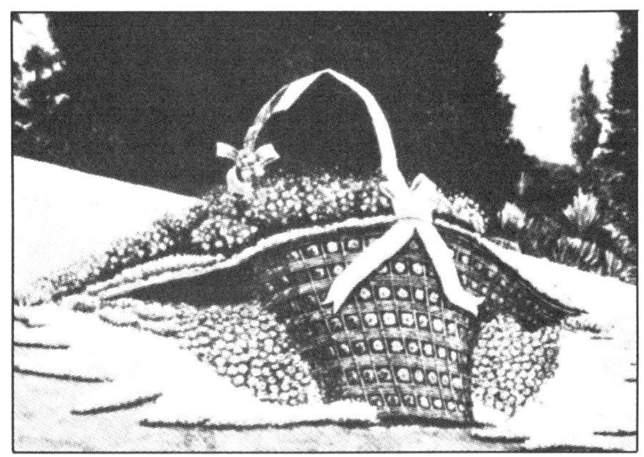

Built against a slope, this carpet bed features a basket made of rattan and metal, which was planted with flowers.

TO BETTER SHOW OFF THE DESIGN, carpet beds were sometimes planted against a slope or mounded in the middle; frequently the plants chosen for the middle were the tallest, with plants dropping down from there to the outer edge. Fashionable "sub-tropical" effects were created with dramatic plants like palms, pampas grass, ornamental banana, and elephant ear. Also highly prized were new, colorful foliage plants like coleus, caladium, and alternanthera, which were being introduced from plant explorations around the world.

THE FANCIEST EFFECTS were seen in public gardens, where the bedding-out of tens of thousands of plants was not unusual. Crowds of people would come to see the latest designs. Simpler carpet beds for private homes were illustrated in scores of books, magazines, and seed catalogs of the period. Right up into the early 20th century, no homeowner with any pretension to style would have been without a bright bit of carpet bedding in the middle of the front lawn.

Carpeting Principles

ALTHOUGH PERHAPS more fun than the relatively tame, earlier bedding styles, high-Victorian carpet bedding is also more complicated and more challenging. In attempting a contemporary recreation, you should keep in mind four key principles: pattern, vibrancy, exoticism, and ease of maintenance.

PATTERN -- Without a pattern, there is no carpet bed. Simpler patterns often look best, especially for small beds. A "bull's-eye" design of three concentric circles can be very striking, and it's an easy one to lay out and keep orderly. The more involved your pattern and the greater variety of plants you use, the more you run the risk of a blurred, muddled design. It's easy to draw a pattern that looks perfectly clear in black and white, but a carpet bed is more than pencil and graph paper; you'll be working with growing things and unpredictable weather. Consider too that your pattern will be seen from an angled, side perspective rather than from straight overhead.

TO KEEP A PATTERN PRECISE, mix the soil to be sure it's equally good in all parts of the bed; set plants close together; and if necessary (it rarely is) use "pinching" or trimming and extra helpings of water or fertilizer to maintain uniform sizes. When buying plants for a certain section, make sure they're all of the exact same variety. Cultivars of celosia, for example, can range from under eight inches to over three feet in height.

Carpet-Bedding Plants

As long as it's bright or bold, almost any plant can be used for carpet bedding. Some authentic Victorian choices are listed here. Many were expensive in those days, or available only to those who had home greenhouses. Today, most are readily available through mail-order seed catalogs or in flats at the supermarket. (A list of catalogs is given on page 69.)

Check mature heights when buying plants or seeds, because cultivars will vary. Many ever-blooming plants flower more continuously if you 'dead-head' them by picking off faded blooms before they seed. This usually is not essential, however.

Carpet bedding was typically done in full sun. Several of the shade plants in this list are basically undocumented as carpet-bedding plants, but they were all available and popular in Victorian gardens. — Scott G. Kunst

AGERATUM — Fluffy masses of powder blue on compact plants (right). Originally 18 inches, by the 1870s dwarf varieties of the plants were available. 6 to 18 inches; sun.

ALTERNANTHERA, telanthera, calico plant — Tropical perennial with small-leaved foliage in yellow-green, maroon, or copper. Very popular then and still common in public designs, but difficult to find commercially. Trimmed to 4 to 8 inches; sun.

ALYSSUM — Low, honey-scented alyssum is as highly recommended now as it was a century ago. Flowers are white, rose, or purple; plant grows easily from seed. Midsummer shearing keeps it neater. 4 to 10 inches; sun.

BEGONIA SEMPERFLORENS — Frequently used in beddings today, it was unavailable here until about 1880, and so is not typically Victorian. Small white, pink, or red flowers with waxy green or bronze foliage. 6 to 14 inches; sun to light shade.

VIBRANCY -- Victorians loved color, be it in the chromolithographs gracing their parlors, the elaborate trim on their Queen Anne houses, or their carpet beds. To be authentic, use only the brightest and most richly colored plants. If that's too much for your modern sensibilities, feel free to make an adapted design using pastel hybrids. Modern cannas, verbenas, geraniums, and many other bedding plants are now available in softer tones.

TO EMPHASIZE both color and brilliance, arrange plants for maximum contrast. Purple verbena is wasted next to blue ageratum, but it positively glows next to the bright gold of California poppies. Plan for textural contrasts too. Planted side by side, the tiny leaves and flowers of blue lobelia and white alyssum are too similar to look their best. But plant lobelia next to the substantial, lobed foliage of dusty miller, and both plants benefit. In a shady bed with perhaps no flow-ering plants, contrasts of foliage shades and textures are especially important. But avoid contrasts <u>within</u> a section; a ribbon of coleus should be <u>all one</u> height and color.

EXOTICISM -- The fashion for carpet bedding flourished with the arrival of everblooming plants and plants with richly colored foliage from expeditions around the world. A design <u>could</u> have been planted with old-fashioned <u>flowers</u> -- maybe johnny-jump-ups, calendula, wormwood, and love-lies-bleeding -- but it wouldn't have seemed a carpet bed because it would have lacked the excitement of the new and exotic. Dramatic, "sub-tropical" foliage plants such as castor bean and elephant ear could make the front yard of a milkman look like that of a sophisticated world traveler.

IN YOUR CONTEMPORARY carpet bed, strive to recapture that look of worldly exoticism. While coleus and petunias no longer seem curious to us, it's hard to imagine ornamental banana seeming anything but bizarre on North Main Street. Other Victorian favorites that can today create a novel, almost freakish effect are caladium, palms, agave, and even cannas. A half-serious rule of thumb might be, "If it looks out of place, use it."

EASE OF MAINTENANCE -- A maintenance-free landscape is a fantasy; even astro-turf requires an occasional vacuuming. And the simplest carpet bed is certainly more work than a bed of pachysandra. Nevertheless, a carpet bed today is a lot less work than it was for the Victorians. After all, you don't have to start all your own plants in a green house, or constantly "pinch" them to keep them low. A few common sense steps will reduce the work even further.

YOUR FIRST YEAR, THINK SMALL. Make a simple design and use plants with which you're expe-rienced, even if they aren't authentic. Stick to your usual gardening practices, and avoid any well-meaning advice to the contrary (in-cluding the advice in this article). Other-wise, the bed can seem like an overwhelming project. As you master the basics and gain confidence, you can move on to fancier work.

CARING FOR HEALTHY PLANTS is a lot easier -- and a lot more rewarding -- than caring for puny, struggling plants. For most bedding plants, choose a sunny site. If you have to work in even light shade, choose plants that can do well there -- or else be prepared to spend a lot of time coddling unhappy plants.

CALADIUM — With heart-shaped leaves marbled & veined in red, pink, or white, caladium adds an exotic color to a half-shady bed. Plants are expensive, but you can start caladium tubers inside early for planting out in late May. Keep well watered. **1 to 2 feet; light shade to shade.**

CANNA, Indian shot — Broad-leaved, sub-tropical, and showy, cannas (right) were practically a Victorian institution. They range from 3 to 8 feet (with smaller, modern dwarfs); in flower, from yel-low to orange to red (with modern pastels); in foliage, from green to bronze. Start the tubers inside for an earlier show. Dig and store in the winter. **1½ to 8 feet; sun to light shade.**

CASTOR-OIL PLANT — For a dramatic Victorian effect, it's hard to beat this towering, tropi-cal plant with its large, palmate leaves. It grows easily from seed, but be careful: All parts of the plant are poisonous, especially the beans. **6 to 10 feet; sun.**

COCKSCOMB, *Celosia cristata* — An old-fashioned plant grown by the colonists, cockscomb was sufficiently bright or grotesque to recommend it to 19th-century carpet bedders (the crested type be-ing more popular than the plumed). There are dwarf and tall vari-eties in rich reds, yellows, magentas, and so on. **8 to 36 inches; sun.**

COLEUS — Another carpet-bed-ding classic, and widely available. Solid colors were the standard back then: deep maroon, bronze, red, chartreuse. Multi-color plants are more popular today, & coleus (right) is frequently sold only in mixed assortments, which mud-dles up carpet designs. Raising plants from cuttings or seeds is easy, though. **8 to 24 inches; sun to light shade.**

DUSTY MILLER, *Centaurea gymnocarpa, Cineraria maritima* — Valued for the striking contrast afforded by its lacy, bright, silver-grey foliage, dusty miller deserves a place in every carpet bed. **6 to 18 inches; sun.**

ELEPHANT EAR, taro, *Colocasia esculenta* — Looking like a giant green caladium (to which it is related), elephant ear adds tropical drama to a shady bed. Keep it well watered & fertilized regularly. For an earlier show, start tubers inside in pots. **3 to 5 feet; shade to half-sun.**

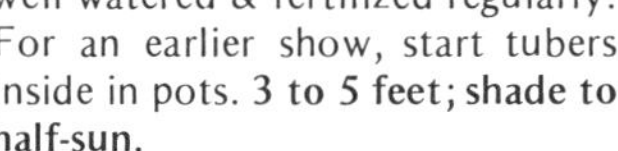

FERNS — Ferns (left) weren't typi-cal bedding plants, but with their fresh, bold foliage they were a Vic-torian passion and will look right at home in a shady bed. Ostrich fern is big, attractive, and tough, although its spreading will have to be controlled. There are many oth-ers. **1 to 4 feet; shade to light shade.**

Before you plant, improve your soil with
fertilizer (high phosphorous for flowers) and,
more importantly, some organic matter such as
peat moss, compost, or manure. Run the
sprinkler on your beds weekly, unless there's
been a good rain.

THE OUTLINE FOR YOUR DESIGN should allow for
easy mowing and <u>no</u> hand trimming. Avoid sharp
interior projections, try for gentle curves,
and leave room for the mower between beds.
You can let your plants grow right over the
edge of the grass and mow into them a little
(be brave), but it's neater to make a mowing
strip; basically it's an open strip separating
flowers and grass, which allows you to mow the
one without running over the other. Brick is
frequently used, but
bare earth is more
Victorian and more
flexible. Dig a
little ditch to keep
the grass from
creeping back in.

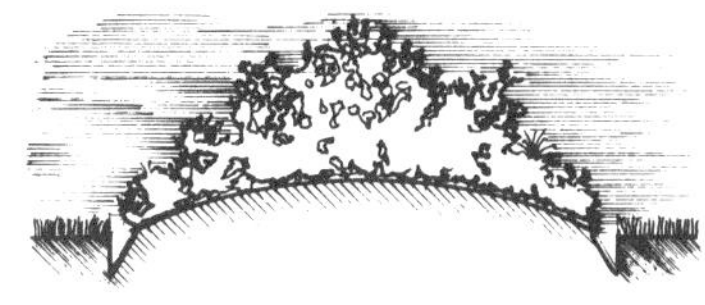

And whatever you do, never ring a carpet bed
with black plastic edging.

TO CROWD OUT WEEDS, set your plants fairly
close together. Mulch can help too, although
it's not the miracle treatment we sometimes
like to believe. Loose, cultivated earth is
an excellent and Victorian mulch; renew it
with a hand-cultivator every couple of weeks.
Other mulches should be as invisible as possible, because the wholesale, decorative use
of mulch is purely a recent practice. Cocoa-
bean shells are one decent choice.

WEEDING WILL BE EASIER if you can reach the
middle of your beds while kneeling at the

This bed in Davenport, Iowa, uses three different colors of
alternanthera; at left are succulents.

outer edge. Four or five feet across is about
tops for this. Wider beds may require special
arrangements such as unobtrusive stepping
stones for access to the middle.

PERHAPS THE MOST IMPORTANT STEP in reducing
maintenance is a psychological one. Things
that we love never seem like work, so plan a
bed you can really enjoy. Use some plants you
love or that have special memories for you.
And remember that the pleasure you get from a
bed positioned so friends and neighbors can
ooh and ahh over it is nothing compared to the
pleasure you'll get from a bed positioned so
<u>you</u> can enjoy it frequently.

GERANIUM — Favored since the late 18th century, geraniums (left) were perhaps the most popular plant for bedding out. Today, how-ever, because many other bedding plants are less expensive, save gera-niums for accents, or raise them yourself from cuttings. Of particu-lar interest are the older forms with variegated leaves. **1 to 2 feet; sun.**

HOSTA, funkia, plantain lily — Valued by Victorians & considered Japanesque, hosta was not typical-ly used in carpet beds but was fre-quently grown in open beds by itself. It can be useful in a shady design, especially because it comes in a wide range of leaf sizes, shapes, and shades of green, often marked with creamy white or yellow. **1 to 2½ feet; shade to light shade.**

IVY — Although infrequently mentioned for carpet beds by the 19th-century writers, English ivy is a useful edging in shady spots. Trimming will keep it in bounds. **3 to 6 inches; shade to half-sun (but avoid winter afternoon sun).**

LAVENDER-COTTON, santolina — This small, shrubby herb with narrow leaves of green & silvery-grey is often clipped low and used as an edging or to mark borders in a design. Perennial to zone 6 (USDA), it survives farther north with winter protection. **Trimmed to 4 to 10 inches; sun.**

LOBELIA -- A low, semi-trailing plant (right) reminiscent of alys-sum, with flowers that are usually intense blue. Excellent for edg-ings. 'Crystal Palace' is a 19th-century variety that is still available. **4 to 8 inches; sun to light shade.**

MAIZE, ornamental corn, *Zea mays japonica* — Maize (right) is much like regular corn, only it has leaves striped in white, yel-low, or rose. It's quite striking, if you can find the seed for it. Start inside for earlier display. **About 4 feet; sun.**

PALMS — House or greenhouse plants were often 'summered' outdoors & brought back inside in the fall. A large palm makes an exotic center for a bed, but full sun will burn most house plants. Check with your florist. **3 to 6 feet; shade to light shade.**

PAMPAS GRASS and other ornamental grasses — These Victorian favorites have gained renewed interest lately. Pampas grass is tall (about 8 feet) and stately, but north of Philadelphia you should

substitute the similar ravenna or plume grass (*Erianthus ra-vennae*), which is hardier. Ze-bra grass (*Miscanthus sinensis zebrinus*, to 10 feet) is another grass for the center of a bed. Fountain grass (*Pennisetum setaceum*, to 4 feet) comes in reddish and green forms; rib-bon grass (*Phalaris arundinacea picta*, to 3 feet) sports bold green and white stripes. There are many others. Sun.

SEVERAL CARPET-BEDDING DESIGNS are reproduced here from books, magazines, and seed catalogs of the period. Copy or adapt one, or let them inspire you to your own unique creation. For other design ideas, look to your own old house -- its fancy interior woodwork, gingerbread trim, or an art-glass window -- or the decorative arts of the appropriate period. Fabrics, linoleum, china, and wallpaper can all be fertile sources for bedding designs.

A CIRCULAR BED is easiest and can be used to illustrate combinations adaptable to more complicated designs. The illustration at right first appeared in <u>Vick's Illustrated Monthly</u> (1878). The center of castor-oil plants is ringed by cannas, caladium (or elephant ear), coleus, and finally dusty miller. Similarly dramatic would be a center of pampas grass ringed by bronze-leaved cannas, tall red salvia, golden coleus, and finally blue lobelia. Simpler, lower variations better suited to a smaller yard would be red salvia, blue ageratum, and white alyssum; rosy red geraniums, purple verbena, and pale pink Drummond phlox; or yellow cannas, tall red cockscomb, and chartreuse coleus.

THIS PINWHEEL-FLOWER CIRCLE is adapted from Peter Henderson's <u>Practical Floriculture</u> (1887). He recommends a red salvia center with petals of red and yellow coleus; for an edging, alyssum, lobelia, or a low succulent would be appropriate. The design is suited to alternating colors of other bedding plants as well, such as pink, white, and purple petunias, verbena, or Drummond phlox; or yellow, orange, and red portulaca or crested cockscomb. Choose plants for the center which will coordinate with the petals.

MUCH MORE ELABORATE circles can be seen in Elias Long's <u>Ornamental Gardening For Americans</u> (1885) (Fig. 4). A simplified version of the top-left design is also shown (Fig. 5). One possible planting would be a center of red salvia in an "asterisk" of blue ageratum, with a red geranium in each arm, surrounded by dusty miller and an edging of golden portulaca. Another possibility would be to plant cannas with bronze foliage and orange flowers in the center of an asterisk of purple

PETUNIA – Too common to be evocative today, petunias (left) were nonetheless very popular, particularly in mid-century single-species beds. Multifloras with their smaller blossoms look most like older petunias; pinks, whites, and purples were the earliest colors. **About 1 foot; sun.**

PHLOX DRUMMONDII, annual or Drummond phlox — Easily grown from seed, this low-growing Texas native (right) carries clustered flowers in bright pink, purple, red, white, & softer tints. 'Dead-head' it to keep it blooming all summer long. **6 to 15 inches; sun.**

PORTULACA, moss rose — This well known succulent (right) is from Brazil, & has ruffled, open flowers in brilliant shades ranging from rosy reds through golden yellows to white. Likes sandy soil. **About 6 inches; full sun.**

SALVIA splendens — Blazing reds are the hallmark of this Mexican wildflower (left), which first became available in the U.S. in the 1840s. It was so popular, it became a carpet-bedding cliche. **10 to 30 inches; sun.**

SUCCULENTS — A variety of succulents were used in Victorian carpet bedding. Some, like carpet echeveria, were valued for their bluish foliage. Others, such as agave, offered an exotic touch. Gold-moss stonecrop (*Sedum acre*) made a neat, low edging, as did the still-popular hens-and-chicks (*Sempervium tectorum* or *Echeveria secunda glauca*). Be aware that not all are hardy. **Sun.**

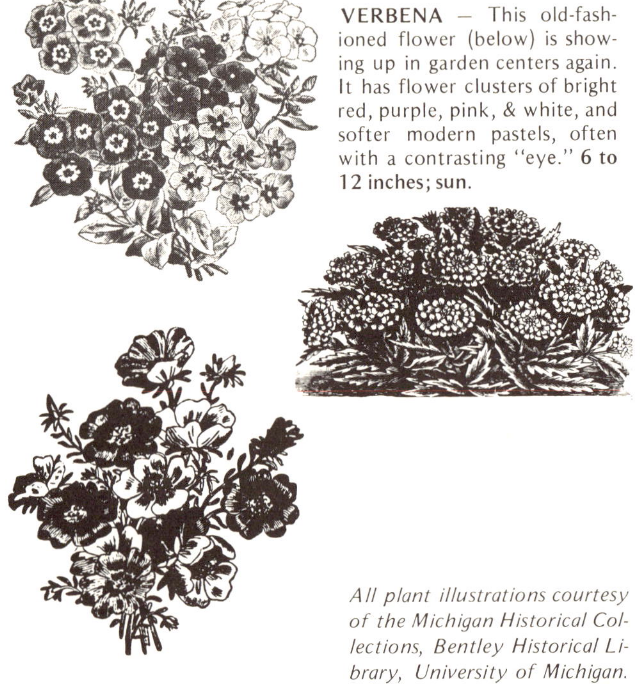

VERBENA — This old-fashioned flower (below) is showing up in garden centers again. It has flower clusters of bright red, purple, pink, & white, and softer modern pastels, often with a contrasting ''eye.'' **6 to 12 inches; sun.**

All plant illustrations courtesy of the Michigan Historical Collections, Bentley Historical Library, University of Michigan.

verbena, with a tall, bronze coleus in each
arm, ringed by low, golden coleus and deep
blue lobelia.

Fig. 4

Fig. 5

Shady Beds

GIVEN A CHOICE, the preferred
location for a carpet bed has
always been in the full sun,
but even a century ago gardeners
were experimenting with carpet beds
in the shade. Today, mature trees
and urban congestion can make a
shady bed the only option for many
old-house owners. But don't despair: Even though less authentic
-- or maybe just not as well documented -- a bed in the shade of a
brownstone or antique elm can be as much fun
as a sunny carpet bed. You won't have masses
of colorful blossoms, but you can have lovely
greens, rich contrasts, and unexpected drama.

ELEPHANT EAR makes a wonderful center plant
for a shady bed. It's easily grown from
large, tender bulbs, and with lots of water
and fertilizer its heart-shaped leaves will be
nearly three feet long on stalks four feet
high. A palm makes another showy choice for
the center. (Like the Victorians, you'll need
to haul it back indoors when the temperature
drops in the fall.)

RING YOUR PALM OR ELEPHANT EARS with one of
the taller ferns: ostrich, lady, toothed wood
fern, or another. Most wood ferns are hardy
perennials, and of course they'll appreciate
the water you provide for the elephant ears.
Ferns alone can make a fine center for a shady
bed too.

AROUND THE FERNS plant a ring of either hosta
or caladiums, both of which are noted for
their attractive foliage. Caladium looks like
elephant ear's flashy little brother, with
foot-long leaves marked with red, pink, or
white. Hosta's greens range from blue through
yellow, and many cultivars are variegated. As
a bonus, hosta also features spikes of white
or lavender flowers in summer or early fall.

RING THIS RIBBON with dwarf ferns or hosta, if
you like, and then for an edging use English
ivy. The hardiest English ivies stay green
through all but the roughest winters, and so

you can extend your shady bed's attractiveness
by allowing the ivy to cover the entire bed as
an underplanting.

OTHER PLANTS that may be useful in a shady bed
are ajunga, myrtle, lily of the valley, or
primroses for an edging; some old lilies --
particularly tiger, rubrum, and gold-band
lilies -- in the center; and astilbe or day-
lilies in between. House plants can be used
too, for example spider plant, sansevieria, or
even African violets. Some bedding plants
will adapt to light shade also -- notably begonia and coleus -- but in real shade they'll
grow slowly, stay small, or bloom sparsely.
For authenticity, avoid the temptation to use
impatiens, the current shade favorite; it's
strictly a recent introduction.

SOIL QUALITY and adequate watering are of
prime importance for success in a shady bed.
Improve the soil with a healthy helping of
organic material to keep it light. If the bed
is in the shade of trees, be prepared to water frequently, because
the overhanging leaves will keep
out rain while the trees' roots
will draw enormous amounts of
moisture out of the soil every
day. A bed under trees often
needs more watering than a bed in
full sun.

ANY POPULAR FASHION is bound to
provoke a certain reaction
against it, and carpet bedding was no exception. In England
as early as 1870, William Robinson
decried carpet bedding as "pastry cook gardening" and called for a return to mixed plantings of perennials and wild flowers. Before
long, Gertrude Jekyll and others were champi-
oning the "cottage garden," although it wasn't
until about the turn of the century that the
reaction really reached America.

HERE, QUEEN ANNE HOUSES and the florid style
of the late Victorians were giving way to
classic and Colonial Revival architecture, and
to a general nostaligia for simpler times,
including the old-fashioned flowers of an
idealized "grandmother's garden." Bedding out
lingered on in public plantings, but by the
1920s few people had anything good to say
about it. Along with Victorian architecture
and decorative arts, carpet bedding was
generally villified for much of this century.

IN RECENT YEARS, of course, Victoriana has
enjoyed renewed respect. Some intrepid souls
have even gone so far as to suggest that carpet bedding might be worth a second look. In
fact in England right now the rage is for open
"island beds," which are nothing more than
Victorian promiscuous beds updated. Certainly, in excess and without sensitivity any
style is laughable. But when handled with
taste and understanding, carpet bedding can be
both striking and evocative. A revival of
appreciation is overdue.

SCOTT G. KUNST heads a firm that does consulting work as well as actual historic landscape design; he also gives lectures and slide shows on
the subject. He can be reached through Old House Gardens, 2315 Park-
wood, Ann Arbor, MI 48104. (313) 973-0304.

Window Parts

Crawford's Old House Store has a good selection of hard-to-find, inexpensive hardware for windows, storm sashes, and window screens.

If you have original wooden storms or screens, three varieties of storm and screen sash hangers are available to you. Two metal hooks attach to the top of the window and two hangers attach to the sash (extra hangers are available so screen and storm can be hung from the same hook). One set, the old-style point 09 hangers (no. 360009), sells for $.95 per pair.

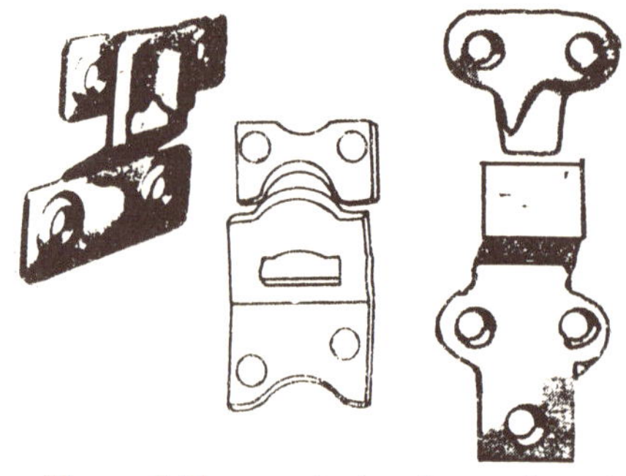

Many old houses had sash numbers to keep track of which storms and screens went where. You need a set for the sill, one for the storm, & one for the screen.

The brass head is embossed with a number, and they're pushed in like tacks. There are four sets, 25 tacks to a set, beginning with nos. 1-25 (no. 360501), for $1.90; the others, from 26 to 100, sell for $1.40 each.

For transom windows there's a catch with striker plates (no. 361410) for $1.70. A 12-in. transom chain with mounting plates (no. 361411) sells for $1.55. All have a plated brass finish.

Postage and handling for all of the above items is extra. To order a catalog, send $1.75 to Crawford's Old House Store, Dept. OHJ, 301 McCall, Waukesha, WI 53186. (414) 542-0685.

Paint for Terne

In our article about standing seam roofing (March 1985), we mentioned the need to prime and paint terne metal to lengthen its lifespan. Terne is known for its ability to hold paint (due to tiny pores in its surface), but only if it is the right paint applied the right way.

If painting an entire metal roof doesn't sound like fun, just try to find the right paint at your local paint store. This hard-to-find stuff, Red Iron Oxide-Linseed Oil paint, has a very slow drying time of about 72 hours. Have you ever heard of such a thing? The firm that makes terne says that brushing the paint into the surface, with its slow drying time, allows the paint to soak fully into the pores of the metal and bond very tightly. Apparently they're right, because the same finish has been recommended for well over 100 years.

Tin-O-Lin National Tinners Paint manufactured by Calbar is designed especially for terne. It is an iron oxide paint ground and mixed in linseed oil. The first coat should be Red Tin-O-Lin (it serves as a rust-inhibitive primer) followed by several color finish coats. You must allow 7-10 days drying time before applying a second coating. For the longest life and greatest protection, terne can be primed on both sides. Underside priming is especially important on flat or slightly sloping roof surfaces.

Tin-O-Lin comes in four colors: Slate Grey, Light Red, Medium Green, and Brown (Black, Duranodic Bronze and custom colors are available). Red is $26.96/gal.; Grey & Brown, $28.20/gal.; Green, $33.40/gal. Five-gallon pails sell for the same price per gallon, less $.20.

For more information on Calbar National Tinners Paint, contact **Calbar, Inc. Dept. OHJ, 2626 N. Martha St., Philadelphia, PA 19125. (215) 739-9141.**

Greenhouses, Conservatories & Garden Structures

"Conservatories were originated by the great garden designers of the 18th and 19th centuries to house tender plants in the captive heat of the sun," says Francis Machin of Machin Designs, Inc. In his design offices and shops in England and in Rowayton, Conn., Machin creates high-quality, period-style greenhouses or conservatories designed to complement rather than detract from old houses.

Machin's structures range in size from 4 sq.ft. to over 5,000 sq.ft. Specifically tailored to the North American climate, they are made with heavy aluminum frames and baked on white finishes.

The conservatories are not designed for do it-yourself assembly. On the East Coast Machin crews can assemble one in 3 to 4 days on your foundation. Elsewhere Machin can send a trained erection supervisor to guide your crew in assembly. The conservatories are not cheap, either in price or quality of materials. For example, an 8 ft. 10½ in. sq. unit, single glazed, with two side walls, one end wall, a pair of doors, opening rooflites, roof blinds, automatic ridge vents, all mounted on your foundation, sells for about $11,575.

No less striking in appearance, design, and quality of construction are the Machin Ornamental Garden Buildings and Landscape Ornaments. The Octagonal Pavilion (pictured) sells for $4,500 plus shipping — seating on five sides sells for an additional $400. On a more modest scale there is the Gothick Covered Seat ($1,150 plus shipping) and a de-lightfully Victorian, freestanding Bird Table ($295 plus shipping). All of these structures are built of treated lumber and have colored fiberglass roofs designed to simulate lead.

The Conservatories brochure is $2 and the Ornamental Garden Buildings catalog is $3. Contact **Machin Designs, Inc. Dept. OHJ, P.O. Box 167, Rowayton, CT 06853. (203) 853-9983.**

Original Morris Wallpapers Available Again

A collection of 24 of some of William Morris' finest hand blocked wallpaper prints has been reissued by the English firm of Arthur Sanderson & Sons, who purchased the original wooden wallpaper-printing blocks of Morris & Company back in 1930. The reissue of these beautiful and exactly authentic wallpaper patterns was timed not only to coincide with Morris' 150th birthday, but also to herald the opening of Sanderson's first U.S. showroom here in New York.

William Morris, an extraordinary 19th-century designer, painter, weaver, pattern maker, novelist, critic, and poet, is credited with reviving interest in the decorative arts in England, called the Arts and Crafts Movement. Morris designed a total of 41 wallpapers and 5 ceiling papers.

Sanderson, well known for their high quality since the 1860s, make and print all their own fabrics and papers. Their craftsmen, in a very slow, time-consuming process, hand print the Morris wallpapers, using the original wooden blocks. Hand-blocked printing produces a unique depth of color and individuality not found in other processes such as silk screening. All of the colors are hand-mixed from raw materials in the quality and character of the original wallpapers. Thirty rolls of a given design requiring 8 color blocks can take eight days to produce (each color has to dry before the next can be applied). No mass production here. The hand-blocked papers are not washable but can be treated with a washable solution. These papers are also supplied with a selvedge that has to be professionally trimmed before hanging. All of the designs in the Morris series can be recolored to suit your particular needs.

How much will these hand-made works of art cost? Hold onto your hat! The retail prices range from $95 to $375 per roll (these are European double rolls, 21 in. by 33 ft. long). The cost of the wallpapers is directly related to the number of blocks (i.e., the time) required to print a given design. The factory claims (probably rightly so) that the production of these papers is very nearly a break-even proposition. But once you see the sophisticated and gentle use of color and the relaxing foliated designs, the price is more bearable.

The hand-blocked wallpapers come in 24 patterns. Sanderson also has 4 coordinated screen-printed wallpapers from

Morris collection, which sell for $57 per roll. They also offer coordinated fabrics to match 8 or 10 of the Morris papers, and sell them for $24 to $73 per yard.

You are encouraged to write for a free color brochure. The color catalog of available wallpapers (which includes the date of each) is $5, and an 18 in. x 24 in. sample of the hand-blocked paper is $10 (refundable with any Sanderson purchase). Since Sanderson deals directly with the trade you'll need a resale number to make a purchase. Sanderson & Sons, Dept. OHJ, D & D Building, 979 Third Ave. (Suite 403), New York, NY 10022. (212) 319-7220.

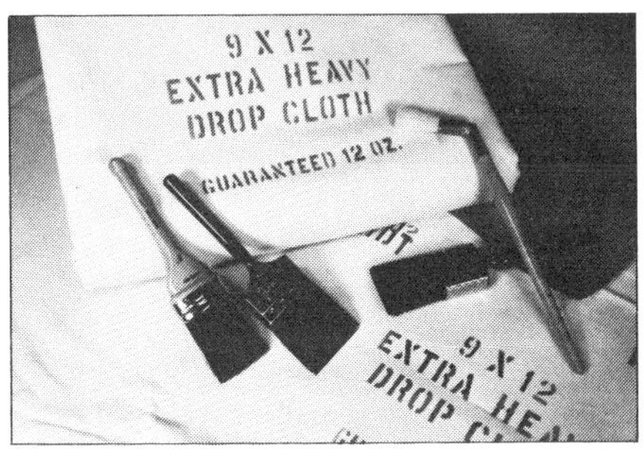

Wolf's inexpensive canvas drop cloth

We've found the perfect gift for old-house owners: a genuine cotton painter's drop cloth, the kind professionals use. They last a long time and are washable. You may not believe this, but there's actually a laundry in New York that specializes in washing drop cloths!

Wolf Paints is our source for hard-to-find painting items, including this great, inexpensive drop cloth. The best ones are tightly woven, 10- to 12-oz. untreated white-cotton canvas, and are usually made in several pieces. The best size is 9 ft. x 12 ft., and Wolf sells them for $19.49. A 12-ft.-x-15-ft. size costs $31. Shipping is extra on all drop cloths.

For more information contact Wolf Paints & Wallpapers, Dept. OHJ, 771 Ninth Avenue, New York, NY 10019. (212) 245-7777.

Air Sealing Homes

An interesting new Canadian manual, *Air Sealing Homes For Energy Conservation*, is currently available in draft form (no pun intended) to Canadian & American readers. This book is jammed with useful, air-sealing techniques for existing houses. It covers the use of sealants, weather-stripping, air vapor barriers, and other products and techniques.

Air infiltration and exfiltration is one of the least understood and least remedied areas of old-house repair. The first section of the manual explains the fundamentals of air exchange, moisture movement, indoor air quality, and sealing air-leakage points. Section two lays out methods for determining what air-sealing measures should be undertaken for a given house. Sealing techniques are prioritized, and sealing packages that fit a variety of situations are examined. The third section looks at the materials and application techniques used to seal up air leaks. An abundance of good illustrations show how to seal up each typical element of a house. Step-by-step 'how-to' work sheets give instructions and outline tools, materials, prep work, and application procedures for each element.

The manual should be of particular interest to architects, contractors, instructors, and homeowners. But there is a limited number of copies available. They're free to Canadians, $20 ppd. for Americans (in U.S. funds, make check payable to Receiver General of Canada). To get yours write to BETT Program, Dept. OHJ, 580 Booth St., Ottawa, Ontario, Canada K1A OE4.

Seed Sources
FOR BEDDING PLANTS

de Jager and Sons, P.O. Box 100, Brewster, NY 10509, $1. Spring and summer bulbs, including a number of old or wild varieties.

Fragrant Path, P.O. Box 328, Fort Calhoun, NE 68023, $1. Not many bedding plants per se, but excellent source of old-fashioned varieties for promiscuous beds.

Park Seed Co., P.O. Box 31, Greenwood, SC 29646 free. General catalog with cannas, caladiums, elephant ears, and some ornamental grasses.

Stokes Seeds, P.O. Box 548, Buffalo, NY 14240, free. General seed catalog. Offers coleus and many flowers in separate colors as well as mixes.

Thompson and Morgan, P.O. Box 100, Farmingdale, NJ 07727, free. Very wide range of seeds, including ornamental corn and banana, and some grasses. Lots of color photographs.

A TYPICAL REMUDDLING: small aluminum windows replace well-proportioned wooden ones, aluminum siding covers original clapboards, asphalt shingles supersede slate, wrought iron and fake brick take the place of the original porch. (photos courtesy of The Butler Eagle)

WHAT MAKES THIS REMUDDLING particularly sad is that that the work was done by vocational/technical students and praised by their teachers and the community. Subscriber Eleanor Gard, who first saw these photos in a local newspaper, describes her reaction.

DEAR OHJ:

THIS NEWSPAPER ARTICLE caused me to choke on my coffee!

I REALIZE 1) the house was unexceptional, 2) not all houses can or should be restored, 3) it is in a depressed area, and 4) a service was done for the community. BUT . . . I also realize that a future generation of plumbers, carpenters, roofers, etc., has been taught to be insensitive to preserving historic architectural elements such as fish-scale shingles and slate roofs. My tax money is going to support this curriculum!

THANKS FOR LISTENING,

Eleanor Gard
Marwood, Pennsylvania

The Old-House Journal®

69A Seventh Avenue,
Brooklyn, New York 11217

NO PAID ADVERTISING

Postmaster: Address Correction Requested

Restoration and Maintenance Techniques
For The Pre-1939 House

May 1985 / Vol. XIII No. 4 / $2.

The Old-House Journal

The Bungalow
and why we love it so

by Patricia Poore

AMERICA HAD a long love affair with the Bungalow--for thirty years a torrid one--and the old flame is being rekindled. This is the story of how an exotic Anglo-Indian word came to mean a new American house style. Bungalows came from India, so say popular accounts, but it wasn't that simple. The word (or variations of it) existed for hundreds of years before any bungalows showed up here. "Bunguloues," temporary and quickly-erected shelter, were referred to by an Englishman in India in 1659; we find "bangla," "bungales," and "banggolos" before the English spelling "bungalow" superseded others by 1820.

THE ENGLISH in India were describing houses built for them by native labor: long, low buildings with wide verandahs and deeply overhanging eaves. Broad roofs, first of thatch and later fireproof tile, enclosed an insulating air space against tropical heat. Then, around 1870, builders of the newly fashionable English seacoast vacation houses called them "bungalows," giving them an exotic, rough-and-ready image.

cont'd on p. 90

In the next issue...
HOLDING A HOUSE TOUR

Special Issue

Should We Spin Off A Newsletter For Bungalovers?

ONCE you've read this issue, you'll be as convinced as we are that Bungalows (and other post-Victorian houses) are <u>the</u> exciting new restoration frontier. We're aching to develop many more articles: regional Bungalows, Bungalow backyard fences, Bungalow curtains and floors and friezes, Bungalow shingles and porches, kitchens and roofs. Furnishings, too, from built-ins to porch swings. And we want everyone to meet the architects and tastemakers who took part in creating the first New American house styles.

WE'VE BEEN gathering and studying early-20th-century books on architecture and furnishing. (Our ground-breaking article isolating different post-Victorian house types appeared in January 1982.) We'd love being the first to publish information that'll help you appreciate and restore your Bungalow (or Foursquare or Prairie-style or Tudor Revival house).

HOWEVER, MOST OHJ subscribers own houses built between 1840 and 1900. In OHJ, we want to keep the balance we've always had -- technical information that can be used by <u>all</u> old-house owners, together with case histories and house-style articles that span the entire 19th century and creep into the 20th. As wonderful and romantic as Bungalows are to read about, we just can't use up all our pages talking about them.

BUT WE could <u>devote</u> a new publication to the period. The OHJ would continue to give basic restoration counsel to a broad readership. In The Bungalow Letter®, we'd be free to lose ourselves in early-20th-century architecture. Like OHJ, it would provide straightforward and well researched articles to help you, whether you're an owner restoring your post-Victorian home, or a historian studying this long-ignored period in American residential architecture.

THE BUNGALOVERS we've met are a proud group of free thinkers who appreciate the solidity, comfort, and history of post-Victorian houses in advance of the fad. To share important (and hard-to-find) information and experiences among this group, we've considered enhancing a subscription to the new publication with membership in The Bungalow Society. Benefits would include a charter subscription to the Bungalow Letter, as well as an annual meeting, information exchange with other members, access to books of the period -- and perhaps reproduction furnishings, too!

SMALL PUBLICATIONS don't have big budgets for "market research," so if you're at all interested, your response now is extremely important to me. You can Xerox this page or write your answers on a separate sheet. Thanks!

Patricia Poore

(1) Would you like us to send you information about a new publication? (no obligation)

____

(2) Would you like more information on joining The Bungalow Society?

____

(3) What is the year and general style of your house?

________ ________

(4) Would you prefer a black-and-white newsletter (at about $18 per year) or a newsletter that included some full-color art (at about $27 per year)?

B&W ________   Color ________

(5) What articles do you need? Help with structural problems? decorating? replacing house parts? landscaping? (Be as specific as you can; attach a separate sheet if necessary.)

____

____

Name ____________________

Address _________________

____

The Old-House Journal®

Editor
Patricia Poore

Production Editor
Cole Gagne

Technical Editor
Larry Jones

Assistant Editor
Sarah J. McNamara

Contributing Editors
Walter Jowers
John Mark Garrison
Roland A. Labine Sr.

Architectural Consultant
Jonathan Poore

Circulation Supervisor
Barbara Bugg

Circulation Assistants
Jeanne Baldwin
Garth White

Special Sales
Joan O'Reilly

Assistant to the Publisher
Tricia A. Martin

Catalog Editor
Sarah J. McNamara

Publishing Consultant
Paul T. McLoughlin

Publisher
Clem Labine

Published by The Old-House Journal Corporation, 69A Seventh Avenue, Brooklyn, NY 11217. Telephone (718) 636-4514. Subscriptions $18 per year in U.S., $25 per year in Canada (payable in U.S. funds). Published ten times per year. Contents are fully protected by copyright and must not be reproduced in any manner whatsoever without specific permission in writing from the Editor.

We are happy to accept editorial contributions to The Old-House Journal. Query letters that include an outline of the proposed article are preferred. All manuscripts will be reviewed, and returned if unacceptable. However, we cannot be responsible for non-receipt or loss — please keep copies of all materials sent.

Printed at Photo Comp Press, New York City

ISSN: 0094-0178
NO PAID ADVERTISING

IN THE VALLEY OF HEARTS DELIGHT

A First-Person Account Of The Bungalow Era

by Paul J. Lukes

MOTHER AND DAD were married in 1911 in the chapel of a mission school in Montana where she had graduated from high school in a class of three. Since my dad was a railroad employee, they took off on a railroad honeymoon. Poor mother. Dad was an RR electrician and signal maintainer and after six months in Watsonville, California, he bumped into the College Park yards in San Jose. (Old timers will remember the bumping system on the railroad.) According to RR rules, employees had to live within a mile of the tracks. So Mom and Dad rode their bicycles around the neighborhood of the College Park tower looking for a place to rent. While Dad worked, mother kept on looking. She had to hurry, I guess, because by that time she was pregnant with me. Old 89 Schiele (now 921 after being annexed to the city) was the place she chose and here she set up housekeeping.

ENCOURAGED BY A WELL-TO-DO aunt of Mother's, the folks bought the place and Dad started immediately to change the rooms around. Mother commented once that when I was born, there was only one room in the house with four walls. Fortunately it was our bedroom. I guess she didn't count the bath.

OUR BUNGALOW was started in 1905 and finished in April of 1906, just in time to be settled on its redwood-slab foundation by the quake of 4/18/06. Our house had two identical porches. One in front and the other on the driveway side. The porch roofs were supported by round redwood pillars that were

in style at the time. The siding is redwood tongue-and-groove, 8-3/4 inches wide with two grooves in each panel to simulate three-inch boards. The roof was shingled with redwood. There were still redwood mills in the mountains to the west of us then.

THE HOUSE WAS PAINTED red at that time, and with two palm trees planted between the sidewalk and the gutter, it couldn't be missed. Mother gave me the impression the house was built by a plumber for himself, but my research shows that the house was built by one carpenter and his helper; perhaps the plumber did the pipework. Anyway, the plumber and his two sons moved in when the house was finished.

GAS LIGHTS lit the house. Some of the fixtures had gauze mantles that cast a white light, and others, mounted on old ceramic tips, produced a yellow fishtail glow. Students had homework to do in those days and I wonder now how we could see to do our work.

ALL THE ROOMS have coved ceilings and all the rooms except the kitchen and the pantry have picture-hanging moulding. Two of the rooms have board-and-batten wainscotting that rises five feet two inches above the floor. The plaster walls rise to a total height of nine feet. The dining room walls are stained dark walnut, but the other room, which used to be Dad and Mother's bedroom, had so many coats of paint that my wife called in a painter and he grained all the walls and doors.

A typical Bungalow window. Gail had the woodwork and wainscotting, which appear in all but the kitchen, grained by a local craftsman.

The maple table and chairs in the dining room came in kits that were shipped in large crates from Wisconsin and then assembled.

OUR BUNGALOW had inside plumbing, but judging by the way the pipes were laid out, I suspect the sanitary sewer line was run down the street after the house was built. There is a small closet off the back porch. When I was growing up there was a pull-chain toilet in it. The water tank was a wooden box with a zinc liner, high on the wall. It was generally considered a man's room, but the ladies used it in emergency. Man, was it cold out there at times, but people who had to use an outdoor privy would probably have thought it was pretty nice.

DAD WAS BORN AND RAISED in a generation of small-town men who had to learn to do anything and everything. Of course it helped that his own father was a mechanical genius. My dad built all the bookcases and china closets in this old Bungalow. Our furniture came from Wisconsin, shipped in big crates as kits, and Dad assembled them. (Solid walnut and just as sturdy as ever today.)

ALTHOUGH WE HAD GAS LIGHTS when we were growing up, Dad had started wiring the house when he was reworking the rooms. I think he was finally moved to finish the job because he wanted an electric radio. We had a battery-operated set before that. Electricity was Dad's specialty, but he didn't exactly trust the PG & E. So when he wired the house, he provided a gas outlet high up on the kitchen wall with a fishtail jet on top to provide light if the electricity failed. Well, it did briefly once or twice. Gave us an opportunity to see again what we had lived with for many years. Dad put another gas outlet in the boys' room. My brother Tom was into chemistry at that time and needed gas for his Bunsen burner. Yes, we lived dangerously, but it was interesting. Incidentally, there's still gas in those pipes.

OUR PUSH-BUTTON SWITCHES, installed when Dad wired the house, are the envy of some old-house connoisseurs. All the switches work, although a couple are getting kind of mushy. The front porch light is an ancient railroad semaphore bulb. We have no idea how old it is, but one thing is certain, if we never turn it off it may burn forever. I saw in a recent issue of OHJ that push-button switches and face plates are available again. I mentioned this to one of our visitors, but like a lot of young people who are reconditioning old houses, they are a little on the shorts.

Dad's Work, 1911-1930

DAD WAS A YOUNG RAILROAD electrician when he and his young bride bought the house in 1911, and being a genius for change, he immediately began to make over the insides of the place and generally for the better. Early on in the project, he bought hundreds of feet of used hardwood flooring from a dismantled lodge hall ballroom. The original floors in this Bungalow were not the best. So

Paul's father installed all the built-in cupboards and china closets in the Bungalow.

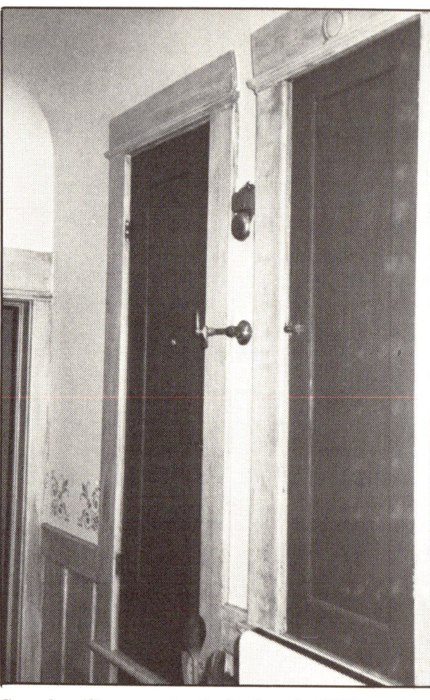

Coved ceilings are typical of early-20th-century homes. Note the gas jet and doorbell on the wall.

The sleeping porch, like the entire house, has Japanese-style rafter ends.

This deck is the only new addition to the exterior of the 1905 Bungalow.

Dad took them up and laid the second-hand maple floors in the living and dining rooms. This wood had a strange grey color that puzzled me. Years later it dawned on me that the color was from a combination of dance floor wax and San Jose street dirt that came in on the waltzing feet of the dancers.

BEFORE DAD got the new (used) maple floors sanded, filled, and varnished, Mother used to let us rollerskate in the dining room when it was raining. I don't suppose Dad would have appreciated us skating on his hardwood floors, but Mother had five kids in the house who had to have something to do. The first time the whole family was allowed in on the newly finished floors was Christmas morning. It was quite an occasion. We had our new electric lights, our shiny new floor, and it was Christmas with the tree and all. Our old dog Queen came running in with us -- it was her first time, too. She rounded the archway between the dining and living rooms at full speed, only to end up scratching and clawing on the slippery floor and landed under the Christmas tree. Dad only laughed. I guess it was kind of a compliment to the smoothness of his floor-finishing job.

IN THE WINTER OF 1919, Dad installed a small gas furnace in the floor of the archway. Visiting ladies often stood over the heat, letting it rise up under their skirts. Once one who had stood over the heat too long started hopping around, grabbing her skirts and slapping her legs. The furnace heat had warmed up the metal on her garters 'til they burned her. I was only eight then and too impressed by this startling performance to think it was funny.

IN 1920 OR THEREABOUTS, Dad built a garage for his Model T. It was the only car he ever owned. Dad's younger brother Dolf was a mechanic for the Ford fleet at the Panama Pacific Exposition in San Francisco in 1915. When the Fair was over, he brought home this car. He really didn't need it because he was driving a big Lozier. He gave the car to his mother and younger brother Mike. When Uncle Mickey went off to WW I, they sold the car to Dad. It had no starter, no generator, and no battery -- eventually no top. When I was a senior in high school, I had one like it -- bought it from a classmate for $5.

BY 1925 when Margaret Alice arrived, our two-bedroom Bungalow was a bit crowded. Because I was the oldest boy, my cot was set up in the dining room, in a tent in the yard, or on the side porch. Eventually Dad (who had a genius for architectural change without doing damage to the outside of the building) reworked the side porch into a sleeping porch for my brother and me. There we slept until we both left for WW II.

The Changing Neighborhood

SAN JOSE WAS A BUSY CITY, the county seat of Santa Clara County. The area, once known as the Valley of Hearts Delight, is now known world-wide as Silicon Valley. Our part of town was annexed to the city about 50 years ago.

IN THE 1880s, a German immigrant named Charles Schiele bought 15 acres in an area of the county known as Alameda Gardens. Charles put a street through his property and named it after himself, so we have Schiele Avenue. Schiele runs between The Alameda and Stockton Avenue. Both streets were served by horsecar lines in those days. The lines on Stockton were abandoned, but the lines on The Alameda became a double-track electric railway.

WHEN CHARLES SCHIELE put our street through, he sold lots on one side only. The other side remained a hayfield surrounded by a six-foot solid board fence until around 1925. Schiele put sidewalks down both side of the streets. Every year a baling crew came to bale the hay. They brought their own chuck wagon and the men slept out in the hay at night. Everything was run by horsepower; not a motor in the organization. Once a year, it was a great excitement for the neighborhood boys.

AROUND 1925, two real estate promoters bought the hay field, took down the fence, and put three streets through it. In no time at all, the lots were sold and little 1920s-style houses covered the field. A new street cut through Schiele Avenue and the sidewalk was torn up at the entrance. Dad brought home some big squares of the sidewalk in his wheelbarrow. He shaped the pieces with his stonemason's hammer and chisel and made a steppingstone walk between our steps and the sidewalk.

IN THOSE EARLY DAYS a mailman delivered the mail from a horsecart with a parasol top and side curtains that could be rolled down in bad weather -- sort of an early-day hardtop. The horse needed no commands. When the mailman stepped off the cart, the horse stopped, and he started again when the mailman came back a-board. I seem to remember that unless Christmas came on a Sunday it was a work day for the mailman. Water-meter readers had the same system, a cart and a smart horse. All utilities were collected door-to-door.

AT ONE TIME, one of our next-door neighbors had several cows. There were two big vacant lots behind our houses where the cows were kept at night. As there were no houses across the street, the cows were led out in the morning and tied to the trees with ropes short enough to keep them from standing in the street. It seems incredible now, but the sight of cows and goats along the grassy sides of streets was a common sight in those days.

THE BOYS IN OUR NEIGHBORHOOD used to play ball in front of our house. That was where the manhole cover was that formed home plate. I can still hear the sounds of ancient bats being pounded on that slightly domed iron base. Once in a while we had to move over when a car came by. One of the neighbor girls had a gentleman friend who sold Maxwells. After a successful sale he'd drive up in front of her house and shout up the block that he had "Sold another one!" The old Maxwell Motor Car Company was bought by Walter Chrysler.

The Lot

OUR LOT IS 140 FEET deep. At one time we had a chicken yard, a girl's play house, a big sandbox, usually a pile of old RR ties for fuel, and a big high swing. When I was about nine years old, I asked Dad if I could try the big saw he was using to cut the ties for the stove. I must have done okay because the job became mine for the next five or six years. Around 1930 the RR began creosoting the ties and that ended our wood supply. Then we got our first, and Mother's only, gas stove.

FOR MANY YEARS we had no garbage service and our kitchen scraps went over the fence to the chickens. One time Mother noticed her wedding band was missing and surmised she must have thrown it to the chickens. Dad bought her another ring, but the original was gone. Years later when the chicken yard became a garden and the girl's play house and the sandpile were gone, Mother was spading in her garden with a spading fork and speared her original wedding band with one of the tines. Stranger than fiction.

LIVING WITHIN TWO LONG BLOCKS of the College Park freight yards, we heard the noise of steam switch engines and the crash of boxcars as they were shunted from one track to an-other. Today the steam engines are gone and the much quieter diesels have taken their place. Most of the train assembly has been moved north to Santa Clara yards where there is room to make up longer freight trains.

The Lukes and their granddaughter on the front porch of their Bungalow.

Gail and I have traveled the length of California and Oregon on Amtrak. We recognize the train as the engineer whistles it through the College Park yards. Some folks object to the train whistles, but not us. Train whistles are a part of old-house living.

The House Today

DURING THE WAR YEARS when the men were away, their wives came home to live with "Granny." They brought little children with them and the house was filled with young voices again. The sleeping porch became a nursery. After the war, when they had homes of their own, the young marrieds lived nearby and eventually there were 23 grandchildren. When the time came when Mother could live alone, her grandchildren were old enough to go live at Granny's house. All these people kept Mother and the old place alive.

GAIL AND I BOUGHT THE HOUSE from the family after Dad and Mother were gone, much to the relief of my brothers and sisters who hated to see the place go to strangers. We lived in a house nearby while we raised our family, but when I retired, we moved back here.

WHEN I READ THE ARTICLE in OHJ about porch pillar restoration, I put our extension ladder up to examine the tops of our front porch pillars. Sure enough, 75 years had taken their toll. I purchased a quart of wood preservative and rot stabilizer. After stripping the paint from all pillars, I poured the preservative from the top. I smoothed the overflow down the sides of the shaft and painted it on the railings. Then I poured on two coats of water seal. My wife didn't like the look of the rails after that, so she painted the whole business with log oil. That didn't look so hot either. When we had the house painted, the pillars and rails were primed with white paint and finished with Cedar, a brand-name color. Looks good, everybody says. We like it, too.

OUR OLD BACK STEPS were getting pretty weary, and Gail wanted a big new redwood deck. So we have it, with built-in benches all around, 11 feet by 14 feet. Actually, it's the only new thing on the outside of the whole house. When one lives in an old place, looking for busy work is no problem. Outside of emergencies, what to do first is the only problem.

A New Craftsman Light Fixture

...the perfect Bungalamp

by Patricia Poore and Jonathan Poore

WE LIVE in a nineteenth-century neighborhood -- but not in a Victorian house. Rather, it's post-Victorian, with glass French doors instead of walnut pocket doors and an utterly simple cove instead of ornate cornice mouldings. How does one decorate a house like this? How does one furnish it?!

TAKE THIS light fixture. There was no light in our dining room and, besides, we needed something pretty to boost our morale during the grunt work. So we thought we'd buy an appropriate period fixture. The dining room shows most clearly a Craftsman influence. In choosing a lamp, we didn't want a Victorian holdover, or a mass-produced glass saucer, or a Colonial Revival chandelier. We wanted a hanging wood lamp inspired by the new architectural styles of the house's period.

NO LUCK. There weren't any in the antique stores because very few high-style fixtures were produced. And the market hasn't yet arrived for post-Victorian reproductions in the Arts and Crafts style. (The one or two Mission fixtures we did find were too small to be the centerpiece of a large room.)

SINCE WE couldn't find an old fixture and we couldn't buy a new one, we set about designing one. Editors at OHJ leafed through old books looking for design inspiration. Jonathan mentioned the project at work and soon his fellow architects were involved. What DiDonno Associates came up with is not a reproduction but something new, based on the "design vocabulary" of the period. Inspiration came from woodwork in Greene and Greene houses and from the linear forms of Frank Lloyd Wright and Scottish architect Charles Rennie Mackintosh.

THE FIXTURE is an Arts and Crafts piece not only in design but also in spirit. Our design is a contemporary interpretation rather than an imitative reproduction. To be inspired by the past, not limited by it, is an extension of the Arts and Crafts philosophy.

WE COMMISSIONED cabinetmaker Brian Trager to make it out of oak. As it was being built, we realized we'd invented a bungalamp, very much in keeping with the materials and details typical of American Bungalows. We hurried over and took some pictures for this issue: It'd be a shame to keep this wonderful design all to ourselves when it's so hard to find the right fixtures for these houses.

IF READERS show any interest, Brian will gear up to produce a _limited_ run of these fixtures. Here are the specs:

- MATERIALS: Oak; leather straps adjustable to 3' long; amber art glass; flat-black canopy and tubing.
- FINISH: Light oak stain; two coats Watco oil; one coat of wax.
- WEIGHT: 23 pounds complete.
- DIMENSIONS: Height 29" (not incl. straps); 18" (short side) x 27" (long side).
- LIGHTING: Six bulbs in glass box, plus two mini-bulbs in neck. Takes frosted globe lights (25-watt recommended, or 40-watt if on a rheostat). Mini-bulbs can be used alone for candle-light effect.
- PRICE:$995 -- finished, electrified, with leather, amber art glass, mini-bulbs, and shipping crate. If you prefer to buy your own glass or commission leaded glass, the fixture can be purchased without glass for $955. (FOB Brooklyn)

THE ART GLASS SHOWN on this page is a beautiful leaded design by Ernest Porcelli. The field is an unusual mottled glass that is opaque and nearly white when the lights are off, but turns a translucent amber-white when illuminated. The dogwood blossoms are pink-and-white glass with green leaves; branches are copper-foil work. If you want a complete fixture like the one shown, cost is $1455. (FOB Brooklyn)

THE FIXTURE would be terrific for Bungalows, Craftsman houses or others in that tradition of natural materials and woody interiors; Prairie-style houses; American Foursquares; Stick and Shingle style and later Queen Anne houses with oak woodwork; in fact, any house built between 1895 and 1930 that is not in the Colonial Revival tradition.

FOR MORE information or to reserve a fixture, please call us at 718-636-4514.

STRIPPING BEAMS

by Bill O'Donnell

Beamed ceilings are featured in many early-20th-century homes, from Bungalows and Craftsman types to Tudor Revival houses. Tastes change, alas, and the beams you inherited may have been painted over. Following is a description of the special techniques that can be used when you're stripping paint overhead.

SEVERAL MONTHS AGO, I moved into a somewhat neglected 1910 house, and the restoration began. The oak beams in the dining room should have been the most impressive thing about the interior, yet I nearly missed them at first. Because of the monotonous green paint that covered the room, they'd all but disappeared into the ceiling plane. Ignorant of what lay ahead, I vowed to return the beams to their original glory.

I SPENT TWO WEEKS struggling in that room, and learned some valuable lessons. As difficult as the task was, the reward was worth the effort. The exposed oak crossing the ceiling changed the room's character tremendously.

PAINT STRIPPING is a messy and irritating job, especially when you're working over your head. To minimize annoyance and disruption, spend an hour or two in preparation. First, remove everything possible from the room; if it's not nailed down, its better off elsewhere. For safety, make arrangements to keep children and pets out of the room while you're working. Not only are the chemicals dangerous, but, in an old house, some paint layers are likely to contain lead. Vacuum the floors and mask them neatly with kraft paper.

VENTILATION is a must when removing old finishes, particularly with chemicals. Turn the thermostat down, open the windows wide, and keep the air circulating with exhaust fans. You'll feel better if you wear a respirator when stripping with heat or chemicals. Fire is always a potential hazard: Many chemical paint and varnish removers contain combustible materials; the fire hazards associated with heat tools are obvious. Common sense and caution will virtually eliminate the danger, but it's smart to keep a fire extinguisher handy.

MANY STRIPPERS-FOR-HIRE use chemical means exclusively -- they don't have to live with the smell and mess. To remove all the paint with chemical strippers though, you would have to use gallons of expensive chemicals and work under a ceiling that was dripping blobs of toxic ooze. I prefer to strip with heat as much as possible, because it's cheaper, cleaner, and less disruptive than using chemicals. I found this procedure most agreeable:

1) Remove as much paint as possible with the heat plate, especially from flat areas.
2) Return to more intricate areas such as mouldings and strip them with the heat gun.
3) Clean up residual paint and varnish with one heavy coat of chemical stripper.
4) Apply a final coat of chemical stripper and wait until it's almost dry. Use a brass brush or steel wool to remove dried chemical-varnish sludge.
5) Clean up with steel wool (or a clean brass brush) and lacquer thinner.
6) Lightly sand out imperfections.

THE HEAT PLATE and heat gun are invaluable paint-stripping tools. The heat plate goes through broad areas in a hurry: Simply hold it close to the surface until paint blisters, then scrape clean with a putty knife. Be careful to remove heat before paint ignites; otherwise, you'll scorch the wood, and the flames may vaporize any lead in the paint. I found it better to leave a thin band of paint between working areas of the heat plate -- overlapping such areas caused small burn lines where the wood had been heated twice. It's easier to return to these bands with the more precise heat gun than to spend hours sanding out burns.

Smothered under layers of paint (left), these beams are barely noticeable. But once the ordeal of stripping is completed (right), the exposed oak brings to life the original character and proportion of the entire room.

MOULDINGS AND CORNERS are best stripped with
the heat gun. The process is identical to
that of the heat plate, although you may want
to substitute a different tool for the putty
knife. The heat gun doesn't <u>seem</u> heavy until
you've held it over your head for a few hours.
To avoid weary arms, I made an armrest for my
scaffold.

A SCAFFOLD is a must if you're spending several hours at a time working above your head.
Scaffolding is a tremendous timesaver because,
unlike a ladder, it has to be relocated only
occasionally. The one I constructed was simple but effective: a 2-ft.-wide platform sitting atop two simply constructed sawhorses.
Be sure to find the optimum height for a comfortable working position before building your
scaffold, so that you're assured a custom fit.
(The armrest was just a place to rest my elbow
while heat stripping -- but it also served as
a convenient place for setting down tools.)

HEAT STRIPPING removes all the layers of paint
down to the original varnish. To ensure a
clean sweep during this stage, I found it best
to work carefully. Working with heat tools at
a hysterical pace will only cost you time in
the long run. For example, pushing a dirty
putty knife back into hot varnish will leave a
paint residue that will require more time to
remove with chemical stripper than varnish
alone. Heat stripping is the neatest and
least offensive way to remove paint, particularly when you're working overhead, so take
full advantage and remove as much paint as
possible before the messy work begins.

HEAT STRIPPING COMPLETED, you're ready to
remove residual paint and varnish. Now
the slime method begins! There are many
chemical strippers on the market, and I've
tried most of them. For this application I
recommend Zip-Strip brand:

● It's non-flammable, thus reducing the risk
of fire.

● It's more viscous than many other brands;
therefore, it hangs on overhead beams long
enough to be effective.
● Although it doesn't produce a pleasant
olfactory sensation, it won't render you
unconscious as quickly as some of the more
volatile brands will.
● It's extremely effective, often doing the
job in one coat.

BEFORE APPLYING THE CHEMICAL, place plastic
dropcloths over the kraft paper that covers
your floor; they'll prevent globs of chemical
from seeping through the paper and destroying
your floor's finish. But you can't avoid getting globs of chemical on yourself, so wear a
hat, a high collar, long sleeves, and rubber
gloves. A faceshield is infinitely more useful than goggles -- I wore mine constantly.

LAY THE CHEMICAL ON THICKLY, catching initial
drips in a large container, such as an alumi-
num-foil roasting pan. Apply as much chemical
as the beams will hold, brushing in one direction only. Let the chemical work for 20 to 30
minutes. Then, while it's still wet, vigorously brush the wood with a brass brush. When
all the paint and varnish has mixed with the
chemical to produce a brown slime, wipe off as
much as possible with paper towels. Stubborn
areas should be brushed again immediately.
After the rest of the stripper dries, it will
brush off easily with a brass brush or steel
wool. The result: original oak beams!

SOME FURTHER CLEAN UP may be necessary. Steel
wool and lacquer thinner removes any hazy film
left by the chemical stripper. Dental picks
or similar objects are effective for digging
into corners. Finally, you'll have to go back
and sand all those scorched areas where you
got over-anxious while using the heat tools.

STRIPPING THE BEAMS was a very unpleasant
task, but, as the photos demonstrate, the
results were dramatic. The oak returned the
proportion and warmth which the room had lost
under all those senseless layers of paint.

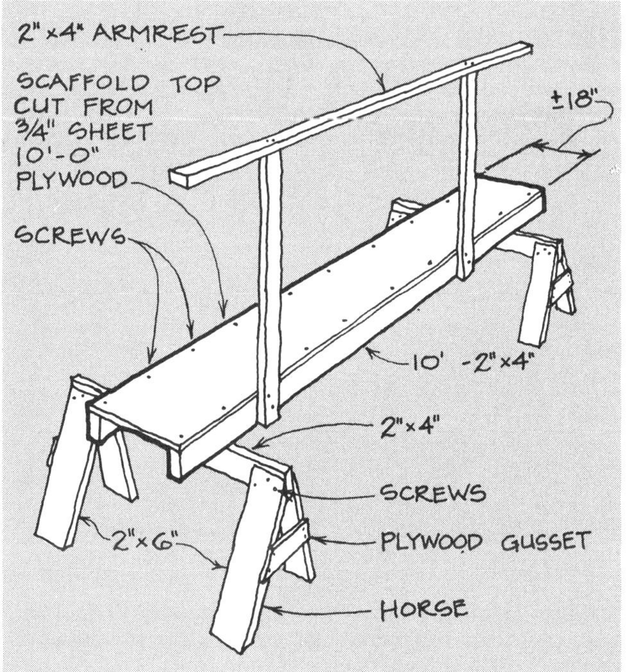

After removing most of the paint with heat tools, Bill finishes up with
chemical stripper and a brass brush.

How To Repair Stucco

by Walter Jowers

IN THE EARLY 1920s, right about the time of the Bungalow Boom, the portland cement industry made a big effort to sell architects, home builders, and home buyers on the "charm, beauty, and permanence" of stucco. This campaign was quite successful; many of the houses built during this period were clad in stucco, and many older houses were remodeled with the material. Before 1900, most stucco houses were finished with lime-based stucco, which is particularly susceptible to water damage. There are still lots of lime-based stucco houses standing, though, and in this article we'll discuss how to distinguish between the types of stucco, and how to repair each type.

Stucco Problems

WATER IS THE CAUSE of most stucco failure. Improper mixing of mortar, poor installation, building settlement, and just plain exposure to the elements account for other stucco problems. Water-damaged stucco usually bulges or falls away from the building, because water causes the coats of stucco to delaminate, and the lath or lath fasteners to fail. (Wood lath can warp, metal lath and nails can rust.) Cracks caused by building settlement or movement of framing members (stress cracks) usually are "clean" cracks, with no surrounding bulging or decayed stucco. Water can, of course, enter a stress crack; then you have both problems at once.

STRESS CRACKS should be repaired only after you've determined what caused them, and whether or not the cracks are still moving. (See "The Crack Detective," May, July, Aug., and Dec. 1981 OHJs.) Similarly, loose or crumbling water-damaged stucco shouldn't be repaired until after you've found and eliminated the offending water source.

WATER DAMAGE to stucco usually comes from one of these sources:
- Rain
- Migration of water vapor from the interior of the building
- Capillary action from the ground
- Leaky plumbing

WATER PENETRATION can be prevented by:
- Proper use and maintenance of flashing, drip edges, and drainage systems on the building exterior
- Use of vapor barriers between the building interior and the stucco
- Proper treatment of the termination of the stucco at ground level
- Repairing leaky plumbing

THE BEST MATERIALS FOR FLASHING are copper, lead-coated copper, terne metal (which must be painted), and a relatively new and very long-lasting material, terne-coated stainless steel (TCS). Galvanized steel is acceptable flashing, but these other metals are better and cost only pennies more. Aluminum, the favorite of many contractors, is questionable; it's flimsy and it tarnishes. It also takes paint poorly, and won't take lead/tin solder at all, which makes it just about un-repairable.

DRIP EDGES are changes in the plane of materials under horizontal projections, such as door and window sills. They interrupt capillary action, causing rainwater to drip away from

Vertical cracking at corners is caused by the different expansion rates of the two surfaces. (In this photo, you can see the metal lath used in earlier repairs of the wall.)

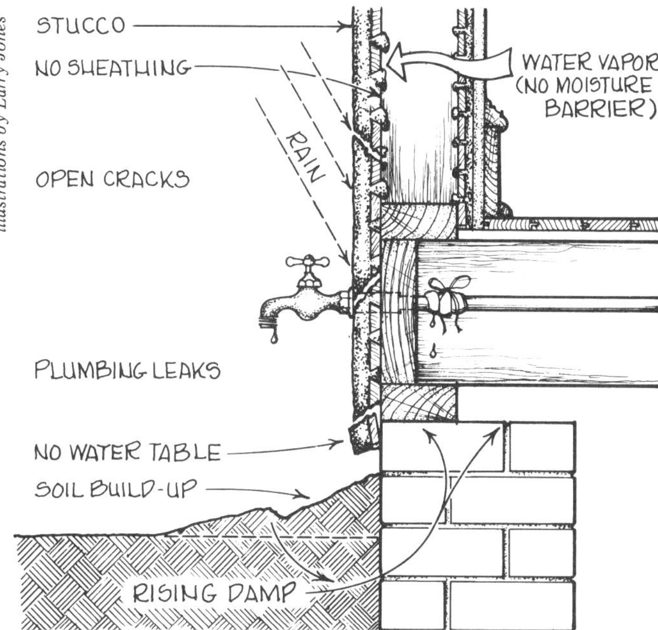

Sources Of Water Damage

the walls of the building. Some drip edges are formed out of flashing; others are integral parts of the house trim, such as window sills. Drip edges are often overlooked as sources of water damage, but they can be major culprits if successive coats of paint or stucco have built up on them and rendered them useless.

GUTTERS must take rainwater away from the house without overflowing or leaking along the way. Rusty gutters with tar patches won't do the job; neither will gutters with broken joints, nor gutters that have settled to the point where they no longer drain to the downspouts. Flimsy aluminum gutters with caulked joints won't do anything well for long. Copper, TCS, or galvanized gutters with soldered joints are best. Accept no substitutes.

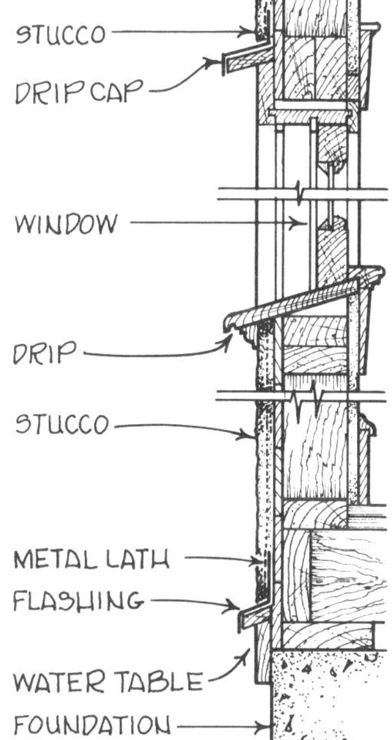

THE MIGRATION OF WATER VAPOR through the walls of a house causes fewer problems than does rainwater, but it can damage stucco (or exterior paint), especially on masonry buildings. (Frame structures normally have a layer of waterproof felt between the wood sheathing and the stucco, which prevents vapor penetration.)

THE AREAS MOST SUSCEPTIBLE to damage from water-vapor migration are the walls outside of kitchens, bathrooms, and chimney flues. If you have damaged stucco near these walls, and

can't blame it on stress cracking or rainwater penetration, then vapor migration might be the cause. Solutions: Make interior walls relatively tighter than exterior walls, by applying vapor-barrier paint on the interior walls, and caulking joints along the interior window trim and baseboards. Vent the bathrooms or kitchens with a sufficiently large exhaust fan. If stucco on a chimney is damaged, line the flue with a non-porous liner (stainless steel is good).

IMPROPER TERMINATION of stucco at ground level often results in water-damaged stucco. Most specifications call for stucco to terminate at least four inches from the ground, but many old houses aren't built that way -- the stucco goes right into the ground. In such a case, you should do everything possible to keep the area dry: Repair and maintain gutters and drains; make sure the ground slopes away from the stucco wall. Only then should you patch the stucco.

STUCCO OFTEN FAILS at 90-degree joints such as those between parapet walls and roofs. Deteriorated or improperly installed flashing is

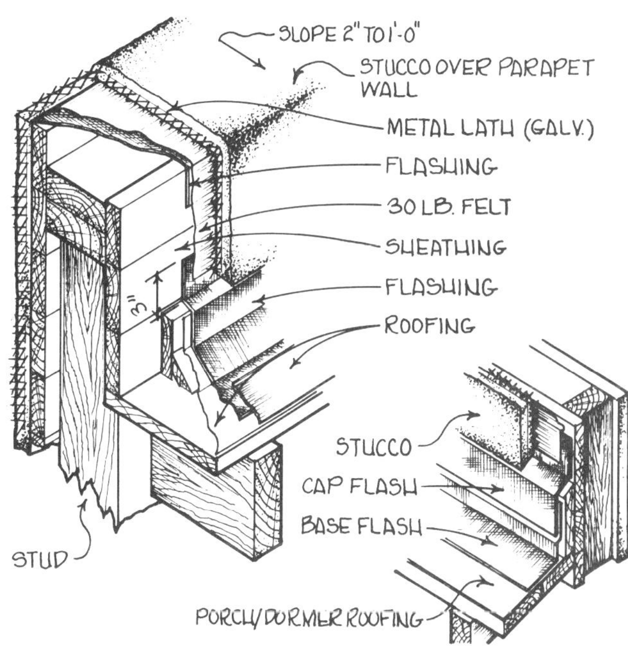

usually the culprit. In such cases, you must remove enough stucco to allow you to remove the old flashing and install new material. The drawings above show some typical flashing details. Consult an experienced contractor before tackling an extensive flashing-replacement job: It might be easier (and cheaper) to re-stucco the whole house, rather than just re-stucco over a lot of new flashing.

Stucco Patching

AFTER YOU'VE FOUND and corrected any source(s) of damage to your walls, the next step is to determine what type of mortar was used to stucco your house. Whatever it was, you'll want to use the same type of mortar for repairs. Generally, 20th-century houses are stuccoed with portland cement, whereas earlier houses are likely to have been built with lime mortar. This isn't a hard-

and-fast rule; some avant-garde masons used portland cement in the mid-19th century, and some conservative masons used lime mortars well into the early 20th century.

TO TEST for mortar type, take a chip of the mortar in question, place it in a container of dilute muriatic acid (available at hardware stores), seal the container tightly, and shake it vigorously. If the mortar dissolves, it's lime. If it doesn't, it's portland cement.

REMOVE DAMAGED STUCCO before you start patching. There are two schools of thought on this subject. Rationale #1: Remove the smallest amount of stucco possible. Why make extra work; you can tackle a small job yourself. Rationale #2: Hire a mason to apply new material all the way to a logical break in the building surface -- for instance, re-stucco a whole wall or chimney. The patch will be less noticeable, and a mason probably won't charge much more to re-stucco a whole wall than to make a patch. Both ideas are reasonable.

TO DETERMINE the extent of the damage, check for spongy areas by pushing against the stucco with your hand. Any areas that move back and forth while making a squishy sound will have to go. Then, tap the stucco with a hammer handle, and listen for the sound of loose stucco -- a succession of sounds, like a tap dance. When you reach an area that doesn't move, and that makes only one solid sound, you've found the good stucco.

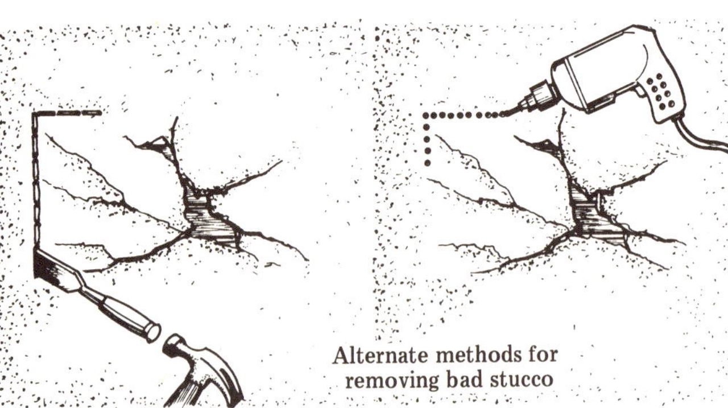

Alternate methods for removing bad stucco

DON'T just start peeling off the loose stucco. If you do, you could de-stucco the whole house before you realize that you're breaking off sound keys along with the bad ones. Make cuts through the stucco around the damaged area, either with a cold chisel or by drilling a series of holes with a masonry bit. Cut to the lath. Then pry off the old stucco with a broad, flat tool such as a nail puller. Cut back the coats of old mortar in square layers, as shown in the illustration (right). Once the old stucco is removed, clean out all the dust, dirt, and loose material with a wire brush. If there's loose wood or metal lath under the old stucco, be sure to nail it back to the sheathing tightly.

Lath Options

THERE IS CONTINUING DEBATE over whether or not one should apply stucco over old wood lath. People who are particularly disturbed by the idea of using "inappropriate" materials in old-house repair can't bear the thought of metal lath imbedded in a wall that originally had wood lath. If you feel this way, be sure to wet wood lath thoroughly with water containing a little photographer's wetting agent (e.g., Kodak Photo-Flo) before applying the new stucco. Professional plasterers nail metal lath over old wood lath (so they know the stucco will stick) and get on with it.

NO ONE should use metal lath when patching an old building that has lime stucco over a masonry base; metal here causes more problems than it solves. The old lime mortars, when deteriorated, simply fall off the building, exposing the masonry underneath. These bricks or stones can withstand weather reasonably well, and the wall can be patched whenever weather and the repair-person's schedule permit. But if you patch the wall with new mortar over metal lath, you've created two new problems: 1) damage caused by the nails used to fasten the lath; 2) should water penetration recur, the patch will cling tightly enough to hold in the water, thus causing further deterioration of the masonry wall.

Applying The Mortar

APPLICATION METHODS are similar for lime or portland cement mortar. The following instructions apply to all stucco work:
● Keep the curing mortar out of the hot sun and away from harsh winds -- either of these conditions can cause new mortar to fail. If you must apply mortar on a very sunny or windy day, set up a lean-to or tarpaulin to provide some shelter for the mortar.
● Don't expose curing mortar to freezing temperatures.
● Cross-hatch the scratch (first) coat of mortar to provide good keys for the leveling (second) coat. Finish the leveling coat with a wood float that has a small nail driven through it (only the nail tip protrudes) to provide keys for the finish coat.

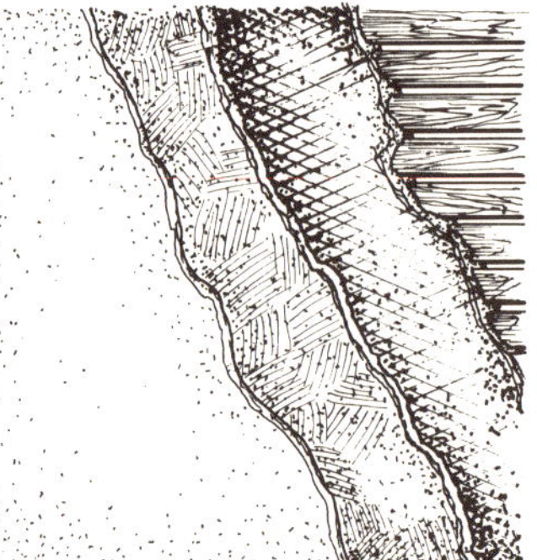

Reading from left to right (that is, from the surface down): finish coat, leveling coat, scratch coat, wood lath.

● Don't make more mortar than you (or your crew) can use in about one hour.
● Throw away partially set mortar. Do NOT try to apply partially set mortar to the wall.

TROWEL ON the scratch coat of new mortar to the same depth as the scratch coat of old mortar. Use your screed to straighten the mortar, and then cross-hatch it. Keep the mortar damp (not wet) by misting it, and apply the second coat 18-24 hours later. If your repair is three-coat work, you must repeat the above process for the leveling coat. When the base coats have cured, trowel on the finish coat. Level it with a screed that rides on the old finish coat (as in the illustration above).

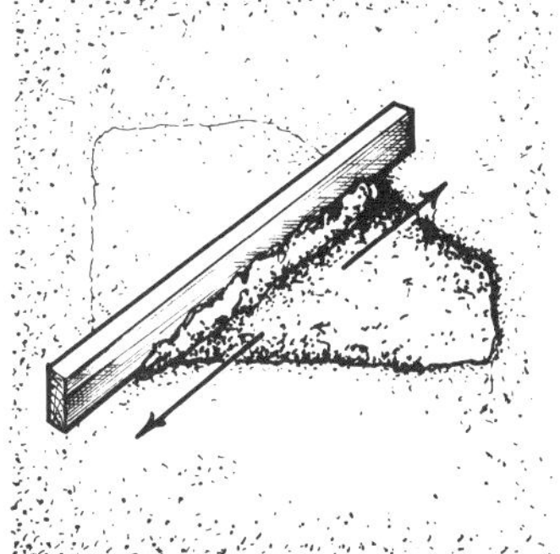

IF YOUR STUCCO has a textured or colored finish, or exposed aggregate, you should at least consult with an experienced local mason before you try to match such a finish. Your State Historic Preservation Office (SHPO) is a good place to ask about local masons with preservation experience.

Mortar Formulas

EYE OF NEWT, tongue of frog ... lime, cement, sand, and water. The recipes for mortar are as arcane as those for witches' brew; it seems every mason has a "secret" formula. And the older the mortar, the more opinions there are on how to duplicate it. The following mortar formulas can be used as starting points for duplicating typical stucco mortar:

High-Lime Mortar
● 1 bag of hydrated lime
● 1 shovelful of white portland cement
● 3 cubic feet of sand (matched to original)
● Coarse aggregate matched to original (not to exceed 15% of total volume of hydrated lime)
● Hair or fiber (for scratch coat) matched to original if possible, about 1 pound of hair per 100 lb. bag of hydrated lime*

Lime/Portland Cement Mortar
● 1 to 1-1/2 bags hydrated lime
● 1 bag portland cement
● 5 to 6-1/2 cubic feet of sand
● Coarse aggregate, hair, and fiber as above

THE MIX ABOVE is a good mortar to use in highly exposed areas such as parapet walls. This mortar may well have been used during the transitional period between soft lime and hard portland mortars.

RELATIVELY MORE LIME makes the mixture more "plastic," but it will also be more likely to

---

*Hair should be clean and free from extraneous materials. Cow hair is best. Cow hair is available from:
Brooklyn Animal Hair Manufacturing Company
175 - 185 Beard Street
Brooklyn, NY 11231
(718) 852-3592

crack because of shrinkage. Relatively more sand or aggregate makes the mixture harder to trowel smooth, and weakens the mortar. Each grain of cement should be in contact with a grain of sand.

IF THE MORTAR was a 20th-century mortar high in portland cement, start with this formula:
● 1 bag of portland cement
● 1/2 bag hydrated lime
● 6 cubic feet of sand
● Coarse aggregate, hair, and fiber as above

THE PROCESS FOR HAND-MIXING all three mortars is essentially the same: Place half the sand required for one bag of cement in one end of the mortar box, spread the cement (portland or lime) over the sand, then lay the balance of the sand over the cement. Place the amount of coarse aggregate or hair required for a bag of cement over the top of the sand. Repeat as necessary until all the required material is in the box. Now, with a hoe (a mortar hoe with two holes in the blade is best) start at one end of the box and pull the hoe toward you in short choppy strokes until you've thoroughly mixed all the material.

NOW POUR THE WATER into the box, and pull the dry material into the water with short choppy strokes. Make sure the hoe cuts to the bottom of the box. Continue to add water, but <u>only</u> as needed to bring the mix to a soft, plastic mass. Keep chopping with the hoe, moving further and further through the wet material. Make your strokes progressively longer, until all the dry material has been wetted and pulled to the end of the box. Then, to ensure a thorough mixing, change direction and pull the mortar to the opposite end of the box. When the materials have been thoroughly combined, the mortar color will be uniform. Don't overmix -- this just hastens the set of the mortar.

IT IS IMPOSSIBLE to duplicate some old mortars precisely; some materials used in the past just aren't available today. (Try to find unpolluted river sand.) The Portland Cement Association provides a service (for a fee) in which they specify modern materials that will match an old mortar in color and density. For further information, contact: Portland Cement Association, 5420 Old Orchard Road, Dept. OHJ, Skokie, IL 60077, (312) 966-6200.

Materials Specifications

THE FOLLOWING SPECIFICATIONS are taken from the <u>Preservation Brief 2</u> of the National Park Service:
● Lime should conform to ASTM C 207, Type S, Hydrated Lime for masonry purposes, or Federal specification SS-L-351B.
● Portland Cement should conform to ASTM C 150, Type I or II, or Federal spec SS-C-192G(3).
● Sand should conform to ASTM C 144, or Federal specification SS-A-281B(1) para. 3.1.
● Water should be clean, free from deleterious amounts of acids, alkalies, or organic materials.

Pandora's Stucco House

A Victorian Goes Tudor

"What's done cannot be undone," said Macbeth — and that applies to a high-quality, architect-supervised remodeling with stucco.

WE GET quite a few letters at OHJ from subscribers who want to know how they can remove old stucco from their houses. Often, someone's research has revealed that the house was once a high-style Victorian dripping with fretwork, and the owner wants to restore some lost details.

WELL, getting off old stucco isn't easy. Quite often, it's applied directly over a masonry base, with no lath in between. It's probably impossible to successfully undo this kind of stucco job. The specifications for installing stucco over brick in those days called for raking out the mortar joints and gouging the brick to provide a better bond for the stucco. So that isn't pretty brick under the stucco waiting for its natural beauty to be restored -- it's a mess, one that's best left alone.

MANY STUCCO REMODELINGS were done for a good reason -- to stop water penetration that occurred because of bad original design. Similar problems beset stucco-remodeled frame houses. Furring strips, stop beads, nail holes, and general woodbutchery are what's hiding under the stucco.

IF YOUR OLD HOUSE is a victim of a stucco remodeling or remuddling, it's almost always best to let it be -- unless you're willing to reface the house after you see what was hidden beneath the stucco.

The Bungal-Ode

HOW MANY HOUSE STYLES have had poems and songs written about them? Bungalyrics abound — one historian claims to know of 22 songs about the beloved Bungalow. Sometimes the melodious word itself provided inspiration, as in this verse first published in no less a mainstream magazine than <u>Good Housekeeping</u> (1909).

There's a jingle in the jungle,
  'Neath the juniper and pine,
They are mangling the tangle
  Of the underbrush and vine,
And my blood is all a-tingle
  At the sound of blow on blow,
As I count each single shingle
  On my bosky bungalow.

There's a jingle in the jungle,
  I am counting every nail,
And my mind is bungaloaded,
  Bungaloping down a trail;
And I dream of every ingle
  Where I angle at my ease,
Naught to set my nerves a-jingle,
  I may bungle all I please.

For I oft get bungalonely
  In the mingled human drove,
And I long for bungaloafing
  In some bungalotus grove,
In a cooling bung'location
  Where no troubling trails intrude,
'Neath some bungalowly rooftree
  In east bungalongitude.

Oh, I think with bungaloathing
  Of the strangling social swim,
Where they wrangle after bangles
  Or for some new-fangled whim;
And I know by bungalogic
  That is all my bungalown
That a little bungalotion
  Mendeth every mortal moan!

Oh, a man that's bungalonging
  For the dingle and the loam
Is a very bungalobster
  If he dangles on at home.
Catch the bungalocomotive;
  If you cannot face the fee,
Why, a bungaloan'll do it --
  You can borrow it of me!

-- Burgess Johnson (1909)

FABRIC ACCENTS for the CRAFTSMAN HOME

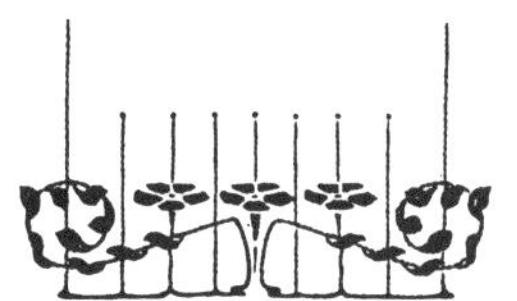

by Brenda Kearse Jowers

N THE QUINTESSENTIAL CRAFTSMAN house, the architectural and decorative features combined to form an unpretentious, restful ambience that served as a statement of the good taste of the homeowner. Decorative needleworks, an integral part of Craftsman interior design, are especially easy to reproduce. These pieces are appropriate for decorating any modest house of the early twentieth century, and anyone with experience in embroidery and applique can reproduce these uncomplicated patterns in the fabrics and colors authentic to the period.

REPRODUCTION CRAFTSMAN PIECES should be done in fabrics that are sturdy and durable, with a rugged and straightforward beauty, as the original pieces were conceived and fashioned not only to be observed, but also to be <u>used</u>.

ROUGH-WOVEN PIECE-DYED CANVAS, which is long-wearing and unobtrusive, is suitable for portieres (curtains that divide rooms, or are hung over cabinet doors), pillows, and chair cushions. The original canvas pieces were dyed in browns "the color of old weather-beaten oak; a sunny, yellowish tone; and a dark russet." Embroidered or appliqued portions were usually done in foliage greens, described as "dark and brownish like rusty pine needles; deep leaf-green; intense green like damp grass in the shade; and very grey-green with a bluish tinge like the eucalyptus leaf."

WINDOWS IN A CRAFTSMAN HOUSE were dressed in light, open fabrics. Craftsman stylists reacted against what they saw as Victorian excess, stating: "Silks, plushes and tapestries, in fact delicate and perishable fabrics of all kinds, (are) utterly out of keeping with Craftsman furniture." In most cases, curtains were either embroidered or appliqued as discussed here, or were done in simple prints.

NET AND CREPE are the best fabrics for window curtains. These fabrics were used in the original pieces to allow softly filtered sunlight into the house, and to give the occupants some view of the outdoors. Linen is appropriate for areas where greater elegance or privacy are desired. Warm natural colors such as pale tea brown, ivory, cream, grey-green, grey-blue, or deep yellow are well-suited to these window treatments.

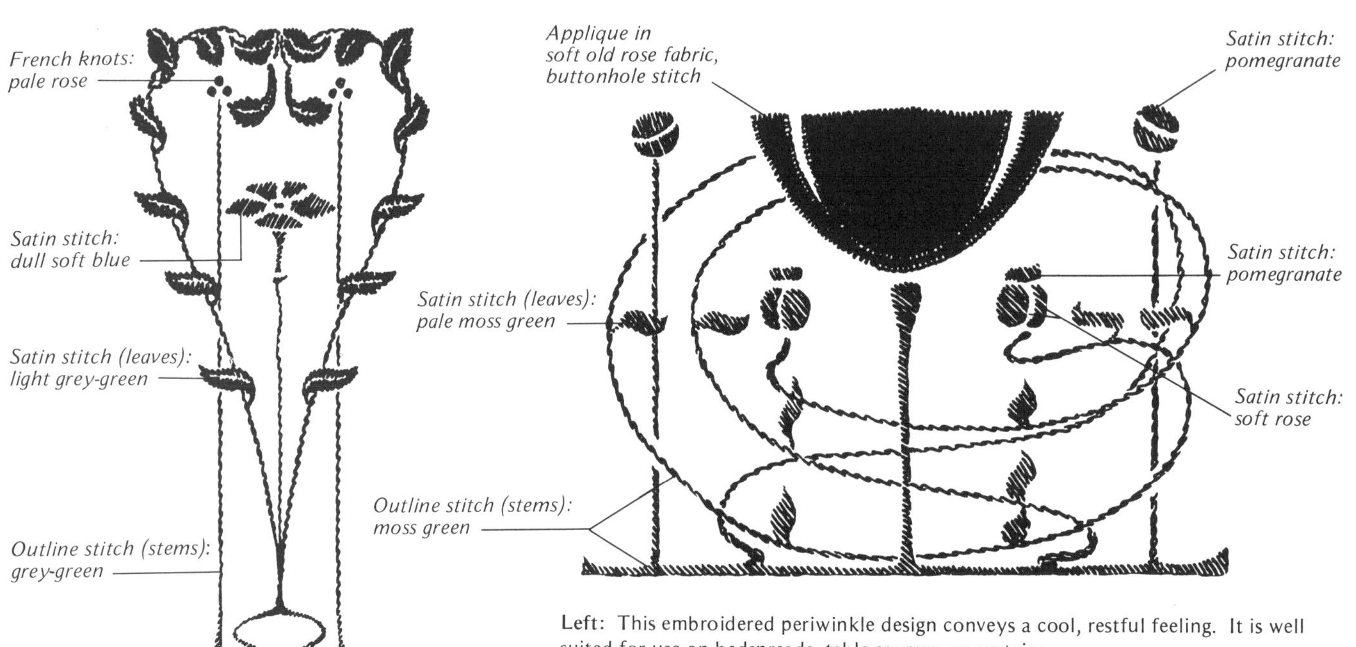

Left: This embroidered periwinkle design conveys a cool, restful feeling. It is well suited for use on bedspreads, table scarves, or curtains.

Above: This poppy design is done in applique and embroidery. Its suggestion of sleep makes it especially suitable for use in the bedroom.

The well-decorated Craftsman dining room. The appliqued and embroidered table scarves are crossed in the favorite Craftsman arrangement. Also notable are the Craftsman rug, the small-paned casement windows, and the recessed sideboard with a stained glass window above.

FOR TABLE SCARVES and runners, as well as bedspreads and towels that receive daily use, homespun, handwoven, or Flemish linen are the best fabrics. The rougher weave of the homespun is most suited for bedspreads. Handwoven linen, and the matte-finish, soft and pliable Flemish linen are best for pieces where a more delicate look is desired, such as table furnishings or curtains. All of these linens can be found in the cream-grey and pale brown colors natural to unbleached linen, and some are available in cream or ivory. All of these colors were used in the original pieces.

UNBLEACHED MUSLIN and rough-woven, dull-finished silk are also well-suited to Craftsman pieces, as the colors and textures of these fabrics blend well with Craftsman furniture and interiors.

LARGE PIECES such as portieres, couch covers, pillows, and table covers are often appliqued. A bold and simple design, cut from linen in a shade that contrasts with the larger piece, is basted into position and then buttonhole-stitched or slipstitched into place. The connecting lines, veins, or stems are done in an outline stitch with linen floss.

FOR SMALLER PIECES such as scarves, curtains, towels, and pillowcases, a simple darning stitch, outline stitch, and occasional French-knot stitch are used. For areas where greater texture or intensity of color are desired, the satin stitch is used.

Table scarf of hand-woven linen; pine cone design in darning stitch

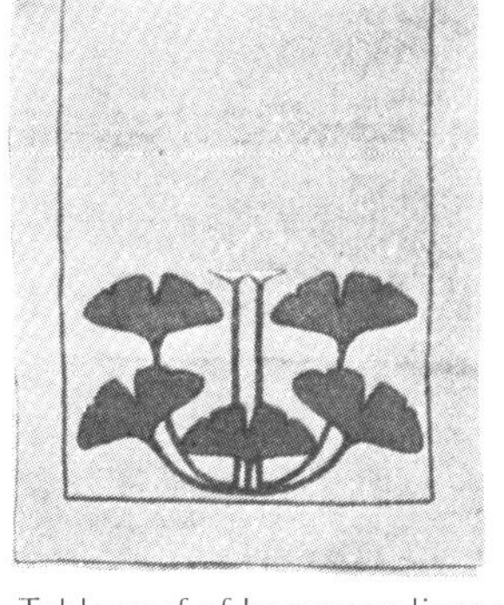

Table scarf of homespun linen; gingko design in applique of deep leaf green (stems in outline stitch of lighter leaf green)

Pillow covered with canvas; pine cone design in applique and outline stitch

Curtain of tea-colored net; design darned with silver-white linen floss

Outline Stitch

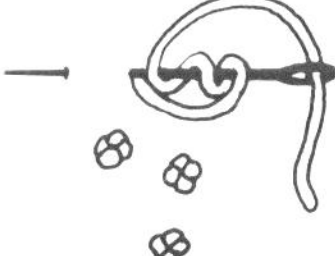

Buttonhole

Satin Stitch

French Knot

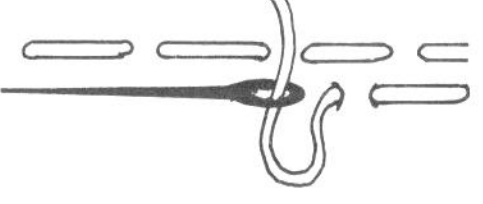

Darning Stitch

DOORS
of the 1920s

What were doors like during the Bungalow Boom?
Here's an inside look from the pages of builder's
catalogs we've collected from the period.

1925

A PERSON WALKING down a street (or more likely, a boulevard) in a new residential neighborhood is greeted, if not by his neighbors,
by the appealing and stylish front entrances
of well-kept houses -- doors that invite the
passerby to pause rather than pass.

1945

SOMEONE WALKING down the same street notices a
lot of "For Rent" signs. Work crews are cutting the larger houses up into apartments to
meet growing demand. Any element that doesn't
fit the remodeling scheme is removed. Goodbye
original doors (especially interior doors).

1965

IN HALF THE NEIGHBORHOOD houses, interior
doors are replaced with hanging beads or
macrame. In the remaining houses, exterior
doors are replaced by opaque, high-security
doors with deadbolt locks.

1985

THE ENTIRE neighborhood is a historic district. The residents are familiar with the
word "remuddling," and want none of it. They
want to restore the houses to their former
state of grace, complete with authentic period
doors. What did the doors look like? Here
are some examples.

This set of french doors, dressed with sheer curtains, is typical of
the period. The screen doors are not the usual wood doors, though —
the frames are metal!

This door, with its large glass opening, was
often used to light a hall or vestibule.

A single french door was often used as an
entrance to a Bungalow or cottage.

An unusual and quite handsome entryway.

  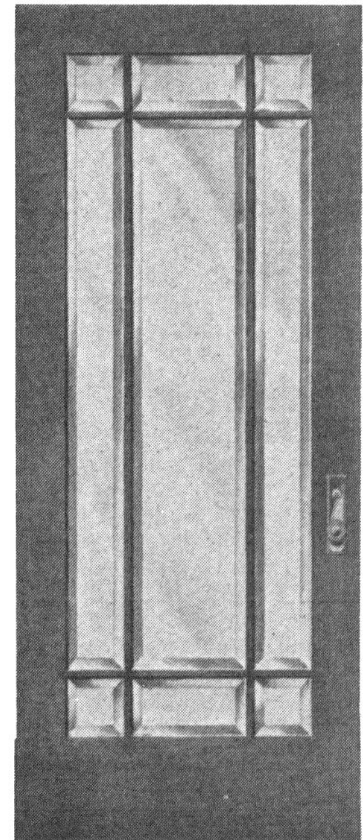 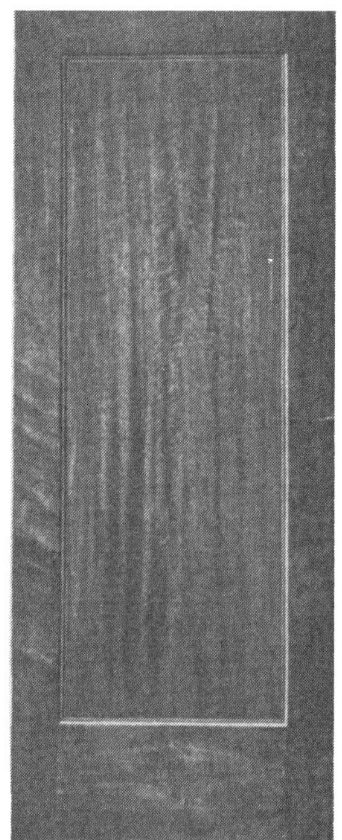

Interior Doors

Exterior Doors

THE MID-1920S DOORS shown here don't include any "famous" doors of the period. There are no examples from well-known architects such as Greene and Greene or Frank Lloyd Wright.

NATIONALLY ADVERTISED in building trade publications during the height of the Bungalow Boom, these doors were used by architects and builders all over the country.

THOUGH SOME of the paneled doors are holdovers from the Victorian period, most of the doors shown here display the simplicity and lightness of form that was characteristic of early-twentieth-century design.

THERE WAS A GREATER use of glass in these doors than in earlier ones; this made houses feel more open, both among rooms and to the outside. Sidelights frequently flanked exterior doors.

IF YOU'RE LOOKING for an authentic door for your early-twentieth-century house, chances are you're looking for a door like one of these. In many parts of the country, these doors are still fairly easy to find at flea markets and salvage yards, and most of them are stock sizes.

continued from p. 71

THE BUNGALOW showed up in America in the 1880s, scattered here and there especially in New England. But it was its development in Southern California that paved the way for its new role as a year-round house and turned it into the most popular house style America had ever known.

The California Bungalow

THE CLIMATE was perfect for a rambling "natural" house with porches and patios, of course, but there were sociological reasons, too, for the American Bungalow's birth in California. Los Angeles and upscale Pasadena, an 1890s resort town, were growing fast. By 1930, Los Angeles would have more single-family dwellings than any comparable city, with 94% of its families living in single-family homes! An essential part of this mass suburbanization was "an innovative, small, single-family, simple but artistic dwelling; inexpensive, easily built, yet at the same time attractive to the new middle-class buyer." Enter The California Bungalow, a term that was in use by 1905 if not before.

THE CALIFORNIA BUNGALOW was soon a well defined new style. Its sympathetic relationship with its site was paramount. The Bungalow hugged the ground. Indoors and outdoors intermingled in terraces, verandahs, screen porches, patios, courts, pergolas and trellises. Natural materials--in California, boulders and wood--made up the exterior and went inside.

THE GREATEST ARTISTS of the Bungalow Style were brothers Charles and Henry Greene, architects who shed their neo-Colonial and Queen Anne motifs to explore the possibilities of a true craftsman-built home. This was after a trip to England by Charles in 1901; he brought back Arts and Crafts ideals probably ten years before that movement would have reached the West Coast of the United States. They took an artistic leap, attempting to synthesize the best of many worlds into a new California vernacular: the adobe and Mission forms of the region, the rugged Shingle style of Richardson in the Northeast, the Italian and Japanese architecture they had studied.

THE GREENES picked the chalet, a folk carpenter's dream, as their base, looking not for a touch here and a touch there but instead the essence of the chalet: an uncomplicated and massive roof, exposed structure. They called the houses "bungalows," not inventing bungalows but transforming them from a lower form of temporary architecture.

Prairie Style & Craftsman Influence

MEANWHILE, 2000 miles away, the Prairie Style was being developed by a group of innovative young architects that would soon be known as the Chicago School. Frank Lloyd Wright would become the most famous, but he was by no means a lone innovator. The Chicago architects were also building one-storey houses, playing off the horizontal lines of the midwestern prairie. The designs were not bungalows in any sense of the Indian root of the word.

BUT, LIKE GREENE AND GREENE, the Chicago architects were influenced by the Arts and Crafts movement, and their simple (by Victorian standards) woody interiors were similar to those of the West Coast Bungalows. Greene and Greene and Frank Lloyd Wright were regularly published in Gustav Stickley's _The Craftsman_ magazine, the mouthpiece of the American Arts and Crafts Movement.

THE CRAFTSMAN magazine was the probably the most important factor in the popular development of the American Bungalow. _Ladies Home Journal_ was also a great Bungalow backer. But directly or indirectly, it was Stickley's appreciation of the Bungalow as an embodiment of Craftsman architectural ideals that gave it its wider appeal.

THE MOST PERSUASIVE VOICE for reform in residential architecture between 1901 and 1916, _The Craftsman_'s message had three major principles: simplicity, harmony with nature, and the promotion of craftsmanship. Greene and Greene themselves might have chanted the words. Their Bungalows, and others in Southern California, were an incarnation of all three principles. The same could be said of the Prairie Style.

STICKLEY BECAME an ardent Bungalow proponent from 1903 onwards, writing such things as [the

A Greene & Greene house as published in *The Craftsman*, 1907; the planned landscape is as noteworthy as the house.

This house by Prairie School architects Tallmadge & Watson was called a "Chicago-type one-storey home" in some Bungalow books; a "Midwest Bungalow" in others.

bungalow is] "a house reduced to its simplest form where life can be carried on with the greatest amount of freedom; it never fails to harmonize with its surroundings..." etc. etc. Stickley's descriptive, profoundly influential prose equated the Bungalow Style with the essence of Arts and Crafts philosophy.

OTHER HOUSE WRITERS soon understood the relationship between Craftsman houses and the Bungalow. In Bungalows (1911), Henry Saylor refers to furniture in "the so-called Craftsman style," later suggesting that "nothing seems so thoroughly at home in the bungalow living-room as the sturdy craftsman furniture of brown oak...." In many people's minds, both tastemakers' and new homeowners', Craftsman and Bungalow were so closely allied as to be the same.

The Builder's Bungalow

T HE BUNGALOW is usually thought of as a small house. Yet at first, in America at least, the style had nothing to do with size. The true Southern California Bungalows at the turn of the century were quite large, with rambling floor plans, extensive grounds, three or five or seven bedrooms, living rooms 20x25 feet, and multiple porches. All of this was about to change.

DURING THIS PERIOD, home ownership was becoming a realizable American dream for a middle class whose numbers were exploding. Speculative building and pattern-book companies were booming. A need existed for a small and simple house that would look good even if plainly built and furnished. The word "bungalow" had been happily adopted, even then with no pure definition, by a public that had read all about them in magazines. It was a type of house that didn't need much hype or hoopla; somehow, it was, and still is, intrinsically appealing. Perhaps a bit radical (bedrooms on the parlor floor?!), it was nevertheless embraced. And anyway, its more radical features were softened by builders who designed for mass appeal.

FIRST TO GO was its strict definition as a one-storey house. At first, builders simply put dormers in the steep roof, allowing room, light, and ventilation for attic bedrooms; such houses they called "semi-Bungalows." Inevitably, more compromise was made; the region and the clientele had changed. Early Bungalows were low-lying, rather rough structures buried in the woods or on a hillside or among the boulders at the seashore. But later

Aladdin described this utterly charming plan-book Bungalow as "rock-ribbed American — a thoroughbred Bungalow and bungalow architecture is American." Then as now, Bungalow lines seemed to be intrinsically appealing.

In addition to publishing Bungalow designs of other architects, Stickley also designed Bungalows himself, like this stone and cement one "suitable for country or suburbs," published in 1909.

builders were creating suburbia. A one-storey house with more than just a bedroom or two was prohibitively expensive: A Bungalow had more foundation, exposed wall surface, and roof in proportion to the space enclosed than did a two-storey house.

EVEN BACK in the 1910s and '20s, architecture writers and critics were aghast at the "misuse" and overuse of the word. Charles White Jr., in his The Bungalow Book of 1923, tells us only that the current definition is "a curious example of how we Americans overwork a word that is euphonious and the meaning of which, because of the word's comparatively recent assimilation into the language, is somewhat uncertain." However, after briefly and pretty accurately recounting the evolution of the true Bungalow, he goes on to show examples that make it clear he's going with the flow: He considers any country or suburban home that is informal and picturesque to be a

Inside Bungalows

*T*HE TYPICAL Bungalow interior, at least as it was presented in the house books of the period, is easier to recognize than a typical exterior. Basically, the Bungalow interior was a Craftsman interior.

IN A COMPLETE DEPARTURE from Victorian interior decoration, Bungalow writers frowned on the display of wealth and costly collectibles. Rather than buying objects of obvious and ascribed value, the homeowner was told to look for simplicity and craftsmanship: "A luxury of taste substituting for a luxury of

cost." How's that for the perfect Craftsman decorating creed?

KEEP IN MIND that both Greene and Greene's Gamble House in Pasadena and a three-room vacation shack without plumbing were called Bungalows. And they both affected what the typical year-round Bungalow would look like. The finest examples of Arts and Crafts handiwork found a place in the Bungalow -- as did rustic furniture and grass matting.

WALLS were often wood-panelled to chair-rail or plate-rail height. Burlap in soft earth tones was suggested for the wall area above, or used in wood-battened panels where panelling was absent. Landscape friezes and abstract stencilling above a plate rail were often pictured.

DULLED, GREYED SHADES and earth tones, even pastels, were preferred to strong colors. Plaster with sand in the finish coat was suggested. Woodwork could be golden oak or oak brown-stained to simulate old English

woodwork, or stained dull black or bronze green. Painted softwood was also becoming popular, especially for bedrooms, with white enamel common before 1910 and strong color gaining popularity during the 'twenties.

IT BECAME almost an obsession with Bungalow builders to see how many amenities could be crammed into the least amount of space. By 1920, the Bungalow had more space-saving built-ins than a yacht: Murphy wall beds, ironing boards in cupboards, built-in mailboxes, telephone nooks.

WRITERS ADVOCATED the "harmonious use" of furnishings small and few. Oak woodwork demanded oak furniture, supplemented with reed, rattan, wicker or willow in natural, grey, or pastels. Mahogany pieces were thought best against a backdrop of woodwork painted white. (Bright white was used most often for bathroom trim; "white" could also mean cream, yellow, ivory, or pale grey.) A large table with a reading lamp was the centerpiece of the living room. (Reading was the family's evening activity before TV.)

RESTRAINT was the universal cry of good taste. Clutter was out -- "clutter" being a relative term: Pottery, Indian baskets, Chinese and Japanese ware, vases, and Arts and Crafts hangings were suggested to satisfy the collector instinct. More affluent households might display (discreetly) Rookwood pottery, small Tiffany pieces, hammered copper bowls, and decorative items from Liberty and Co. A watercolor landscape or two, executed by the amateur painter of the family, was the ultimate Arts and Crafts expression for the Home.

Top: 'A characteristic Craftsman interior,' showing built-in furniture, reading table, and open floor plan.
Center: A dining room from The Wilson Bungalow *(1910), so similar to Craftsman rooms. Note burlap wall panels.*
Bottom: Corner of a softly furnished Craftsman living room, 1905. Note frieze, built-in seat, simple mantel, open doorway.

Bungalow. These same writers continued to wrap Prairie houses in the Bungalow blanket: In White's book, an early residential design by Frank Lloyd Wright is captioned "A Bungalow of the Midwestern Type."

WHAT REALLY HAPPENED during the Bungalow building boom is that the Bungalow was no longer a pure structural type, but a broader house style. A <u>house</u> could be built "along Bungalow lines." Some historians call these houses "bungaloid," but that's an unfortunate and unfair word. We cannot look back now and say that literally millions of homes, many of

in popular taste was already apparent: The same catalog also included an unbound supplement entitled "Colonial Bungalows," which were nothing more than tiny, inexpensive houses with Colonial motifs.

BY 1928, the fat Home Builder's Catalog was full of Colonial Revivals, unremarkable "suburban homes," and houses with vaguely English lines. There's also an odd hybrid labelled "a duplex bungalow". . . even its previously respected definition as a single-family (if not single-storey) home had been thrown aside. The scattered use of the word

Aladdin, 1921

A house sold as a Colonial Bungalow. In the '20s, "bungalow" sometimes just meant small size; at least this one has a pergola.

Home Builders Catalog, 1928

Two of the three bedrooms are in the upper half-storey, making this popular design a semi-Bungalow.

Wilson Bungalow, 1910

Labelled a Bungalow in 1910, this house fits none of the standard definitions. But it's clearly a house of "the bungalow period."

them picturesque, well built, and stylish, were aberrations. Instead, let's accept the fact that the definition of Bungalow broadened over time. This was "the bungalow period" of residential architecture.

The Beginning of the End

ANYWAY, as early as 1908 the word with the fashionable cachet was being used for many small houses that had only the vaguest bungalow allusions. In the 1920-1 Aladdin Homes catalog, more than half the models were, stylistically and in name, recognizable Bungalows. But the inevitable change

"bungalow" in the catalog was more a case of the copywriter searching for a synonym than any reference to style.

IRONICALLY, the 1920s was the boom period for bungalow building even as its decline began. Instead of "simple, rustic, natural, charming," the bungalow glut was beginning to change the connotation of the word to "cheap, small, and vulgar." You knew the bungalow bust was coming when Woodrow Wilson described President Warren Harding as "bungalow minded" and meant that he had a limited thinking capacity. It was unprecedented suburban growth, no longer bungalove, that kept the bungalow strong through the late '20s.

AFTER the Second World War, as we all know, the word came back to mean a cheap vacation house by the seashore (usually in New Jersey, usually painted aqua or coral) -- not so terribly far from its first incarnation in England in the early nineteenth century.

IT'S THAT CRUEL last association that the Bungalow has had to live down. But happily, the darling of the first quarter of the twentieth century is back in favor. First-time homebuyers are rediscovering its undeniable charms. And just this year, a major architectural journal published the design of a brand-new bungalow court in California. We think a Bungalow Revival would be every bit as sensible as the Bungalow itself.

FLASH: We just saw barely-off-the-press pages from a new book called *The American Bungalow*, by Clay Lancaster. We loved it so we ordered a supply. See Bookshop page in back of issue. —*P. Poore*

by Larry Jones

Mission Light Fixture

Besides their wide variety of reproduction Victorian lighting fixtures, the St. Louis Antique Lighting Company is the only source we've uncovered for a stock lighting fixture in the Mission style. This exact reproduction of a 1912 fixture has a shade 22 in. wide; it measures 40 in. high (counting the wooden chain from which it depends). The four-sided shade has an oak frame that supports four triangular art-glass panels. The glazing is available in three colors: caramel brown, sky blue, & kelly green. (The fixture is also available without the glass.)

You can order the Mission Oak fixture with a light, medium, or dark stain, finished with a high- or low-gloss lacquer; or you can stain it to match your own woodwork. It comes pre-wired, ready to install, & takes one standard bulb. (Reproduction bulbs of this period are available from Bradford Consultants, Dept. OHJ, 16 E. Homestead Ave., Collingswood, NJ 08108, (609) 854-1404.) At extra cost, silk or beaded fringe can be added to the shade; the working wooden chain can be lengthened or shortened. The fixture costs $480 plus shipping.

They also have a patterned glass shade 2½ in. square, which is suitable for the wall sconces or hanging fixtures of Bungalows. It's the No. 418 PR, & sells for $10.50 plus shipping.

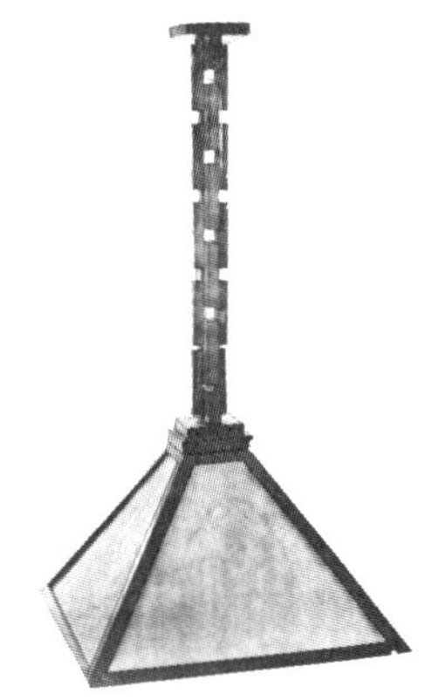

Send $3 for a portfolio/catalog to St. Louis Antique Lighting Co., Dept. OHJ, PO Box 8146 St. Louis, MO 63156. (314) 535-2770

Arts & Crafts Copper

If your Bungalow needs a beautifully handcrafted, custom-designed, copper fireplace or range hood, you need to see Matthew Richardson. He's supplied interior designers, architects, & homeowners with items ranging from light fixtures to friezes, custom made from their drawings. He'll make just about anything except kitchenware.

Matthew works in the Arts and Crafts tradition — nothing looks machine made or mass produced.

His catalog has some interesting copper garden light fixtures appropriate for Craftsman and Prairie-style houses. The lights mount on 4-x-4 posts (not included) and come ready to wire up. They're finished in a green patina and range in price from $60 to $108 (plus shipping).

Send $2.50 for the latest catalog, with light fixtures, friezes, planters, weathervanes, and wall sconces. Write **Contemporary Copper, Dept. OHJ, PO Box 69, Greenfield, MA 01302. (413) 773-9242.**

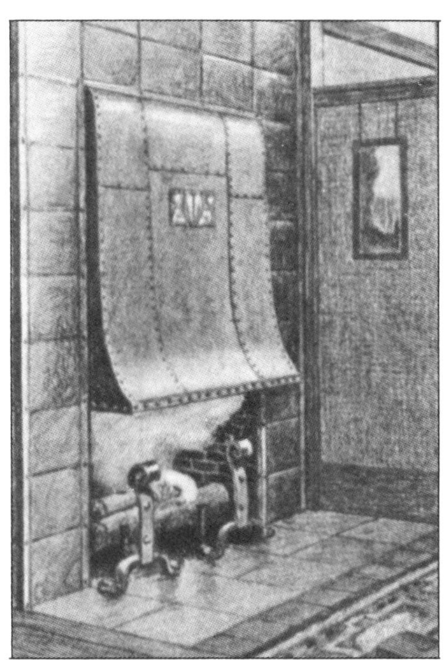

Copper fireplace hood & andirons from 'Craftsman Homes' by Gustav Stickley.

Roll Window Screens

Bungalows and other post-Victorian houses often have casement windows that open by swinging out. The usual screens made for double-hung windows won't work with these; fixed interior screens prevent access to the window.

For years Walsh Screen Products has been making an ingenious device: the Rolled Screen. Designed for casement windows, it works like a window shade. The screen is mounted on the inside of your window frame, and rolls up when not in use, giving an unobstructed view and admitting lots of light. The Rolled Screens, custom made to fit your windows, are said to last up to 25 years, because they're made of bronze and aren't constantly exposed to the weather.

The Rolled Screens are available for any window width from 12 to 48 in., & range in price from $47.65 to $88.30. Contact **Walsh Screen Products, Dept. OHJ, 26 E. Third St., Mount Vernon, NY 10550. (914) 668-7811.**

Custom Made Hardware

Ready-made household fittings such as hinges & firesets, which have the hand-wrought, rugged, simple design qualities

common to Bungalows and Craftsman furniture, are almost impossible to find — we've looked. But we did find Joel Schwartz, a master blacksmith whose sculptural custom ironwork, including gates, railings, grilles, and furnishings, graces such buildings as the Renwick Gallery of the Smithsonian Institution.

Joel can supply Bungalow owners with custom-made, period-style hardware and accessories to suit their needs. He does not do hinges & latches. (A good source for these would be other blacksmiths who are well versed in Early American designs.) But Joel will make andirons, fenders, and even fireplace hoods which

can add charm to any fireplace nook. He'll work from your sketches or create original designs.

Metal accessories of the Craftsman period shouldn't look machine-made. Rugged designs with a structural quality and simplicity matching that of Craftsman furniture are best. Wrought iron should have a dull silver look, with its high points polished; copper usually has a deep mellow brown glow; brass is often finished to a soft greenish dull surface.

For a 20-page portfolio of Joel's work, send $3.50 to **Joel Schwartz's Forge and Metal Works, Dept. OHJ, PO Box 205, Deansboro, NY 13328. (315) 841-4477.**

Mission Oak Doors

The Renovation Concepts' collection of high-quality hardwood, period-style doors has expanded to include two Mission Oak models, the Carmel & Riviera.

The Carmel uses a 3/8-in.-thick, oak-faced plywood panel for its single flat panel design. Until now, if you wanted this old-style design, you usually had to have the door custom made. The Riviera is another hard-to-find style, featuring real divided lights. When used in pairs (usually between the dining room and living room), the Riviera doors make excellent 'French doors.'

Both door styles are made of solid red oak, with mortise-&-tenon and dowelled construction, and exceed AWI "Premium-grade" specifications. They're warranted and are available in 3 ft. x 7 ft. x 1-3/8 in. size. The Carmel sells for $465; the Riviera, $540 (FOB, Minneapolis). If you need doors of a different finish, style, or size, give the company a call. Brochures on the doors & other quality restoration items are free. Contact **Renovation Concepts, Inc., Dept. OHJ, 213 Washington Avenue N, Minneapolis, MN 55401. (612) 333-5766.**

Wallpapers & Borders

We know that Victorian Collectibles has an unusually large collection of original wallpaper designs that date from the 1860s well into the 1930s. So we asked if they had any designs of interest to Bungalow owners. Sure enough, the next day's mail brought several photos of original wallpaper borders.

Our favorite, the Poppy, falls somewhere between the Art Nouveau & Art Deco periods. The colors are red, brick red, and soft green. Originally an 18-in. border, the paper is available in that size as well as in a 9-in. size. In the original

Arts & Crafts Furniture

Coly Vulpiani's workshop produces superb, high-style furniture of the Arts & Crafts movement. Coly gained a reputation by researching & restoring Mission furniture for dealers & collectors. With a thorough understanding of the construction, coloring, & finishing of these pieces, he started custom-manufacturing furniture in the Stickley tradition.

The Vulpiani workshop now produces reproduction & original designs inspired by such designers as C.R. Mackintosh, Greene & Greene, Frank Lloyd Wright, and Joseph Hoffman. The pieces range in price from $250 for a small table to $7,000 for a unique bed inlaid with copper and pewter.

colorways, the borders are available on order for $19 per yard. (It's possible to have a mural produced from this design, which will cover an entire wall; write for details and prices.)

Renderings in Craftsman magazine often showed a rug matched to the wall decoration, & that's just what this company has done. They've adapted the Poppy design to a 100%-wool, hand-knotted and carved rug that's made in India to your size requirements. It's about ¾-in. thick and sells for about $40 per sq.ft.

Here's another special border/rug combination. Their Nouveau Fleur border, originally made in a 9-in. height, is available by custom order in its original size & colorways. It's hand-stencilled, hand-painted on canvas, and comes ready for mounting. A spectacular 100%-wool, handmade rug has been adapted from its design. It can be ordered in any size and sells for $40 per sq.ft. (Rugs are made to order, so be patient — it can take as long as ten months to receive one.)

Victorian Collectibles will soon have available an 18-in. border called 'Walk in the Park.' Its landscape scene has also been adapted into a hand-painted wall mural, which can be adapted to fit various sizes. It comes via custom order in a 4-panel set 12 ft. wide by 9½ ft. tall.

All hand-printed and painted products are custom made. The rugs can be purchased in standard 6x9 and 9x12 sizes. To find out more about their vast array of wallpapers, borders, fabrics & canvas

Coly produces an extraordinary fumed-oak hall table designed by Mackintosh in 1904. It sells for $3,000. To produce the distinctive red-brown finishes common to furniture of this style, the workshop has developed a chemical process that substitutes for the very disagreeable method of fuming oak with ammonia.

Besides supplying the pieces listed in their catalog, the workshop can reproduce virtually any piece of Arts & Crafts furniture a client desires. For the color catalog, send $2 to **Vulpiani Furniture and Finishing Workshop, Dept. OHJ, 8 Bridge Street, Florida NY 10921. (914) 651-7331.**

Ceramic Tiles

Barbara Rosen began making Arts and Crafts ceramic tiles for Coly Vulpiani's Mission furniture reproductions and for fireplace surrounds. These handmade, sculptured tiles are available in a wide variety of custom colors, designs, and sizes. The 4x4-in. tiles sell for $8 each; 5x5, $10 each (plus shipping). Barbara also accepts commissions to reproduce existing tile designs. Her tiles are suitable for kitchens, countertops, fireplaces, & entryways and bathrooms.

A great gift for the Bungalow owner: hot plates & trivets each containing four handmade tiles set into oak trays. The small size costs $50; the large, $60 (plus shipping). Barbara will send you photos or slides of her work for a $1 handling fee. For further information, contact **Barbara Rosen, Dept. OHJ, 8 Bridge St., Florida, NY 10921. (914) 651-7331.**

panels, and plaster mouldings, send $2 for an information packet to **Victorian Collectibles, Dept. OHJ, 845 E. Glenbrook Road, Milwaukee, WI 53217. (414) 352-6910.**

Bungling of the month

FOR THIS special issue, we found a bungalow remuddling -- or "Bungling." This Bungalow in Tupper Lake, New York, would be unrecognizable were it not for the lawn ornaments. Gone are the special Bungalow characteristics. The front is covered in darkly stained fiberboard shingles; the end wall, with vertical siding. The welcoming porch is gone, as is the dormer that gave light to the upstairs bedroom. What's left is just a box, indistinguishable from any tract house of the past forty years. (Thanks to Daniel D. Reiff of Fredonia, New York, for the photos.)

The Old-House Journal®

69A Seventh Avenue,
Brooklyn, New York 11217

Restoration and Maintenance Techniques
For The Pre-1939 House

June 1985 / Vol. XIII No. 5 / $2.

The Old-House Journal

Removing Interior Woodwork

Clever Ways To Avoid Destroying Your Trim

by Gordon H. Bock

WOOD TRIM is perhaps <u>the</u> indispensable feature of an old house's interior: a humble grace note that brings character and elegance to featureless walls. People who own an old home wouldn't dream of removing it -- unless they have to strip paint, refinish the floors, rebuild the windows, re-plaster the walls, or install new wiring, plumbing, or insulation. Then they face a nightmare of damaged walls and split wood (and it's getting harder to find replacement stock mouldings of even so recent a time as the 1930s). But removing trim isn't a terribly complicated job if it's done with forethought and patience.

cont'd on p. 108

In the next issue. . .
RESIDENTIAL SCAFFOLDING

Letters

YOUR ARTICLE in March about the water level was most interesting. I have a suggestion, however, that does away with the glass tubing ends, couplings, etc. Just buy an appropriate length of clear polyethylene tubing and use as instructed in the article. PE tubing is relatively inexpensive (a 50-ft. section runs about $7), provides clear ends of the water level that can be easily seen, and also allows the user to see if there are any bubbles in the length.

I'VE USED clear tubing to align a series of windows on a house I rebuilt in Wilton, Conn.; more recently, to align kitchen cabinets in the 1845 house I'm rebuilding in Upton.

James F. Balderson
Upton, Mass.

WARNING! Regarding the March article <u>All About Wall Canvas</u>: Imperial <u>Wall</u> Cover No. 9962 MAY NOT BE PAINTED <u>ATTRACTIVELY</u>.

JUST FINISHED a project involving some horrible walls. For reasons not important to this letter, it was almost imperative that the walls be painted. I have used various liners in the past, but this project required a miracle, and the Imperial product looked like the one. The is-

sue of painting was discussed, and I even checked the literature, which specifically said, "may be painted."

AS A WALLCOVER, the product is superior. But when it came to paint, I had a problem. The paint raised the synthetic fibers, giving a hairy surface. Since the problem arose with the first brush-full of paint, I had time to investigate many possible solutions before proceeding, including shellac, enamel undercoater, latex enamel, oil enamel. Nothing worked.

THE RESOLUTION CAME when the regional distributor gave us -- free of charge -- the wallpaper of our choice to cover the mess. The distributor admitted that ours was not the first such complaint. His comment: "The manufacturer said it can be painted -- they didn't say that it would look nice."

BY THE WAY, the rest of the article was excellent and accurate. Just wanted to warn the unwary.

Janet Walheim
St. Davids, Penn.

[WE CALLED Stephen Wolf, who in turn contacted the factory. They've decided to drop the "may be painted" from their product literature. -- Ed.]

Attention ARCHITECTS, RESTORATION CONTRACTORS, BUILDING SCIENTISTS, and PRESERVATIONISTS

Meeting of the Association for Preservation Technology

I was bowled over reading the program for APT's annual technical conference to be held in **San Francisco**, Sept. 5-8. It promises to be the most rewarding meeting ever.

Technical sessions include concrete stabilization, terra-cotta repair, mechanical and electrical systems, metals, substitute materials, interior finishes, transportation systems, adobe stabilization, landscape, and roofing.

Keynote speeches focus on the restoration of the Statue of Liberty and the cable car system. Planned social functions allow informal exchange among members — perhaps the most important phase of an APT meeting.

Technical tours — many to places not usually open to the public — relate to conference topics and take advantage of the history and beauty of the Bay area. Tours include stabilization of concrete at Alcatraz; masonry, iron works, and terra-cotta tours; the Gladding-McBean terra-cotta factory; cable-car tour; landscape tour of Golden Gate Park. Also: tours of Victorian interiors; Art Deco tour of Oakland; State Capitol tour; and a visit to Bradbury & Bradbury Wallpapers factory.

Training courses held prior to the conference, Mon. 9/2 — Wed. 9/4: APT's intensive technical courses are internationally famous for the high caliber of faculty and course material. Topics this year: Deterioration and Preservation of Architectural Concrete. Analysis and Preservation of Historic and Modern Paints. Seismic Retrofit. Maritime Preservation. Cost is $585; includes tuition, materials, tours, room & meals for 3 days & 3 nights.

APT members won't want to miss this one — and of course, **registration is open to the public.** Meeting registration is $110 before Aug. 15. (Student, APT member, and per-day rates available.) This short notice is incomplete — I urge all preservation professionals to request further information. Write or call the Conference Chairman:

> **Bruce D. Judd, AIA**
> **Pier 9, The Embarcadero**
> **San Francisco, CA 94111**
> **(415) 421-1680**

or, if you like, you can call me for more information about APT.
— *Patricia Poore*

The Old-House Journal®

Editor
Patricia Poore

Production Editor
Cole Gagne

Senior Technical Advisor
Larry Jones

Assistant Editor
Sarah J. McNamara

Contributing Editors
Walter Jowers
John Mark Garrison
Roland A. Labine Sr.

Architectural Consultant
Jonathan Poore

Circulation Supervisor
Barbara Bugg

Circulation Assistants
Jeanne Baldwin
Garth White

Special Sales
Joan O'Reilly

Office Manager
Tricia A. Martin

Catalog Editor
Sarah J. McNamara

Publishing Consultant
Paul T. McLoughlin

Publisher
Clem Labine

Published by The Old-House Journal Corporation, 69A Seventh Avenue, Brooklyn, NY 11217. Telephone (718) 636-4514. Subscriptions $18 per year in U.S., $36 per year in Canada (payable in Canadian funds). Published ten times per year. Contents are fully protected by copyright and must not be reproduced in any manner whatsoever without specific permission in writing from the Editor.

We are happy to accept editorial contributions to The Old-House Journal. Query letters that include an outline of the proposed article are preferred. All manuscripts will be reviewed, and returned if unacceptable. However, we cannot be responsible for non-receipt or loss — please keep copies of all materials sent.

Printed at Photo Comp Press, New York City

ISSN: 0094-0178
NO PAID ADVERTISING

A Midwestern Cinderella

by Roberta Holm

ONCE UPON A TIME there was a little house whose simple beauty lay hidden and unappreciated behind a decaying pseudo-bungalow facade. Uncovering its real identity would take either a fairy godmother or lots of money. A clergyman and his wife, the Robert Crosses, admired old houses, but had neither lots of money nor a belief in fairy god-mothers. They did, however, believe that where God guides, He provides. So they bought the little house and went to work.

THEIR HOME HAD ITS ORIGINS in the mid-19th century, a time when the rivers of the northern Midwest provided the only access into its forests and prairie lands. The promise of a good livelihood in logging white pine lured pioneers from New England. Two small settle-ments of hardy folk faced each other across the rapids of the St. Croix river -- one in what would be Wisconsin, the other in the future Minnesota. Soon the river was jammed with logs headed for markets all over the booming USA.

ABOVE THE DALLES on the Minnesota side, the beautiful lumber was used to build a community of houses that 130 years later would tell of the settlers' New England roots. Simple frontier houses, they were built in the Greek Revival style with a few concessions to the builders' experience. W.H.C. Folsom, an influential early businessman and politician, hired carpenters from Maine to build his home.

The Folsom house, now owned by the Minnesota Historical Society, has French doors and open verandahs on the first and second floors, features Folsom added to his plans after a trip to New Orleans. Others followed suit. (Sometime early, a wag named the area "Angels Hill" for the supposedly snooty people who lived there.) There was a romantic streak in these folks, and French doors, despite their inappropriateness in a northern climate, were popular innovations.

THE HOUSES THEMSELVES did not experience forever-after beatitude. They all went through hard times during the past century. Gradually, and most recently through the efforts of architect William Scott, who has restored three of the homes, their uniqueness in the architectural history of the state has been recognized. Restoration of all of them by private owners is almost complete and the Angels Hill district is now listed in the National Register of Historic Places.

NONE SUFFERED MORE disgrace than the Thomas Lacey House, 1858. Its original open-porch facade with French doors and its shutters and bargeboards were discarded for a World War I bungaloid cover-up. A boxy wooden awning angled over the old doors that were cut down to window size. Narrow siding, small single-paned windows, and the first bathroom on Angels Hill made the owners proud,

Restoration of the original Greek Revival facade began with the demolition of the pseudo-bungalow porch and awning.

Half-way through the restoration. The Crosses duplicated a piece of the original bargeboard that they found under the eaves.

but obliterated the house's real Greek Revival identity. The owners destroyed the gracious entrance into the house by installing the bathroom there. A clumsy carpenter had framed in the porch off the kitchen and installed oversized six-over-six windows to make a sunroom, and created new space upstairs by adding a dormer.

THE CROSSES HAD LIVED in New England during Bob's seminary days and had loved the simple beauty of its architecture. Angels Hill has a similar feeling, and the Crosses were attract-

ed to it after they had raised 11 children in a big house in Minneapolis. The restored houses on the Hill were well beyond their financial resources. This Cinderella house, however, stood sadly with its "For Sale" sign out in front. It had no appeal as it was, and the Crosses went through it reluctantly. But there were discoveries to be made! Behind the ugly porch they found the original French doors and Greek Revival surround. Although difficult to see, the original house was there, waiting to be revived with TLC and money. Could they do it? With the big house in Minneapolis unsold, but with faith in Providence to see them through, they borrowed money and purchased the house "as is" in December 1980. They jumped into the restoration.

THE WORK PROCEEDED with compromise for practical and financial reasons -- whenever the compromise did not drastically affect the desired authenticity. The first step was to strip the interior of the hole-riddled plaster, the buckled veneer floors, the lowered acoustical-tile ceilings, the ancient electrical wiring, and the plumbing. Care was taken with the old woodwork that, back in the 1850s, had been put into place before plastering. It was left in place so that the new plasterboard would relate to it in the same way the old plaster walls had. The Crosses watched for other original details they could salvage, like old iron clothes hooks, lock boxes, and door knobs. Stacks of old doors and windows in the shed were rescued.

The Crosses kept the framed-in sunroom, but installed period windows and a new roof to make the room look like it belonged to the house.

Smith Treuer working on the bargeboard in his shop. He owns the Murdock house, sister to the Crosses' home.

Nancy used two pine doors to make this fireplace surround. The left panel opens for storage.

AN EXPERT LOCAL CARPENTER completed an under-girding of the house. Although the 2-by-12 floor joists were eternally sturdy and the sills perfect, changes in weight bearing required new support posts. In the basement the waste drain that had angled wall-to-wall five feet off the ground, was lowered into the floor. The heating plant was upgraded with new duct work, which vastly improved headroom and made an otherwise unpleasant cellar useful for laundry and storage.

BOB AND NANCY WERE HARD PRESSED when family and friends asked for explanations during these first few months. The outside wreck was all that could be seen and the interior work was anything but impressive. Bob and Nancy's descriptions and diagrams couldn't bridge the credibility gap -- all that borrowed money at 17% interest! An architect's drawing finally convinced a few people that the Crosses weren't quite mad.

AS WITH MOST small frontier houses, the original floor plan had many small rooms not appropriate for large family gatherings. The largest, the living room, measured 15 feet by 15 feet. This attractive square with exposure to light through the French doors was just the sunny space the Crosses had dreamed of for a study. Nancy, a writer and icon painter, and Bob, a clergyman and lecturer, both demanded ample space for desks, bookcases, and storage. They added stock kitchen cabinets with shelves built in above all the way to the ceiling for storage.

The Crosses had to rip a bathroom out of the front hallway.

ZERO-CLEARANCE FIREPLACE UNITS are relatively inexpensive and fairly efficient heaters. For the kitchen, the Crosses choose a single-faced unit from Sears. They used a double-faced fireplace unit in the study/living room wall. Both fireplaces, without installation costs (which were minimal) and including all chimneys, cost just over $3,000. The fireplace surround for the living room was found at a salvage yard. Nancy designed the fireplace surround in the study from pictures of New England houses with panels around the fireplace which disguise storage space. She made her panels by cutting pine doors in half, using one half on each side and the bottom panel of a second door for the insert above the mantel. The left-hand panel hides a small storage area of shelves above and beside the firebox. Cupboards, fireplace surround, and book shelves were painted a soft maize to complement the forest green and maize wallpaper.

ALL THE FLOORS, original four-inch white pine boards, were sanded and stained. The kitchen is carpeted with handwoven rugs made on the loom of a neighbor, Cynthia Holmberg. Nancy had collected old fabrics, cut them into strips, hand-sewed them together and wrapped them into 80 seven-inch balls. From them, Cynthia wove strips of rugs that Nancy laid side by side on the floor. Then Nancy tacked the ends and whip-stitched the seams together. The rug can be taken up in sections, machine-washed and dried, and put down again in very little time. Old hooked rugs made by Nancy's

Grandma Harlton in the '30s and '40s, along with braided rugs made by Nancy's mother, Bea Vercoe, and a commercial braided rug found at the Salvation Army for $20.00 cover the floor of the study. Two wool "orientals" from Sears are on the living room floor. Total cost for all the floor coverings was under $800.00!

WINDOW TREATMENTS, TOO, were done with very little money. Fabrics found at $1 per yard at a fabric outlet were, heaven forbid, polyester! The styling, with inexpensive braids and lace, made this practical but out-of-sync fabric fit into the old house. The study windows were left bare while the kitchen curtains were made from dusty blue fabric, and the living room curtains were made from cream-colored fabric. The bedroom windows were dressed with lace panels from Sears and home-sewn unbleached muslin ruffles. Cost for the entire house was under $80.00. Nancy found suitable though not authentic wallpapers in discount stores, outlets, through mail order, and in bulk bins at lumberyards.

THE CROSSES REPLACED the inappropriate siding with hardboard, half as expensive as cedar and indistinguishable when painted. They found six-over-six sashes, some with wavy antique glass, in the shed and replaced the single-paned windows with them. They joined the sunroom to the garage and the kitchen wing with a hipped roof, which made the addition look like it belonged on the house. They found wooden shutters (not always the right size, but alterable) at an offbeat lumberyard. Bob also found short lengths of wide pine crown moulding to face the bargeboards for only fifty cents per foot. (Digging around in this lumberyard and in big discount chains saved a lot of money.)

NANCY AND BOB RAZED the old lean-to. A two-car garage now takes its place. They added gables at right angles to the kitchen wing gables, New England barn fashion, to create shop space and a large screened-in porch under one roof.

TO IMITATE A BAY that had been added to a nearby house in the 1880s, the Crosses had an Anderson window installed on the south side of the house. The natural light that comes through the window is important to the interior -- and the stock bay looks remarkably good. Other money-saving moves -- finishing the job without an architect, doing all the decorating and interior finishing themselves, having a friend design and execute the bargeboards in his shop -- all helped the Crosses complete their rehabilitation with a minimal amount of money. One money-saving effort backfired, however. The Crosses fell into the temptation of using a friend-of-a-friend weekend contractor to repair the roof. The nightmare that followed would have made a reputable roofer desirable at any price!

THE CROSSES MOVED into their house before it was completed and finished the details over the next two years. They credit their Cinderella-turned-princess not to a fairy godmother, but to an even higher source. It seems appropriate to add, "May they live there happily ever after."

How To Hold A House Tour

Persuasion, Planning, Publicity

by Ron Pilling

THERE'S NOTHING LIKE A HOUSE TOUR to show off the neighborhood. Thousands of historic and not-so-historic communities have them every year and the results are always the same: House sales increase, bringing new neighbors and eventually more restored homes. The population becomes more aware about your neighborhood and what's going on there. Valuable publicity is generated about your efforts and those of your neighbors. Your local preservation association pockets some well-earned money. And everyone has a lot of fun.

ALSO, some things don't happen on House Tour Day: No one "cases" your house and returns to carry off your stereo, or worse, your new brass faucets. The tax assessor doesn't prowl around. Your guests don't track mud on your oriental rugs or fall down the steps and sue you for everything you're worth. Our house has been in 20 tours, and I've been the neighborhood chairperson for four of them, so I speak from experience.

AN ANNUAL House Tour, Open House, House and Garden Pilgrimage, or whatever you choose to call it, can be the single most important event on your community's calendar. I can happily testify that few things are more rewarding for an old-house person than to see hundreds of well-dressed strangers, each with a ticket and a brochure, standing on the sidewalk in front of your home, saying, "I had no idea ..." and "Such wonderful things in these old houses ..." and "These people deserve a lot of credit ..." My favorite is the guest who comes up and says, "You know, my wife and I started our married life in an apartment on your third-floor front in 1927. I remember then that the house had ..."

THE TOUR CHAIRPERSON faces two major projects:
1) Getting enough neighbors to open their homes to make a respectable tour. It should take at least two hours for your guests to see every home -- then they'll feel like they've gotten their money's worth.
2) Getting a lot of pre-tour publicity. If you get publicity, you'll get visitors. Our efforts attracted decent crowds even when the weather wasn't cooperating.

Persuasion

IT TOOK THREE YEARS of arguing with neighbors before we could pull off our first tour, just because we weren't prepared to counter their objections. Here's what you'll hear when you propose an open house:

"WE CAN'T OPEN BECAUSE OUR HOUSE ISN'T FINISHED YET."

THE BASIC ASSUMPTION here is that people only want to see completed homes. Exactly the opposite is true. Sure, guests will want to see rooms that are decorated and furnished, but they also come to learn about what has to be done to get a room to that point. They want to see what you had to work with. Many will be looking for hints on how to tackle the specific problems of their old houses.

ONE YEAR a neighborhood homeowner, who had barely begun, hung signs around the house which explained his plans: "There will be a closet here"; "That peculiar smell is the six layers of linoleum -- they are going to go!" It was a big hit. So if you wish to sponsor a tour that will really tell about old-house work, show visitors some before along with the pristine.

"I DON'T WANT TO OPEN MY HOUSE BECAUSE I DON'T WANT TO SUBJECT IT TO THE WEAR AND TEAR."

THERE COULD HARDLY BE a crowd more respectful of your home and your things than open-house visitors. Every year we see people tiptoeing around our oriental rugs. We have to beg people to go into rooms and walk on the wood floors. Bottlenecks form at the front door as guests carefully remove every gram of dirt from their shoes.

SMOKERS remain on the sidewalk until the last puff is history. Very seldom will anyone bring a young child on a tour (they want to enjoy themselves, after all). In short, when the door is closed on the last departing guest, the place will be in the same shape as it was that morning.

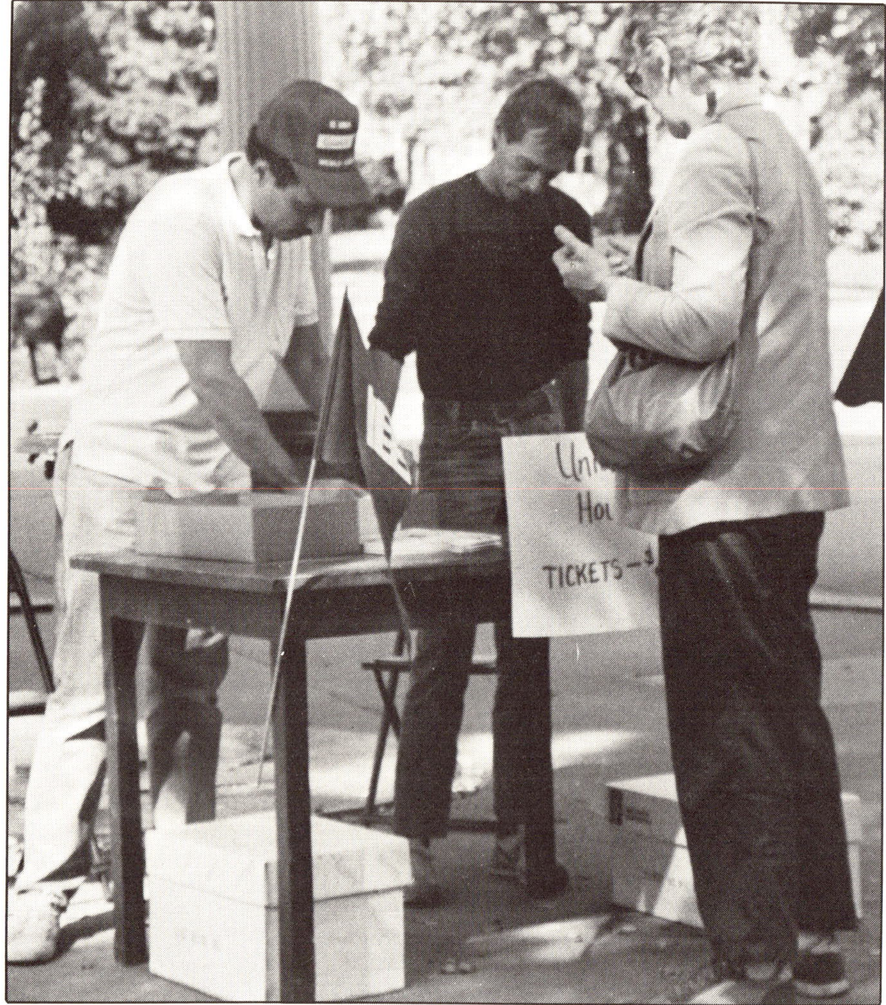

If possible, sell tickets in a public place that's at the tour center and easy to find. This table was stationed at a gazebo in the center of a park. Note the pennant on the table; each open house sported one, so guests could easily spot the places they could visit.

month.) Other than that, there's something special about every old house. If there wasn't, no one would go to the trouble of trying to save them.

WHEN PRESENTED with this objection, try reminding the homeowner of some of the things he or she may have forgotten: an especially nice tin ceiling or a leaded glass transom. Make clear the benefit guests will receive, or what they'll learn, by having visited the home.

Planning

PUT TOGETHER the tour committee. There are a lot of details to cover. The tour date, for one. Don't schedule it for a time when everyone is out of town, or when it would clash with other neighborhood open houses. Spring and fall, along with the Christmas season, are the most popular times. We have our tour when the leaves in our park are at their autumn best.

MANY TOURS have a particular theme. There are art tours, food tours, literary tours, garden tours, and a host of other great ideas. For your initial open house, merely the fact that it's the first tour will probably be enough to generate publicity and attract a crowd, but it'll be necessary eventually to distinguish your tour from others. (I'll explain more about this when we come to "Publicity.")

COMMITTEE MEMBERS will have several major chores. Assign a member as house liaison, to advise participating homeowners of the progress of plans. One may want to take care of preparing a tour brochure; another, publicity. The entire committee should handle the logistics, because how a tour is organized affects every aspect of the planning.

ASSUMING that the publicity is good, the goal is to assure that all the visitors enjoy themselves. Logistically, the tour has to be easy to follow and to understand. Organize the tour carefully, to minimize walking. Clearly explain how to locate open houses. Sell tickets at an easy-to-find public place. We have a gazebo in the center of our park, where we set up for the day.

THE TOUR BROCHURE, or guide, is very important. It not only gets guests around the neighborhood, but it's also what they take home at the end of the day. It should look professional. The cover of every one of our tour guides has featured either an original work of art or a historical picture. A gra-

THIS NOTION is a difficult one to dispell. I can only report our experience, which is that thieves do not come on house tours. Why should they spend five dollars when so many people make it so easy for them to get in for nothing?

I'M NOT SUGGESTING that one shouldn't take precautions. Have guests show tickets to gain admittance to houses. Try to round up enough friends or relatives so that rooms are watched. Of course, don't leave your jewelry lying about in easy reach, and put away any other small valuables. It's possible to make it understood that the tour is security-conscious without being blatant about it.

HUMILITY is an unwanted virtue on an open house. There are houses in any community which the tour chairperson may choose to politely ignore. (You know, the ones whose owners clean up after their dogs only once a

cious letter of welcome from the chairperson is included. We also advise the public about how we plan to use the tour proceeds.

HOUSE DESCRIPTIONS are short, emphasizing the features of the house, any significant house history, special collections of the owners, decorating themes, or upcoming projects. A map shows each house, with a number corresponding to the one accompanying its description. Numbers are then posted on doorways, along with something that makes it easy to spot tour houses. Over the years we've used potted plants on front stoops, dried flower arrangements on doors, or special house-tour pennants.

THERE ARE MANY MORE CONSIDERATIONS. How much should you charge? Check other local tour prices. Do you want to feed guests, or at least provide them with liquid refreshments? You could suggest that they visit a popular local restaurant or coffee shop. One year a neighborhood businessman served wine and cheese in his office at our tour.

WE'VE ALWAYS TRIED to make the tour friendly and at the same time classy. We pamper our guests, and this objective is woven throughout the entire planning process. When people leave our neighborhood after having seen some 20 homes, they feel as though they've spent the day with friends. This attitude is present from the first committee meeting; from our experience, it keeps people coming back to the tour year after year.

Publicity

SUPPOSE you gave a house tour and nobody came? Good publicity is the key to a successful tour, and it isn't so hard if you go about it the right way. Begin by writing a good press release. This is a one-page document that you can send to small weekly or monthly papers, and which they'll probably publish verbatim. In fact, if they can't use it as is, they probably won't print it at all. There are a million neighborhood festivals and fairs all competing for newspaper space, and the release that's easiest for the editor to use is the one that will get printed.

THE PRESS RELEASE should have all the features of a good newspaper article. The lead should be catchy. The first paragraph should present the most important facts: date, time, location, and so on. Tell readers why they'll benefit from coming to the tour -- what they'll learn, the unique things they'll see, how much fun they'll have. Tell them a bit about what's happening in your community. Make them feel that if they don't visit you on tour day, they'll really miss something special. Include a phone number for information -- no newspaper wants to take calls from people asking about your tour.

TO MAKE THE RELEASE even more effective, send with it an 8x10, black-and-white photo of something tour-related: maybe people preparing for the tour in an interesting room, or a good picture of a row of houses or house facades. Small papers are always delighted to get first-class pictures for free.

The huge pot of yellow mums was used to identify the tour houses (note also the number on the door frame). Nevertheless, some of the guests still needed directions. So the author's wife Pat — wearing vintage clothes for the tour — points things out for a visitor.

WRITE A SHORT COVER LETTER thanking the editor and explaining why readers will want the information in the release. Put the letter, release, and photo in a large envelope, along with a piece of stiff cardboard, and mark the outside "PHOTO -- DO NOT BEND." Find out the editor's name and mail it directly to him or her, about six weeks before the tour. Do this for every small local paper you can find.

THE LARGE DAILY PAPERS are another matter; competition here is much stiffer. First, for months in advance, scan every arts and entertainment section, every home repair section, and every leisure feature section for events calendars. Cut out every calendar you find, and then send in a press release (no photo, but still with a good cover letter) for each specific column.

ALSO CUT OUT feature articles on topics related to antiques or old houses. Their writers need a steady stream of topics, and it's to these journalists that you want to make your pitch. Four or five months in advance, send the writer a polite letter plus the press

It's a wonderful sight — a constant stream of well-dressed strangers with brochures, visiting your neighborhood for the first time. And the long-term benefit is an increase in house sales, more restored homes, and a greater awareness of the need for preservation.

release. Make sure he or she understands that you'll do whatever's necessary to help put together a good pre-tour feature. Make things as easy for the writer as possible. Give suggestions of photos, and offer to make arrangements with the staff photographer. Explain why readers will be forever thankful to the writer for having told them about the tour.

PAY SPECIAL ATTENTION to home features. The most valuable piece of publicity we've ever gotten was the house article in the Sunday magazine section on tour day. Some papers run a feature with lots of pictures of a private home, usually a unique one. Contact that reporter months in advance, with a good house already lined up.

SINGLE OUT all these reporters on the large papers. They probably won't want to do anything until the last moment, but don't let them forget you. As plans progress, drop them notes to advise them. Then, unless they contact you directly, phone them three weeks before the tour and offer your organizational services. It is imperative that you stay in close touch at this point. Make it clear that they are important to you, and that you will do anything you can to help.

RADIO STATIONS and television channels run community announcements. A post card will do, sent in about two weeks before the tour. Go through the phone book for the appropriate addresses, and send cards marked "Community Announcement" to everyone on the airwaves.

PUBLICITY is all-important, and tours must be planned so as to garner the most press. But we discovered that after about four years, it was difficult to get a reporter to give us any space at all -- we were old news. So we've had to come up with a gimmick every year to make the tour special. Here are some worth considering:

● There's a cooperative artists' gallery nearby, so we asked members to display their work in open houses. This angle sparked reporters' interest, and we got great press. Result: record attendance.

● A kitchen tour. We asked homeowners to prepare some special family recipe, usually a dessert item, that they could serve in small pieces to 500 guests. Then we printed the dessert recipes on House Tour Recipe Cards. The food reporters loved it. It was a lot of work, but it got results.

● Another neighborhood couples their tour with seminars on old-house work. They get local experts to talk and demonstrate in the church hall, school auditorium, or private homes.

● Is there a special local business? We have a little-known gourmet baker, and he prepared a treat for guests this year. Both he and we got great publicity.

● If the tour is scheduled for the holidays, take advantage of this -- perhaps homes decorated with handmade reproductions of Victorian Christmas ornaments; maybe even demonstrations of ornament-making.

THERE ARE SOME THINGS you can do directly to tell people about the tour. We've distributed flyers in other historical areas nearby, addressing them specifically to the residents there. We offer a dollar off to a party bringing the flyer to the tour, which makes it easy to determine how well the flyers worked.

ALSO CONSIDER sending invitations to local church groups or community associations. You could offer tickets in advance at a reduced rate to the ladies' circles at churches, for example. Groups like these often plan organized day trips, so why not cash in on it?

Pleasure

SURE, it all sounds like a tremendous amount of work. The first time around it is, but it gets a little easier year after year. The cold, hard fact is that a house tour is the best vehicle for getting people into your neighborhood, attracting new neighbors who'll fix up now-derelict homes, and telling the public about your efforts.

YES, IT IS WORK. But on tour day, when you've smiled for four or five hours and tried your humble best to fend off hundreds of generous compliments, you'll agree that it's worth it.

Bare Chimney Breast

WE RECENTLY EXPOSED the brick chimney in our kitchen. Though it was once covered with plaster, now it appears as originally constructed. The mortar is soft and crumbly. I'd like to coat the brick to give it a light gloss. Is there a coating that will give the brick a gloss and prevent the mortar from crumbling all over the floor?

--Terry N. Trantow Bingen, Wash.

DURING THE 1970s, the misconception grew that old chimney breasts were meant to be exposed. Actually, exposed interior brick is rare, used most notably in Prairie School and Craftsman architecture of the early 20th century. That kind of brickwork is excellent, with hard, uniform bricks and narrow joints pointed with portland cement mortar.

IF BRICK CRUMBLES, is soft, or is laid haphazardly, however, it wasn't meant to be exposed. It sounds like your chimney bricks were originally plastered. New plaster (or furred-out Sheetrock) is the best coating: appropriate, low-maintenance, and non-crumbling.

IF YOU'RE REALLY in love with the bare brick, you can try a polyurethane masonry sealer, or a good urethane varnish. It may yellow over the years and it won't cure really crumbly mortar, but it will help. Latex masonry paint in a brick color would be effective, too.

Why Use Primer?

PLEASE TELL ME what the benefit is of using a primer before painting exterior wood. Wouldn't a first coat of thinned paint do just as well?

--Edmund R. Kuser Delta, Pa.

MODERN PRIMERS are specially formulated to do three things:
● Penetrate bare or weathered wood, providing a sealed base for the topcoat of paint -- without peeling.
● Provide a uniform coat that allows excellent adhesion of various finish paints.
● Cover everything from bare wood and putty to different colors of paint, so that the finish coat will be an even color.

THINNED PAINT will penetrate wood fibers better than unthinned paint would. But thinned paint won't have the other special properties of primer. Also, over-thinning paint may give it unpredictable drying, coverage, and wearing characteristics.

Parging Problems

I HAVE ENCLOSED some samples of a coating that is on the bricks and the stone foundation and window sills of our 1875 house. (Apparently, the previous owners preferred this stuff to tuck-pointing.) What is it and how do we get it safely off the bricks? The coating is very thick, and as it chips off, part of the brick comes with it.

THE COATING FAILURE is most acute on the front porch addition, as you can see in the photo. (We plan to remove this porch later, and replace it with a more appropriate wooden one.)

--Terry & Elizabeth McCloskey Hammond, Ind.

THE COATING on your house is a colored portland cement parging (like stucco) with several layers of white paint on it. "No-maintenance" coatings such as this often were installed on moisture-damaged brick and stone, to put the damage "out of sight and out of mind," or on bricks needing pointing, or for reasons of taste.

THERE'S NO GOOD WAY to get the coating off; it was trowelled directly onto the bricks, not on wire lath that could be pulled away. To remove the coating would mean taking some of the brick surface with it. You're going to have to live with the coating, so you need to keep it in good repair.

THE COATING could be failing because it was installed over water-damaged bricks in the first place...and now the parging, too, is falling victim to water penetration. Have you inspected to see where water might be coming from? Check gutters, flashings, drip edges, and drainage around the foundation. Also, make sure kitchens and bathrooms are properly ventilated.

ONCE YOU'VE repaired the sources of water damage, your best bet is to scrape off any loose paint and parging and keep your bricks painted with a latex masonry paint (a brick color would be preferable to white).

---

continued from p. 97

THE MAIN TOOL for removing trim is a short, flat prybar. Often used in pairs, it's designed for just this kind of work. You'll also need these tools for your woodwork-removal toolkit:

- Clawhammer
- Nail puller or pliers
- A couple of putty knives
- A pair of sturdy work gloves

YOU WON'T NEED a screwdriver to pry woodwork loose. Screwdrivers leave chewed-up edges on the wood, because they're too narrow to distribute the prying force over a wide area.

TRIM CAN BE "GLUED" onto the wall by excessive paint buildup or wallpaper that overlaps the wood. Cut through them with a knife or scraper before pulling away the trim, so you don't flake paint or rip wallpaper. Repair any splits or defects in the trim itself before it's removed. Mending the wood at this stage is easier than trying to reassemble splintered pieces after the trim is off.

NOTE THE CONSTRUCTION of a corner before you work on it. Generally, outside trim corners are mitred (both pieces cut at 45 degrees); inside corners are coped (one board cut with a coping saw so that it fits the contour of its mate at 90 degrees). The coped board was installed after its mate, so remove it first; then you can cover any evidence of your initial prying when the trim is nailed back into place. Pry each board at the edge or joint exposed by the board you've just removed.

The coped board, which was installed in this interior corner after its mate, is removed first.

Taking It Off

TO REMOVE MOULDING, gently hammer the bent edge of the prybar between the wall and the wood at one end of the trim. The tops or bottoms of windows and doors are good places to begin prying. If you're removing baseboards or ceiling mouldings, begin at the corners. Start in an inconspicuous place, because you're likely to gouge or dent the wood or the wall with your first effort.

After you've freed the corner, hold the gap open with another prybar and continue prying at the next nail.

POSITION a wood shingle or a wide-bladed putty knife to protect the wall from the prybar, and lift the end of the prybar carefully, using the wall as a fulcrum. Work the wood away from the wall until you see a nail. Hold open the space between the wood and the wall with another prybar or a wood shingle, and then pry at the exposed nail until a second nail is visible. Continue prying in this manner down the length of the board, working at the nailed spots only, until the trim is free of the wall. Once the whole board has been pried out and is suspended by a few nails, you can usually tug it away from the wall by hand.

VERY SOFT TRIM WOODS can show marks from the prybar even if you're careful. Use two wide putty knives, one to protect the wall and the other to protect the trim. Insert them at the edge of a board and tap them in until a gap is opened. Then slide the prybar between them and continue prying in the normal manner.

Either of the base shoes used in this mitred outside corner can be removed first.

Using two prybars in opposite directions is the easiest way to remove the stop moulding of a window.

SOMETIMES YOU HAVE TO SEPARATE two mouldings from each other; for instance, when you're removing the stop moulding from a window. Use two prybars next to each other and work them in opposite directions. (The handles can face the same way or in opposite directions -- whichever works better.) Opposing prybars exert a lot of force, so work carefully. The inside window sill, or stool, is the first board the carpenter installed. Therefore it can't be removed until you've pried off the casings above it and the apron below it.

IN MOST CASES, the nails holding the woodwork will be small-headed finishing nails. They'll either pull through the trim and remain in the wall, or come away with the trim. To remove any finishing nails still in the wood, take a nail puller or pliers and pull them out <u>from the back</u> -- never hammer them through the front of the board. The nail heads were originally set below the surface and filled with putty; knocking them through the front can dislodge the putty and splinter the wood around it.

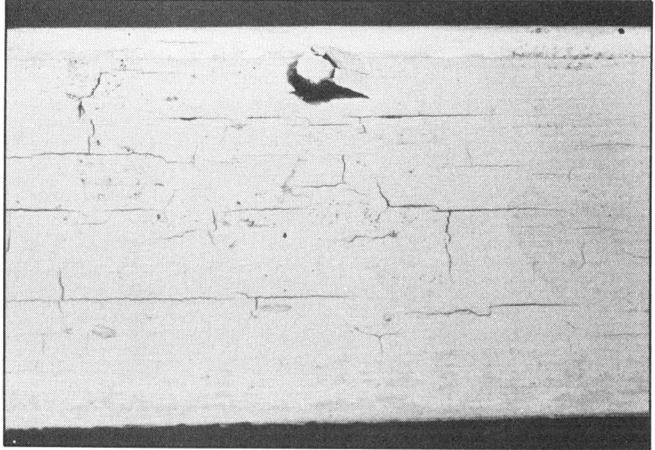

Don't try removing leftover nails in the board by hammering them through the front — you'll damage the surface.

IF YOU'RE UNLUCKY, your trim was secured with large-headed common nails. Pry the moulding about 1/4 inch away from the wall, as described above. Then, with a wood block, tap the moulding back against the wall. The offending nail heads will protrude enough for you to either: (1) remove the nails with your prybar, using a wood shingle or putty knife under the prybar to protect the moulding, or (2) cut the heads off the nails with your wire cutters. If the nails are thin enough, use the second method and avoid further prying.

COMMON NAILS can't be pulled through from the back of the board, so if any are left in the wood after you've removed it, cut them with heavy wire cutters, close to the back of the board. Then file down any protrusions of the nails, so they don't scratch the other pieces when you bundle up all the woodwork.

AFTER YOU REMOVE all the trim, prepare the pieces for temporary storage. Number each one on the backside, and note its location on a map of the room. Stamp the numbers into the wood. If you just write on them in pencil or ink, it can be erased by paint remover or light sanding. Then, once a complete set of mouldings for, say, a window has been removed and numbered, it can be tied in a bundle and labeled: "Living room, north wall, left."

Reusing The Trim

REINSTALLING TRIM is much like fitting brand new trim. We can't cover the whole trade of finish carpentry here, but we can outline some steps and shortcuts that will help you reinstall trim with good results.

The best way to remove nails is by pulling them out from the back of the board with pullers or pliers.

THE TOOLS required:
- Hammer (12-oz. clawhammer preferred)
- Handsaw (backsaw or dovetail saw preferred)
- 12-in. combination square
- Ruler (Rulers are more accurate than tape measures)
- Coping saw
- Nailset

Also: white or yellow glue, wood putty, and sandpaper for final touch-ups.

TO REINSTALL a piece of trim, position it temporarily by tacking it in place with two finishing nails, partially hammered in. If the fit is right, nail the board back in place with finishing nails. To avoid putting more holes into the woodwork, nail through the existing nail holes -- but at an angle, so the nail will go into new wood. (If the trim piece is less than 5/8 inch thick, nail in new positions.) Hammer the nail until it's one or two blows from being flush with the wood, then set the nail about 1/8 inch below the surface with your nailset.

If you strike the wood with the face of the hammer -- no matter how lightly -- you'll leave a disfiguring dent that'll be all too obvious when the woodwork is finished. Once the nails are set, fill the holes with putty, and wipe the patches clean with a rag, or sand them as necessary.

TO AVOID SPLITTING THE WOOD, never nail closer than two inches from any board ends. If you're working with delicate or thin strips, blunt the nails on a hard surface or snip the tips before using them. This causes them to act more like a punch than a wedge when they penetrate the wood. With hardwoods such as oak, you can prevent splitting by drilling pilot holes for the nails. Use a drill bit with a diameter slightly smaller than that of the nails.

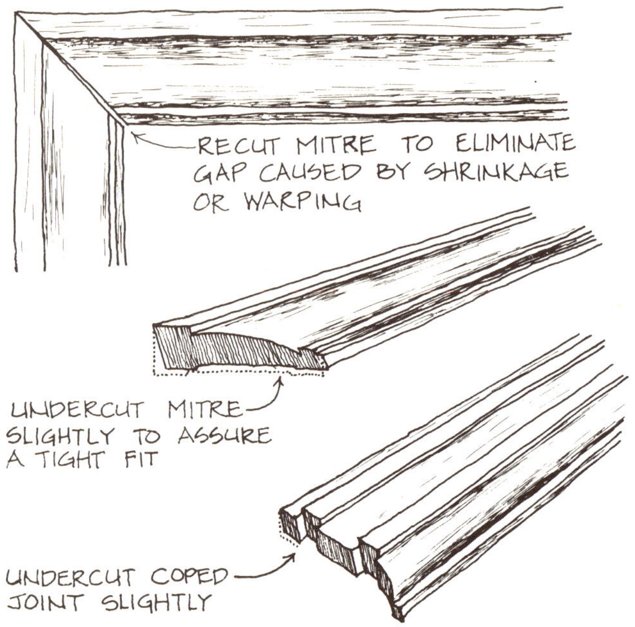

MITRED CORNERS that have been pulled apart by warping or shrinking wood can be brought closer together by undercutting with a saw on the hidden side of the mitre, on one or both of the mating boards (see illustration at bottom left). If the crack is still objectionable, you'll have to fill it. Use putty or caulk if the wood will be painted. If you'll be applying a clear finish, use linseed-oil putty tinted with stain or oil colors, or white glue mixed with sawdust.

Using New Moulding

SOMETIMES YOU JUST DON'T have all your original moulding. In such cases, you'll have to install pieces that aren't pre-measured and pre-cut. When mitering trim around "picture frame" enclosures such as windows, doors, or raised-panel wall mouldings, measurements for length are made to the "short point," or inside edge, of the rectangle; that is, to the points that will be on the short sides of the trim board when the mitre is cut. Cuts measured this way produce neat joints and accurate lengths. Measure, cut, and fit one mitre at a time.

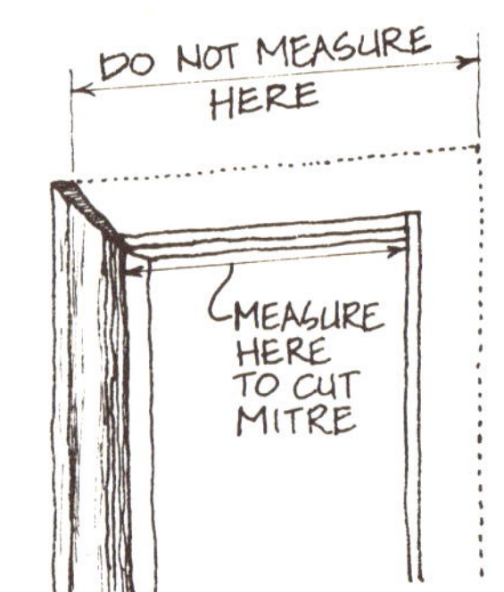

For greater accuracy when cutting trim, mark your boards with a knife rather than a pencil. You can line up your saw more accurately with this sharper line. And, of course, remember to cut on the waste side of the line.

THERE ARE TWO TECHNIQUES for making a profile for a coped joint. The first, which works best with smaller mouldings, is to initially cut the piece to the correct length in a mitre box. The sawn edge along the moulded surface then becomes the profile to be cut with a coping saw. When making this cut, undercut slightly to assure a tight joint.

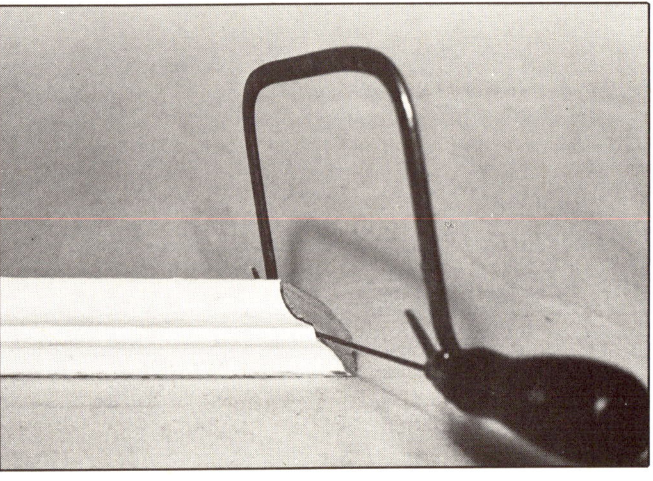

One technique for making a profile for a coped joint is to cut the piece in a mitre box. Then saw along the edge, undercutting slightly so the cut will match the contour of the trim.

Another technique is to set a compass to the width of the lumber, butt the boards at a right angle, and draw a compass along the joint so it scribes the profile of the board.

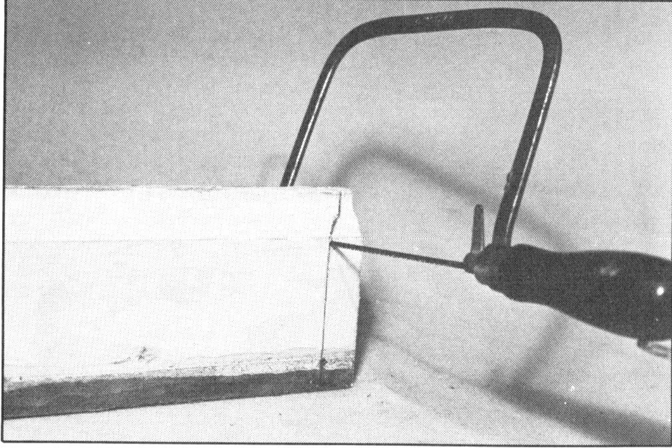

Then you cut along the line . . .

. . . and the finished profile is identical to the trim.

THE SECOND TECHNIQUE, which is usually used on larger lumber such as baseboards, is to scribe the profile. The board to be coped is butted at 90 degrees against the board with which it will mate. A compass or pair of dividers, set to the thickness of the board, is then drawn up along the inside of the corner, so that it draws the profile of one board onto the other. This line is then cut with the coping saw.

COPING is also necessary when ending a window apron or a milled chair rail. In most cases, the trim stops without meeting another board, so it should have the profile returned for a finished look. The ends can be coped to make a moulded edge that matches the front. An alternate method is to mitre the board and return the profile with another small mitred piece glued on the edge. Both techniques produce nice results.

IF YOU HAVE TO MAKE a ceiling moulding, baseboard, or similar long piece of trim from two or more pieces of wood, join them in a scarf joint rather than butt them. This joint is made with two matching, 45-degree mitres. Position it on a wall stud for good nailing. It's much less obtrusive in the finished job, and resists shifting when the house settles.

A CLEVER WAY to mitre a 45-degree angle without the benefit of a square or mitre box is the "mirror-saw trick." It works best on small mouldings such as 5/8-inch (or smaller) cove or quarter-round. And it's fine where absolute precision is unnecessary, such as for woodwork that will be filled and painted. (Don't try it on very deep or wide pieces because the saw may wander.)

ALL YOU NEED is a shiny saw blade, so you can see the reflection of the piece being cut. Most people can't "eyeball" a precise 45-degree angle, but almost anyone can recognize an accurate right angle. A right angle is what you see in the saw blade when it's set at 45 degrees. Set the saw at the proper length on the moulding and then pivot it on this point until a right angle is formed by the moulding itself and its reflection in the saw. Then cut. When measured afterwards, it turns out the cut is exactly 45 degrees -- or certainly close enough. Works every time!

The "Mirror-Saw" Trick: Pivot the saw on the trim until the reflection in the blade is 90 degrees to the board being cut.

Instant Color Match

Old-house owners often need to have paint custom mixed to match existing paint colors, old paint chips, wallpaper samples, carpet, or fabric. Many of our readers know how hard it can be to get a paint store to match a color. And if they do, the paint they mix often doesn't match. Benjamin Moore & Co. has ended all that trial-and-error mixing with the introduction of a computerized spectrophotometer. The machine reads a 1/4-inch-diameter sample to be color matched, and in seconds prints out a color-matching prescription. Following this prescription, the dealer can mix the color within minutes. Best of all, the computer stores the prescription for future use, and the homeowner gets a printout of it, which can be refilled by many Benjamin Moore dealers across the country.

The Computer Color Matching System is now used by Benjamin Moore dealers in over 140 locations throughout the nation. (One dealer in Florida has found the system very useful in matching Art Deco exterior pastels.) Call your local Benjamin Moore dealer or write **Benjamin Moore & Co., Dept. OHJ, 51 Chestnut Ridge Road, Montvale, NJ 07645. (201) 573-9600.**

Shaker Village Colors

Speaking of painting: The City of Shaker Heights, Ohio, has a beautifully produced, 22-page booklet to help owners of post-Victorian homes choose exterior paint-color combinations. Taken from a booklet produced by the architect/developer in 1925, it illustrates full-color paint schemes for a variety of 1920s houses: English Tudor, 'Jacobethan,' New England Vernacular, Federal, Spanish, Georgian, Dutch Colonial, French Classical, Bungalow, and Prairie Style.

To make the booklet even more useful to today's old-house owners, the Sherwin-Williams Paint Co. dug into its archives and came up with current paints that authentically match the original colors. A separate folder containing these color chips is included in the booklet, along with descriptions of the colors, instructions on where to use them, and painting tips.

There's a limited supply of 'Shaker Village Colors' left. To get a copy, send $3 to **Heritage Director, Shaker Heights City Hall, Dept. OHJ, 3400 Lee Road, Shaker Heights, OH 44120. (216) 752-5000.**

Color Consultant

Bob Buckter claims to have been San Francisco's first exterior color consultant. You may have seen many of his earlier projects illustrated in the 1978 book *Painted Ladies.* Bob currently designs both interior and exterior color schemes to suit clients' tastes and to harmonize with adjacent neighborhood buildings. Designing paint schemes with contrasts in both color and sheen are his specialty. Through the careful placement of color, Bob can make largely unnoticed architectural elements leap into prominence.

He charges $75 per hour plus expenses for consultation. But working directly with the client at the job site isn't always possible, so Bob also offers design consultations by mail, for $275. For color placement by mail, Bob uses a color specification sheet, indicating high-quality paint available in the client's area. He numbers photos supplied by the owner to show what color goes where. (You need to supply him with sharp 3x5-in., 35-mm photos.) Send for a free brochure from **Bob Buckter Color Consultant, Dept. OHJ, 3877 20th Street, San Francisco, CA 94114. (415) 922-7444.**

Color Service

Selecting exterior paint colors for old houses and then figuring out where to use them is a very tricky business at best. There's probably nothing more disappointing, expensive, and downright embarrassing than picking paint colors from those little swatches, buying all the paint, and then being horrified with how it looks on your house. One way to protect yourself is to hire a colorist who's a professional paint-color consultant.

Jill Pilaroscia of San Francisco Color Service is a colorist with over nine years experience in San Francisco. But you don't have to live in the Bay Area to benefit from her experience and talent. Jill currently provides distinctive polychrome color schemes for building owners by mail. She'll send you detailed instructions about which areas of the house should be photographed. Then, from your photos and color preferences, she'll propose three appropriate color schemes. She supplies sample color chips and a detailed diagram of where to place the colors. You'll also get a pamphlet that has color-placement hints and help on how to beware of color surprises.

This service will cost you $200, but think of it as insurance against living with a technicolor fiasco. Besides, she may come up with a color scheme you never would have thought of! Contact **Jill at San Francisco Color Service, Dept. OHJ, 855 Alvarado, San Francisco, CA 94114. (415) 285-4544.**

DECORATIVE FINISHES: Painting, Stencilling, Gilding, and Murals

Gold Leaf Studios

Bill Adair is a master gilder and founder of Gold Leaf Studios in Washington, D.C. Bill and his crew have worked their magic on the Nebraska State House, the Hearst Castle at San Simeon, and the White House. They've just completed what is probably the nation's tour de force in gold leafing, the Benjamin Franklin State Dining Room for the Secretary of State. But Gold Leaf Studios still deals with smaller projects of homeowners. Objects large and small get the same museum-quality restoration attention, not only to leafing and gilding but also to the painstaking replacement of missing elements and the stabilization of decayed materials. The studio rescues such items as furniture, looking glasses, architectural objects, sculpted pieces, and picture frames.

With Bill's experience at the frame-restoration shop of the National Picture Gallery, the studio can help you find and restore picture frames appropriate to your house's period. There's even a variety of them for sale at the studio. Bill also has a fine poster that identifies and dates picture frames; it's available for $12.50 ppd. from the **Professional Picture Framer Association, Dept. OHJ, P.O. Box 7655, Richmond, VA 23231. (804) 226-0430.** For $17.50 ppd., they offer Bill's book *The Frame In America, 1700-1900.* It's an illustrated history that includes gilding and repairing techniques, plus methods of frame construction.

Bill warns against refinishing your gilded pieces with 'Green Grunge': gold spray paint. Also beware of bronze powders and other cheap, gold-leaf substitutes. If you want to be a do-it-yourself gilder, the studio sells a complete kit with glue, burnishers, gilders tip, burnish clay, gilders cushion, quick size, casein paste, a book of gold leaf, and thorough instructions, all for $99.85 ppd. Contact **Gold Leaf Studios, Inc., Dept. OHJ, 930 F Street, Suite 200, Washington, D.C. 20004. (202) 638-4660.**

Restoration Stencilling

Sally Hopkins and her firm, Restoration Stencilling, specializes in the restoration of stencilling on the walls and ceilings of late Victorian structures. Her past efforts include stencilling floors, ceilings, friezes, floor cloths, and even window shades. Sally works mainly on the West Coast, but is willing to travel outside the Northwest to work on stencilling, gilding, marbleizing, and graining projects. Her work isn't limited solely to the Victorian Period; she's also well versed in Craftsman designs and can create contemporary custom stencils.

Have you found old stencilling you want revived? Well, Sally cautions against cleaning it with any sort of liquid cleaner — that will simply dissolve or ruin it. Instead, take a photo of the design and make a pencil tracing of one repeat of the design. Then try to match the original colors with paint chips from your local paint store. For more information contact Restoration Stencilling, Dept. OHJ, 1416 E. Second Street, Port Angeles, WA 98362. (206) 457-6676.

Folk–Art Murals

For over 20 years the Whiggins Brothers have become well known for their traditional interior folk painting in New England; their work has carried them as far as Texas. The second-generation family business has particular experience with the restoration and design of 19th-century stencilling, especially that of Moses Eaton Jr. Besides their stencilling, glazing, and marbleizing talents, the Whiggins Brothers create folk-art murals in the style of Rufus Porter. They do a range of adaptations from original designs, working in styles appropriate to houses of the 19th and 20th centuries. Write **David Whiggins of Whiggins Brothers, Dept. OHJ, Hale Road, Tilton, NH 03276. (603) 286-3046.**

Wallpaper Restoration

Sheila Foster of Manchester, Vt., restores wallpaper. Not by the usual method of carefully uncovering built-up layers or duplicating old wallpapers with new; she repaints faded and damaged wallpapers by hand. Using latex and acrylic paints, Ms. Foster meticulously retouches every detail to create a color match that's almost indistinguishable from the undamaged portions.

Her most notable project to date was her restoration work in the dining room at the Robert Todd Lincoln House in Manchester. An attic water tank had leaked, showering the dining room wall for six hours. Ms. Foster repainted the intact but badly stained wallpaper, returning all the damaged areas back to their original colors. She charges $50 per hour (plus milage) for consultation — refundable if you decide to hire her. The actual painting costs $25 per hour. Write to **Sheila Foster, Dept. OHJ, P.O. Box 318, Manchester, VT 05254. (802) 362-1038.**

SUBSCRIBER Lawrence Sommer and photographer Wade Lawrence spotted this house while working on a historic structures survey in Minnesota. This remuddling may go in the history books itself. Not so much for the second-floor fenestration -- jamming square pegs into round (-top) holes is a standard remuddler's foible. (The same thing's been done to the two houses that flank this one.) What's truly amazing about this house is the remodeler's showcase on the ground floor. From the sidewalk up, there's fake brick; a rectangular picture window punched into the wall; vertical aluminum siding; and phony wood shingles, complete with their very own phony shed roof. But the _piece de resistance_ is the company name emblazoned on the siding. To quote the poet Robert Burns, "O wad some Pow'r the giftie gie us / To see oursels as others see us!" -- CG

The Old-House Journal®

**69A Seventh Avenue,
Brooklyn, New York 11217**

NO PAID ADVERTISING

Postmaster: Address Correction Requested

Restoration and Maintenance Techniques
For The Pre-1939 House

July 1985 / Vol. XIII No. 6 / $2.

The Old-House Journal

Return To Awnings

by J. Randall Cotton

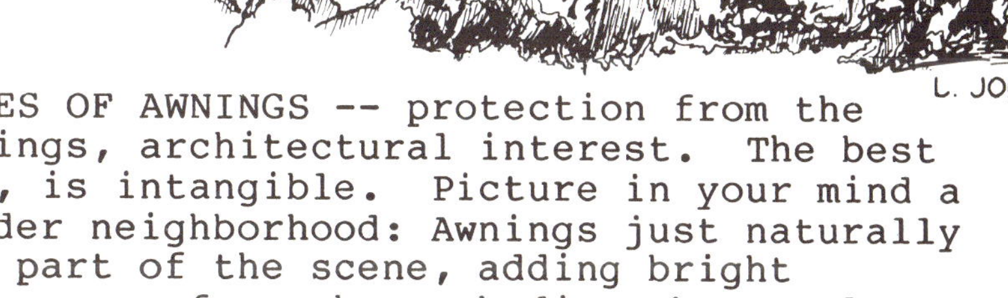

AH, THE ADVANTAGES OF AWNINGS -- protection from the sun, energy savings, architectural interest. The best payback, though, is intangible. Picture in your mind a typical street in an older neighborhood: Awnings just naturally ought to be an integral part of the scene, adding bright splashes of color to the rows of porches, shading the people who seek respite on a hot summer afternoon.

UNFORTUNATELY, modern conveniences such as air-conditioning have made awnings less common along the streetscape. But more and more old-house owners are deciding that awnings are just what they need to complete their restoration -- and cool off their homes, too! We're happy to say that awnings are still readily available in traditional styles, colors, and materials. In fact, thanks to an array of modern but compatible fabrics, they now come in a greater range of colors, and will last longer than ever before.

cont'd on p. 126

In the next issue...
WOOD CORNICE REPAIRS

You Know You've Got An Old House When...

by Patrick Kee, Ida Grove, Iowa

... the living room light dims whenever you run the Dust Buster.

... you get personal Christmas cards from natural gas company executives you don't even know.

... everyone in town insists "that isn't the color the house used to be" -- but no one remembers for sure what color it was.

... a 4-ft. step ladder is useless to you.

... a 6-ft. Christmas tree is 'just too small.'

... the only man who knew where your city water shut-off is died in 1919.

... your change dish includes plaster washers, finish nails, and a radiator key.

... the local lumber yard can supply only one out of every ten items you want.

... once or twice a year, when you're walking down that long upstairs hall, you feel like someone is behind you -- but you never, ever turn around to look.

... you get more evening phone calls from siding salesmen than from your mother.

... you walk four blocks in the dead of winter because you refuse to use the parking lot 'they' tore down the old courthouse to build.

... you'd rather read a paint-chip chart than the sports section.

... you think one of these days a loose attic floorboard will yield Old Man Smith's unbanked hoard of gold coins AND the original blueprint of the house.

... you start writing notes to future owners and hiding them behind the wainscotting and mop boards.

... the terms 'warmth' and 'patina' replace 'worn out' and 'dirty.'

... you're willing to ruin your vision needlepointing upholstery for a footstool you could crush with one good squeeze.

... you feel there's nothing amusing or quaint about the wardrobe of Sherlock Holmes and Dr. Watson.

... people are talking about 'tennis elbow' or 'Army arches,' and you want to tell them about 'scraper knuckle' and 'rung foot.'

... you drop someone from your guest list for referring to your Bungalow as a Victorian.

OHJ's next issue will be the August-September double issue. Look for it in early September.

The Old-House Journal®

Editor
Patricia Poore

Production Editor
Cole Gagne

Senior Technical Advisor
Larry Jones

Assistant Editor
Sarah J. McNamara

Contributing Editors
Walter Jowers
John Mark Garrison
Roland A. Labine Sr.

Architectural Consultant
Jonathan Poore

Circulation Supervisor
Barbara Bugg

Circulation Assistant
Jeanne Baldwin

Special Sales
Joan O'Reilly

Office Manager
Tricia A. Martin

Catalog Editor
Sarah J. McNamara

Publishing Consultant
Paul T. McLoughlin

Publisher
Clem Labine

Published by The Old-House Journal Corporation, 69A Seventh Avenue, Brooklyn, NY 11217. Telephone (718) 636-4514. Subscriptions $18 per year in U.S., $36 per year in Canada (payable in Canadian funds). Published ten times per year. Contents are fully protected by copyright and must not be reproduced in any manner whatsoever without specific permission in writing from the Editor.

We are happy to accept editorial contributions to The Old-House Journal. Query letters that include an outline of the proposed article are preferred. All manuscripts will be reviewed, and returned if unacceptable. However, we cannot be responsible for non-receipt or loss — please keep copies of all materials sent.

Printed at Photo Comp Press, New York City

ISSN: 0094-0178
NO PAID ADVERTISING

A Scaffolding Primer

With Basic Guidelines On The Use Of Welded Tubular-Frame Scaffolds

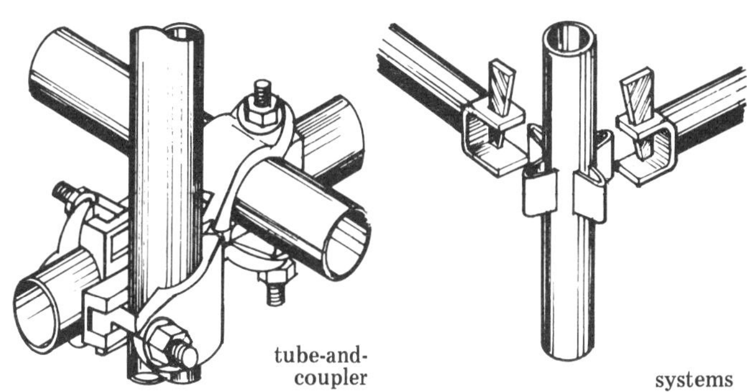

A welded tubular-frame scaffold assembly, set up with putlogs (trusses) to bridge large obstructions on the ground.

by The Old-House Journal Technical Staff
Illustrations by Larry Jones

THIS IS AN ARTICLE for people who know nothing about scaffolds. Our intention is to familiarize you with scaffolding so you'll know when to use it (it can be safer than an extension ladder) and what options you have. No magazine article can make you a skilled scaffold erector, however. Only you know whether you've got enough experience and information to erect safe scaffolding for your particular needs.

SOMETIMES you have to tackle a job that you can't do from the ground and shouldn't do from a ladder. Cornice restoration is an example: It requires access to the whole cornice; tools and materials have to be handy; workers need both hands free to do the work. Scaffolding fits the bill. Other old-house jobs that often require scaffolding include masonry repointing, major repairs to gutters and soffits, residing and reshingling, whole-house paint stripping and repainting, and building a porch or addition.

Scaffolding Types

YOU MAY HAVE SEEN some of these kinds of scaffolding being used around the neighborhood. Each type is right for some jobs, inappropriate or dangerous for others.

● Built-up scaffolding -- A temporary elevated platform, built from the ground up, used to support workers and materials. There are several types of built-up scaffolding.

● Welded tubular-frame scaffolding -- Built-up scaffolding consisting of metal frames with braces and various accessories. This is the most common type of scaffolding, used by contractors as well as homeowners.

● Tube-and-coupler scaffolding -- Built-up scaffolding consisting of tubing that serves as posts and beams, with special couplers that join the various members. This type of scaffolding is quite popular in Europe. It has to be erected by experienced crews.

● Systems scaffolding -- An American hybrid similar to tube-and-coupler scaffolding. Parts are field-assembled by the use of proprietary pipes, wedges, etc. It's useful on complicated jobs, where it can be built to conform to odd shapes. Easier to erect than tube-and-coupler, but should still be erected by an experienced crew.

● Shoring -- A common type is similar to welded tubular-frame scaffolding. It's not really scaffolding, but rather temporary support and bracing that holds up structural members (instead of workers and materials) during construction or repair.

SPECIAL THANKS to the following for their help:

Joe Budd, Scaffolding & Shoring Institute, Cleveland, Ohio.
Kenneth J. Buettner, Vice-President of Your Scaffold Equipment Corp., Long Island City, N.Y.
Warren Duncan, Waco International Corp., Houston, Texas.
Alan Keiser, Havertown, Penn.
Victor D. Saleeby, Executive Vice-President of Scaffold Industry Association, Van Nuys, Cal.

Drawings adapted from *A Guide To Waco Scaffolding* and *SIA Membership Directory & Handbook*.

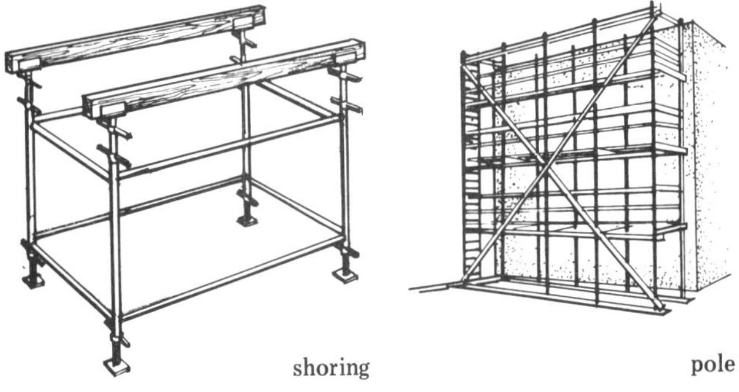

● **Pole scaffolding** -- Built-up scaffolding made of wood; the "original" scaffolding before welded-tube types came along. Still used today by contractors whose experienced carpentry crews understand how to put it up. Can be used for carpentry, painting, or masonry work.

● **Rolling scaffolding** -- Built-up scaffolding with wheels, usually used indoors. It can be used outdoors on, say, a fully paved flat perimeter for work at low heights.

The Worst Can Happen

by Alan D. Keiser

WHEN MY FRIENDS at The Old-House Journal asked me to comment on an article about the basics of erecting and dismantling exterior scaffolding, my first reaction was "don't publish it." The reason for this is simple: Erecting and dismantling scaffolds is extremely dangerous work. I know this from tragic first-hand experience. I was lucky — I survived a 40-foot fall from a scaffold that collapsed while I was dismantling it. I had earned a reputation for being cautious and for being safety conscious. Nonetheless, the worst happened. It's important for every non-professional (and professional as well) who sets up and takes down scaffolding to never forget that the unexpected *can* happen in this very dangerous work.

Because our readers must deal with scaffolds at times, despite the danger, I think The Old-House Journal should lay out the basics. However, my advice is, quite frankly, don't set up and dismantle scaffolding yourself. If you're working at a height greater than 10 feet, hire a professional to do it. The risks are too great and the results of a misstep can be catastrophic. This is work best left for the professional.

If you can't find a professional to do it or if you insist that you do know enough to do it safely, then be sure to do all your homework. Be sure you do in fact know what you are doing. Follow *all* safety rules and guidelines. Above all, do not ignore them because someone says, "Oh, nobody bothers with that, it's okay." It's imperative that you do everything possible to even the odds.

This article provides basic advice. Read the article critically, then go find out as much additional information as you possibly can. At the bare minimum, when you are erecting and dismantling a scaffold, follow these four rules:

1. Have a step-by-step plan of action before you begin the work, so you'll be able to predict what *could* go wrong.
2. Be aware of your environment and changes in the environment (weather, people, weight of materials, the scaffolding itself). Change your plans if conditions change.
3. Never hurry.
4. Never "fly tired."

Alan D. Keiser is former Director of the National Trust's Restoration Workshop at Tarrytown, N.Y.

● **Built-out scaffolding** -- Scaffolding that is built out from the wall instead of up from the ground or suspended from above. It can be economical in some circumstances as it saves the renting and erection of very large scaffolds. It is used more in new construction than in repair work, and usually at greater heights than we come up against working on our houses. For old-house applications, it should be built by an experienced crew.

● **Swing staging** -- Also known as suspended scaffolding, this is a scaffold platform suspended by wire or ropes from an overhead support system. It's useful for repair work that requires a short stay in a location before moving to another (e.g., window washing, painting a cornice or window trim, minor masonry work). Most cities and towns require users of swing staging to have a rigger's license, because it's dangerous for inexperienced workers and, sometimes, for people below.

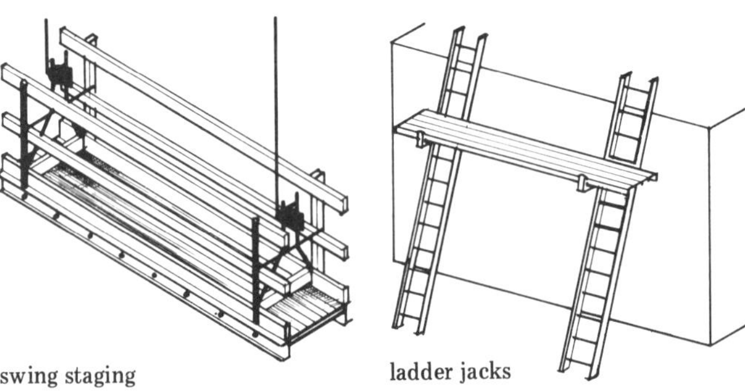

● **Ladder jacks** -- Made up of metal jacks that attach to the rungs or side rails of an extension ladder to hold a work platform. <u>Must</u> be tied into the building. Not to be used for heavy (masonry or carpentry) work or for heights above one storey, but they're fine for light work such as painting and window repair at heights around 10 feet or so.

● **Trestle-ladder scaffold** -- Specially designed step-ladders that extend to hold a platform. Used for the same kinds of jobs as the ladder jack, but is self-supporting. Useful and safe for jobs such as work on a porch ceiling.

● **Pump jacks** -- A popular form of scaffolding that uses spiked 2x4s, foot-operated jacks, and planks. Often used by masons and other workers who need to move up and down a wall surface at short intervals, and who load building materials onto the platform. Okay for use at low heights, but must be braced or

---

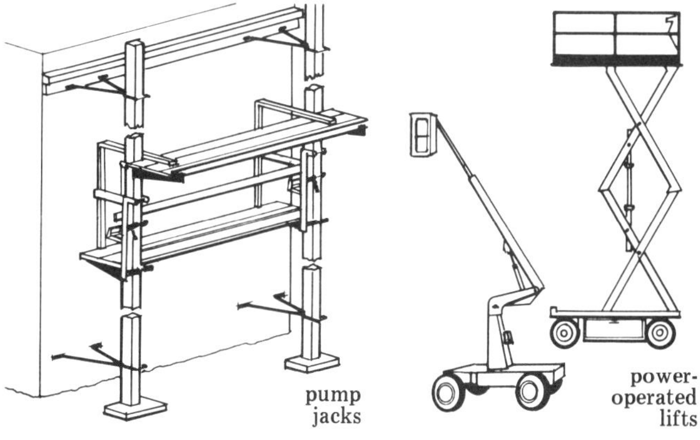

anchored to the building or may buckle even as low as 20 feet. Safety features such as guard rails are often omitted, so we recommend that only experienced workers use them.

● Power-operated lifts -- Scissor lifts, cherry pickers, hydraulic personnel lifts ... these motor-driven lifting devices are designed for specific tasks such as working on electrical lines. Sort of expensive because you're hiring an operator along with the machinery. But because of their speed and flexibility you might consider renting one for inspections or a quick job like putting a cupola or tower roof in place.

WELDED-TUBE SCAFFOLDING is the most common and available type of scaffolding, useful for most residential projects, and relatively simple to understand, assemble, and work from safely. The system's modular form, though, makes it inflexible when used around highly complex buildings (such as Queen Anne houses, with their projecting bays, oriel windows, turrets and balconies). If your scaffolding has to reach around tricky projections, you may have to use more versatile "systems" scaffolding. Ask your supplier.

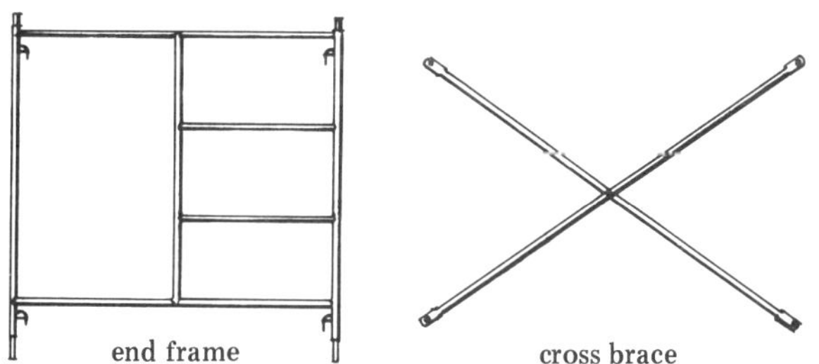

BUILT-UP SCAFFOLDING has to be put up much like a building: It needs a proper foundation, structural members must be straight and plumb, and the whole construction has to withstand loads and stresses. If it's poorly erected, it is extremely unsafe, and may tip, move, or buckle.

SOME OLD-HOUSE OWNERS think nothing of renting and erecting scaffolding themselves. If the equipment is in good condition, written instructions provided, and safety accessories used, they may be perfectly safe doing so. An intelligent and cautious handyperson should have no trouble erecting scaffolding up to 20 feet or so on firm, level ground.

WHEN THE JOB is at all complicated, however, we recommend that a professional crew erect, move, and disassemble the scaffold. If you're a novice, consider all of the following to be "complications": scaffolding to higher than the second storey; sloping ground; sunken or clay soil; difficult setups such as over a porch or around a projecting bay. Working from safely erected scaffolding is <u>much</u> less dangerous than erecting and dismantling it.

BEFORE PLUNGING AHEAD, take into account these sobering thoughts:
● Mistakes or oversights aren't merely inconvenient or expensive; they can kill you.
● Each scaffolding setup is different; there are lots of considerations and only experience can tell which require special adaptations, accessories, safety equipment, etc.
● There are many types of scaffolding and within each type, different brands are non-generic. You can't interchange parts because fastening devices and accessories vary from brand to brand. So obviously, we can't give you all the "how-to" here.

FINISH READING this article even if you've decided to hire the scaffolding setup done. (And if you've decided to hire out the whole job, it still falls to the owner to do regular inspections -- you may have to climb the scaffold for a look now and then.) You'll want to know something about what a safe scaffold looks like before you go up.

Renting A Scaffold

TRY THE YELLOW PAGES under "Scaffolding Equipment -- Rental." In some cases, there <u>will</u> be companies specializing in scaffold rental. The person behind the counter may even know what he's talking about and may be able to supply a professional crew to erect and disassemble for you.

BUT DON'T COUNT ON IT. This is a "renter beware" situation. If you do find a serious scaffold-rental place, you're not going to be an important customer. (They'll be used to dealing with contractors who rent often and in large quantities.) If you're forced to deal with an all-purpose rental company (the kind that also has baby carriages and garden tillers), you may find poorly maintained equipment and little advice. In either case, you'd better know as much as you can about what you want before you walk in the door.

YOU CAN ALSO CALL the Scaffolding Industry Association (SIA) in Van Nuys, Calif., at 818-782-2012. They may be able to give you the name of a member (a scaffold dealer) in your area.

KEEP IN MIND that you should not mix scaffold brands. Because you want to find a company that has a large enough inventory to supply all the parts you need from one manufacturer, it pays to go out of your way (even many miles to another town) to find a serious scaffold rental company.

IF YOU CAN'T FIND what you need, <u>and</u> the written instructions to use it <u>safely</u>, <u>and</u> a crew to erect and dismantle the scaffold,

Welded Tube Scaffolding Parts

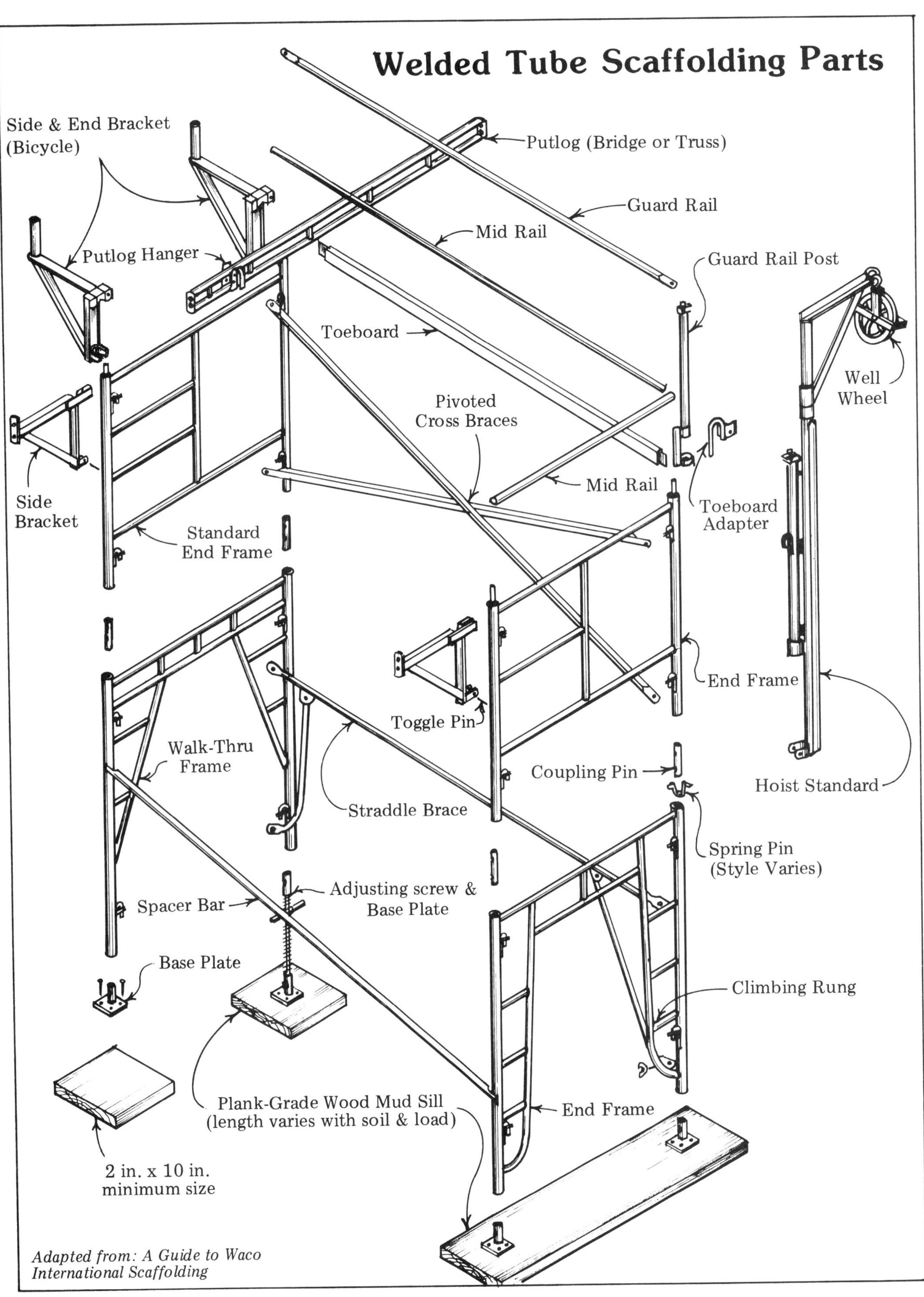

Adapted from: A Guide to Waco International Scaffolding

seriously consider hiring the work done -- the contractor's crew will come with their own scaffolding.

BY THE WAY, if the job will take longer than eight to twelve months, look into buying rather than renting scaffolding. It may be cheaper. And when you rent, come prepared to pay a BIG (refundable) deposit -- maybe as much as the cost of the scaffolding.

Basic Components

WELDED TUBULAR-FRAME scaffolding is modular, as shown in these illustrations. Length of a section is determined by the diagonal brace that spans between the two end frames. Narrower sections are stronger, and so used for heavier loads such as bricks. Section lengths around 8' are for medium-duty loads such as lumber. Ten-foot spacing is light-duty -- for jobs that don't require significant loading beyond the weight of the workers. (The industry booklet noted at the end of the article explains exactly what setup you need for various loads.)

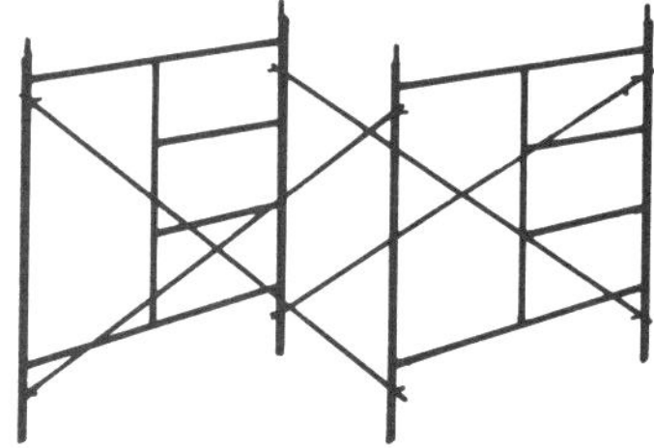

THE FRAME SECTIONS can be tied together to make any <u>run</u> length. A greater run means renting more scaffolding -- but don't fall into the trap of not renting enough. You'll waste time and money moving the scaffold from place to place. Every time a scaffold is moved, it has to be largely disassembled.

METAL FRAMES come in varying heights to allow fine-tuning the height of the <u>towers</u>. Taller frames are <u>usually</u> used at the bottom of the tower (they're easier to walk under); shorter ones usually used at the top. (The opposite is true if the terrain is extreme in slope.) Generally, it's better to build a scaffold a little short than a little tall: Stretching is less tiring than stooping. (Stretching <u>up</u>, that is -- stretching <u>out</u> is dangerous.)

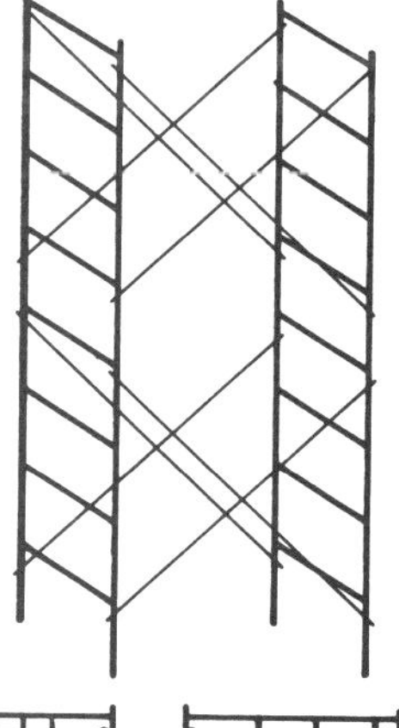

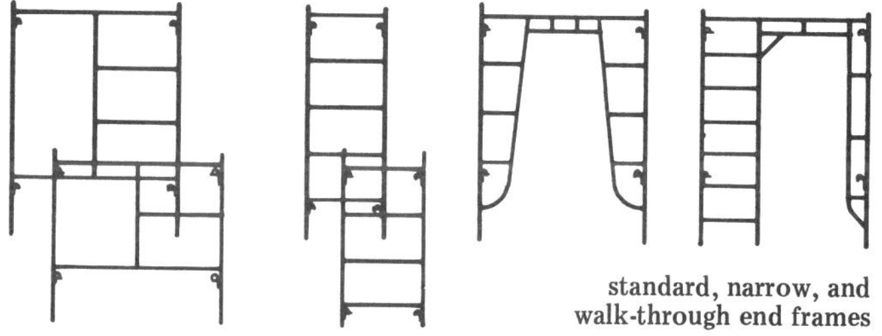

standard, narrow, and walk-through end frames

SOME NEWER scaffolding frames have an integral ladder -- convenient, but hard to climb because it's plumb vertical. You can rent an access ladder to tie to the scaffolding. Most people find a ladder easier and safer to climb than the widely-spaced rungs of the scaffold itself.

Parts & Accessories

INSPECT ALL THE COMPONENTS carefully when the crew arrives with the scaffolding. Make sure all locking devices work properly. Inspect the welds for failure. Reject badly rusted or bent metal parts. Also reject planks with warps, splits, or unsound knots.

WHETHER YOU'RE experienced enough to set up your own scaffold or just checking the crew's work, here are some important flags:

● Wooden 'mud' sills are used to support scaffolding on soft ground. The scaffold legs should have base plates which must be securely fastened to the sills. DO NOT allow the use of swivel bases to correct major out-of-level conditions. Don't allow support "sandwiches" of concrete block, boards, and shims.

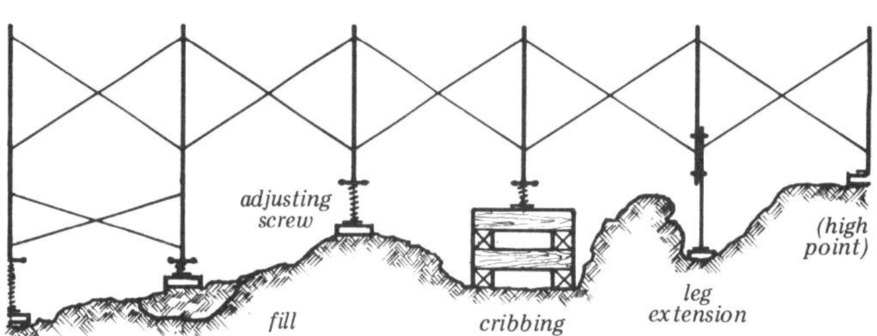

Ways To Level Scaffolding

● Each leg also has an adjustable screw jack, necessary for keeping the whole scaffold plumb and level. After each tier of scaffolding is assembled, the crew should check the assembly for plumb (in both directions) and level, and correct discrepancies before moving on to the next tier. Out-of-plumb or out-of-level scaffolding is subject to uneven loading and instability -- the higher the scaffold, the more dangerous this is.

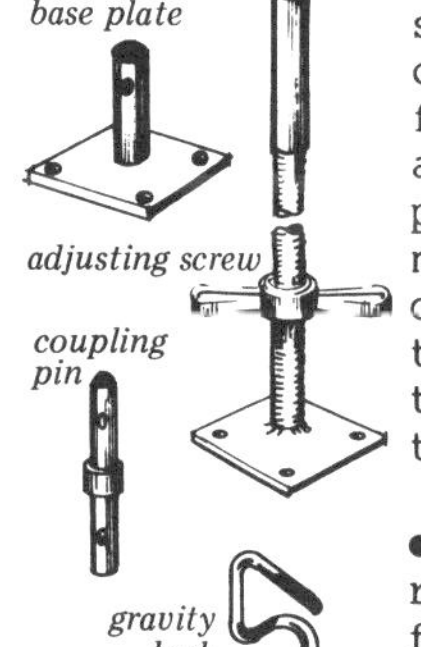

● Although many codes don't require that the scaffolding frames be locked together vertically, and the rental company may tell you "nobody uses uplift pins," THEY ARE NOT OPTIONAL. ALWAYS INSIST THAT UPLIFT PINS (locking pins) BE USED. You never know when or why you might have an unexpected need for protection against uplift: uneven loading on the platform, wind ....

● Guard rails, midrails, toeboards, screening, and all other safety features required by local codes or useful on your job must be installed on every work platform. They are <u>not</u> optional. You may be told that some accessories aren't used. Take it upon yourself to find out what the accessories are for, then insist on them.

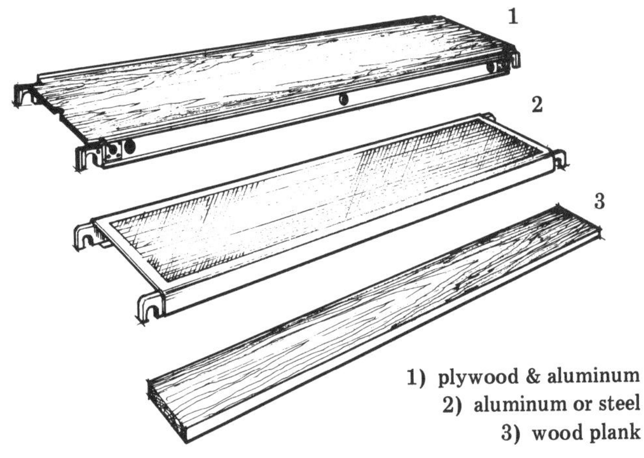

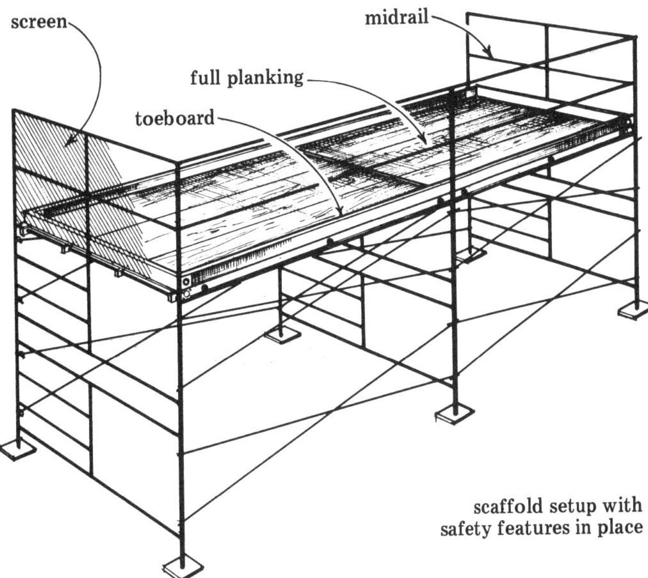

scaffold setup with
safety features in place

● Some setups require additional parts. Side
or end brackets (called "bicycles") extend the
work platforms; novices shouldn't work on ex-
tended scaffolding more than ten feet high.
Hoists safely lift materials to the platform;
working with a hoist from heights is tricky
and requires experience. Bridges (called
"putlogs") are used for reaching over obstructions or projections; experienced crews should
set these up.

WE RECOMMEND the use of prefabricated flooring
made especially for scaffolding. There are
many types -- some wood, some metal, some
combinations of the two -- all of which have
locking devices that fasten securely to the
scaffolding frames. Prefabricated flooring
systems are generally stronger, lighter, and
easier to walk on than are plain wood planks.
Use flooring made by the same manufacturer as
the scaffolding.

IF YOU CAN'T GET prefabricated flooring, be
sure your scaffold is floored with only scaf-
fold-grade planks, lapped and secured to the
scaffold with #9 wire. (See OSHA specs.)

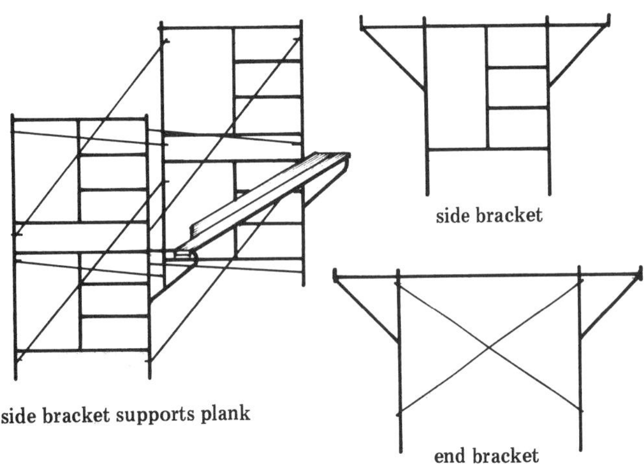

side bracket supports plank

Anchoring To An Old Building

WHEN THE SCAFFOLD reaches a height four
times its minimum base dimension (20 ft.
if you're using standard 5-ft. deep
scaffolding), the scaffolding must be anchored
to the building or braced to the ground. If
you're going forty feet up or more, the scaffold must be secured to the building again at
the 40-ft. level, and at 20-ft. increments
thereafter. (These numbers are just
guidelines; refer to local codes or the OSHA
standards.) Again: Novices should not work at
heights above 20 or 25 feet.

SOME COMMON ANCHORING METHODS are hard on old
buildings; some downright destructive. Old-
house owners should be aware of alternatives
that can avoid damage to the building.

● Be sure each working platform is fully
"floored" without gaps in the planking. If
you'll need to work
at several levels
simultaneously, you
would find cross-
bracing would be in
the way. For cases
like this, use strad-
dle braces.

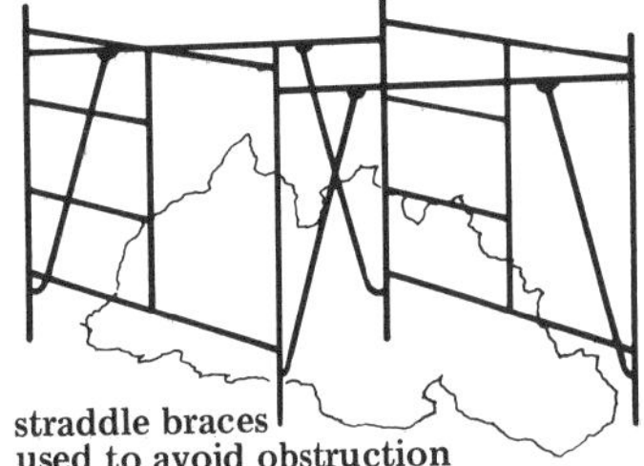

straddle braces
used to avoid obstruction

ABOUT PLANKING: It's
not as easy as it
used to be to get
good scaffolding planks. According to the
Scaffold Industry Association Newsletter:
"Lumber grading authorities project a declin-
ing supply of lumber...for scaffold grade
planks. This means (you) must be more vigi-
lant in culling out bad planks."

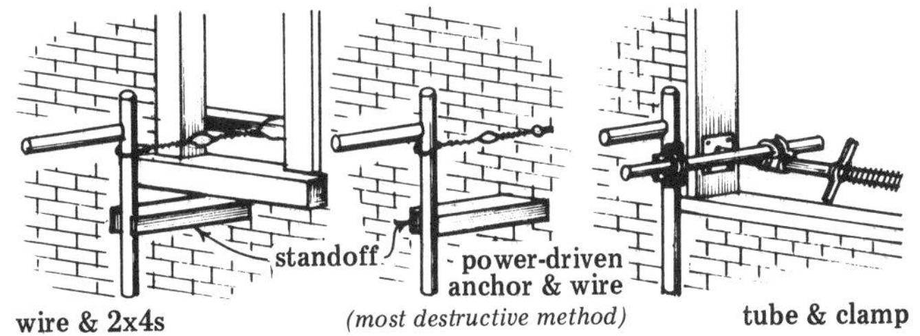

THE EASIEST and least destructive way to tie
scaffolding to the house is through window
openings, with the tube-and-clamp technique or
with wire and 2x4s. But the house may not
have enough conveniently located windows to
allow enough anchor points.

IF IT'S A FRAME HOUSE, the crew can drill
through the siding and anchor the scaffolding
to wooden framing members with screw eyes.
Later, holes can be filled with dowels (glued
in place with waterproof glue) and painted.

IF IT'S A BRICK OR STONE HOUSE, though, it's
difficult to make invisible patches in the
bricks or stones. So drill holes in the
mortar joints, install stainless steel sinkers, and use the sinkers as anchor points.
When the job is over, point over the sinkers
with matching mortar. (Beware that soft lime
mortar may not adequately hold anchors.)

IF YOU'RE DEALING with a stucco house (where
installing sinkers would cause great chunks of
stucco to fall off), or a museum house (where
even minimal damage is taboo), you won't be

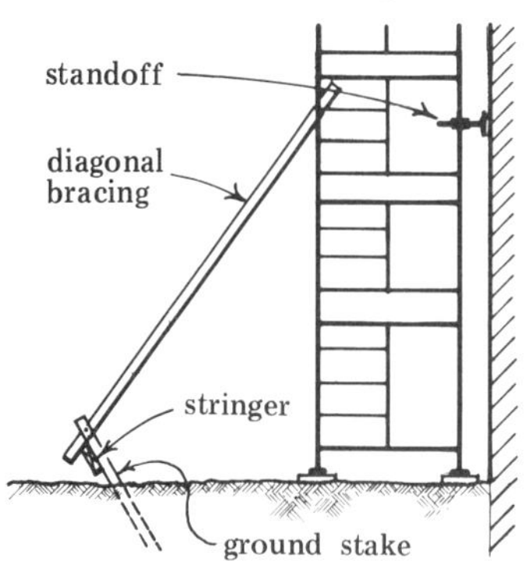

able to anchor scaf-
folding to the house
at all. In such
cases, the scaffold
can be braced.

YOU CAN'T build scaf-
folding more than
four times as high as
it is wide without
anchoring it, and
here you can't anchor
the scaffolding to
the building, so your
only choice is to
make the base wider.
Diagonal braces are used to effectively widen
the base. The surest way to brace is to sink
multiple stakes into the ground, tying them
together with wood stringers and anchoring the
scaffold to the stringers.

IF THE SCAFFOLD is secured using any of these
slightly unusual methods, pay very close
attention to the condition of the anchoring
system when you make your daily check.

A Daily Checklist

NOW THE SCAFFOLD has been erected -- either
by you, because you're much more experienced than this article could have made
you, or by a scaffold crew. Every day, check
the following things before you climb:

● The sill under each scaffolding leg must be
in place and level. Washouts from overnight
rain, or overloading, can cause sills to become unstable.
● All base plates and adjustment screws must
be in firm contact with their supports, and
the whole assembly must be snug.
● Frames must be plumb in both directions.
● If there is a gap between the lower end of
one frame and the upper end of another frame,
adjust the leveling feet to bring the frames
in contact. If that doesn't cure the
misalignment, the frame is out of square and
should be replaced.
● All cross-braces frame-to-frame along the
run must be secure.
● All locking devices must be secure, including clamps or wire ties for planks.
● All ties between the scaffolding and the
building (or all angle braces between the

scaffolding and the ground) must be secure.
● Safety equipment such as guard rails,
midrails, and toeboards must be in place.
● Access ladders must be securely fastened to
the scaffolding frames. Check out the locking
devices before you climb.

Working Safely From A Scaffold

CLIMB ONLY on the integral ladder or
securely fastened access ladders. Don't
climb on the braces, which were not
designed to bear a person's weight. (Besides,
it's easy to fall off them.) Don't hang outside the scaffolding frames. Wear a hard hat
-- not just to protect you from falling objects, but even more to keep you from bumping
your head on the unfamiliar protuberances of a
scaffold.

PAY SPECIAL ATTENTION to housekeeping on the
work platform. Accidents happen when people
slip or stumble. Common offenders are tools
laid on the scaffolding floor, spills, and
electrical cords. Keep the platforms clear at
all times. At the end of every day, clear
debris away from the scaffold base.

HAVE A WORKBENCH on the platform to keep tools
off the floor. Tools belong on the bench, in
your hands, or in a tool apron. If you spill
something, wipe it up immediately and cover
the residue with a non-slip surface if need
be. Keep electrical cords out of the way by
duct-taping them to the midrails or, if absolutely necessary, to the flooring.

DON'T USE THE SCAFFOLDING when wet or icy
conditions exist. Rain, dew, and ice make
ladders and planks slippery. At _all_ times,
wear non-skid shoes.

NEVER SET planks, ladders, or any kind of
extension on the guard rails to use them for
greater reach. This is just plain stupid, but
we've seen it done.

BURGLARS MAY BE delighted by the easy access
to windows you've provided. And don't forget
that a metal scaffold looks like a big jungle
gym to kids. Make the scaffold less attractive by removing lower floor planks at the end
of the day.

If you plan to erect or work from scaffolding, we urge you to read the
following publications first:

Guide To Scaffolding Erection & Dismantling Procedures (S101), $.50
Recommended Steel-Frame Shoring Erection Procedure (SH 304), $.50
Scaffolding Safety Rules (S 100), $.25
Steel-Frame Shoring Safety Rules (SH 300), $.25
Slide shows also available; free publications brochure.
Scaffolding, Shoring, & Forming Institute, Inc., 1230 Keith Building,
Cleveland, OH 44115. (216) 241-7333.

A Guide To Waco Scaffolding, $1.00 (an excellent 23-page booklet that
describes this firm's equipment but applies to others as well).
Waco International, Inc., 7575 Dillon Street, Houston, TX 77061.
(713) 641-6558.

Membership Directory & Handbook, $55.00 (includes just about every-
thing on scaffolding, including standards, definitions, illustrations,
OSHA standards, etc. — for $85.00, you can join the Association and
receive the SIA Newsletter).
Scaffold Industry Association, 14039 Sherman Way, Van Nuys, CA
91405. (818) 782-2012.

First: Commit Mildew Murder

I HAVE A PROBLEM with a bathroom in my 1905 house: The paint on the ceiling is starting to crack terribly and mildew is all over. I've tried to remove the mildew, but nothing works -- it keeps coming back. I tried to paint and wallpaper, but they both peel right off. Nothing stays up!

WHAT can I do about the peeling paint and the mildew, and what coverings can I use on the walls and ceilings?

--Sondra Babcock Oak Park, Ill.

THE PROBLEMS you describe are sure signs that there is too much water vapor in the bathroom.

EXCESSIVE water vapor (mostly from showers, which weren't common in 1905) allows mildew to grow, and causes paint and wallpaper to peel. The simplest solution: Crack a window during and after showers. The best solution: Install an exhaust fan sized for the room.

YOU CAN KILL the mildew with Clorox, or a commercial mildewcide. You have to kill mildew before you repaint or hang wallpaper; if you don't, the mildew will continue to grow through the new paint or paper. Re-paint with a high-gloss mildew-resistant paint, or re-paper with mildew-resistant wallpaper.

Removing Sap From A Terne Roof

MY HOUSE has a terne roof that has been stained black in places by sap from over-hanging pecan trees. I need to repaint the roof, and I've tried to clean the sap off with TSP and other soap-type cleaners, to no avail. Any ideas on how to get the sap off?

--P.J. Breitling Trenton, Ill.

FIRST, try scrubbing the sap off using turpentine or mineral spirits as a solvent. They're flammable, so don't use steel wool or a wire brush (or anything that could make sparks) for a scrubber -- use old towels.

IF THAT doesn't work, try a strong alkaline cleaner like those used to clean masonry buildings. ProSoCo's T-534 and T-547 (available through ProSoCo distributors) are two such cleaners.

IF THE SAP stands up to all this, you'll have to use a chemical paint stripper. (This will, of course, attack the existing paint.) Thoroughly rinse off the paint remover residue, dry the metal roof surface, and prime bare areas immediately. If you leave bare terne exposed overnight, it could rust.

Gutters For A Circular Roof

MY QUEEN ANNE house has a circular front porch. If the porch roof ever had gutters, they are gone now. Water from the roof collects at the base of the porch and is causing the lattice to rot. I'm having trouble finding a contractor to install new gutters. Can't anybody install gutters on a circular roof anymore?

--Tony Restino Springfield, Mass.

A GOOD sheet-metal contractor -- not a "roof-and-gutter man" who works only with pre-fab vinyl and aluminum -- will be able to make a new gutter system for your porch. Insist on gutters formed out of copper, terne-coated stainless steel (TCS), or galvanized steel, with soldered (not caulked) joints.

MAKE SURE the perimeter of the porch roof (soffit, fascia, rafter ends) is free from rot and properly painted before the new gutters are installed.

Where's The Linoleum?

DOES ANYONE still make linoleum rugs -- not wall-to-wall vinyl, but real enough linoleum rugs which were common in the '30s?

--Anne Kenney Wichita, Kansas

YOU'RE IN LUCK. You can still get linoleum rugs from (where else?) Linoleum City, 5657 Santa Monica Blvd., Hollywood, California, 90038.

THIS COMPANY and over 1300 companies that offer hard-to-find products and services for old houses is listed (where else?) in the OHJ Catalog. (See the facing page -- please -- for further enlightenment.)

General interest questions from subscribers will be answered in print. The Editors can't promise to reply to all questions personally—but we try. Send your questions with sketches or photos to Questions Editor, The Old-House Journal, 69A Seventh Avenue, Brooklyn, NY 11217.

If Only I'd Read Those Pages...

by Walter Jowers

LONG BEFORE I became a contributing editor, I was a loyal OHJ subscriber. Each issue would wind up a dog-eared wreck, because I'd always refer to it in all my own restoration work. I'd read The Old-House Journal from cover to cover ... sort of. I'd just skip those last few pages in the back (and go right to "Remuddling"!). After all, there was work to do. Life's too short to read ad pages.

THEN LAST YEAR, when I left Nashville and came to work at OHJ, I walked into a lot of office hubbub I didn't understand. There was a special telephone marked "Catalog Hot Line," and it rang all the time. Only certain people (Catalog Editors) were allowed to answer that phone, and one of them had to be near the phone at all times. Company rule.

EVERY NOW AND THEN, a Catalog Editor would jump up and yell something like, "Somebody still makes busybodies!" Or, "A new company is making Arts and Crafts furniture!" After witnessing a few of these outbursts, I decided to get to the bottom of this Catalog business. I asked the Chief Catalog Editor, "Are you thinking about publishing some sort of directory of arcane old-house goods and services?"

THIS put the Chief Catalog Editor into a snit that she's not over yet. "We've been publishing The Catalog for TEN YEARS! Where have you been, Mister How-to from Tennessee? Where-to-find-it is just as important as how-to-do-it." "Well, pardon me all to pieces," I said. "Why don't you ever advertise the thing?"

THAT put the Production Editor into a snit that he's not over yet. "We advertise it in every issue. Big ads. In the back of the Journal. Didn't you even see the one with the elephants? I designed that one myself." He produced a Catalog ad and read: "Whether your house was built in 1730 or 1930, you've undoubtedly encountered sales clerks who insist, 'they don't make that anymore.'" Then the Chief Catalog Editor and the Production Editor spoke in unison, like a Greek Chorus: "Well, they DO still make thousands of authentic products and services for the sensitive rehabilitation of old houses."

THEY WENT ON to tell me the salient facts: The Catalog has grown from a listing of fewer than 50 restoration-oriented companies into a 200-plus-page book, listing over 1300 companies -- companies that provide products and services to a demanding restoration market. Our Catalog includes sources from all across the country. Its Company Directory tells you the full address, phone number, and what literature is available at what price.

SO I LOOKED at a copy of the Catalog. And the more I looked, the more I found in it:
● A meticulously crafted index (so you can find anything, whether you know the right name for it or not)

● Good-looking product displays from listed companies (some in full color!)
● Listings for small and large companies (some of which have been around long enough to have made <u>original</u> old-house parts) -- not only sources for reproductions, but also antique warehouses and old-house services.

EACH COMPANY gets listed by product or service; by company name; and by city and state. And they're high-quality companies -- <u>not</u> importers of tacky brass hardware and colonial paper-towel holders. No aluminum siding either. <u>Good stuff!</u> People who make full-size porch posts (saving you from the scourge of modern wrought iron). People who'll put a bent-shingle roof on your house....

"I COULD HAVE USED THIS BOOK when I was restoring my Bungalow," I said. "I must have spent a few hundred dollars on phone calls searching for just the right this or that." "We did our part," the Chief Catalog Editor said. "We've spent thousands of hours and dollars tracking down all these companies and checking to make sure their products and services are of the highest quality."

A historic moment: Walter Jowers discovers the OHJ Catalog.

AS MY PUNISHMENT for not knowing about the Catalog, I was assigned to answer all the mail from OHJ readers who want to know where to buy hard-to-find things. I'm tied to my desk, telling people where to find fancy faucets, library ladders, hoosier hardware.... The volume of mail is tremendous, and that's because an awful lot of you don't know about the Catalog, either. I can't answer the same where-to questions day in and day out, meet deadlines, <u>and</u> learn to live in New York. I could crack under the strain.

IF YOU NEED SOMETHING for your old house, from adzes to wrought iron, look in the Catalog. Everything we know about where-to-find-it is in there. If you don't have a Catalog, buy one. It's cheap -- only $10.95 to subscribers ($13.95 to Outsiders -- still a bargain). Just check the box on the Order Form, or send a check to The Old-House Journal Catalog, 69A Seventh Avenue, Brooklyn, NY 11217. And be sure to read our ad pages in future issues. Don't make my sad mistake, and discover an invaluable resource after it's (sob) too late. 🏛

Awnings cont'd from p. 115

FABRIC SHELTER was common as far back as ancient Rome; awnings probably evolved from Mediterranean and Middle-Eastern countries, where tents and canopies were traditionally used for shelter from the hot, sunny climate. (To this day, awnings enjoy a greater popularity in southern European countries than they do here.)

THE AMERICAN ROMANCE with awnings began in earnest during the 1890s. Soon there was hardly a town of any size without at least one local awning fabricator. The awning-maker worked with traditional canvas, which is a heavy, woven material usually made of cotton. The early canvas awnings were most often painted, in either solid bright colors or stripes. Occasionally the undersides would be painted with a floral pattern, to add visual interest for anyone looking out the window.

AWNINGS ARE MOST APPROPRIATE for late- and post-Victorian house styles -- especially Queen Anne, Colonial Revival, Bungalow, Spanish, and the many Period-Revival styles. They were most commonly featured on porches, but a house with all its windows and doors sheltered by awnings was certainly no rarity. And as any old photograph demonstrates, the quintessential American downtown "Main Street" had both sidewalks covered by a nearly continuous canopy of storefront awnings. They served not only as shelter for window shoppers, but also as a natural place for advertising. Seaside resorts, shuttered-up ghost towns in the off-season, sprang to life in the summer; one of the first signs of activity was the putting up of the porch awnings that added to the colorful and festive atmosphere of the resorts.

AFTER WORLD WAR TWO, fabric awnings fell from favor, replaced by aluminum awnings. These were more permanent and featured movable louvers that allowed the summer breezes to pass through the house. Metal awnings can imitate fabric awnings in shape and color, but they can't provide the romantic appeal of canvas awnings; they're also inappropriate for anything other than post-war homes.

BOTH CANVAS AND METAL AWNINGS have largely disappeared from houses during the past 30 years, due to the popularity of air-conditioning and the corresponding decline in the use of porches as living spaces. Of course, awnings are still widely used on commercial buildings, where their sheltering and advertising functions are as important as ever. And there are still pockets of resistance where awnings remain common, particularly in sunny Florida and California.

The Advantages Of Awnings

● COOLING -- Window and porch awnings shade the sun's rays, and keep the house from getting uncomfortably hot in the summer. Effectively placed awnings allow you to keep the windows open while reducing, by up to 75%, the heat gain from direct sunlight. Awnings are seven times more effective at reducing heat gain than window shades or other inside devices.

● ENERGY-SAVINGS -- According to the National Bureau of Standards, even if you air-condition your home, awnings can give a 10- to 15-degree cooling effect. And that can reduce up to 25% the cost of running your air-conditioner. You can increase the efficiency of window-mounted air-conditioners by keeping them in the cooling shade of awnings. (Warning: Keep awnings at least 10 inches from window units.)

● WEATHER PROTECTION -- Awnings mounted over entries provide shelter from the rain.

● REDUCTION OF GLARE AND SUNLIGHT -- Awnings protect interior fabrics, paintings, carpets, and drapes from fading.

● COVER-UPS -- Some unsympathetic alterations to old houses, especially modern window replacements, can be partially disguised or subdued by a sheltering awning.

● AESTHETICS -- Colorful awnings can add to or complement the architectural character of an old house. They add character to even plain, unstylish older homes. A dark, drab house can be brought to life by bright striped awnings. The many interesting awning shapes available can soften severe wall planes.

In this glimpse of 1917 Chicago, storefront awnings are a natural part of the streetscape.

Awning Types

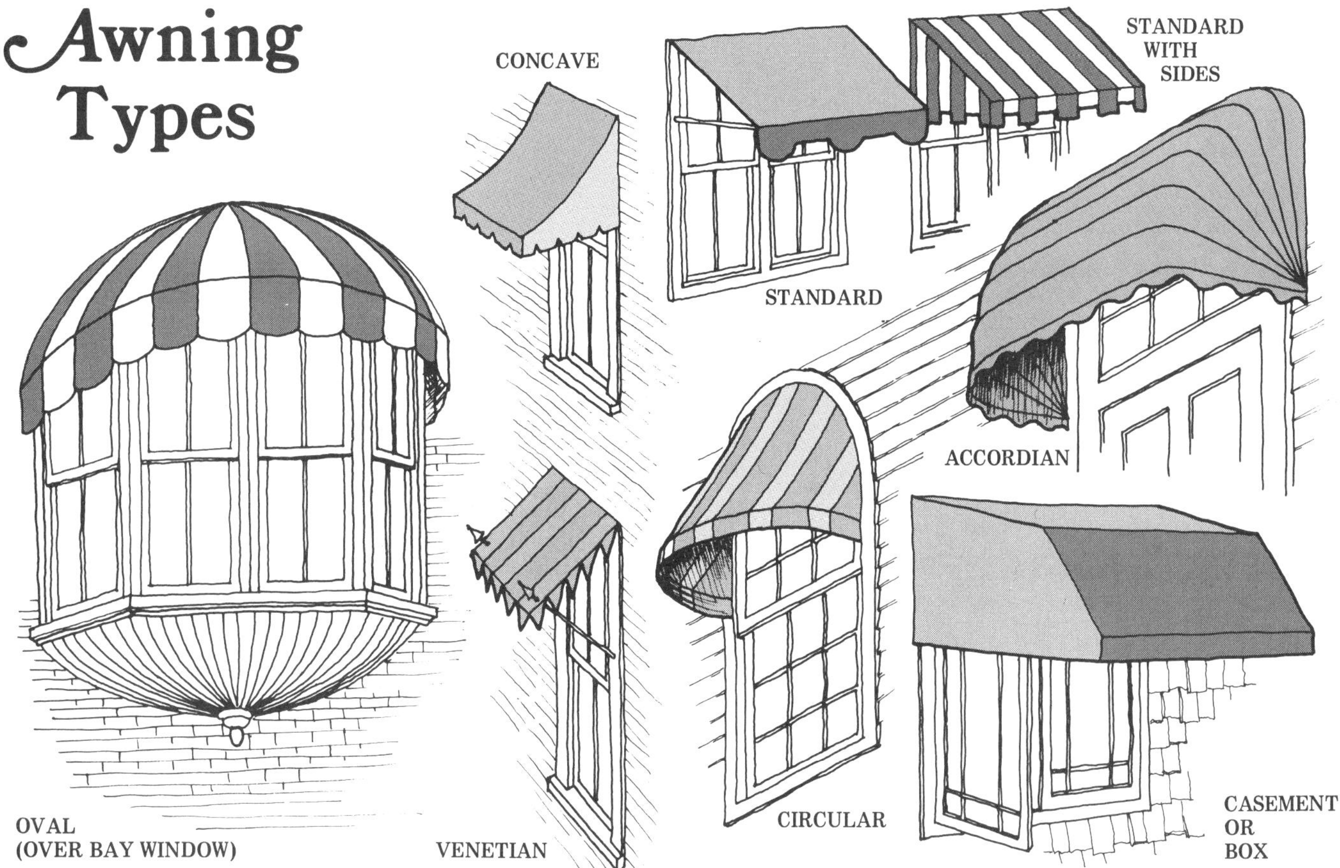

BUT THERE ARE DISADVANTAGES to awnings. They aren't particularly inexpensive, and you'll have to put in some maintenance to protect your investment. Furthermore, all awning fabrics will eventually deteriorate, and their colors fade. Modern fabrics last longer, but expect to replace them every six to twelve years.

What's Available

IF YOU KNOW AWNINGS only from earlier times, you'll be pleasantly surprised by the array of fabrics, finishes, and hardware available today. These advances often come out of Europe, where they remain years ahead of America in "awning technology." Many fabrics are only for specialized commercial applications. For homes, there are really only three to consider (although they go by many trade names):

1) CANVAS -- This, the traditional material, is the least expensive. It's also the short-est-lived, generally surviving about three to seven years. It's available with a painted surface in a wide variety of colors and stripes. (The paint colors will fade in a number of years.)

2) VINYL-COATED CANVAS -- It costs 10 to 20% more than painted canvas, but should last from seven to ten years. In addition, the vinyl coating comes in many colors, is easily wash-able, and has better sun-darkening properties. However, the vinyl gives a hard, shiny finish, and so is used mostly for commercial purposes.

3) ACRYLIC -- This is probably the best bet for old-house owners. Acrylic awnings are about as expensive as vinyl-coated canvas, but they last from seven to twelve years. Because the threads are dyed before the fabric is woven, acrylic is highly fade-resistant. It's available in many colors and striped patterns, and has a non-shiny, natural-looking finish that's equally attractive on both sides of the fabric. These materials often go by their trade names, such as Sunbrella, Sunflair, or Argonaut (see list of suppliers, page 139). Because acrylics are generally not painted or coated, they 'breathe' easily and last longer.

Shapes & Types

AWNINGS are available in many shapes; the most traditional ones are shown in the illustrations. The standard, straight-topped type can be used for most window and porch applications. You might want to add side panels (also called "drops"), which shield against angled sunlight. Other options include the various decorative-edged valances, which were common in early awnings and add architectural interest.

A CASEMENT OR "BOX" AWNING will be necessary if you have casement windows; the Venetian type is particularly appropriate for Spanish- and Mediterranean-style houses of the 1920s and '30s. If you have arched windows or an arcaded porch, consider using circular-headed awnings. It's possible to put a straight-topped awning over arched openings, but that would destroy the original intent of the

Circular awnings emphasize the arcaded porch on this 1930s Spanish Bungalow.

SOME AWNINGS are fixed; that is, they don't fold up. Fixed awnings include the Venetian, circular, and accordion types, as well as large patio canopies.

house's architecture. Accordion awnings, popular in Europe, can add an elegant look, particularly over doors, but they're more expensive. So are the other complex shapes such as convex, concave, and oval.

THE OLD-FASHIONED AWNING MECHANISM has the side bars of the awning hinged near where they are attached to the structure. By pulling on a cord connected to the front transverse bar, you can raise the awning up against the house. The cord is tied off on a cleat that's mounted near the window. This is the simplest mechanism, and still the most popular. Its one drawback is that it requires more maintenance, because the raised awning may hang in unsightly folds that collect rainwater and debris.

THE EUROPEAN-TYPE retractable awning is fairly new to this country. The two arms supporting the awning are hinged at the middle, like elbows, and can retract flat against the house as the awning itself rolls up. It operates by a hand crank or electric motor, which can even be controlled by automatic photo-electric and wind-sensitive devices. The retractable awning has no need for side braces, and therefore has a very 'clean' appearance, which may be too modern and streamlined for old houses. It can also be very expensive, running over $1,000 for large patio or porch awnings.

Colors & Designs

MOST AWNING FABRICS are available in a large range of colors. It's best to choose a color that complements your house, rather than one that exactly matches it. Blues, reds, browns, greens, and tan were common awning colors. Consider your selection in the same way you'd consider a trim color.

HISTORICALLY, striped awnings were usually white alternated with primary colors. This was very popular, and still is: A red-&-white-striped awning looks great on a brick house with white trim. As a general rule, striped awnings are best on more informal houses, like Bungalows, Queen Annes, or Spanish Revivals; for Colonial Revivals, solid colors are preferred because they don't 'complicate' the more formal and restrained lines. Fringe or decorative borders (which are painted or

Simple, solid-color porch awnings work well with the restrained lines of this Florida Post-Victorian house.

appliqued on) along the valance edges are also historically correct and still available today.

Where To Get Them

DO-IT-YOURSELF KITS are available (see sources list, page 129). They can save you considerable cost, but have a major drawback: They're available only in certain incremental width and depth sizes. Awnings should generally be mounted <u>within</u> the window opening,

Traditional Valance Designs

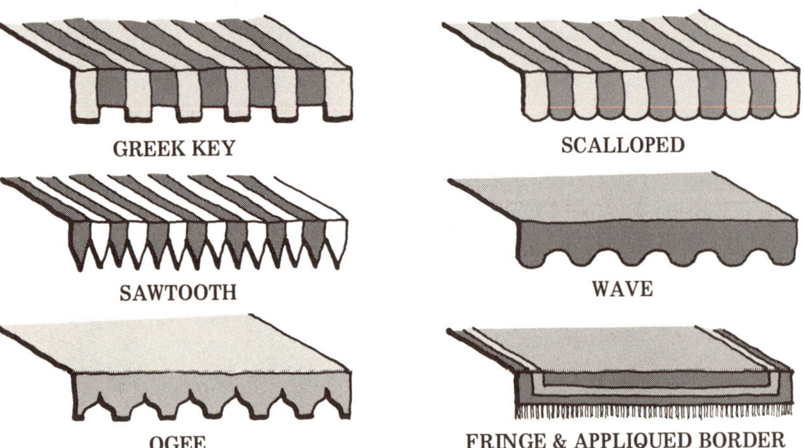

Awning Sources

European-type Retractable Awnings by Brand Name
(available from local awning dealers):

Solair — available in four projection sizes in 8- to 20-ft. widths.
Astrup, Dept. OHJ, 2937 W. 25 St., Cleveland, OH 44113.

Sunesta — five projection sizes; widths 7 ft. and up.
Canvas Products, Dept. OHJ, P.O. Box 3235, Jacksonville, FL 32206.

Sun-Tamer — widths 6 to 40 ft., prices $600 to $1300.
Levolor Lorentzen, Dept. OHJ, 1280 Wall Street, Lyndhurst, NJ 07071.

Sunvisor — a do-it-yourself retractable, available in 3 widths.
Architectural Concepts, Dept. OHJ, 3 Westchester Plaza, Elmsford, NY 10523.

Do-It-Yourself Patio Canopy Kits:

Fiesta Patio Canopy — choice of 56 colors and stripes; up to 25 ft. wide and 12-ft. projections.
Anchor Industries, Dept. OHJ, 1100 Burch Dr., P.O. Box 3477, Evansville, IN 47733.

Awning Dealers:

All American Awning Company, Dept. OHJ, 89 E. Lancaster Avenue, Paoli, PA 19301.

Astrup (see above listing; they also have many regional dealers).

Atlas Awning Company, Dept. OHJ, 38 12th St., Ronkonkoma, NY 11779.

Bronx Window Shade & Awning Company, Dept. OHJ, 372 E. 162 Street, Bronx, NY 10451.

Major Acrylic Fabric Tradenames:

Cabana Cloth — by Graniteville Mills, through Astrup dealers.

Sunbrella — by Glen Raven Mills, through Anchor Industries dealers.

Sunflair — through Canvas Products of Jacksonville.

Awning Supplies:

An automatic stitching awl (with self-feeding thread in the handle), perfect for awning repairs, is available for about $5 from **U.S. General Supply Corporation**, Dept. OHJ, 100 Commercial Street, Plainview, NY 11803.

For temporary repairs of rips, use nylon adhesive ripstop spinnaker tape from **E & B Discount Marine**, Dept. OHJ, 980 Gladys Court, Edison, NJ 08818.

For cleaning synthetic fabrics, use Sailbath, a liquid concentrate used with warm water; also available from **E & B Marine**.

directly on the frame; it can be hard to find a ready-made awning for the sometimes odd sizes of old windows and doors.

MOST AWNINGS are still custom made by local awning dealers, who fabricate them from fabrics and hardware manufactured by major suppliers. Most local awning-makers do mainly commercial work, but should accommodate your needs as an old-home owner. Ask to see swatch samples of the fabric, and check the warranties of both the fabric manufacturer and local installers.

WHERE DO YOU PUT THE AWNINGS? The most common place is on porches and sunrooms. Fixed patio canopies (ranging from $1,200 to $1,700) are also popular. Even though this is a less traditional use for old homes, a patio canopy can be quite compatible.

IF YOU CAN AFFORD IT (a standard window awning should run $60 to $120), awnings on all the major window openings will look more appropriate than just a few. If expense is a consideration, the south, sun-facing elevation is the logical choice for selective placement.

THE AWNING FRAMEWORK should be attached just inside the window opening, on the window frame. If this isn't possible, attach it just outside the opening. On brick houses, always make attachments in the mortar joints, not in the brick itself. Set screws in silicone caulk to prevent moisture infiltration.

Traditional red-and-white-striped awnings look great on both wood houses and brick houses.

Maintenance

YOU'LL HAVE considerable investment in your awnings, so it makes sense to give them routine, year-to-year preventive maintenance.

● CLEANING: Follow the fabric manufacturer's directions. A hosing down or a gentle scrubbing with a soft-bristle brush will usually do the trick. Do not use harsh detergents;

common soap can be used if
necessary. Bird droppings,
soot, industrial contaminants,
and organic "droppings" (like
mulberries) should be cleaned
off regularly.

● DRYING: Moisture can cause
mildew, so don't let rainwater
or snow stand in the folds of
furled awnings; lower them so
they can dry out after wind
and hail storms. Chronic
standing-water problems can be
corrected by installing stra-
tegically placed grommets for
drainage.

● STORAGE: You'll greatly pro-
long the life of your awnings
by removing and storing them
in the off-season. Keep them
in a dry, well-ventilated place, away from
sunlight. If the awnings are retractable but
not removable, they should retract into protective, shedlike housings designed to repel
water and snow.

● HARDWARE & FRAMES: Rust causes fabric to
deteriorate rapidly, so inspect the hardware
for corrosion at the beginning of each season.
(Most modern frames are made of aluminum or
anodized steel, which eliminates this problem.) Clean out any winter debris from the
mechanisms, and lubricate according to the
manufacturer's directions.

● ORGANIC MATTER: Keep trees and shrubbery
away from awnings -- sap, berries, and bird
droppings can be especially damaging. Organic
stains can sometimes be cleaned with benzene,
but spot-test first.

● REPAIRS: Small rips or tears can be fixed by
gluing or sewing small patches over the damage
on both sides of the awning. Allow three to
four inches overlap around larger tears.
(It's a good idea to purchase a yard or more
of extra fabric when you buy the awnings.)
Sewing repairs can be done with heavy canvas-
upholstery needles, either straight or curved;
thread from your canvas dealer; and a protective leather sewing palm.

Awning Mechanisms

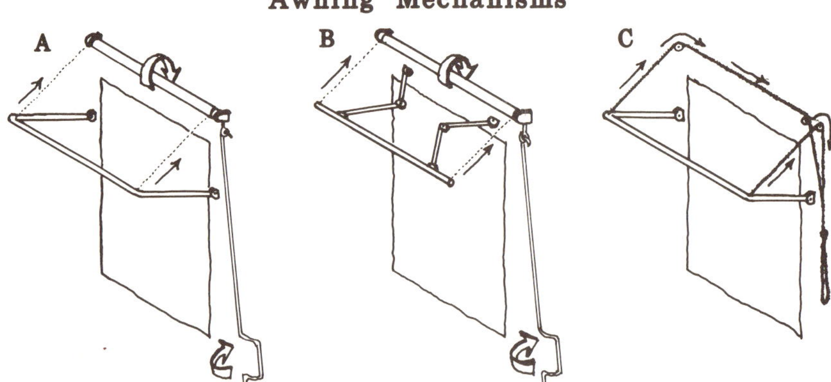

Awning A is rolled up by a hand crank; awning B, with retractable hinged arms, is also operated by a crank. Awning C is raised by a cord attached to the front transverse bar.

On this Florida Spanish Colonial Revival, the awnings have appliqued borders that emphasize their Greek-key valance design.

Informal Furniture—most for outdoors, some appropriate inside

High Victorian Wicker

We're proud to announce that really high-quality, high-style Victorian wicker furniture is once again being made in this country. Dissatisfied with the quality & styles of wicker furniture available from abroad, Classic Wicker of Los Angeles, California, decided to make their own. Currently with a crew of 20 crafts-people, Classic Wicker is turning out an elegant array of intricately woven and beautifully styled wicker rockers, plant stands, settees, lounges, chairs, tables, and more. This furniture would turn any porch into an elegant outdoor living room (in fact, it's elegant enough for the parlor).

Our favorite pieces are the Granada rocker ($460) & Comfort chaise lounge ($925), which are dead ringers for turn-of-century originals. The prices aren't cheap — but neither is the quality and craftsmanship. (The rocker requires up to 28 hours to construct.) You can expect wicker furniture of this quality to last and become a family heirloom. All of the furniture is made with solid wood frames and tightly woven wicker, finished in polyurethane. Available finishes include natural, antique brown, & white (designer colors cost an additional 5%).

Prices are FOB Los Angeles. OHJ Scoop: Although not in their product line yet, Classic Wicker will make a turn-of-century porch swing — all they need is an order. Send $2.50 for a brochure and price list to **Classic Wicker, Dept. OHJ, 8532 Melrose Avenue, Los Angeles, CA 90069. (213) 659-1121.**

Redwood Porch Swing

Here's a Craftsman-inspired porch swing that really looks comfortable. Constructed out of heavy redwood, the Alfresco has a deeply contoured seat & a generously sloping back. Finished with oil, the swing has level arms and is suspended from four points with 80 feet of sisal rope. It has bronze fasteners and can be assembled in ten minutes (the seat & back come fastened with dowels). The swing sells for $199 ppd. Alfresco also offers an Adirondack rustic chair for $89 ppd. For brochures call or write **Alfresco, Dept. OHJ, P.O. Box 1336, Durango, CO 81301. (303) 259-5743.**

Victorian Swing in Pine

Classic Architectural Specialties produces a porch swing with Victorian-style ornamentation, which might be just what your front porch needs. Made from white pine, the 4-ft.-long swing comes with chains and hardware, unfinished & unassembled (in four sections). It sells for $210 plus shipping. A 5-ft.-long version is available by special order; write for details. Send $2 for catalog to **Classic Architectural Specialties, Dept. OHJ, 5302 Junius St., Dallas, TX 75214. (214) 827-5111.**

Rustic Willow Furniture

For almost a century one Georgia family has practiced the craft of bending & carving willow branches into beautiful rustic furniture for gardens, porches, or indoors. The individual character of the shaped wood makes every piece a unique work of folk art. Held together mainly by the tension of bent branches, all the furniture is handmade — they even take measurements using the width of a hand. The only tools are a hammer, tree saw, and machete.

The furniture is available in two styles: the butterfly style, with a flat seat designed to use fitted cushions; the classic style, with a rounded seat that's comfortable with or without cushions. Our favorite pieces are the rocker ($275 plus shipping) & the 54-in.-long porch swing ($375 plus shipping). There's a wide variety of other pieces, including chairs, a fern stand, tables, children's furniture, a loveseat, wall basket, hutch, headboards, & even a bird house. Send $2 for a catalog to **American Folk Art, Dept. OHJ, 354 Kennesaw Avenue, Marietta, GA 30060. (404) 344-5985.**

The Brumby Rocker

The famous Brumby Jumbo Rocker, produced from 1875 until World War II in Marietta, Ga., is available once again as an exact reproduction. Using old Brumby equipment, each rocker is carefully formed from Appalachian red oak and "Blue Tie" cane. The rocker's large size, curved back, wide arms, and good balance all add to its comfort. They come in a natural lacquered finish or two stain colors for $455; white is $475 (shipping extra). A matching caned footstool is also available in rocking or stationary styles, priced from $265 to $275 plus shipping. Brumby rockers accompanied President Carter to the White House.

Also produced from prime aged red oak is the Melson Swing, a sturdy porch swing, that comes in 4-, 5-, and 6-ft. lengths. Mortise-and-tenon joints and posturized seats and backs provide a strong yet comfortable swing. The swings are complete with chains and hardware, and come in antique oak finish, white enamel, or unfinished. They range in price from $295 to $430 (shipping extra).

Send for a free brochure of these and other chairs & rockers from **The Rocker Shop of Marietta, Georgia, Dept. OHJ, 1421 White Circle, N.W., P.O. Box 12, Marietta, GA 30061. (404) 427-2618.**

Victorian Porch Swing

Green Enterprises produces a beautifully detailed oak porch swing with a cane seat. In fact, it looks almost too nice to leave out on the porch! It comes complete with scrollwork, turned pendants, and other Victorian decoration, in either white or hand-finished oak. The 4-ft. size sells for $275; 5-ft. size, $325 plus $15 shipping. For further information contact **Green Enterprises, Dept. OHJ, 43 South Rogers Street, Hamilton, VA 22068. (703) 338-3606.**

Classic Rope Hammock

The 'Original Pawleys Island Rope Hammock' was invented in the late 1800s on Pawleys Island, S.C., by Captain Josh Ward, a river boat pilot. For nearly a century the cool and comfortable cotton rope hammocks have been handknitted exactly the same way. Three sizes of hammocks are available. We suggest you get the large deluxe size; it holds two people comfortably and sells for about $114.95.

The hammocks come complete with hanging hardware and instructions. If there isn't enough space between trees or on your porch, a sturdy tubular steel stand is available. You should also consider purchasing one of their two hammock pillow designs, which snap into place. For the dealer nearest you, contact **Pawleys Island Hammock Co., Dept. OHJ, P.O. Box 308, Pawleys Island, SC 29585. (800) 845-0311.**

For information on 1300 OTHER companies, see the new edition of The Old-House Journal Catalog.

The Presidential Rocker

The Presidential Rocker sold by L.L. Bean is supposedly the only piece of furniture President Kennedy took with him from his Senate office to the White House. The angled, steam-bent back posts and the Malaysian rattan seat and back are designed to provide firm support and good posture, with natural "spring." The 4-in.-wide arm rests are set low and won't interfere with handwork or reading. The oak rocker comes assembled, finished in light walnut stain, and sells for $169 (call to verify), plus $16 shipping. For a free catalog contact **L.L. Bean, Dept. OHJ, 3210 Birch St., Freeport, ME 04033. (207) 865-3111.**

Courting Swing

William Fisher and a crew of local boat builders in Maine produce this high-quality porch swing of Honduras mahogany. The 4-ft.-wide swing is finished with no less than seven coats of white polyurethane marine paint; the mortise-&-tenon joints are shellacked for weatherability. Bronze fasteners are used throughout, and the swing is supported by Dacron line spliced in the best marine tradition. Part of the Estate line of garden furniture produced for Smith & Hawken, the swing sells for $680 plus $8 shipping, and comes assembled. For a free catalog write **Smith & Hawken, Dept. OHJ, 25 Corte Madera, Mill Valley, CA 94941. (415) 383-4050.**

WHO EVER HEARD OF WHITE OAK SHINGLES?

BY LARRY JONES

NESTLED just off Virginia's Blue Ridge Parkway atop a 2700-foot peak, surrounded by hardwood forests, is the Blue Ridge Shingle company. From this small mill, white oak shingles are available again -- and there's an interesting story behind it.

C.R. HARRIS, a former engineer, and his son Christian had restored an 18th-century log structure and opened the Shenandoah Longrifles Museum. Then, in the nearby town of Stanton, the Harrises discovered a delapidated shingle mill that had closed around the turn of the century. Even after securing the antique shingle-cutting machinery, it took the family another two years to restore it and set up a working shingle mill. With the exception of a modern power plant, carbide-tipped saw blade, and a few new safety features, the shingles are manufactured just as they were originally. Each shingle is finished, graded, and packed by hand.

TODAY, white oak shingles are pretty much a forgotten roofing material, but historically they were commonly available in the eastern, midwestern, and western states. It's still possible to spot 60- and 70-year-old, white-oak-shingled roofs in Pennsylvania, Maryland, Virginia, Missouri, Kansas, Colorado, and other states. Why, even George Washington, apparently impressed with the long life of white oak shingles, specified them for use on Mt. Vernon buildings.

IT'S UNCLEAR just why the shingles disappeared from the marketplace until now. Says Michael Contezac of the U.S. Forest Products Lab: "White oak was used extensively for shingles and shakes during the settlement of the Middle Western States, and the highly desirable characteristics of this species created so many other applications that its use for shingles became limited."

WARD HITCHINGS of the National Forest Products Association offers the following technical explanation for the durability of white oak shingles: "White oak is unique among wood species since the longitudinal vessels in it are occluded by membranes known as tyloses, which resist the penetration of moisture, rendering the wood resistant to decay. White oak has been used for a number of years in wood ship building, which tends to support its classification as a highly durable wood species." (Railroad ties, mine timbers, and whiskey barrels are also popular applications for this tough wood.)

WHITE OAK SHINGLES weather quickly to a distinctive dark, slate-like, grey color. The lifespan of these shingles, properly laid (applied over open sheathing), is considered greater than that of comparable red cedar shingles. Unlike red cedar, oak shingles do not split readily and have to be sawn to the desired width. The result is greater installation time but less waste.

THE SHINGLES come in 18-in. and 24-in. lengths; widths vary from 3 in. to 9-1/2 in. The best grade is number 1, Red Label, which is 100% heartwood, 100% edge grain, 100% clear, uniform taper and butt thickness. Also available are no. 2, Blue Label and no. 3, White Label grades. The Red Label, Butt Style, Colonial Williamsburg shingles sell for $162 per square (18 in.), or $174 per square (24 in.). Other varieties include Butt Style Williamsburg Chamfer or Williamsburg Round, Boston and Boston Ridge, Shenandoah Valley Ridge, and starter courses.

THE RECOMMENDED METHOD is to lay the shingles over 1x4 (or wider) sheathing, spaced with centers equal to the weather exposure at which the shingles are to be laid -- but never more than 10 in. As a general rule, 7-1/2 in. maximum exposure is recommended for 18-in. shingles and 10-in. maximum exposure for 24-in. shingles. The longest lasting wood-shingle roofs always have plenty of ventilation on the underside, and weather exposures less than 1/3 of the total shingle length (known as a 3-ply roof). A 4 in 12 is the minimum recommended roof pitch for these shingles.

THERE ARE PRICE BREAKS for quantities over 100 squares per order. To obtain complete information, including prices and application instructions, contact the Blue Ridge Shingle Company, Department OHJ, Montebello, VA 24464. (703) 377-6635.

Shingle cutting on a restored shingle-mill

SUBSCRIBERS Jackie and Steve Scarbrough sent us these photographs: "This house is in an old neighborhood in Knoxville, Tennessee. Most of the old Victorian homes are experiencing beautiful revivals. (My husband and I own a Victorian that we take great pride in.) My stomach turned when I came across this poor house, stripped of all its embellishment and character. Besides the obvious gross replacement of windows, and the substitute siding, where's the front porch? Where's the front door? Steps leading to a blank house."

The Old-House Journal®

69A Seventh Avenue,
Brooklyn, New York 11217

Postmaster: Address Correction Requested

Restoration and Maintenance Techniques
For The Pre-1939 House

August-September 1985 / Vol. XIII No. 7 / $2.

The Old-House Journal

Salvage of Original Clapboards

by John Obed Curtis

IN THE EARLY MORNING HOURS of Monday, December 2, 1974, an unusually high wind brought down a massive portion of an ancient maple tree. It fell thunderously against the north end of our 18th-century house, shattering a large area of asbestos siding (with which the house had been clad in the late 1950s). The damaged siding was no real loss, because we intended to remove it and expose the underlying and -- we hoped -- original clapboards. But the damage done by the tree would admit water behind the siding. There was no hope of it drying properly, so we had to re-schedule our priorities to put siding removal and clapboard repair at the top of the list.

cont'd on p. 156

In the next issue . . .
OLD-HOUSE REWIRING OPTIONS

Letters

A Stripping Story

JUST READ the article about stripping brick (Jan.-Feb. '85). Perhaps you'd be interested to know that I had my 1917 _frame_ house chemically stripped. The experience was unforgettable, with hundreds of gallons of water-stripper-paint-sludge filling up window wells. (The only way to empty them was to open their casement windows and then figure out how to clean up the basement floor.) It destroyed the lawn, too. Periodic inspections (I'm on assignment in Brazil) reveal that the new paint is holding firm, and that flora/fauna are all doing well. (Even my neighbor's lawn furniture recovered!)

ALL THE DETAILED exterior woodwork had been obliterated by cracking layers of paint, so I'd been heat-gunning and repainting for several summers. The call to Brazil forced a quick completion. No regrets, but I wouldn't want to clean up that mess again.

Jim Dierks
Rochester, N.Y.

Bungaloquacity

I HAVE BEEN READING OHJ for five years and find it fascinating but often inapplicable to my current home. I think your "Bungalow Letter" will reach a whole new audience in cities like San Antonio which were only tiny villages in the 19th century.

Charles Allen Foster
San Antonio, Texas

MY HOUSE was built in 1922. I have every issue of OHJ and do not really think an additional publication is needed. You have aided me just fine the way you have mixed periods in the past.

Betty Ann Smiddy
Cincinnati, Ohio

[Our response to May's Special Bungalow Issue was overwhelming! While most respondents want the separate publication, others asked us to expand OHJ to cover topics related to post-Victorian houses. More on this next month. --P. Poore]

Trim Removal

ENJOYED Gordon Bock's lead article on interior woodwork (June 1985 OHJ), but was surprised to find no mention of a technique I've found very useful -- especially for old redwood casements, etc., which split easily. Once the trim piece has been parted (using the techniques Bock describes) by as little as the thickness of a hacksaw blade, then such a blade can be used to cut off nails behind the trim. This saves a lot of strain on the wood. A thin sheet of coke-tin (or a flattened tin can) can be used to protect walls or other nearby woodwork.

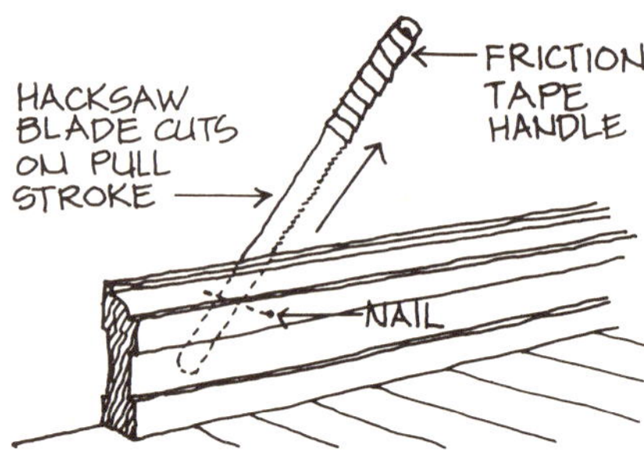

STANLEY and others make a handy handle-gadget for use with hacksaw blades, but of course in a pinch a handle can also be made by wrapping friction-tape around the hacksaw. In this situation, hacksaw blades work best if inserted so that the cutting takes place on the "pull" stroke.

Jim Tyler
San Francisco, Ca.

No Butts About It

THE ARTICLE "All About Wall Canvas" in your March 1985 issue states that non-cotton lining fabrics are always butted at the seams. However, Glidden's Glid-Wall -- a fiberglass material -- is double-cut at the seams, not butted. Having hung both double-cut and butted-seam wallpaper, I prefer the double-cut because the seam is smoother and less noticeable. For a fabric which is to be painted, a smooth seam is most important.

W.D. Smith
Atlanta, Ga.

The Old-House Journal®

Editor
Patricia Poore

Production Editor
Cole Gagne

Senior Technical Advisor
Larry Jones

Assistant Editor
Sarah J. McNamara

Contributing Editors
Walter Jowers
John Mark Garrison
Roland A. Labine Sr.

Architectural Consultant
Jonathan Poore

Circulation Supervisor
Barbara Bugg

Circulation Assistant
Jeanne Baldwin

Special Sales
Joan O'Reilly

Office Manager
Tricia A. Martin

Catalog Editor
Sarah J. McNamara

Publishing Consultant
Paul T. McLoughlin

Publisher
Clem Labine

Published by The Old-House Journal Corporation, 69A Seventh Avenue, Brooklyn, NY 11217. Telephone (718) 636-4514. Subscriptions $18 per year in U.S., $36 per year in Canada (payable in Canadian funds). Published ten times per year. Contents are fully protected by copyright and must not be reproduced in any manner whatsoever without specific permission in writing from the Editor.

We are happy to accept editorial contributions to The Old-House Journal. Query letters that include an outline of the proposed article are preferred. All manuscripts will be reviewed, and returned if unacceptable. However, we cannot be responsible for non-receipt or loss — please keep copies of all materials sent.

Printed at Photo Comp Press, New York City

ISSN: 0094-0178

Right: The Matthew Busey house in 1870. With the aid of this photo, Marylee MacDonald was able to rebuild the home's jettisoned ？＿ ＿ porch and belvedere.
Above: Family reunion — Matthew Busey, wife Sarah, and their six grown children pose on 804 West Main's front porch.

Urbana Renewal

How One Woman Defeated Her Family's Doubts

By Jacqueline A. MacDonald

"IT'S A FIXER-UPPER!" Marylee MacDonald's eyes lit up as she stood in front of the ivy-shrouded brick expanse at 804 West Main Street in Urbana, Illinois. Marylee's spouse, Bruce Rittmann, remained silent. The realtor who accompanied them arched his brows and looked at Marylee as if she were crazy. The house had, after all, been condemned by the City of Urbana and had thus stood vacant for nine months.

THE TRIO pushed through the overgrown mass of bushes and cobwebs to the front door. Entering, they were assailed by a cloud of dust and the combined smells of grease, mould, excrement, and general mustiness. Bruce, peering around cautiously with a flashlight, frowned at the crumbling plaster and the peeling, institutional blue paint (the color asylums are painted to calm inmates). To his left, the flashlight revealed a bull's-eye scribbled on the wall with chalk, the plaster underneath it and surrounding it pockmarked where darts had hit. Longingly, Bruce recalled the newly remodelled, ready-to-occupy homes the realtor had shown them that morning.

WHILE BRUCE DUBIOUSLY eyed the crumbling plaster and the graffiti, Marylee danced around the house pointing out the graceful, curving staircase, the elegant high ceilings, and the uniquely embellished, cast-iron fireplace mantels. For years, she'd wanted to restore an old house.

BRUCE THOUGHT Marylee was crazy when she suggested they buy the place -- especially after a trip down the precarious, rotting, rickety basement stairs nearly landed him in the hospital emergency room. Nevertheless, a day later, the MacDonald/Rittmann team signed the contract and won custody of the abused old house. In January, 1980, the couple and their four children moved from Palo Alto, California, to Urbana, Illinois, where Bruce would start his job as a University of Illinois civil engineering professor and Marylee would found the "Women Working" construction company.

THE HOUSE'S "FAMILY VIBES" courted Marylee from the start. "When I first walked into the house, it had such a good family feeling," says Marylee. It's no wonder: the house was built to withstand the exuberance of six children. Matthew Busey, who built the house in 1869, rejected the strict rules his Victorian contemporaries imposed on children -- he was a family man. To the horror of his peers, Matthew kept an overstuffed chair in one corner of his parlor for his six offspring to use as a trampoline; he allowed the children to slide down the stairway bannister; and he let his granddaughter set up a make-believe school in the belvedere. On holidays, Matthew Busey's house was so full of kids and relatives that the dining room table had to be turned diagonally across the room to seat everybody.

Top left: John and Ted stand in front of the Busey house shortly after the MacDonalds moved in. Notice that the belvedere and front porch are missing, and that the shutters are louver-less.
Right: Restoration underway: Here, the belvedere has been restored, front porch construction has commenced, and louvered shutters replace most of their phony stand-ins. The door to the right of the main entrance was bricked over when the MacDonalds moved in.
Below left: Sisters Kristin and Terry Jensen paint some of the 2,080 hand-cut shutter louvers.

THE FAMILY SPIRIT lived on in the Busey house until 1975, when it was sold to a developer. He rented it to unsympathetic University of Illinois students who kicked holes in the plaster, scribbled on the walls, and installed acoustical tile ceilings and fake panelling. While reckless students trampled the dwelling's dignity, the ill-meaning developer waited greedily for interest rates to drop so he could replace the Busey house with a cheap apartment unit. Meanwhile, the Busey family spirit receded into the brick walls.

FORTUNATELY, interest rates remained so high that the developer gave up his plans and sold the house to Marylee and Bruce. Unfortunately, while Marylee immediately sensed the house's value and spirit, it took the rest of her family a while to catch on. From the start of her old-house adventure, Marylee faced lots of resistance from her family as well as from the decaying house.

THE FIRST LINE OF RESISTANCE was Bruce: Marylee persuaded him to sign the joint-ownership contract by pointing out that none of the other Urbana properties they'd seen was large enough to house their four kids, and by promising she'd have 804 restored within six months. She reminded Bruce that their son Teddy had camped in a backyard tent until the California rainy season drove him from his leaky retreat -- all because he didn't want to share a bedroom with his brother. Bruce's initial hesitancy disappeared after a few weeks in residence; he, too, felt the Busey spirit. He fell in love with the place almost as much as Marylee had, spending evenings after work and weekends working on the house.

BUT THEN, Marylee had me to contend with. I'm her oldest child, her only daughter. I was 15 when we moved in, at the height of my adolescent rebellion and ever critical of my mother's activities. Full of resentment after leaving California's mountains and oceans for Illinois' tabletop-flat cornfields, I wasn't moved by the so-called Busey family spirit.

AFTER A FEW MONTHS in residence at 804, the house, in my eyes, looked worse than when we had moved in. My mother had cleaned up the dog droppings (gifts from the house's former occupants) in the attic; she'd hired two men from Manpower (an unemployment agency) to scrub the layers of grease off the kitchen walls; my bedroom was finished, with freshly stripped woodwork and a new coat of plaster (applied by John Pickens, a 79-year-old, partially blind plasterer trained at the prestigious Chicago Plastering Institute; he became the saviour of the house's decrepit interior plaster). But the other rooms in the house were in shambles: cracking plaster, peeling paint, bathroom sewage still flowing uphill thus causing clogs and an unbearable stench. The rooms that looked the worst were the ones Mom claimed she was restoring: All the plaster had been torn off the living room walls and a bare light bulb dangled precariously from the ceiling.

MOM'S DINING ROOM WORKSHOP annoyed me the most. Instead of a table and chairs, our dining room was furnished with a tablesaw and sawhorses. The floor was perpetually littered with sawdust, nails, and a medley of hand tools. Worst of all, tablesaw debris crept under my bedroom door daily, dirtying the fur-

The parlor at its most depressing stage: All the plaster is torn off the walls, and a bare light bulb dangles from the ceiling.

Restoration survivors Bob, Ted and John relax in the finished parlor, a haven of sanity while the rest of the house was in shambles.

niture I polished each night. Unfortunately, I didn't realize that a house being restored always looks worse before it looks better.

ONE SUMMER DAY stands out in my mind as being particularly depressing. Walking up 804's front path, I was confronted by a structure which looked like it was on the eve of destruction. Plaster was flying out of one of the upstairs windows onto the lawn. A hand reached out another window knocking down shutters. By the end of the day, our front yard was a rubble heap of plaster and the house, missing its shutters, looked naked. It looked ready to be bulldozed, not restored.

AS I LOST FAITH that our house would ever be complete, I became a recluse, confining myself to my bedroom and refusing to invite friends to the house. All my friends lived in clean, newer homes. None of them had yards full of plaster; none had mothers perpetually clad in overalls, fingernails purpled from poorly aimed hammers, hands covered with varying mixtures of paint, glue, and tile grout. I was embarrassed because my mom and my house were different from my friends' moms and houses -- when you're an adolescent, you want to be the same as everybody else.

AT THE DEPTH of my despair, four events sweetened my sour attitude toward Mom's endeavor. The first was meeting descendants of the family that built the house. Three months after we moved in, David Busey, driving through Urbana on a visit from his home in El Paso, Illinois, noticed that there was work going on in his grandfather's house. In his youth, he had expressed his loyalty to his grandfather by mowing 804's then quarter-acre lawn every Saturday. He had many happy memories stored away in the Busey house, and

watching the house deteriorate year after year had depressed him -- at age 68, he didn't have the energy to restore the house himself. When David Busey saw that someone was actually trying to save the old place, he was elated.

AND MY FAMILY was elated. For, along with the gratitude he expressed, Mr. Busey sent us a picture of the house taken in 1870, a year after it was built. The photo confirmed my mom's suspicion that the house originally had a front porch and a belvedere. (Without them, the house looked too tall and boxlike, resembling a giant half-gallon milk carton). The photo aroused my hope that the house could return to its past glory days.

SECOND, some mysterious findings provoked my interest in the house's history:

● We discovered a hidden stairway. (What kid wouldn't be excited by such a find?) A past resident had walled in the back stairway to accommodate heating ducts. Repairing the floor above the hidden stairway, Mom noticed that the floor boards didn't match up. Poking a hole through the floor, she discovered the stairs, all intact except the bottom two, with the original stairwell wallpaper preserved.

● We discovered writing behind the wallpaper. Laura Busey, one of the six children who grew up in the house, had used the newly plastered wall to practice her alphabet. Her older sister Clara had used the same wall to practice skills which later admitted her to the University of Illinois' art program.

● Behind one mantelpiece, we uncovered letters and bills dating back to 1870. Apparently, the 1870s agricultural depression hit Matthew Busey hard: Bills dated 1877 admonished him for postponing his payments.

Marylee lounges in her restored belvedere (obscured by trees in the photo to the right.)

THIRD, my mother hired Kristin Jensen, whose persevering enthusiasm made me regret my lack of faith in the house. Kristin recreated the 52 louvered exterior shutters someone had destroyed, along with the porch and belvedere, in a post-Victorian attempt to convert the Italianate house into a Federal-style manor. This immense project involved hand-cutting 2,080 individual louvers -- 40 for each shutter. Kristin modelled her shutters on the four surviving originals. (The rest had been replaced with fake shutters nailed into the house's brick walls.) Later, Kristin helped my mom design and build the belvedere and porch, using the 1870 photo as a guide. Kristin's zeal for the old house convinced me my mom's project was feasible, after all.

THE FOURTH EVENT that increased my confidence in a seemingly hopeless restoration project was the parlor's completion, after 18 months of work. The parlor walls were plastered and papered with a period reproduction. An elegant but simple brass chandelier with six etched glass globes replaced the bare light bulb. The cast-iron mantelpiece was stripped of its peeling white paint and polished glossy black. The floor, at last void of sawdust and paint flakes, was refinished and carpeted with a 100-year-old Busey heirloom Mrs. David Busey gave us. Bright sunlight shone through lace curtains decorating the room's ten-foot windows, at last cleared of blinding cobwebs and overgrown foliage. Once seated on the green velvet parlor sofa, one could forget the tablesaw and plaster dust in the adjacent dining room. The parlor was a sign of what was to come; it boosted the family morale.

AS THE MONTHS PASSED, I became proud instead of embarrassed to show my house to friends. Most of them were very supportive of the restoration project and tolerant of the dirt it engendered. The only exception was a boyfriend whose first reaction to the house was, "Couldn't you at least sweep your stairway?" I refused all his later invitations to movies.

GRADUALLY, the common ordeal we were surviving strengthened the family bonds; my brothers and I even volunteered to work on the house. Of course, our "help" was occasionally a nuisance instead of a benefit. I wasn't too skilled with the heat-gun, often scorching the woodwork I was stripping. And my poor brother Ted, who hadn't quite learned to coordinate his growing limbs, ended up in the hospital when he tried to help: In one unlucky weekend, Ted spilled chemical stripper in his eyes, broke his arm, burnt all the skin off his calves with boiling water, and ended up in a minor car accident en route to the emergency room -- all in the process of trying to strip the woodwork in his bedroom.

DESPITE SUCH DISASTERS, the house took shape -- sagging floors unbent with hydraulic house jacks, creaking staircase bolted back into the wall, dining room wallpapered and tablesaw replaced with antique furniture, front porch and belvedere completed. Strangers slowed their cars outside the house to stare in awe at the Italianate manor's new exterior embellishments and period paint job; passersby asked to tour the interior. Two such visitors introduced themselves as Busey grandchildren: Sally Reston, wife of New York _Times_ columnist James Reston, sent my mom a congratulatory letter after her visit; Mrs. Mabie, now retired in Florida, asked with delight to visit the restored belvedere, and her eyes sparkled as she recounted her childhood exploits in the room atop the house.

THE BUSEY HOME'S VITALITY, dormant for so long, has been renewed. It's no matter that the restoration lasted three-and-a-half years instead of the predicted six months, because my family will have a lifetime to enjoy the restoration's results. Though I now live at a college 1,000 miles from home, the house still attracts me like a magnet. As I lounge in the sitting room during those long-anticipated college vacations, I feel enveloped and replenished by the house's family spirit. Someday, I hope I'll restore my own spirited old house; but even then, the Busey house will captivate me.

RESTORATION WOOD CORNICE AND REPAIR

BY LARRY JONES

A CORNICE ADDS architectural interest to an old building. In fact, on many commercial buildings and urban rowhouses, the cornice is the only notable detail. Nobody likes to maintain cornices, though, because they're so big and out of reach. Beware! An unmaintained cornice is worse than just an eyesore. Water penetration through a rotted or open cornice could damage the building wall and roof. And a severely deteriorated wood cornice is dangerous. Decorative elements might fall off, and the whole structure could even pull loose.

INEVITABLY, the cornice either has to be torn off or restored. The trick is to get up there and fix it right, so that repairs last for decades. A good restoration might involve design modifications as well as flashing and woodworking repairs and a paint job -- all of which are discussed here.

Cornice Types

WOODEN CORNICES have been built in every size and shape imaginable, yet there are only three basic methods for attaching them to buildings.

THE PARAPET CORNICE is probably the most common type of cornice, used on both wood and masonry structures. It's built on top of a parapet wall (which extends above the roof of a building) and projects out over the facade, often partially supported by its decorative brackets. The decorative portions of the cornice, which extend down the facade, are frequently attached to the surface with spike boards. (See illustration on next page.)

THE TOP-OF-THE-WALL CORNICE may, from the street, closely resemble the parapet type. But its overall design is more lightweight, and allows for deeper panelled decorative surfaces. This cornice usually rests on a masonry wall or facade that stops at or slightly above the roof line; instead of being attached to the face of the building, it supports itself structurally. If left unchecked, water damage eventually can cause the entire cornice to fall from the building. (See illustration on p. 143.)

THE FLUSH-MOUNT CORNICE is most commonly seen on facades between floors, usually between the first and second floor of a three- or four-storey building; or it may be surface-mounted on a parapet. This cornice type is often attached to the wall through spike boards (surface-mounted or set into the masonry). Sometimes floor joists or other interior supports extend through the facade to support the cornice. (See illustration on p. 143.)

Inspection

TO ROUGHLY ASSESS its condition, examine the cornice through a pair of binoculars. Study it from a variety of angles, looking for loose or missing pieces; signs of water damage; overall sagging; and separations between the cornice and the building.

IF YOU SEE SOMETHING that requires closer inspection or repair, it's time to plan your ascent. Forget about using a ladder for all but the smallest jobs; ladders are simply too dangerous for high work where you have to move around a lot. Unless you have some experience as a rigger (and in some cases, the required city license), forget about using suspended rigging, too. Your best bet is to rent welded-tube scaffolding from a local scaffolding rental company and have them erect it. (See "Scaffolding Primer" in the July 1985 OHJ.) Even if you're hiring a contractor to repair your cornice, you might want to brave the heights of the scaffolding yourself: at first, for a close look at the condition of the cornice; and later, for regular inspections of the repair work in progress.

DURING THE FIRST INSPECTION, hunt out any missing, damaged, severely deteriorated, and non-original elements. Old photos of your building, and intact cornices on similar buildings, are the best sources of information about original details. And take some photos of your own while you poke around the cornice; they're quite useful for jogging your (or your contractor's) memory of how the parts go together. Photos are also invaluable references for off-site work. If you want a millwork shop to duplicate a bracket, it may be easier to take photos and measurements to the shop than to remove and take along a bracket.

WOODEN CORNICES that sit on parapet walls or are attached to facades can be found atop stone, brick, stucco, and wood-frame structures. Building stresses such as settling can cause masonry walls to deteriorate, creating cracks that weaken the wall. Moisture damage is a frequent problem. On wooden structures the facade, parapet wall, or "false front" which holds the cornice may start to bow, arc outward, or sag from the cornice weight; it

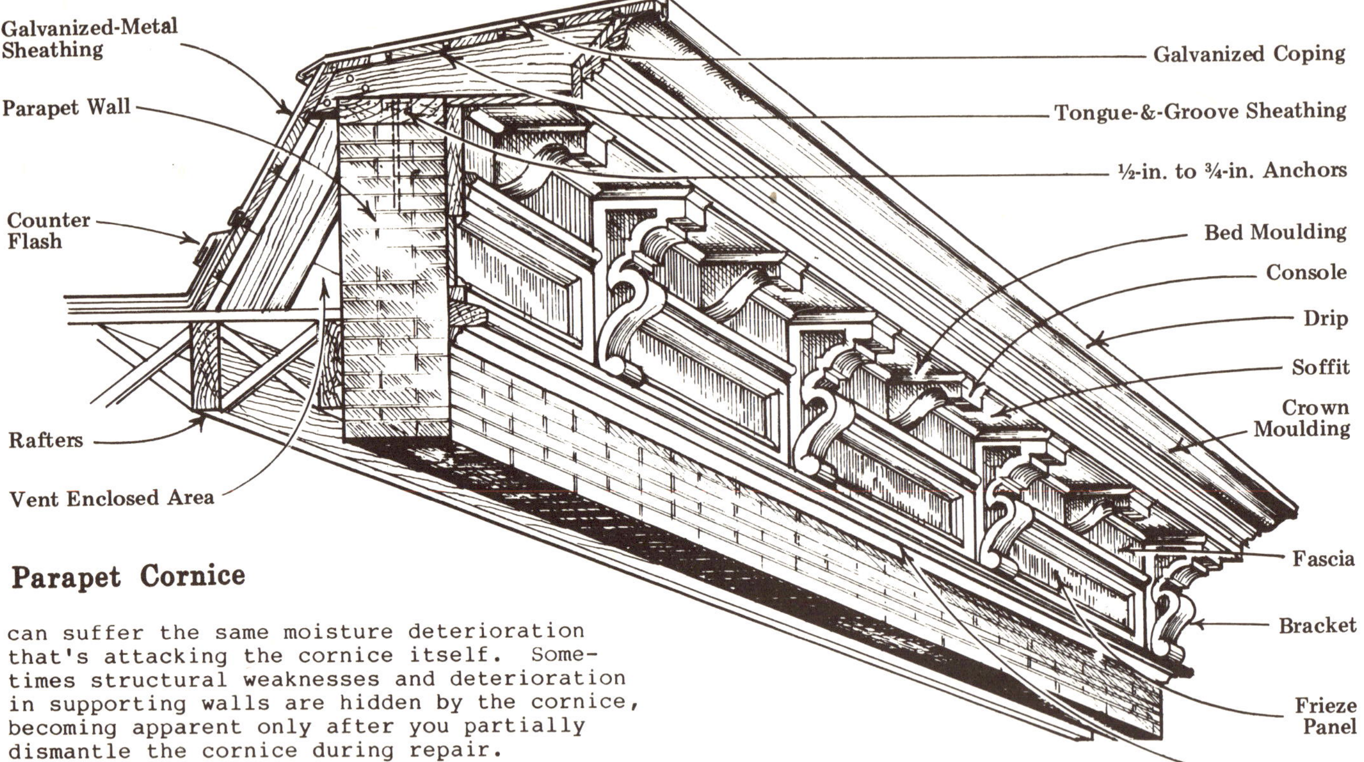

Parapet Cornice

can suffer the same moisture deterioration that's attacking the cornice itself. Sometimes structural weaknesses and deterioration in supporting walls are hidden by the cornice, becoming apparent only after you partially dismantle the cornice during repair.

MOST OF THE DETERIORATION you'll find will be moisture related. Trace leaks back to their sources and look for weakened, water-damaged structural members. Use an ice pick, awl, or knife to probe (gently) for deteriorated wood.

PAINT FAILURE and subsequent wood decay start at joints where moisture and dirt collect. Some particularly susceptible areas:
● horizontal projections (foot mouldings)
● mitered or butted joints (frieze mouldings)
● exposed end grain
● laminations of built-up pieces (brackets or trusses)
● vertical surfaces washed by rainwater (crown moulding, fascia, frieze panel)
● areas where flashing was ineffective or has failed (crown moulding)

WOODEN CORNICES seldom fall from buildings in one big piece. (They just give up a few chunks at a time.) But look twice before you pull, bang, or lean on an old cornice. On masonry buildings, cornices were commonly fastened to spike boards; over the years, these boards are likely to have warped; their fasteners to have rusted. This can cause the cornice to warp and twist away from the building. Be very cautious around a loose cornice -- it must be supported or secured before you work on it.

Spike Boards

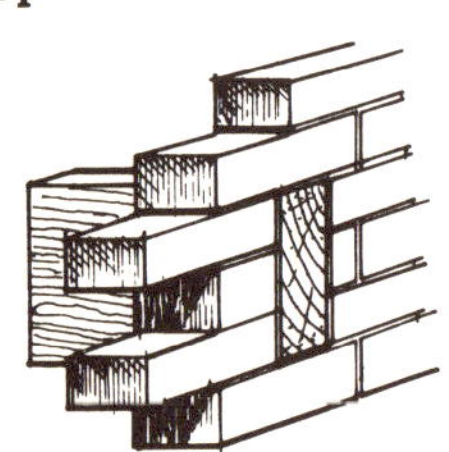 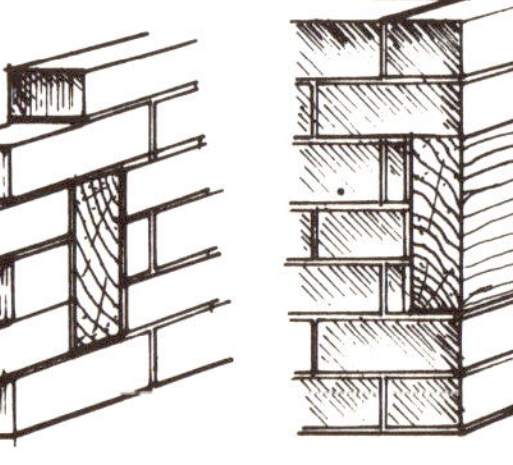 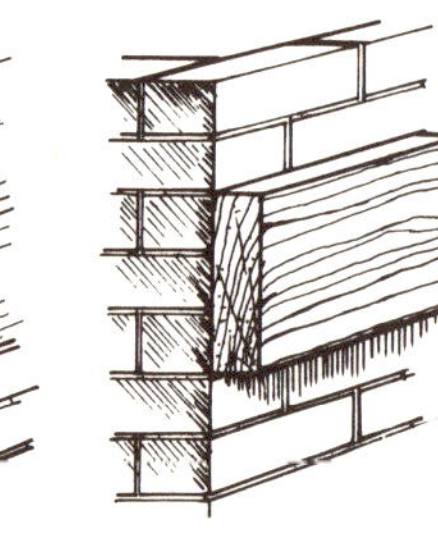

Through-Wall Mount   Inset, Flush Mount   Surface Mount

Problems With The Wall

THE CONDITION of the parapet wall is often overlooked when restoring a cornice. But cornice deterioration may have spread to (or, occasionally, started with) the roof, parapet, or facade wall. Although this article deals mainly with simple cornice repair, it's important to look for structural weaknesses in the wall as well.

MOST WELL BUILT CORNICES mounted on masonry parapet walls have shed roofs (or properly designed coping and flashing) to protect the back of the wall from the weather. Some masonry and most wood-frame parapet walls are

With few horizontal surfaces to trap water, this cornice has held up well. The primed (white) pieces are replacements; duplicates of each replaced element have been set aside, in case any future replacements are needed.

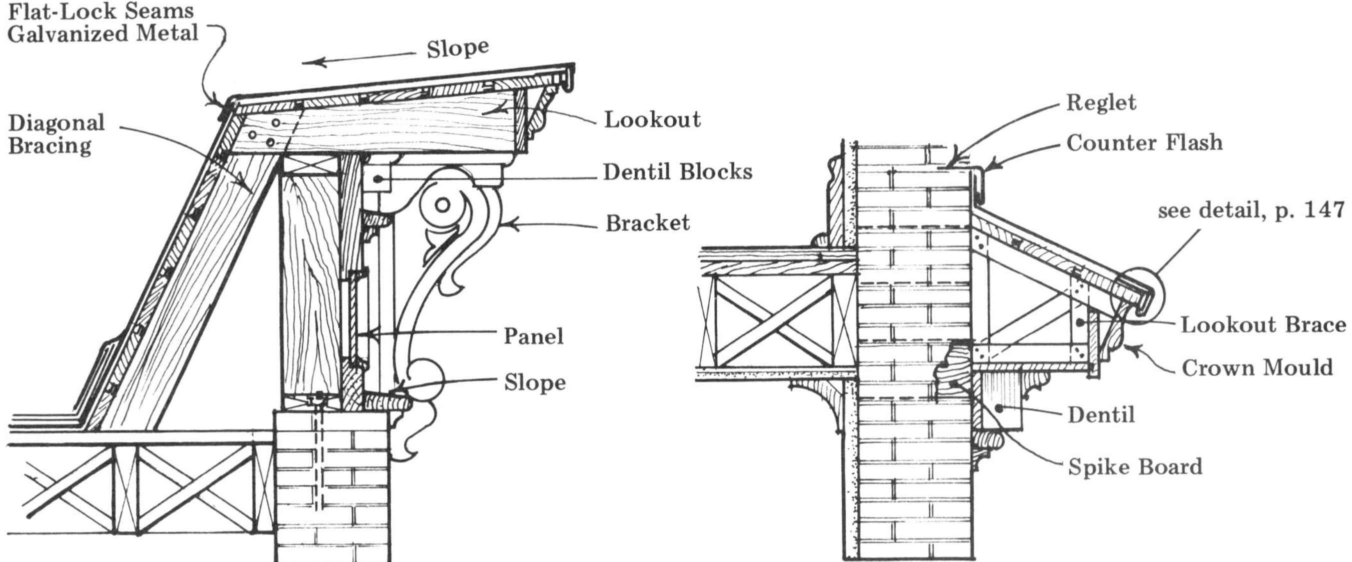

Top-Of-The-Wall Cornice

Flush-Mount Cornice

shielded by metal copings, wall pans, flashings, and counterflashings. (Black asphalt-type roofing cement is the least effective, shortest-lived, and most irreversible way to protect the backs of parapet walls.)

MISSING OR CORRODED coping and flashing can cause extensive water damage to the back of the parapet wall, and even spread decay to the roof structure. Old sand-lime mortar joints left exposed to the weather will sometimes expand, causing the wall to gradually arc toward the cornice, creating a structurally unsound condition. But the most common masonry deterioration is erosion from weathering. The wall may have to be repointed, or in some cases dismantled down to sound bricks or stone and then relaid.

WOOD-FRAME PARAPET WALLS frequently can be strengthened by removing the exterior sheathing from their backs, and bolting new structural timbers alongside existing ones. For major repairs to strengthen unsafe parapet walls, seek the advice of a structural engineer.

A CORNICE that's coming loose from its moorings must be temporarily stabilized before any repair work begins; this can be done with built-up shoring. NOTE: This is dangerous

work and should be done only by experienced professionals. Don't try to secure a loose cornice unless you're absolutely sure of what you're doing.

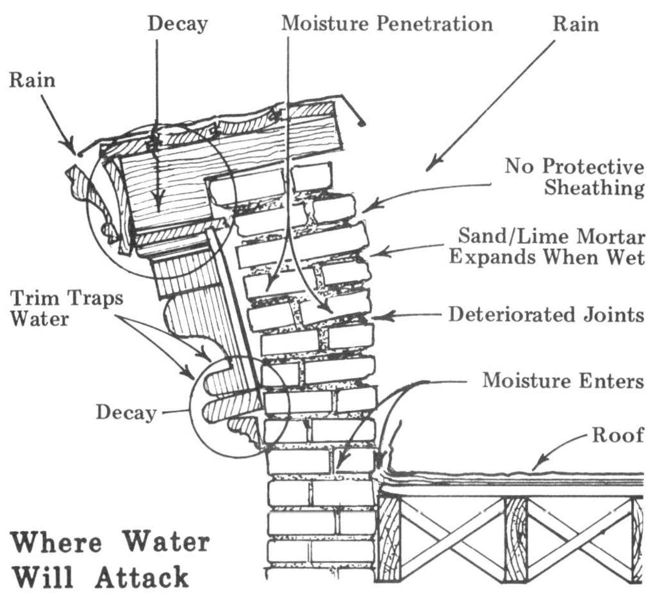

Where Water Will Attack

Cornice Structure And Anchors

THE INTERNAL FRAMEWORK of a wooden cornice varies considerably with the size and complexity of the cornice. The simplest, smallest cornice may have no enclosed interior spaces; larger ones may have spaces big enough to crawl into. The framework for most cornices consists of 2x4s (sometimes 2x6s). Whatever the design of the rough structural framing, it's obviously constructed to resist the downward pull of gravity. For instance, closed soffit designs, such as the flush-mount cornice illustrated at the upper right corner of this page, frequently have a boxed framework with diagonal bracing for added strength.

MOST CORNICES were built in place, so their structural-support systems are such that the

Notice the deflecting bricks in the parapet wall on the left side of the photo. They indicate that the cornice has begun to lean back, creating an unsound structural condition.

cornice can't be removed from the building in one piece. Therefore it's usually easier to repair it in place on the building. A cornice with unsound structure will probably have to be partially disassembled to reveal the nature and condition of its internal support system. Again: Make certain that the cornice is temporarily supported before going into it.

A GOOD WAY to gain access to the interior cornice framework is to come in from the top. By carefully removing sections of the roof covering and wood sheathing below, you should be able to look directly down in at the structural supports. Make your repairs from the top, trying to avoid removing either the decorative trim or facing boards. A lot of these brittle pieces get broken during removal and reinstallation.

WOODEN GUSSET PLATES, diagonal bracing, and additional framing members are all ways to strengthen the existing structural frame. (The design and sizing are best specified by an engineer.) Use screws rather than nails to securely fasten interior framing members; for really strong joints, use waterproof glue with the fasteners. You'll save a huge amount of time and frustration if you use an electric screw gun. If that's not in your budget, try a standard multi-tip ratchet screwdriver. Use treated lumber to replace deteriorated members if wood rot is likely to recur.

TO REANCHOR A CORNICE that's pulled away from the building, you have to know how it was attached, and understand what forces have been acting on it to pull it loose. Remember that cornices, except for some flush-mounted ones, rest most of their weight on the top of the facade wall; the elements fastened to the front of the facade are largely decorative. You're not likely to find many heavy anchors attached to the facade.

WHEN THE FRONT of a cornice has pulled away from the building, you may be able to pull it back again by installing anchors (either the through-wall variety or expansion bolts). In work on old buildings, always avoid using masonry anchors or bolts that are shot into the

masonry with a powder charge. Installation of too many anchors, especially through-wall, can seriously weaken masonry parapet walls, so plan your repairs carefully and get professional (engineer's) advice.

A SEVERELY DETERIORATED CORNICE -- one that can't be shored up and refastened -- may have to be removed. Certain cornices can be lifted free with a crane and lowered to the ground; others have to be dismantled piece by piece. If there's enough left to work with, you may want to restore the old cornice in the shop, using epoxies or traditional carpentry repairs. Even if the structure has to be rebuilt, you might be able to salvage some of the decorative parts, saving money as well as original materials. Try to exactly duplicate missing or unsalvageable pieces; if you can't afford exact duplicates, then save whatever old pieces you can and fill in with replacement pieces that match in size and general shape or profile. Plywood used on exposed panels nearly always ends up looking like plywood, so avoid using it.

Design Changes

SOME CORNICES are better designed, and therefore weather better, than others. Once you understand the weathering characteristics of your cornice, you might be able to improve on its original design without noticeably altering its appearance. For instance: An original foot moulding can collect water, dirt, and bird droppings on its flat, projecting top surface. It would save wear on the cornice if you replaced the offending moulding with a new one of similar design but with a sloping top surface.

REMEMBER the "shingle principle" when modifying cornice design: All joints and fastener holes are to be overlapped from above to shed water. The tops of large horizontal projections aren't visible from the street, so flash them. Keep in mind that you have to provide an exit for water (both liquid and vapor) that might get inside the cornice.

PROVIDE ADEQUATE VENTILATION for closed interior spaces: Moisture buildup leads to peeling paint and wood decay. If your cornice has no boxed-in enclosures, then there's nothing to ventilate. But cornices with enclosed spaces (and a history of paint failure and rot) should be vented. If possible, provide plenty of cross ventilation from the soffit through the cornice and out the back side of the parapet wall or lean-to shed. Vents are screened to keep out rain, snow, birds, and insects. The small, ready-made, circular, painted-aluminum louvered screen vents are easy to install, but admit far too little air; they're useful in only the smallest enclosures.

Water has gotten inside this cornice through the deteriorated roofing and flashing. It's weakened the interior supports, causing the cornice to sag — and to pop off pieces onto passersby. A cornice left in this condition is bound to fall off eventually, giving all cornices a bad name and fueling public resentment against them.

Repair Of Decorative Trim Parts

DECORATIVE WOOD TRIM and mouldings often warp
and pull away from the surface: Nails rust off
or the wood decays around the fasteners, allowing them to pull out. Loose trim can often
be reattached after you clean out any debris
that's collected behind it. After removing
the trim, cut the remaining original nails and
reposition the piece. If you're using nails
to reattach the trim, blunt their ends or pre-
drill pilot holes to reduce the chances of
splitting. Renail through new holes in sound
wood; the old holes have probably gotten too
large to give a tight hold.

USE ONLY high-quality, long-lasting fasteners
to re-attach loose pieces:
● Hot-dipped galvanized finishing nails, or
brass or stainless steel marine wood screws.
They won't rust.
● Self-starting drywall screws. These screws
can rust, so use them only where they can
either be countersunk and plugged over, or
covered with another element.
● Galvanized screws for use with a screw gun.
Be sure the heads aren't visible from the
surface of the cornice.
● Monel "Anchorfast" boat nails. They have
the holding strength of similar-sized screws
(due to their ring-shank design) and won't
corrode or rust.

REPLACEMENT PARTS are best fashioned out of
the same wood originally used in the cornice
(although some restorations have used parts
cast in fiberglass-reinforced plastic or high-
density foam). New wood replacement parts
should have the grain running in the same
direction as the original, ideally with no end
grain exposed to the weather. Weldwood phenol
resorcinol is an excellent waterproof exterior
wood glue for repairing splits or attaching
decorative pieces. Available at most hardware
stores, it comes in two parts that have to be
mixed together. (It shrinks on setting, so
use it only as a glue, not as a filler.)

The hole in this wooden cornice is being filled with filler epoxy,
which will be sanded down to the proper contour and smoothness.
To ensure the best bond between wood and epoxy, all the surface
paint around the area to be filled has been removed.

Wood And Metal Patches

COVERING PROBLEMS with a metal patch sounds
seedy: "If you can't fix it right, slap on a
patch." Well, with cornices, that's not always a bad idea. Maybe your cornice has missing pieces, and the ugly gaping holes are
letting in birds, animals, or water. Maybe a
full-blown cornice restoration is low on your
list of budget priorities. Consider using
reversible metal patches.

THE MOST COMMON patching material is galvanized steel. It will last indefinitely -- if
it's kept painted. Terne, terne-coated stainless steel, and copper are also good patching
materials. (If a patch will touch metal
flashing, they both have to be made of the
same metal to avoid galvanic corrosion.)

A METAL PATCH should overlap the hole by at
least one inch all around; more if necessary
to reach sound wood. Pre-drill holes in the

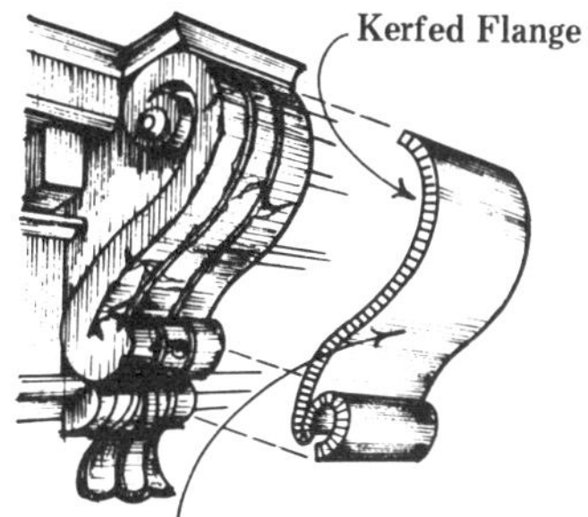

patch 1/2 inch in
from the edge and an
inch or less apart --
this helps the patch
follow the contour of
the area being
repaired. (Use gal-
vanized nails to re-
fasten a galvanized
or terne patch; cop-
per nails for a cop-
per patch.) Prime
the back of the
patch. Set the patch
in a bed of high-
quality, paintable, exterior-grade caulk
before nailing. Wipe off excess caulk, then
prime and paint the front of the patch.

A CARPENTER'S "dutch-
man" is a long-last-
ing and good-looking
repair. It involves
skillfully hand-saw-
ing or chiseling out
a damaged area to a
prescribed size and
shape, and then cut-
ting a wood piece to
fit the opening
exactly. Glue the
patch in place with
epoxy or waterproof
glue, secured with
dowels or screws. A
dutchman, properly
sanded and painted,
is a smooth and
almost invisible, permanent repair.

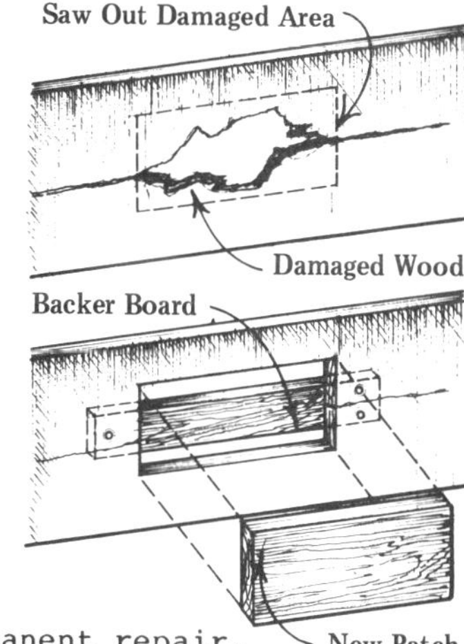

MOISTURE-DAMAGED, rotted, cracked, split, and
even missing wood cornice elements can be
repaired, filled, and reconstructed using two-
part, high-performance epoxies that are specially formulated for this purpose. Epoxies
allow you to patch in place; they're quick,
easy to apply, easy to tool and finish -- but
they're not cheap. However, unlike the less-
expensive auto-body fillers and latex wood
fillers, high-quality epoxies adhere well and
stay put.

AS A GENERAL RULE OF THUMB, if 40% or more of
a wooden piece has rotted, it's more cost ef-

fective to replace it. Below that percentage, epoxies are an excellent way to retain many original wood pieces that otherwise would have to be removed. (Millworks have never been keen on tooling up to make a 12-in. length of crown moulding, and there's certainly no point in replacing all 30 feet of moulding when only a foot has deteriorated.) Where many intricate wood replacement pieces would require many hours to produce and install, consider patching with epoxy thickened with compatible fillers (available from the epoxy supplier).

EPOXIES CAN BE USED to consolidate even rotted wood, reducing its tendency to soak up moisture. This is particularly handy for the decorative millwork on cornices, which tends to trap moisture and lose paint. For proper adhesion, paint and varnish have to be removed from wood before treating; if it's wet, the wood will have to dry out. Low-viscosity epoxy can be brushed, poured, or injected into rotted wood until it's fully saturated. For best adhesion, pre-wet deteriorated wood with either low-viscosity or regular epoxy, before you apply the epoxy filler. Filling large areas usually requires several applications. (Epoxy gives off heat as it cures, so you want to apply only a thin layer at a time. <u>Don't</u> apply in direct sunlight; watch it, and keep a hose or fire extinguisher close by.)

FOR MORE INFORMATION on epoxies and their uses contact the following firms:
● Gougeon Brothers, Inc., makers of the WEST SYSTEM (free catalog; manual, $2): Dept. OHJ, P.O. Box X908, Bay City, MI 48707. (517) 684-7286.
● Abatron, Inc., makers of LIQUID WOOD and WOODEPOX (free brochure): Dept. OHJ, 141 Center Drive, Gilberts, IL 60136. (312) 426-2200.

This decorative cornice has typical crown-moulding decay caused by the failure of the drip flashing and roof. Arrows on the photo indicate where (A) the mitre-cut, curved crown moulding has fallen apart at the saw cuts; (B) the frieze trim has dropped off because water rusted the nails; and (C) a pigeon has made its home.

Repairing Galvanized Steel

GALVANIZED STEEL is the most common coping and flashing material found on old cornices. Left unpainted, it eventually rusts. Rusting is the most common type of sheet-metal deterioration (although wind and thermal stress can pull joints apart and work anchors loose).

REPAIR RUST-OUTS in galvanized steel by soldering a patch over the damaged area:
• Thoroughly clean the area to be patched of all rust and/or roofing cement — get down to the clean, shiny metal.
• Cut a patch from the same galvanized metal, about two inches larger than the hole.
• Fold the edges under 1/2 inch & snip off the corners; this makes the patch stronger and takes off easily damaged sharp corners.

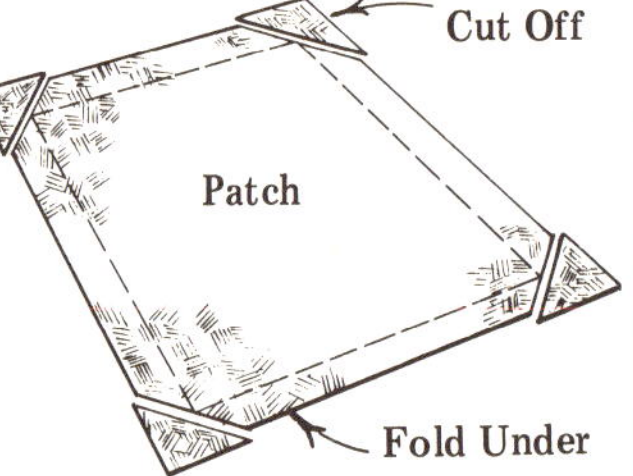

• Place a weight (a brick is good) over the patch to hold it firmly to the metal. If the patch is on a vertical surface, clamp or tack-solder it in place.
• Brush rosin flux around the patch edges.
• With either a 3- to 5-lb. propane-heated soldering copper, or a 200-watt electric soldering iron, melt 50/50 lead-tin solder into and over the seam. It's critical that the patch not move until after the solder cools, or else the solder will start to break. If the patch moves, start over.
• After the solder cools, wipe the patched area with mineral spirits, then prime all the bare metal with a suitable metal primer.
• DON'T try to weld on a patch, and don't try to solder with a blowtorch. High-heat methods can damage light-gauge metal and start fires in a wood cornice.
• DON'T use asphalt roofing compound or cheap aluminum-based roof coatings to make patches. These repairs seldom last one summer, and are hard to undo.
• For detailed painting instructions, see "Painting Galvanized Metal" in the January-February 1984 OHJ.

Cornice Roof & Flashing Repair

EXAMINE THE CONDITION of the cornice roof and flashing. Most water damage can be traced to deteriorated, ill-designed, or non-existent roofing and flashing. The least satisfactory cornice-roof coverings are granulated building felt, asphalt shingles, and mopped-on coatings. Use the longer-lasting materials listed below. Remember, one good leak could go unnoticed for quite a while before the costly damage begins to show on the outside of the cornice -- or inside your building.

GOOD METALS to use for cornice roofs, coping, and flashing are: copper (16-20 oz.); lead-coated copper (16-20 oz.); terne-coated stainless steel (24-26 ga.); terne metal (IX 40#); and galvanized steel (22-24 ga.); also 3-lb. hard lead or 4- or 6-lb. chemical grade, animonial, or copper-bearing lead. (6-lb. lasts the longest.)

FLASHING on masonry buildings is often set into a reglet. If the joint packing (usually mortar or caulk) fails, the flashing may pull out and allow water to enter behind it, resulting in moisture damage. Often it's possible to clean out the joint and re-anchor the flashing in the reglet by installing lead wedges, then re-packing the joint with mortar that matches the original.

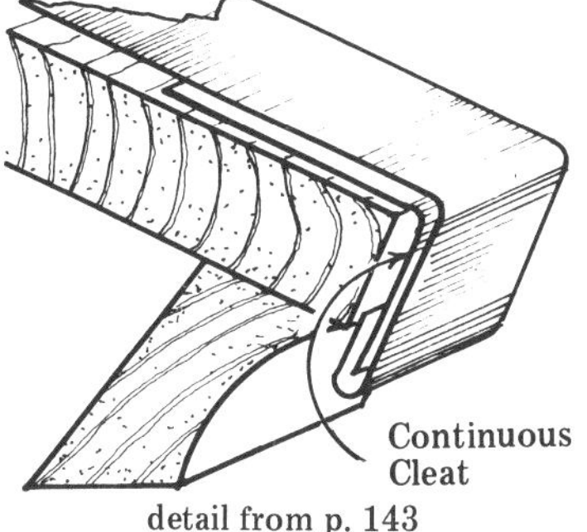

detail from p. 143

BE SURE to install an effective drip edge along the front of the cornice where the crown moulding meets the roof; this forces water to drip free rather than run down the front of the cornice.

Caulk And Putty

WOOD PUTTY, fillers, and doughs are misused cure-alls for every type of exterior wood deterioration. Exterior fillers work fine for covering small nail holes, but shouldn't be used to fill joints or seams. They can't expand and contract with the wood, and so larger patches usually fail in short order -- wrecking a good paint job, forming a trap for moisture, and opening up the wood to further decay.

SEALANTS, more commonly referred to as caulks, come in four common varieties: polysulfides, silicones, acrylics, and butyls. Of these, polysulfides tend to provide the greatest elasticity without breaking away from the seam or joint. They're also sandable -- meaning you can fill a seam and sand flush for an imperceptible joint. Their disadvantage is that they're slow to dry (up to 10 days); they usually can be painted just after installation, but can't be sanded until dry. Polysulfides work best with two-sided seams; if the sealant is attached to three sides, one side may pull loose. For best adhesion the seam should be a minimum of 1/8 inch wide and 1/4 inch deep.

This cornice is really for the birds: The missing scrolls on the consoles and brackets are now a sparrow motel. All the missing parts had surfaces that trapped water, dooming them to fail.

COMPARED TO POLYSULFIDE, the other sealants dry very quickly, in 24 to 48 hours. Silicone rubber can't grip nearly as strongly or take as much expansion and contraction as polysulfide can, and although some varieties can be painted, it can't be sanded. Acrylics are less expensive, shorter-lived polymers; limit their use to tight narrow joints. Butyls work in applications similar to acrylics. They're somewhat stringy to apply, can't be sanded, and may be painted when cured to a rubber.

SEALANTS are indispensable for sealing joints and seams on cornices where expansion and contraction movement will occur, where dissimilar materials meet, or where two or more objects are joined together. Horizontal seams and joints on cornices are notorious for opening up and trapping all kinds of debris and moisture, so be sure to allow yourself plenty of time to caulk all the open seams you find on the cornice. It's also a good idea to bed elements being reattached to the cornice in sealant, at least around the perimeters. But don't use sealants as fillers or adhesives.

Primer / Paint

YOU'LL HAVE TO SCRAPE peeling paint before you can repaint. Don't remove any paint, though, until you've looked for ghosts: Missing pieces often leave behind a clue to their contour in the form of a paint line, or ghost. You might also want to test for original paint colors before you remove paint down to bare wood.

PAINTING is the last step in restoring your cornice, and one of the most important. Here are some things to keep in mind while planning the paint job:
● Prepare the surfaces properly -- remove flaking paint, dirt, oil, etc.
● Use paintable sealants.
● Use primer that is compatible with the topcoat of paint -- primer and topcoat from the same manufacturer is best.
● Back-prime all decorative elements before you install them.
● Never leave primed wood exposed to the weather for longer than 48 hours before applying the topcoats.
● High-gloss alkyd enamel works well as a topcoat on exterior wood. High gloss paints are slightly more weather resistant than those with lower sheens. You can get good results with a semi-gloss alkyd paint or latex paint, though.
● Don't use cheap, substandard paint, and don't try to get away with applying only one topcoat -- always apply two. (You don't want to have to do this again next year.)
● Don't spray paint a cornice; it has too many sharp angles and recesses to be properly covered by spraying. Brush paint carefully, making sure to get every nook and cranny.

AT LEAST ONCE A YEAR, you should make a routine inspection of the cornice, and make whatever small repairs and touch-ups are needed. If possible, wash the painted surfaces of the cornice annually -- the paint job will last longer. Once the cornice is restored, you may be surprised to find that your efforts have set off a trend of cornice restoration in our area. No one seems to notice the beauty of cornices until one gets restored.

From *The Book Of Building And Interior Decorating* (1923)

English Revival Interiors

by Jacqueline A. MacDonald

THE END of an era is often marked by a swing in the opposite direction. Thus, the intense architectural eclecticism of the Victorian era was replaced by a yearning for simplicity. The romantic notion of constructing homes that resembled the unadorned, stuccoed and half-timbered cottages of sixteenth- and seventeenth-century Tudor England was part of this post-Victorian back-to-nature movement.

SIMPLICITY -- or the appearance of simplicity -- became the number one rule for interior decoration in the 1910-1930 Tudor Revival in America. Ornate Victorian ceiling medallions made way for exposed ceiling beams. Natural wood panelling and rough plastering (or restrained wallpaper) replaced the outmoded fancy wallpaper. (Allen Jackson in The Half-Timber House, circa 1919, noted that rough plaster "may seem rather ascetic to one who is used to having bunches of roses nodding at him from his wall, but when he has become accustomed to it he will never go back to the other....") Large fireplaces, as opposed to small coal grates, were re-introduced as the central focus for living rooms. Tudor Revival was a romantic return to the era when the hearth was "the lounging-room, library, study, and smoking room" (as Jackson said) of every English manor house.

PERHAPS the most dramatic change was in furnishings. No longer were rooms cluttered with doily-covered furniture. Rooms were sparse by comparison to the previous era. Knick-knacks were apparently tossed in garbage cans. Simple muslin curtains were preferred over elaborate drapes for the diamond-paned casement windows of Tudor Revival houses. In their 1920 mail-order catalog, Curtis and Companies hit the nail on the head: "There is no pretense about the English House. Its charm lies in its informality, its simplicity. It is built for comfort, not for show."

THESE authentic period photos provide a document of what the interiors were actually like. If you have an English Revival house, the pictures, more than words, will help you with your restoration.

(above) Compare the authentic Tudor interior pictured on the left (The Great Hall at Great Dixter, Northaim, Sussex — fifteenth century) with the Tudor Revival living room on the right (the former residence of William H. Wheelock, Esq.) . Notice especially the similarity of the timbered ceilings.

(below) "It may be accepted as an axiom that in the half-timber house the more panelling we can have the better," Jackson said, describing this room. Panelling and rarer sculpted plaster ceilings were the only ornate features of Tudor Revival. Notice that the fireplace is without a mantel — no space to store Victorian knick-knacks!

Goodnow and Adams in **The Honest House** (1914) say this Forest Hills, Long Island, bedroom owes its charm to the substantial old furniture and the gay English chintz quilt and curtains.

The stair hall in "The Belfry," a half-timbered house in Katonah, New York.

A timbered ceiling, rough plaster walls, and tile floor are features of this sparsely furnished English Revival dining room in Riverdale, New York.

Goodnow and Adams recommend muslin curtains and a row of flower pots (planted with geraniums) to decorate the English-style kitchen window. This kitchen is in Forest Hills.

Restoring My Mechanical Doorbell

by Spencer Hines

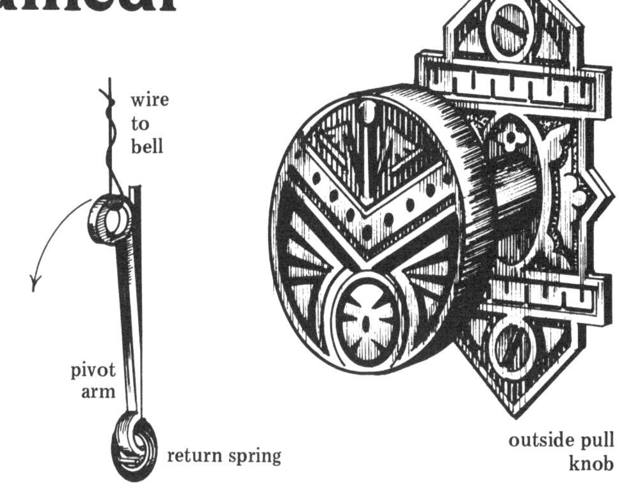

EARLY IN THE COURSE of restoring our 1889 Queen Anne house in Hyattsville, Maryland, my wife and I noticed a strange but use-ful-looking device on the interior frame of our front door. It was a pivoting strip of metal with holes in either end, set into the door moulding. On the outside of the door frame, right about doorbell height, was the outline of a hole that had been filled with wood putty. We concluded that we had discov-ered the remains of a mechanical doorbell, and decided to restore it ... if we could only find out how it was supposed to work.

MORE URGENT REPAIRS diverted our attention from our doorbell restoration for quite a while, until we had a breakthrough: Our coun-ty government decided to de-Victorianize a Colonial mansion as part of a restoration pro-ject, and recruited me to help salvage archi-tectural elements from the building. Imagine my delight when I found on the door of this house the same metal fitting that was on mine! The broken remains of the bell mechanism were also there. Unfortunately, no knob or spring mechanism was left. I bought the broken bell mechanism and took it home for further study.

THE BELL was a complex firebell-type device, activated by a pull wire. A metal rod forced back a little copper hammer until it suddenly sprang forward, hitting the bell. A one-way catch then forced the rod back to its original position. Now I understood what I had on my door -- it was the lever that linked the out-side pull knob with the bell mechanism.

MY PATIENT (but determined) wife took on the job of finding the parts we still lacked. At Hyattsville Hardware, an anachronistic (in the best sense of the word) establishment that stocks vintage hardware, she found two tension springs that were just the right size. Then, at the local electrical supply house, she found a modern bell (part of an electric bell) that was the right size and shape. She bought the whole electric bell, and the electrical supply store happily helped her redrill its center hole to fit its new home.

I ASSEMBLED the bell mecha-nism, then turned my attention to finding a proper pull knob. I knew what it was supposed to look like (from the OHJ arti-cle on mechanical bells, Octo-ber and November 1979), but I couldn't find a satisfactory reproduction. So I bought a cabinet knob and adapted it. I screwed the escutcheon to the moulding and used the knob's bolt as the base for a spring that held the knob tightly against the escutch-eon. Then I fastened a wire to the bolt, threading it through the wall.

SOME TIME LATER -- after all that work adapt-ing the cabinet knob -- I visited an architec-tural antiques store. A thoughtful clerk, who was kind enough to listen to the story of my house restoration, rummaged through an old drawer and produced a beautiful Aesthetic-Movement-style brass pull knob that fit perfectly with the house's original hardware. It, too, was incomplete: The original spring mechanism was missing.

ONCE AGAIN, Hyattsville Hardware helped me out by supplying a compression spring just the right size. The pull knob assembly fit com-fortably into the hole in the moulding. With the escutcheon screwed down, the knob could be pulled out nicely, and then the spring would snap it right back into place -- just the way it was supposed to work.

I ASSEMBLED the whole system, using old paint marks on my moulding as a guide for mounting the bell mechanism. I ran a wire from the pull knob to the built-in lever on my door, then stretched another length of wire taut between the lever and the bell assembly. It worked! After many years, our doorbell was once again making its tinny clang.

WITH OUR MECHANICAL DOORBELL finally complete, our only difficulty is that most people don't know what it is. But they're learning....

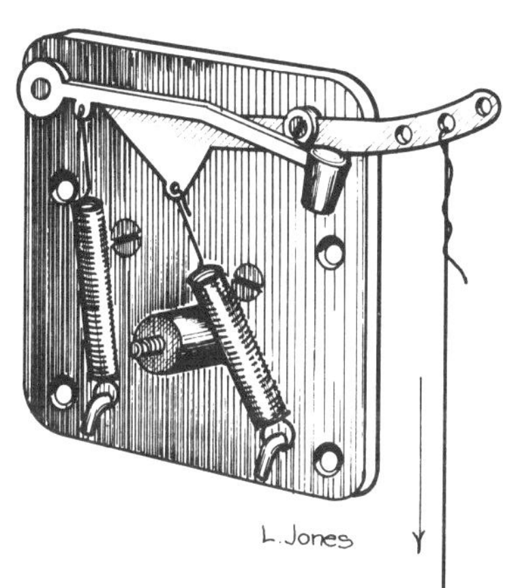

Restoration Products *by Larry Jones*

Paint Companies With Historic Paint Colors

'Who makes historical paint colors?' is a common question we get from readers. There are many choices these days; here's a rundown of who's got what. Bear in mind that some colors are documented originals while others are adaptations.

Allentown Paint Manufacturing Co., Dept. OHJ, P.O. Box 597, Allentown, PA 18105. (215) 433-4273. Breining's Ready Mixed Oil Paints, linseed oil/alkyd exterior paints. 12 colors originally produced from 1855 to 1913. Color card is $3.

Benjamin Moore & Co., Dept. OHJ, 52 Chestnut Ridge Rd., Montvale, NJ 07645. (201) 573-9600. Historical Color Collection, 18th- & 19th-century colors, alkyd enamels and latex paints. Free interior and exterior color charts.

Finnaren & Haley, Inc., Dept. OHJ, 2320 Haverford Rd., Ardmore, PA 19003. (215) 649-5000. Authentic (Colonial) Colors of Historic Philadelphia, alkyd oil base and acrylic-latex paints. Free chart of interior and exterior colors.

Fuller O'Brien Paints, Dept. OHJ, P.O. Box 864, Brunswick, GA 31520. (912) 265-7650. Cape May Victorian Colors and Exterior-Interior Heritage Color Collection. Victorian Color chart, $1.30; Heritage Color Collection, free.

Martin-Senour Co., Dept OHJ, 1370 Ontario Ave., N.W., Cleveland, OH 44113. Williamsburg Paint Colors, interior and exterior latex paints. Color chart, $1. Order from Colonial Williamsburg Foundation, Dept. OHJ, Craft House, P.O. Box C, Williamsburg, VA 23185. Call (800) 446-9240 for the dealer nearest you.

Muralo Co., Dept. OHJ, 148 E. Fifth St., Bayonne, NJ 07002. Georgetown Colors in 100% linseed oil and latex paints; also calcimine paint. Write for name of distributer – no literature.

The Old-Fashioned Milk Paint Co., Dept. OHJ, P.O. Box 222H, Groton, MA 01450. (617) 448-6336. Genuine milk paint in powder form in eight colors. Send $.60 for color sample card.

Pittsburgh Paints, PPG Industries, Inc., Dept. OHJ, One PPG Place, Pittsburgh, PA 15272. Historic Colors of the 18th and 19th centuries are greyed tints and shades that complement old homes of all periods. They're available for interior and exterior in alkyd, oil, latex, and acrylic paint. Free color folder.

Pratt & Lambert, Dept. OHJ, 75 Tonawanda St., Buffalo, NY 14207. (716) 873-6000. Early American Colors from Greenfield Village duplicate colors of the 18th and 19th centuries; available for interior and exterior in latex. Color cards, $.50.

Sherwin-Williams Co., Dept. OHJ, P.O. 6939, Cleveland, OH 44101. (216) 566-2332. Heritage Colors, 40 historic paint colors documented in the book *Century of Color: Exterior Decoration for American Buildings 1820-1920*. The colors are available in either latex or oil-based paints. $2 color card.

Stulb Paint & Chemical Co., Inc., Dept. OHJ, P.O. Box 297, Norristown, PA 19404. (215) 272-6660. Old Sturbridge Paint Colours and Old Village Paint Colours, authentic 18th- and 19th-century colors, for interior or exterior use. Available only in oil-based paint. Color cards, $1.

If you don't find what you're looking for in the Restoration Products pages you're sure to find it in The Old-House Journal Catalog.

Renewer & Remover

Restore-x Exterior Paint Remover and its companion, Weathered Wood Renewer, are relatively safe and economical for stripping (prior to repainting) or renewing weathered, stained wood.

The Exterior Paint Remover is a professional-strength, lye-based (sodium hydroxide) product that will remove paint and heavy-bodied stains from wood, masonry, and metal. It comes ready to use; a gallon covers from 150 to 200 square feet when brushed or rolled on. After a waiting period, the surface is scrubbed with a stiff brush and the old finish is rinsed off. If the chemical remover dries out before it is rinsed off, it can be reactivated and softened by misting it with water. After rinsing away the sludge, you neutralize the wood with an oxalic-acid conditioner that should also bring back the color of the wood.

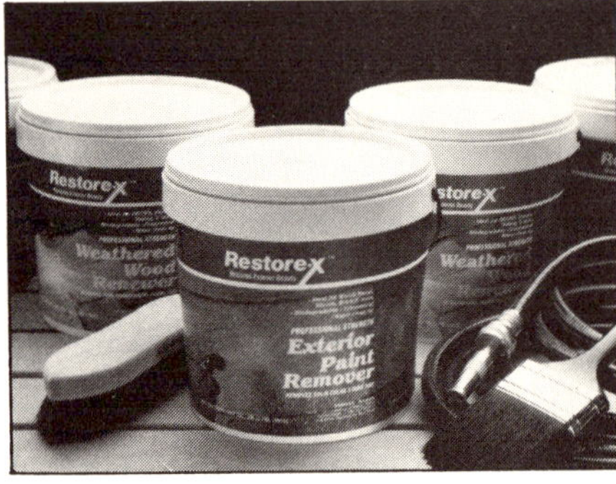

The product's drawbacks are similar to those of other chemical paint removers. The water rinse will probably raise the grain. You have to wait until the wood is thoroughly dry before repainting. Also, the manufacturer suggests that in some cases a high-pressure (not garden hose) rinse is necessary to remove the paint. High-pressure washes can cause damage similar to sandblasting. Nevertheless, the product offers a convenient way to buy an effective and economical paint remover.

The Weathered Wood Renewer, chemically similar to the Remover, will remove both weathering discoloration from unfinished wood, and semi-transparent stain from previously treated wood. It's intended to give siding, decks, fencing, and outdoor furniture the look of new wood. Neither product works on baked-on enamel finishes, epoxies, or plastic/polyurethane-based clear finishes. Restore-x is sold nationwide at lumberyards and building suppliers; for the dealer nearest you and a free brochure, write to Restec Industries, Inc., Dept. OHJ, P.O. Box 2747, Eugene, OR 97402. (503) 345-1142.

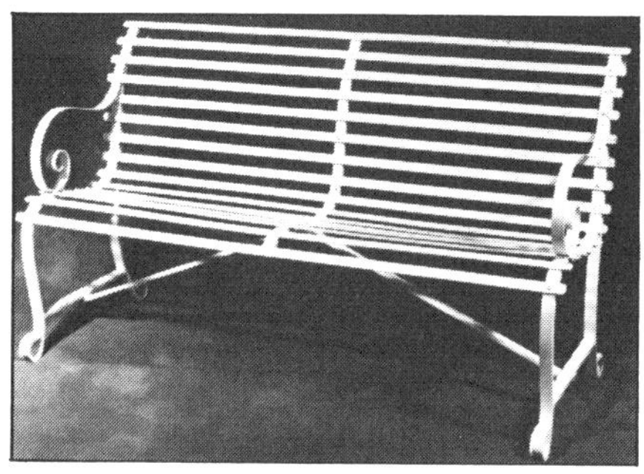

Iron Park Bench

We're not talking about oak-slatted promenade benches here, but rather those old-style, all-iron park benches. Wikco Industries's Clear Creek Bench is an exact replica of a design that's over 100 years old. It's made of the same channel and flat wrought-iron as the original. The bench is all metal, weighs 75 lbs., and comes in white, black, or green enamel (other colors available on special order). The price is $189 plus shipping from **Wikco Industries, Inc., Dept. OHJ, Route 2, P.O. Box 154, Broken Bow, NE 68822. (308) 872-5327.**

Garden Trellises

Wooden ornamental trellises, arches, and rose arbors are all-but-forgotten garden and landscape features that may enhance your old house. A handsome trellis can screen unwanted views; act as an entry or focal point; separate parts of a garden; support vegetable, fruit, and flowering vines; or serve its original purpose of supporting climbing roses.

The Trellis Garden has unpainted wooden trellises, arbors and arches, made from cypress, red cedar, redwood, and mahogany. Well built, sturdy, and easy to assemble, they range in price from $210 to $325, plus shipping. Also available are matching garden benches and even Gothic Cottage and Country Church bird feeders. Their catalog ($3, refundable with an order) contains a handy listing of plant material suitable for trellises. Order from **The Trellis Garden, Dept. OHJ, P.O. Box 64, Rydal, PA 19046.**

OLD–HOUSE & GARDEN

We've discovered some wonderful, old-fashioned items for the old-house yard and garden.

Tree Fences

If you've spent any time in New York City, you've probably seen little hoop-shaped iron fences surrounding the sidewalk street trees. For over a century these sturdy, decorative fences have served the dual purpose of protecting trees and forming a small flower-bed enclosure. Today tree fences are more popular than ever, for street trees on Main Street as well as in front of townhouses.

Italian Art Iron Works in Brooklyn will custom make and ship tree fences to any OHJ readers who need them. The fences cost $18 per running foot, plus shipping. They're heavy enough to rest on the ground without stakes; if a car does bump one it'll move rather than bend. These strong fences are made out of ½-in.-diameter steel rod with an angle iron base. They're usually 12 inches tall (taller ones can be made to order), with rods formed to a 10-in. radius only. When measuring, add ¾ inch to each 10 inches of length. (If you needed a 20-in.-by-40-in. fence, they'd make you one 21½ in. by 43 in.)

The fences bolt together at the corners and come in the standard color for street-tree fences: gloss black. There is no brochure, but you can call or write **Italian Art Iron Works, Dept. OHJ, 38 Bergen St., Brooklyn, NY 11217. (718) 875-1362.**

Wooden Screen Doors

The Oregon Screen Door Company makes a number of period style doors in fir, priced from $138.05 to $314.55. The doors come as kits or assembled. You can replace the screens with glass storms or other decorative panels. They will even stencil paint old-style designs on the screens. Send $3 for a brochure to **Oregon Screen Door Co., Dept. OHJ, 330 High St., Eugene, OR 97401. (503) 485-0279.**

Adirondack Chair

Westport makes a folding version of the classic Adirondack Chair. It's ideal for use on cottage porches, lawns, and even indoors. This chair is solid as a rock yet folds up for storage to a mere 10 inches wide. Made from kiln-dried white oak, the chair comes unfinished. It can be painted, stained, or left unfinished to weather to a grey color. The Westport Fold-Away Adirondack Chair sells for $125 plus shipping. Order it by phone or mail from **The Pottery Barn, Dept. OHJ, 231 Tenth Ave., New York, NY 10011. (212) 929-0753; outside NY State, (800) 847-4048.**

1888 Burpee's Catalog

Larry Jennings, an OHJ reader in California, mentioned to us that the Burpee Company at one time was offering reprints of their 1888 Farm Annual of garden, farm, and flower seeds. We contacted the company and discovered that they still have a limited supply of the reprints available; as long as the supply lasts they'll sell them to OHJ readers for $2 each. The catalog has a beautiful color cover and is loaded with black-and-white etchings of vegetables, fruits, and flowers. It's an excellent resource for anyone trying to plant a period-style garden; there are interesting planting tips, and some of the varieties listed are still available. Order Burpee's 1888 Catalog (9466-4). Write to **Burpee's 1888 Catalog Offer, Dept. OHJ, 300 Park Ave., Warminster, PA 18974.**

From Elegant Townhouse To Plain Rowhouse
The Party-Wall House

by James C. Massey and Shirley Maxwell

ROWHOUSE, townhouse, party-wall house -- the name may vary, the facade may be plain or fanciful, the style anything from Colonial to Queen Anne to Colonial Revival to 1980s Developer's Tasteful. Whatever you call it, however you dress it, it is the early urban residential form most frequently found in America's older cities.

STYLISTICALLY, rowhouse facades bespeak their eras. This remarkably versatile concept can embrace virtually any vertical treatment and any type of embellishment: You can find rowhouses with tiny stoops or ample porches; with the flat surfaces of the Federal period or the towers and bays of the Romanesque.

WHATEVER THE "STYLE," the distinguishing characteristic of the rowhouse is the presence of at least one party, or common, wall that's shared with a neighbor on one or both sides. The idea was (and is) to fit as many building lots on a block as possible -- a clear benefit to the developer. That done, the building itself spreads upward and backward, rather than outward, to accommodate the needs and tastes of the occupants. Most often the narrow, streetfront facade has two or three bays, usually with a front door at one side and two windows at the other. However, the grander townhouses of the wealthy may have four bays, whereas the rowhouse dwellings of the less affluent occasionally have as few as one.

THE TYPICAL ROWHOUSE has two or three storeys rising above a high basement, but some (particularly in Boston, Philadelphia, and New York) may stretch to four or even five. The single-storey rowhouse is largely a 20th-century phenomenon. A twin, or double, house is closely akin to today's duplex. The flounder, a regional phenomenon, is really a half-house built on the party line, with its roof sloping sharply to one side. The bandbox house is sometimes associated with the early rowhouse; it's built at the rear of the lot, with one room on each of its two or three storeys.

Dating The Rowhouse

CLUES to the age of the house are provided by rooflines, dormers, and windows. The high-pitched gable and gambrel roofs of the 18th century gave way to lower pitches in the second quarter of the 19th century. Flat roofs with a rearward slope became common around the time of the Civil War, only to be replaced in the 20th century by the gable once again. Dormers moved from the simple, shed-roofed projections of the early 18th century to more ornate, gabled and pedimented structures, often with round-arch heads and

pilasters, in the latter part of the century. After 1810, the low, segmental-arch dormer became common.

THE AGE OF THE HOUSE is also suggested by building projections, which became ampler and higher with the passing decades, and by construction methods and materials. Rowhouses of frame construction, although built well into the 19th century in later and smaller cities, are usually found only in the earliest sections of major older cities, where fire codes were firmly in place by the late 18th century. (One visible result of the codes are fire walls: masonry walls between rowhouses, which project above the roofline to prevent sparks from traveling from one roof to another.)

BRICK BECAME STYLISH; so did, from the mid-19th century until about 1900, smooth-faced brownstone (actually sandstone, most often) laid in even, rectangular, "ashlar" patterns. In the very late 19th century, more heavily textured "rock-faced" stone was popular. The type of bricks used and the method of laying them (the "bond") varied over time. Hand-cast, 18th-century bricks tend to be rougher than the smooth, hard, mechanically formed pressed brick (or "Philadelphia" brick) of the late 19th century. Flemish bond, alternating end and side faces of the brick, is found more frequently on facades of 18th-century buildings (and on the Colonial Revivals of the 20th century). The 19th-century structures are more likely to have either all-stretcher bond, displaying only the long, side faces of the brick, or common bond, in which rows of headers (end faces) occur after every three, five, or seven rows of stretchers.

THE INTERIOR CONFIGURATION of 18th-century rowhouses is typically expressed by a main block with side stair hall, a rear wing (probably containing the kitchen and possibly other rooms as well), and a "piazza," the passageway that connects front and rear and contains the stairs. In the 19th century the piazza disappeared, to be followed in the early 20th century by the wing. The house became slightly wider, with more and larger windows front and rear, as the "airtight" concept gained influence. The floor plan of most late-19th- and early-20th-century, urban, three-bay rowhouses is so standardized that a visitor from Philadelphia would have no trouble finding his or her way to the bathroom in a Washington, D.C., counterpart. The plans generally allowed for a stair hall, kitchen, and one or two other rooms on the first floor; two or three bedrooms and a bath on the third floor.

THE REAR YARD may have access to the street by means of a covered side passage carved out either from one or both of the houses or through an alley along one side. Rear alleys often facilitate "back-door" services.

Reading The Old House
The Rowhouse

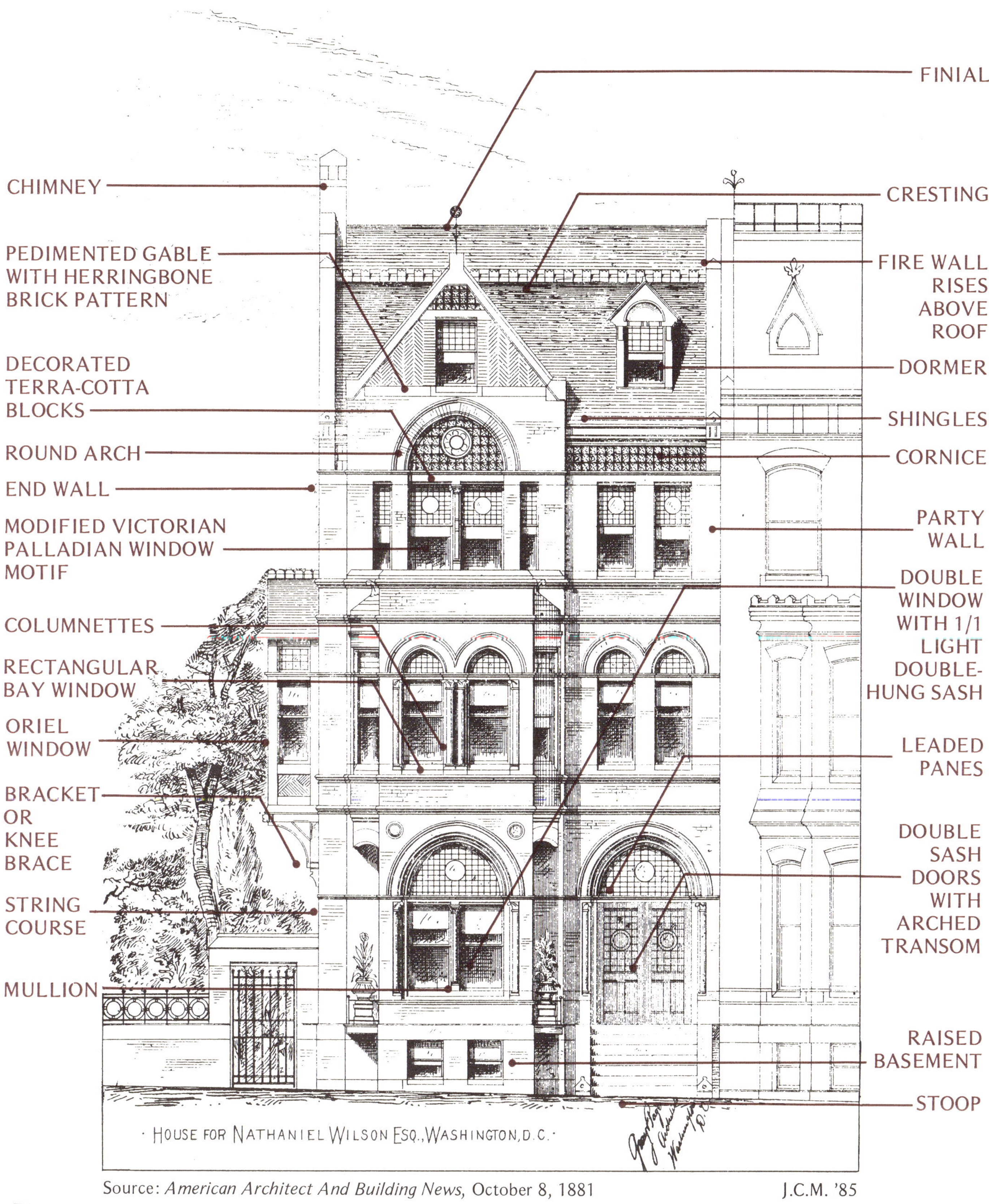

Source: *American Architect And Building News*, October 8, 1881　　　　J.C.M. '85

Clapboards

continued from p. 135

WARM WEATHER came in early spring, and we began removing the asbestos. A tack puller was used to "start" the galvanized-copper, serrated nails, so they could be drawn with a claw hammer. We saved usable nails, and piled up asbestos shingles for removal to the town dump. (Strips of tarpaper underlayment were salvaged to become several gardening-seasons-worth of cut worm collars around the tomato plants.) Sawn wood lath had been liberally used at each clapboard course to fir out the wall into a flat plane to receive the asbestos shingles. We salvaged several bundles of lath and later employed it more traditionally, for the replacement of a missing plaster ceiling.

WHEN WE REMOVED the 1950s-vintage work, we discovered that all of the original 18th-century clapboards had indeed survived, except for the bottom seven courses, which had been replaced in past sill repairs. We also learned why the previous owners had chosen the not-inexpensive expedient of asbestos-shingle siding: Many of the surviving clapboards were cracked, and a discouragingly large proportion were extremely loose because of rotted segments around the large, hand-wrought, "rose-headed" iron nails that secured them to the building.

IN A TECHNIQUE peculiar to some 18th- and early-19th-century New England buildings, the clapboard ends weren't square-butt-jointed (as is customary in modern construction); they had been shaved thin, in long tapers that overlapped one another. This procedure was more labor-intensive than the usual butt joint, but it did create a more dependable weather seal. However, long-standing neglect and an absence of paint had significantly contributed to the deterioration of the original clapboard covering. Most surfaces retained virtually no paint; at other areas, the remaining paint residue could be removed with a whisk broom.

IN SOME INSTANCES where they abutted window frames, clapboard ends had also rotted from the lack of caulking and paint. In at least two areas, it was unhappily apparent that exterior side-wall sheathing beneath the clapboards had also deteriorated from chronic water intrusion. Obviously, the clapboarding had to be entirely removed. We had to decide whether to re-clapboard the entire north end of the house using new material, or to attempt to salvage, repair, and re-use as much of the original 18th-century fabric as possible.

PRESERVATION WON OUT. The wonderfully textured, lapped-joint clapboards, with their

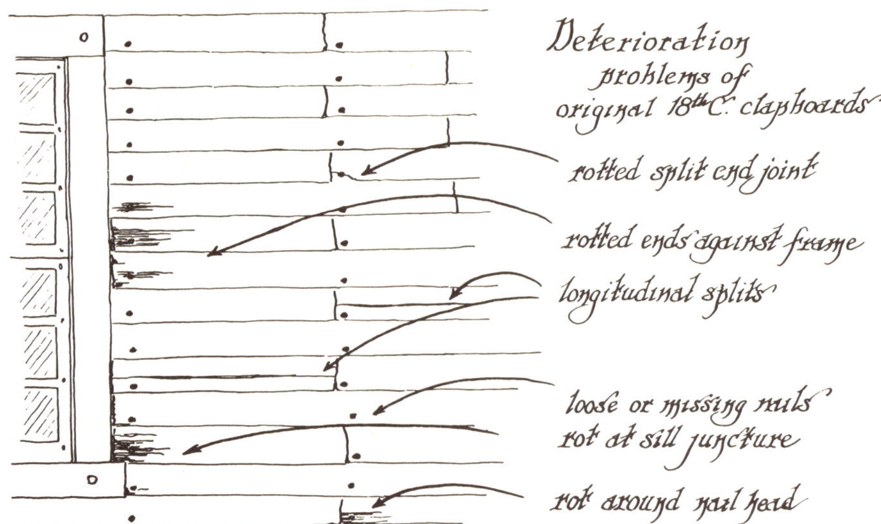

Luckily, only a window and some of the siding were damaged when this maple tree smashed into the house.

The clapboards of this 18th-century house are lap jointed, their ends tapering and overlapping rather than merely butting.

narrow exposure to the weather, were original to the house; their loss would have sacrificed much of the character and visual interest of the north end of the building.

Taking It Off

BEFORE REMOVING THE CLAPBOARDS, we numbered them sequentially with colored chalk, to assure accurate replacement. To guide matching during their re-installation, simple symbols were chalked overlying all joints. Corresponding numbers and index marks were chalked on window frames and cornerboards. As a final precaution in the interest of accuracy, we made a visual guide for alignment by drawing a series of diagonal lines across the clapboards. We used a different color chalk for each area of the wall.

USING A TACK PULLER, a cat's paw, a small curved wrecking bar, and a claw hammer, nails were carefully drawn and saved for re-use. True wrought-iron is malleable, and it's a simple matter to straighten bent nails with a regular hammer, using a short section of railroad track as an anvil. (No heating is required.) In this fashion, the clapboards were carefully removed and stored to await future conservation efforts.

WE DISCOVERED that areas of the underlying sheathing boards, which averaged at least a foot wide and a full inch thick, had deteriorated too, especially at the ends that abutted window frames. In many instances, the rot was sufficiently advanced that we could not renail to the side-wall studs and posts. Consequently, we had to remove and salvage sidewall sheathing as well as the clapboards. Those boards, too, were systematically marked with chalk prior to removal, and the large,

hand-wrought nails were saved and straightened for re-use. Sheathing boards, like the clapboards, were stored under cover for future reapplication.

WITH THE NORTH WALL opened to the building's frame, it seemed only sensible to install insulation (even though this was back in the halcyon days of 37-cents-per-gallon fuel oil). Three-inch-thick glasswool, backed with kraft-paper vapor barrier, was friction fit between the studs and the posts; the depth of the in-wall cavity permitted material of no greater thickness. This endeavor was a do-it-yourself project of several weeks' duration, so we tacked large, heavy-gauge polyethylene plastic sheets over the exposed wall every day at the end of the work.

WE RENAILED SHEATHING BOARDS to the frame after cutting rotted ends back to sound wood that could be secured to the next stud. Where cutting back to the next stud would have meant removing an excessive amount of good wood, we instead spliced on a new piece using a mitred joint. We securely fastened the piece to the original board by screwing an inch-thick plywood batten behind the joint on the inside. (Fortunately a local lumberyard had a supply of full-inch-thick, rough-sawn pine, in widths as great as 14 inches.) After we re-installed the sidewall sheathing, we covered the boards with red rosin building paper as an additional seal against drafts.

Making The Repairs

NOW WE TURNED OUR ATTENTION to the stored clapboards. A few clapboards were split longitudinally, and these were relatively simple to repair. We cleaned the split edges just as any surface should be cleaned preparatory to gluing. Then we mixed a two-part epoxy cement and applied it to the facing surfaces. Several parallel-jaw, wooden furniture clamps were used to hold the pieces overnight until the glue had thoroughly dried.

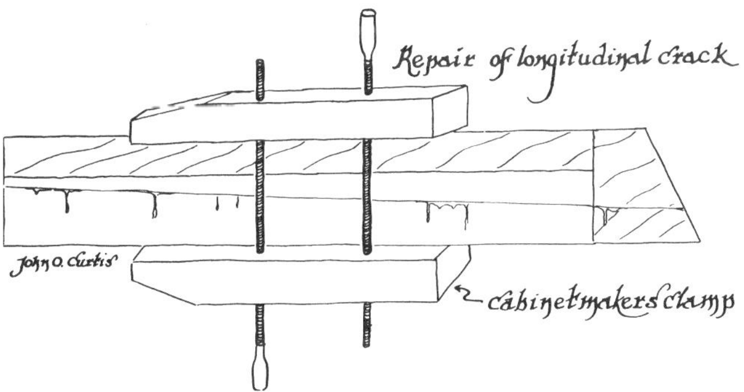

BEFORE THE ASBESTOS SHINGLES had ever been applied, long-term unpainted exposure to the weather had severely deteriorated the clapboards, primarily around the wrought-iron nails. But the major portion of each clapboard was still sound, so the sensible approach was to develop a technique whereby the rotted sections could be cut away and the resultant void patched with sound new material.

WE TOOK ADVANTAGE of the table saw's mitering capabilities, cutting away the damaged portions of the clapboards in an angled cut. The undercut assured that the patch would be mechanically wedged in place, beneath the angled edge of the sound wood, when the clapboard was renailed to the building. Again using epoxy-resin adhesive, we glued the patch in place and clamped it overnight for curing. We deliberately cut the patches slightly oversize, so they could be trimmed to conform smoothly with the adjoining original wood.

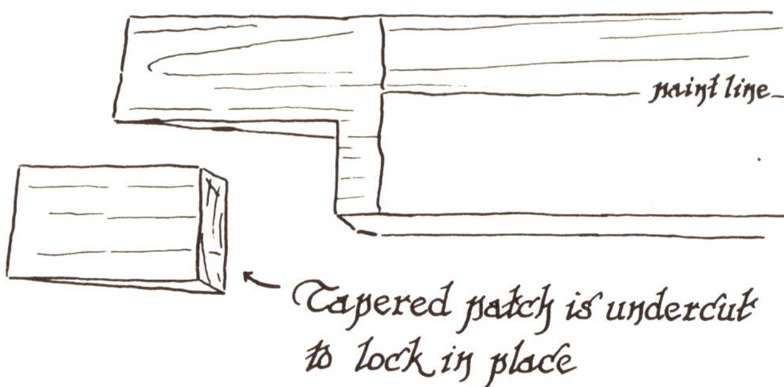

A FEW CLAPBOARDS were simply too far deteriorated to be successfully repaired in this manner. Rather than discard these, we used them as the stock for cutting patches. This procedure assured that the original clapboards and the patches would be compatible in texture, wood species, and rate of expansion and contraction. The clapboards we'd sacrificed to patch others were replaced with appropriate square-edged hemlock clapboards from the local lumberyard. These were back-primed prior to installation.

REGULAR EPOXIES such as Devcon or Elmer's worked quite well; the "five minute," quick-setting types provided a less strong joint. The thicker pigmented epoxies didn't yield as tight a joint and were harder to work with. None of the two-part cements were of special formulation; all were "off-the-shelf," proprietary adhesives, purchased at the lumberyard or hardware store. Buying them in such small quantities was by no means the least expensive course, but it was convenient and approximately eight packages sufficed to repair clapboards for <u>one</u> end of the house up to plate level. That, certainly, is cheaper than buying new clapboards. Also, not every jointed end of every clapboard required such repairs.

WE HAD TO DRILL PILOT HOLES in the patched areas to admit the thick, square-shanked, wrought nails. Because the clapboards had been marked prior to removal, our sequential re-installation resulted in an excellent finished appearance, nearly identical to the original untouched wall.

Here you can see the patches made in the rotted ends of the clapboards. (Note the large heads of the wrought-iron nails.)

AS ADDED INSURANCE against possible fracture of the glued joints, we drove an additional hot-dipped, galvanized wire nail through the unpatched section of each clapboard, immediately adjacent to the patched section in which the original hand-wrought nail had been used.

ALL BOARDS were lightly wire-brushed in preparation for painting. Epoxy-resin cements are vulnerable to degradation by ultra-violet light, which breaks down their adhesive capabilities, so it was imperative to paint the glue joints immediately. Exterior grade primer was applied; following several weeks' drying time, a finish coat of paint completed the job.

SUCH A LENGTHY and tedious project is not recommended for those impatient souls who want quick results. It was a labor of love. The result is the preservation of most of the 18th-century clapboards, their irregularities and visual interest punctuated by wrought-iron nails with which they were refastened ... all intact. It was also a successful experiment in using the technology of modern adhesives to conserve a wall surface created by traditional handcraft technology. As of this writing, just a decade later, the joints have survived a succession of New England winters and are still holding well, though the wall is admittedly due for another coat of paint. Work on an old house is never finished.

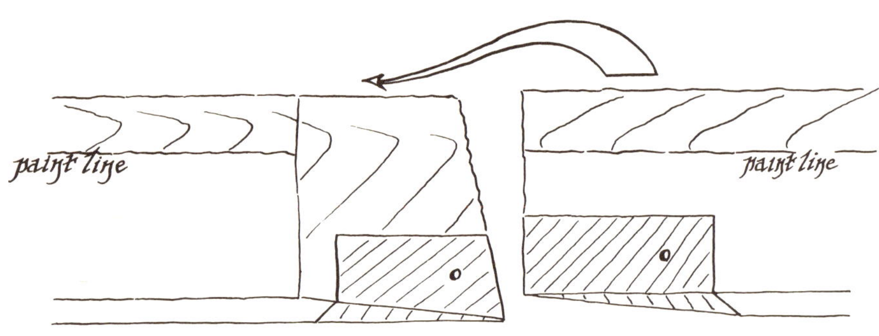

JOHN OBED CURTIS, Director of the Curatorial Department at Old Sturbridge Village, has first-hand experience in the art of restoring and maintaining an 18th-century house.

How To Hook Paint

YOU KNOW THE PROBLEM: You're two storeys above the ground on a wiggling extension ladder, and you're trying to hold a gallon of paint in one hand while brushing with the other. You can let the can dangle from a hook on a ladder rung, but that's still pretty inconvenient. Every time you dip the brush in it, the can swings and sways, and you have to continually reach between the ladder rungs.

PROFESSIONAL PAINTERS solve this problem by using a pot hook. You can buy one at a well-stocked paint store, or you can fashion your own from a paint-can handle. A pot hook keeps the paint can perfectly steady against the right side of the ladder. The can can't swing back and forth because it's nestled in the channel of the ladder rail. A pot hook is also advantageous because it holds the wire handle of the paint can off to one side -- out of your way.

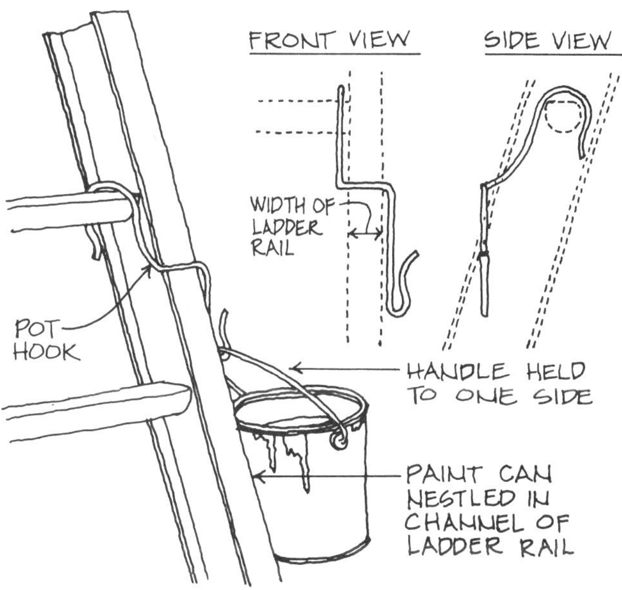

UNFORTUNATELY, you won't find a left-handed pot hook ready-made. So if you're a southpaw, you'll have to make your own.

> Lee Gardner
> Rowley, Mass.

A Rust-Buster

THE January-February 1985 "Ask OHJ" had a letter about the problems of rust stains in clawfoot tubs. I too have a clawfoot with bad rust stains that I couldn't get out. But here's a remedy I found in a book that's probably as old as our clawfoot tub. Form a paste by mixing together small amounts of cream of tartar and hydrogen peroxide. Let the paste sit on the stain for at least a few hours. I let it sit overnight, and when I used the shower the next morning, it all went down the drain. This also works well around the sink plug -- mine was brass, and came clean like new.

> Mrs. R.M. Acosta
> Brooklyn, N.Y.

Another Rust-Buster

I JUST READ in the January-February issue about a person having troubles with rust stains in a clawfoot bathtub. Here's the solution: Lay three or four sheets of paper towels over the stain and saturate them with white vinegar. Let them stand for one to three hours (depending on the stain). Then remove and rinse thoroughly. If a three-hour soaking doesn't work, leave it on overnight or up to 10 hours.

> Dennis Lane
> Eureka, Ca.

On Cleaning Candlesticks

'BUTCHER, baker, candlestick maker' goes the old nursery rhyme. That the third profession should rate mention with two of the most familiar trades indicates the recognition accorded the contrivers of ornate cast-metal candlesticks designed with endless small curlicues and crevices, which were the delight of rococo Victorian fancies.

BUT AFTER USE, candlewax finds its way into these designs, defying easy removal. How Victorians handled this vexing problem is more than I know. The problem is how we can do it in our modern kitchens without damaging the candlestick and without spreading wax over everything within ten yards of the operation. Take heart, kind reader -- a clean and easy solution is at hand!

I SPREAD a double thickness of paper towels on the drainboard and hold the candlestick at an angle above the paper. With the other hand I click on my trusty heat gun (purchased from OHJ) and direct a current of hot air at the offending encrustation. Like magic, the wax melts away onto the absorbent paper. No chips, no waxy scums, no work, and no damage! Then quickly, I rinse the candlestick in hot water under the sink faucet to remove the last trace of wax; then I dry it with a dishtowel. Goodbye paring knives, scrapers, large-scale messes, stopped drainpipes, and frazzled nerves!

> Roy A. Swayze
> Eutaw, Al.

Tips To Share? Do you have any hints or short cuts that might help other old-house owners? We'll pay $15 for any short how-to items that are used in this "Restorer's Notebook" column. Write to Notebook Editor, The Old-House Journal, 69A Seventh Avenue, Brooklyn, NY 11217.

A CORNICE is an important visual element on any building -- but it's especially significant in urban row-house architecture. Take away the cornice, and all that's left is a brick wall ... unless the brick wall disappears, too, under a spanking-new skin. In this case, every element that bespoke the period and style of the house has been covered over. Proportion was lost, along with the patina of age that graces even the plainest old masonry. The cover-ups are old standards: permastone on the foundation; implausible aluminum "clapboard" above; standard new windows that don't match the originals; the "modernized" entry -- an all-purpose contractor's device that has little in common with an old urban row-house. The decision to cover the cornice finished the job. To apply the aluminum, corner brackets (like those of the unremuddled neighbor at left) were hacked off and discarded. Fortunately, the rest of the cornice remains under the aluminum. Perhaps in the future, it will again see the light of day.

The Old-House Journal®

69A Seventh Avenue,
Brooklyn, New York 11217

Postmaster: Address Correction Requested

Restoration and Maintenance Techniques
For The Pre-1939 House

October 1985 / Vol. XIII No. 8 / $2.

The Old-House Journal

Routing Wiring

How To Get From Here To There With Very Little Plaster Repair

by The OHJ Technical Staff

HAVE YOU EVER FOUND yourself dreading the arrival of an electrician? Sure, you want to use an air conditioner in your bedroom, but not at the price of a month's worth of plaster repair. And if she or he removes a section of decorative cornice moulding, the damage may never be repaired. Don't panic: There are ways to conceal wiring with little disruption to finished surfaces.

THIS ARTICLE IS NOT about wiring an old house. You and your electrician can decide how many circuits you need, where switchboxes should be located, etc. What follows is an outline of some of the tricks used to navigate wiring through walls, floors, and ceilings with minimal disruption to finished surfaces. Whether you're running the electrical cable yourself or coaching an electrician, you'll find these tips and techniques to be invaluable timesavers.

cont'd on p. 168

In the next issue...
THE QUEEN ANNE PARLOR

BUNGALOW RESPONSES

I WISH TO TEMPER your interest in starting a new, more specialized version of OHJ. I also happen to be an Art Deco/ Moderne enthusiast, but I would certainly not advocate an "Old Art Deco House Journal." What of the Georgian or the Romanesque fans? Will they clamor for their own edition? I would hate to see your OHJ efforts diverted to serve a special interest. Although the styles may change, the materials, tools, and tricks of the trade are generally the same; the OHJ should continue to serve this market.

If you choose to ignore my advice and plan a new publication, yes, I would like to hear about it. Any bungalow news is good news.

--Ray Ott
West Chester, Penn.

SORRY I don't share your gushing love of bungalows (or your cutesy plays on the word). I'm glad you'll be shunting all that to a different publication --as long as you aren't then distracted from the job of maintaining the quality of dear old OHJ.

--P. Sontagh

I WOULD NOT recommend that you start a separate publication devoted to bungalows. A great many of your readers have an interest in old houses of a variety of styles, and would not appreciate having to order a number of different magazines to get the variety. For instance, read back over your past issues to see how many people have bought more than one old house over the years. They are not all necessarily of the same vintage.

I recommend against starting a spin-off newsletter for bungalows. All of your readers would be better served by a single journal about "Restoration and Maintenance Techniques for the Pre-1939 House."

--Charles L. Gellert
Washington, D.C.

I AM WARY about your possible new publication. I thought the May OHJ was terrific, especially the details about fabric accents and sources for borders.

But...if you begin a bungalow publication, I would probably not subscribe because I do not have a bungalow. I might thereby miss information. My greater fear is that OHJ might become too Victorian and my type of house [1902 medieval-revival shingle] would slip through the cracks and be covered by neither. Personally, I would prefer to see a special annual issue on bungalows in OHJ with details integrated into other issues, rather than a spin off.

--Nancy Schrock
Winchester, Mass.

I AGREE, bungalows are nice. So are a lot of other styles, too. Why not have a regular Bungalow feature in OHJ? I do not feel there is a conflict between them and older styles.

--Sarah Peterson
Alameda, Calif.

I BELIEVE your Bungalow Letter would be more successful as an extension of OHJ, not as a replacement. My largest concern is that you don't ignore the other post-Victorian house owners, just so the bungalow people can have their own magazine.

--Peter St. Denis
Plano, Illinois

WELL, we asked for it and we got it: an overwhelming response to the Bungalow Spin-Off Survey. Almost everybody likes the idea of more articles about post-Victorian houses. But--as the letters above indicate--some thoughtful readers suggest that we just expand OHJ to include articles for everyone to read.

Readers worry that choosing one publication would mean missing important articles in the other. Yet few people are eager to pay for two publications that might overlap. Others are concerned that owners of older buildings would never learn to appreciate post-Victorian houses if they don't read about them in OHJ itself.

Taking into account readers' concerns along with the practical aspects of publishing, we've decided that an enhanced OHJ is the way to go...so all readers will get all of our unique information.

As I write this (in July), we're busy planning the expansion. Look for the details in next month's issue.

The Old-House Journal®

Editor
Patricia Poore

Production Editor
Cole Gagne

Senior Technical Advisor
Larry Jones

Assistant Editors
Sarah J. McNamara
William J. O'Donnell

Contributing Editors
Walter Jowers
John Mark Garrison
Roland A. Labine Sr.

Architectural Consultant
Jonathan Poore

Circulation Supervisor
Barbara Bugg

Circulation Assistants
Jeanne Baldwin
Elaine Lynch

Office Manager
Tricia A. Martin

Catalog Editor
Sarah J. McNamara

Publishing Consultant
Paul T. McLoughlin

Publisher
Clem Labine

THE OLD-HOUSE JOURNAL *(ISSN 0094-0178) is published ten times annually for $18 per year by The Old-House Journal Corporation, 69A Seventh Avenue, Brooklyn, NY 11217. Telephone (718) 636-4514. Application to mail at second-class postage rates is pending at Brooklyn, New York, and additional mailing offices. POSTMASTER: Send address changes to* THE OLD-HOUSE JOURNAL, *69A Seventh Avenue, Brooklyn, NY 11217.*

Subscriptions in Canada are $36 per year, payable in Canadian funds. Contents are fully protected by copyright and must not be reproduced in any manner whatsoever without specific permission in writing from the Editor.

We are happy to accept editorial contributions to The Old-House Journal. Query letters that include an outline of the proposed article are preferred. All manuscripts will be reviewed, and returned if unacceptable. However, we cannot be responsible for non-receipt or loss — please keep copies of all materials sent.

Printed at Photo Comp Press, New York City

Seduction in South Dakota
My Unexpected Conversion To Old-House Living

by Betty Dove Wright

LAST SUMMER I learned that housing prices in South Dakota were dirt cheap compared to those in southern California and I was elated. I'd had a long-held, but private, dream of owning a snug little summer home in the Black Hills. I had spent part of my childhood there, and loved the beauty and freshness of the pines and mountains. The historic town of Deadwood was not only picturesque, it was home. For the first time I told my children of my plan to escape the hot, smoggy California summers to a little old house on a wee bit of land in that clean, clear air away from the hustle-bustle and hard work. During summer vacations from my job as professor of nursing in Pasadena, I could "live in a house by the side of the road and be a friend to Man."

MY FIVE DAUGHTERS didn't see it that way. Unaware that the whole foolish idea had been simmering in my dreams for years, the project came to be known as "Mom's Latest Dementia." There had been others: I had enrolled in college at the age of 39 in order to become a registered nurse while still raising a husband and five daughters and had stayed until I had earned a masters degree; at the age of fifty I had gone off to England to spend a year learning to be a midwife; at the age of 59 I had gone back there for another year to study cancer nursing. One would think my crazies would have become commonplace, but then, by definition, crazies never do.

IT TOOK US ONLY AN HOUR to find my house, since there are fewer than 500 in the whole town. I really didn't need four bedrooms or two living rooms, but the location and the price were even better than we'd hoped for. The original varnish on the carved woodwork meant that sloppy layers of paint would not have to be removed before covering it all with fresh, clean white paint. The wood panelling on the stairway could stay because its original surface would contrast nicely with the white woodwork. The floors, once delivered of the smelly green shag carpeting, now glued and stapled in place, would be cleaned and re-covered with a soft baby-blue pile of easy-care nylon. It was no problem that one of the pair of sliding doors between the two living rooms was stuck: I would find a good strong teenager to help me push the panelled door back into its hiding place between the walls, leaving the wide doorway between the east and west living rooms uncluttered. Identical doors, at a right angle to these, between the west living room and the dining room, could be hidden and ignored. The expanse of baby-blue would be uninterrupted.

THE PINKISH-BEIGE ASBESTOS shingle siding, under which Nan discovered the original clapboard, was certainly <u>not</u> going to be removed. I found the color pleasant and the siding was in good condition. Anyway, it would save me the trouble of having to paint the house every five years or so.

THE FIRST TO COME AROUND was Number Three Daughter, Nan. To refurbish an old house had been a dream of hers since childhood. She had been known to lose sleep from excitement after merely driving past an old relic ripe for re-doing. Her dream, however, ran counter to mine. Before she agreed to join me in my expedition to buy the old house, I warned her that mine was not to be one with cutesy gingerbread, dung-colored wainscotting, garish cabbage roses, or, horror of horrors, bathtubs with legs. I explained that great clouds of dust accumulated under those tubs. Nan, always the pragmatist, replied: So clean it out! I told her I could put up with antiquities only if they were unobtrusive, easy to care for, and didn't interfere with the soft pastel effect I was seeking. She swallowed hard, but consented, provided I promised to do nothing that she could not undo when I was gone.

My house and its companion, which is identical though slightly larger. We're gleefully removing asbestos shingles — everyone in town is fascinated!

Number Three Daughter Nan and the one working pocket door between the double parlors. Luckily the woodwork had never been painted.

A grandchild of a former owner had several old photographs of my house. This one, dated 1937, shows the rear of the house.

plane. The wood shaving had lain there, protected, for 80 years. At that moment I felt a sort of oneness with the nameless folk who had so carefully sawn the decoration on my stairway, who had installed the dining room window lopsided and then fitted the baseboard below it to minimize the crookedness, who had painstakingly built the orderly panels and decorative beading of my stairway wall nearly a century before.

AFTER I RETURNED to Pasadena, while yet again telling of my find, someone asked me, "What are you going to do with your house?" To my astonishment, I heard myself reply: "I am going to restore it as perfectly as I can for a bed-and-breakfast."

BUT THE HOUSE had to have a new roof, now. The master bedroom ceiling was badly damaged from water leaks. Bidders for the roof job talked to me of asphalt, fiberglass, scaffolding, flashing, pitching, and other intangibles. I paid little attention. Then somebody mentioned wood shingles, tax credit, and restoration, all in the same breath. Roofs are strange stuff, but a tax credit is something I can relate to. It seems that Deadwood is a designated Historic District. I learned that if I had the roof done right, that is, appropriate to the age of the house, it could earn a tax credit for me. On that basis I could go along with a wood shingle roof for my 1905 house. But remuddling, although I had not yet heard the term, was what I was after.

NAN HAD TO RETURN HOME, but I still had a few vacation days left. I set to work stripping dirty, painted wallpaper from the front living room -- the one with the bay windows. Even with a six-foot step ladder, my 5'2" height would not let me reach the 10-1/2-foot ceilings, but I made great headway with the walls. It gradually dawned on me, as I soaked and scraped, that I was uncovering successive periods of room-decoration taste, going back as far as my own 62 years could take me. I suspected that Nan would want to see this before I obliterated it. Even the four hold-out daughters (who were beginning to relent) should find it interesting, as would their families. I let the wall stay as it was and turned my attention to the floors.

AS I SCRUBBED AND SCOURED and pried zillions of staples, I wondered again and again about the peculiar design of concentric circles, side by side and row by row, that had been painted on the perimeters of the floors. I tried to figure out how it was done and why.

AT THE FLOOR'S EDGE a piece of quarter round was missing and I could peer through the opening and see the sub-floor. I saw, lying between wall and floor, a wood shaving still curled as it had come from the carpenter's

IN THE WEEKS that followed I subscribed to OHJ and bought all the OHJ Yearbooks and read them cover to cover. I sent for catalogs and literature from everywhere. I wrote to the South Dakota SHPO*, and he wrote back -- several times. I memorized the information he sent. I bought books I could little afford. I returned to Deadwood in November and again in December. I measured, poked, pried, and spent hours alone in my house. I haunted the Office of Recorder of Deeds and the Deadwood library. I asked questions and I got answers. I found a former grandchild of my house who had an album of old photos: not enough photos, not the right photos, but photos.

BACK IN PASADENA I went to see an accountant and I took notes. At school I would not allow myself to think of my house until my teaching chores were done. School was paying the bills, and I am not willing to give up the pleasure I get from my teaching.

ON JANUARY 24, exactly five months after we first saw the house, I sent in my application to the SHPO and National Park Service stating that for the next five years I promised to love, honor and obey the Secretary of Interior's Guidelines and to: strip off the asbestos siding and restore the underlying clapboard; restore the graining on the downstairs floors; rehang the balky pocket door between the double parlors; uncover and restore the turned columns on the front and back porches and install appropriate railings and balusters; rebuild the chimneys; hang wallpapers by Bradbury & Bradbury featuring huge terra-cotta-color sunflowers, and, I swear it, to install not one but two clawfoot bathtubs. And then to paint the house in three colors: Rookwood Clay, Rookwood Amber, and Rookwood Dark Brown.

ALL OF THE ABOVE in pursuit of a $5000 tax credit? No way. All of that dissipated long ago. All of the above because a curly wood shaving spoke to me of history.

*Affectionately pronounced "ship-o," State Historic Preservation Office(r)

NEW LIFE FOR OLD
BATHROOMS

Ajax, Not Demolition, Is Usually The Answer

by Bill O'Donnell

PUT AWAY that wrecking bar! Save your budget! Sure, we know that bathroom is filthy and disgusting, and you're afraid to go in there barefoot. But you needn't rip it out and start from scratch. Even the most horrendous bathroom can be made shiny and sanitary, usually without the expense of new fixtures or tiles. We're going to use a rubber bucket, latex gloves, a scrub brush, and steel wool as our restoration tools -- along with a healthy measure of old-fashioned elbow grease!

Wall Tiles

IN MOST OLD HOUSES, bathroom tile was professionally installed by skilled masons and should last for many generations. The majority of tiles will be securely fixed to the wall; it's rare that you'll have to reset more than a few tiles. The first step is to clean any mold, mildew, and soap scum off the tile, so you can better appraise the situation.

ALMOST ANYTHING will clean glazed wall tile. To remove built-up scum, blobs of paint and caulk, and greasy dirt, methodically and gently scrape each tile with a single-edge razor in a holder. Then rinse with ammonia in water.

FOR HEAVY-DUTY cleaning of glazed wall tile, use a non-abrasive scouring agent (like Bon Ami or Ajax Liquid) with a sponge and hot water. Then thoroughly rinse off the scouring agent with lots of water. Wipe dry with a terrycloth towel.

FOR A SUPER-NEGLECTED glazed tile surface, the Ceramic Tile Institute recommends this four-step poultice method: First, coat the tile with an undiluted neutral soap (animal fat soap, for example). Allow to dry and stand for several hours. Next, mix additional soap with warm water, and wet down the tile. While still wet, sprinkle with scouring powder and scrub with a stiff brush. Rinse thoroughly with water, and dry with a terrycloth towel.

GROUT LINES will probably still be dark with mold and mildew. Household bleach kills these fungi. Mix bleach and hot water and apply to the grout with a stiff old toothbrush. Choose a dilution depending upon the degree of mildew, the amount of ventilation available, and your ability to breathe chlorine. A good solution is one part Clorox to three parts hot water, but you may have to tolerate a 1:1 mixture. A cup of trisodium phosphate (TSP) and 1/2 cup detergent added for every gallon of bleach solution will accelerate its action.

WHILE YOU'RE SCRUBBING mold and mildew off the grout, keep a dental pick, awl, or similar tool handy. As soon as you notice any loose grout, dig it out. It's easier to remove it now than to search for it later. After you've thoroughly washed the tiles and removed all the loose grout, vacuum all the open joints left between the tiles. (Use the crevice attachment.) Loose bits of old grout will mar the finish of new grout.

Tile Repair

BEFORE REGROUTING areas of tile that need it, you have to replace any broken or missing tiles. Also check for any tiles that may be a little loose; subsequent movement of the tiles could spoil the appearance of your new grout.

MODERN GLUES and adhesives won't work well for tiles set in cement. A good material for resetting such tiles is Structolite. Mix the Structolite to a fairly thick consistency, so you can easily set the tile to the proper depth. After the Structolite sets up a little, but before it's completely hard, clean any excess material from between the joints.

NOW YOU'RE READY TO GROUT. (See the March '84 OHJ, and read the grout manufacturer's instructions for proper grouting techniques.)

Fixtures

OLD NEGLECTED bathroom fixtures can be especially grungy. Hard-water deposits, ground-in dirt, and rust stains make them appear unsalvageable. Worse, the porcelain finish may be scratched, gouged, or partially worn through. Damaged fixtures won't look as offensive after a good cleaning, so the first step is to remove dirt and stains.

SCRUB THE FIXTURES with Bon Ami, Liquid Ajax, or other non-abrasive cleanser and hot water. This will remove all the surface grime and

The prospect of sitting naked in this bathtub is enough to gross out anybody — but even this mess can be brought back to life!

give you a clearer picture of the filth that remains. Follow with full-strength vinegar on hard-water deposits, and a thorough rinse.

FOR REALLY resilient, ground-in grime, you'll have to use a mildly abrasive cleaner like Ajax or Comet. Sprinkle the powder all over the fixtures, and wet with just enough water to form a thick paste. This acts as a poultice, bleaching the porcelain and drawing out stains. Allow to stand for several hours, keeping it moist. Then add some more cleanser and water, and scrub the dickens out of the sink, tub, or toilet with a stiff-bristle scrub brush. Rinse thoroughly with plenty of warm water.

AFTER YOU'VE USED the above-mentioned cleaning procedures, you may still be dissatisfied with the appearance of your bathroom fixtures. Abuse, repeated abrasive cleaning, or a constant drip-drip may have worn away some of the porcelain, permitting deep penetration of rust stains. Crazed or chipped enamel may have allowed dirt to work its way down into the iron or clay body underneath, turning the cracks or chips dirty brown. Often these problem areas can be cleaned, but some of the methods may be damaging to the already-worn porcelain. So when it's time to bring on the artillery, always test its destructiveness in a small inconspicuous area before proceeding.

THE MAJORITY of rust stains can be removed with readily available commercial products sold in most hardware stores. Stay away from the sodium hydroxide crystals or other caustics packaged as rust removers; we've yet to find one that works effectively on stains (although they will do a job on your nasal passages). Naval jelly, muriatic acid, and dilute phosphoric acid are all quite effective for removing stubborn rust stains. Any chemical that will remove rust deposits deserves special respect and appropriate care when handling. Also, these preparations are not to be poured all over your fixtures just before you take off for the weekend: You don't want to leave them on your porcelain one second longer than is necessary to remove the stain.

Resurfacing?

FIXTURES that have received an inordinate amount of use or abuse over the years may be rough, pitted, nicked, or heavily crazed. Once you've cleaned your bathroom fixtures, you must decide if you can tolerate these imperfections. Although many people have reported satisfactory results from professionally applied, urethane-based coatings, the new surface usually doesn't hold up for more than two to five years (less if the applicator was not meticulous about preparation). If you consider the fixture priceless and irreplaceable, it is possible to have the clay or iron base reheated in a kiln to accept a new porcelain finish. In most cases this is prohibitively expensive, though; it's cheaper to buy and install reproduction or salvaged fixtures.

OUR BEST ADVICE is to clean your fixtures thoroughly, then learn to love their minor imperfections and blemishes. A rough, pitted porcelain surface is a little harder to keep clean than a new one, but if you keep up with it, it's no big chore. If you can't tolerate the ancient appearance of your antique fixtures, replace them with suitable reproductions. (Check the OHJ Catalog for sources.)

Tile Floors

THE STANDARD SOLUTION for a dirty or damaged floor is to cover it with linoleum or vinyl tiles. This solution is temporary at best. Most of the time it's just as easy to clean and repair tile floors as it is to cover them up with whatever is on sale at the home center. Original tile floors are worth saving; not only are they attractive and historically appropriate, but they're also long wearing and, when properly repaired, watertight.

THE FIRST STEP in restoring a tile floor may be finding the darned thing. It's not unusual for the floor to be hidden under half a dozen layers of linoleum. Removing the offensive layers is usually no problem. Linoleum does not stay put very well once water has gotten underneath it, so if you can lift one corner, you may be able to roll the whole floor up in one sheet. If it resists, gentle prying with a wide-blade putty knife should do the trick.

IF THE LINOLEUM resists your efforts, try using a heat gun. The heat will penetrate the linoleum and soften the mastic (glue) that holds it down. If you move the heat gun along slowly, you should be able to lift the linoleum in small sections with a wide putty knife. A wallpaper steamer may also be used for this purpose. After the mastic cools, most of it can be removed from the tile by knocking it free with a putty knife, or scraping it off with a single-edge razor blade.

WHEN YOU FIRST EXAMINE your tile floor, you may consider covering it back up. Resist the temptation; after a good scrubbing you'll see that it's worth saving.

HERE'S THE PROCEDURE for cleaning a heavily stained and soiled tile floor:

1. Vacuum thoroughly, then remove surface dirt with a quick detergent-and-hot-water mopping.

---

2. Scrub the floor with scouring powder, <u>hot</u> water, and scrub brush. Use #00 steel wool wherever gummy deposits exist. Rinse well with water and repeat process on bad areas. This step should take at least an hour for a small bathroom.

3. Mix Clorox and <u>hot</u> water 50/50 and spread evenly over the floor. Let stand until it has evaporated. This will bleach the floor and fade deeply imbedded stains. (Bathroom floor tile is unglazed to keep it non-slippery -- but it does stain.) Rinse with clear water.

4. If necessary, scrub grout with a stiff old toothbrush dipped in muriatic acid. Be sure to wear goggles and rubber gloves, and provide adequate ventilation. <u>Completely rinse muria- tic acid off the grout immediately.</u> Muriatic acid works by dissolving some of the grout, so it's important not to let it stand any longer than necessary.

IF STAINS AND DISCOLORATIONS remain after such a thorough cleaning, you may be able to remove them with a poultice; one that works well on stubborn stains in floor tile is made of lac- quer thinner and corn starch. (<u>Warning: Lac- quer thinner is extremely flammable.</u>) Pour lacquer thinner over a small section of the floor, and sprinkle corn starch on it. Mush together to form a wet paste. The corn starch draws the solvent up out of the tile, taking the stain with it. You'll see the snowy-white corn starch turn grey-brown as it absorbs the stain and dries. Pick up the dry powder with a wide putty knife and dispose of it.

REGROUTING may be necessary. Regrouting a floor is identical to grouting wall tiles -- actually it's a little easier because you're working on a horizontal surface. Be sure to follow the manufacturer's instructions for mixing and curing the grout.

CEMENT PATCHES may exist around toilets and tubs -- plumbers fixing a leak are generally unconcerned about the damage they do to tiles. Fortunately, insensitive patchwork is usually confined to inconspicuous areas behind fixtures. If the tiles and patch are approximately the same color, just paint false grout lines on the patch. If not, smooth the patch level with a cold chisel and paint in false tiles. Sure, close inspection will reveal your time-saving trick -- but few will notice at first glance.

Caulking

YOU NEED a flexible sealant around fixtures and in cor- ners. Movement between fix- tures and walls, and between tiles set in two different planes, will cause grout to fail in very short order.

BEFORE CAULKING, thoroughly clean the joint. Remove all loose grout, caulk, soap film, and mildew. Use an elastic, non-porous, high-quality sili-

cone sealant from a major manufacturer. (Dow- Corning #784 White Fungicidal is one example.)

WHEN SEALING around a bathtub, first fill the tub with water, so the joint is at its maximum width. Apply the sealant by pushing the noz- zle along the joint rather than pulling it. Dip your finger in water, and use it to smooth the bead. Be careful not to get the stuff near your eyes, and wash thoroughly after han- dling the sealant. Any blobs or drips can be cleaned up with a razor blade after the caulk has set.

Final Touches

CLEANLINESS goes a long way toward making an old bathroom look like a well-cared-for an- tique. There are also several low-cost things you can do to spruce it up a little. For in- stance, replacing that gawdy 1960s light fix- ture with something more suitable can make a tremendous difference. A bright shower cur- tain will draw your attention away from the minor nicks and stains left in the bathtub. If you use a pipe collar to cover that gaping hole where the water feed passes through the floor, you'll improve the appearance of the entire room.

THE IMPORTANT THING at this point is to look for low-cost measures that improve the general appearance of the bathroom. Painting the trim or stripping the door, replacing the broken cover plates, buying a new mirror or hanging a thick, colorful towel on a handsome towel rack will help the room a lot, yet may require less than $20 worth of materials.

Using only the techniques described in this article, the author transformed that nightmare shown on page 165 into this veritable work of art.

Wiring cont'd from p. 161

Electrical Risers & Feeders

UNLESS YOU ARE CONNECTING into an existing circuit, the first step in routing wiring is to bring power from the panel box in the basement to the floor on which you plan to work. Ideally, your house will contain unobstructed voids running from the basement to each floor above. If you take a little time to find those spaces now, you'll save a lot of work and aggravation when it's time to route the wire. Check for the existence of:

● PIPE CHASES -- Check plumbing to bathrooms, kitchens, and radiators. Waste pipes are vented to the roof, so they run the entire height of the building.

● ABANDONED FORCED-AIR DUCTS -- Houses that were once heated with hot air will have unused ducts running through the walls. In city row houses, these can usually be found in the brick common walls. Check for patches in the brick walls of your basement. If you're really lucky, the old hot-air registers will still exist in the rooms, eliminating the need for detective work.

● DUMBWAITERS -- Abandoned dumbwaiters are easy to find because of their large size. Re-opening a dumbwaiter will provide a beeline to the floor on which you're working. If your dumbwaiter is still functional, there should be ample space around it for you to run cable without interfering with its operation.

● VENTILATION SHAFTS -- Even though most ventilation shafts don't run all the way down to the basement, they are helpful for running wiring between upper floors.

● VOIDS NEXT TO CHIMNEYS -- The framing around interior chimneys frequently has ample space to run wiring.

IF YOU can't find any vertical through-floor voids in your house, you'll have to bring wiring up one floor at a time, using the methods outlined below.

Planning And Preparation

ONCE YOU'VE BROUGHT a new circuit up from the basement or decided where to hook into an existing one, you'll route wiring to the exact location where the fixture or switch box will be added. We'll describe various ways to neatly circumvent obstacles -- but the first step is to carefully plan your project.

CONSIDER the type of framing the building has. If the house has balloon framing, vertical runs through walls will have fewer interruptions; a house with platform framing has plates and sills which impede vertical runs at each ceiling and floor. Find out which way the joists run, and if they change direction anywhere. If the building is masonry, is the plaster directly on the brick, or are the walls furred out? You don't have to be an architect to successfully route wiring, but the more you know about your house's construction, the better off you'll be when deciding which path will offer the least resistance. (See the December 1980 OHJ for information on house-framing systems.)

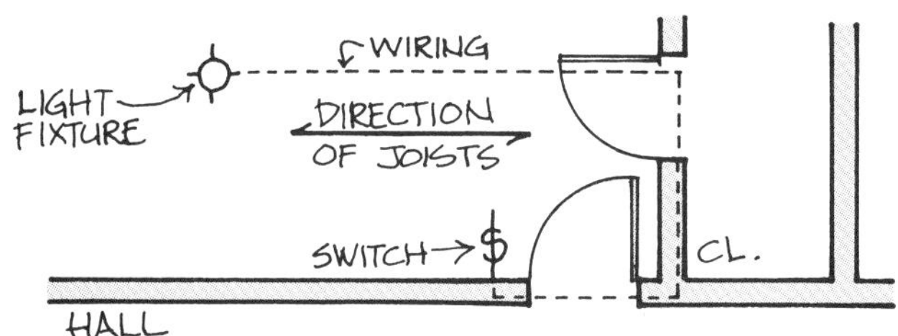

NEXT CONSIDER what is above, below, and behind the area being wired. If there is a cellar, attic, or other unfinished space above or below, that is where to make your horizontal runs. If there are closet interiors, garages, or other unfinished spaces adjacent to the area being wired, take advantage of them for vertical runs. Neat patching is not critical in unfinished spaces. Also, look for mouldings that could be used to conceal wiring. Baseboards, window aprons, and other mouldings can be easily removed to route electrical cable behind them. When the mouldings are reinstalled, they conceal the wire without the need for plaster patching.

Tools

YOUR CABLE ROUTING tool kit should include:

FISH WIRE -- steel tape about 3/16 in. wide and 1/16 in. thick; also called a snake. Fish wire is flexible enough to go around corners, yet stiff enough not to buckle when being pushed through partitions. Get several pieces of varying lengths.

COLD CHISEL AND HAMMER -- for cutting holes in plaster.

KEYHOLE SAW -- for cutting lath.

POWER DRILL -- with carbide-tipped bits (for drilling in plaster), spade bits (for boring beams), and a bit extender.

PLASTER PATCHING MATERIALS -- to repair finished surfaces after the wire is routed.

Running Wire

YOU'LL ROUTE WIRING either parallel to the studs or joists, or perpendicular to them. You must also be able to cross from a wall to a ceiling. Following are instructions for dealing with these three main conditions. If you adhere to these basic guidelines, you'll be able to conceal electrical cable with minimum disruption to finished surfaces.

Parallel To Studs

NEATLY CUT A HOLE in plaster where you plan to locate your switch, outlet box, or fixture; cut a second hole where the power source is located. Attach wire to loop on end of fish, and pull fish back through. A reverse bend on the end of the loop will keep the fish from getting snagged while being withdrawn.

TO RUN WIRE FROM one floor to another, start by removing the baseboard on the upper floor. Use a bit extender and spade bit to bore a hole through the top plate in the partition wall of the floor below. Then, neatly cut a hole in the plaster wall about six inches from the ceiling of the lower floor, or at the firestop if one exists. Insert your fish through the hole in the plate, and pass it to the hole in the wall of the floor below. Attach the wire to the fish and pull up to the floor above. Cut a hole at the bottom of the top wall so you can continue to run the cable up. Now notch the floor plate on the upper floor and staple the wire into the notch. The reinstalled baseboard will conceal most of the damage.

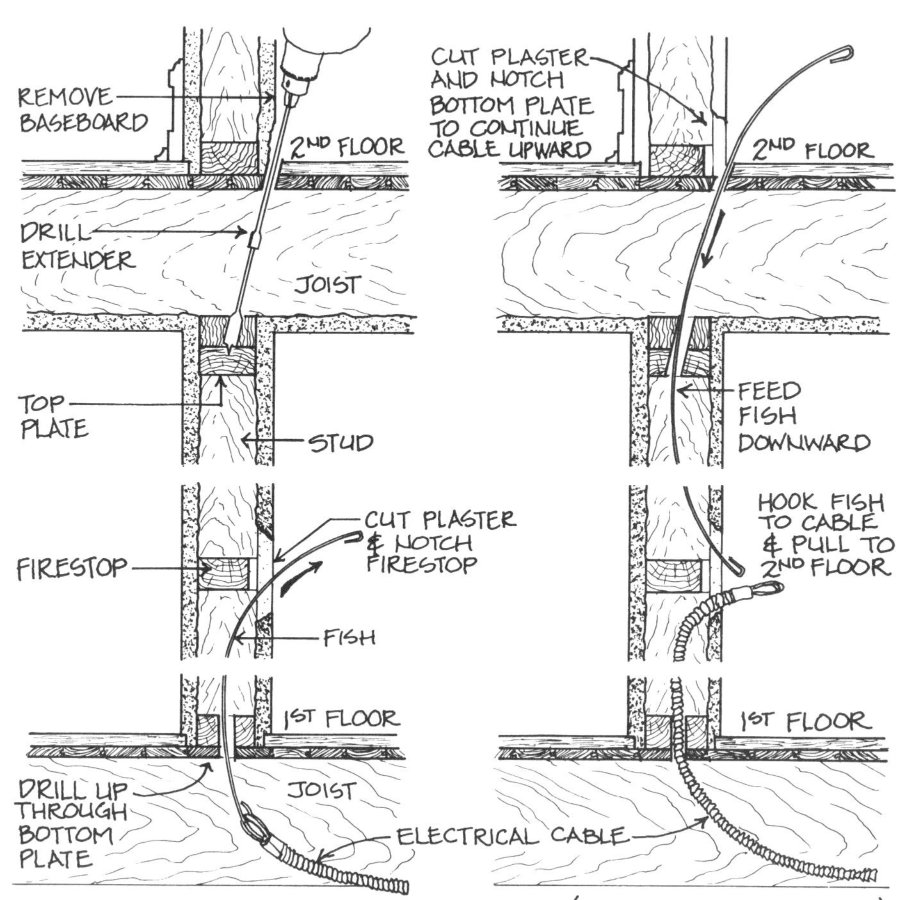

FISHING FROM FLOOR TO FLOOR (PARALLEL TO STUDS)

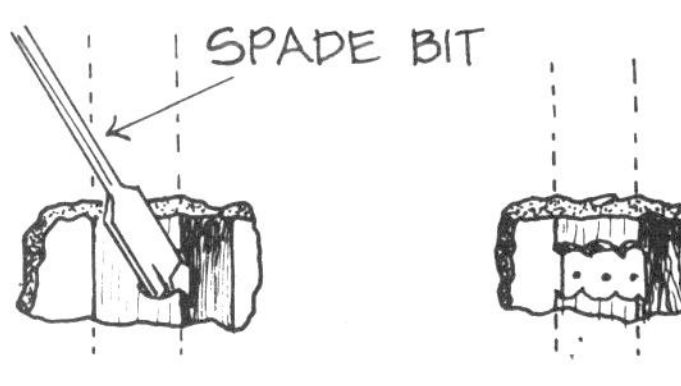

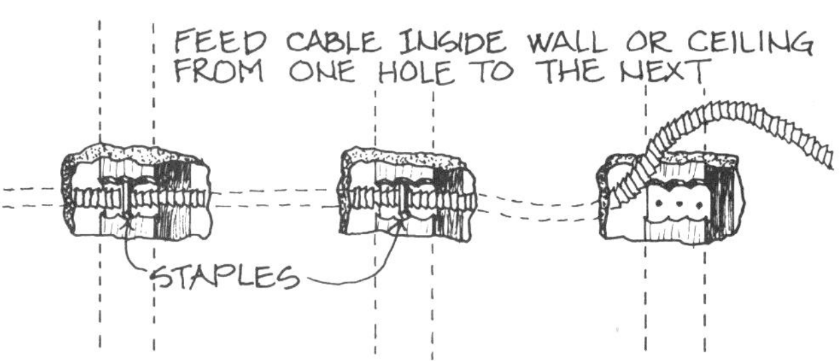

FISHING ACROSS JOISTS OR STUDS

Perpendicular To Studs

OCCASIONALLY, you'll have to run wire across the framing members within a wall or ceiling. On walls this can be done behind the baseboard. You can bring the wire down to the baseboard with a simple vertical run, carve a channel in the plaster behind the baseboard, notch the studs, string the wire across, and run the wire back up with another simple vertical run. When you're finished, most of the mess is covered by the baseboard.

IF YOU CAN'T RUN WIRE horizontally behind the baseboard or other concealing moulding, or if you're running wire across the joists in a ceiling, cut a small hole in the plaster at each stud. Notch the studs or joists, and fish the cable one section at a time across the wall or ceiling. This also applies when you encounter solid blocking or firestops while running parallel with studs or joists.

WHILE RUNNING HORIZONTALLY across a wall, you may encounter a door, window, or other obstacle. If you hit a door, you can remove the casing and run the wire between the jamb and framing studs. Spacer blocks between the jamb and stud may have to be notched. With windows, you can remove the interior casing, run the wire down under the apron, and back up the other side. (See the June 1985 OHJ for trim-removal techniques.) If the original plasterer did a meticulous job, you may have to cut channels in the plaster under the wood trim.

FISHING AROUND A CORNER

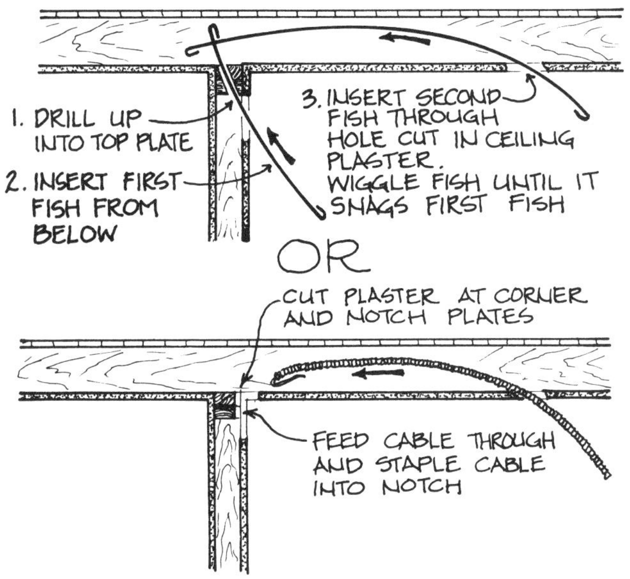

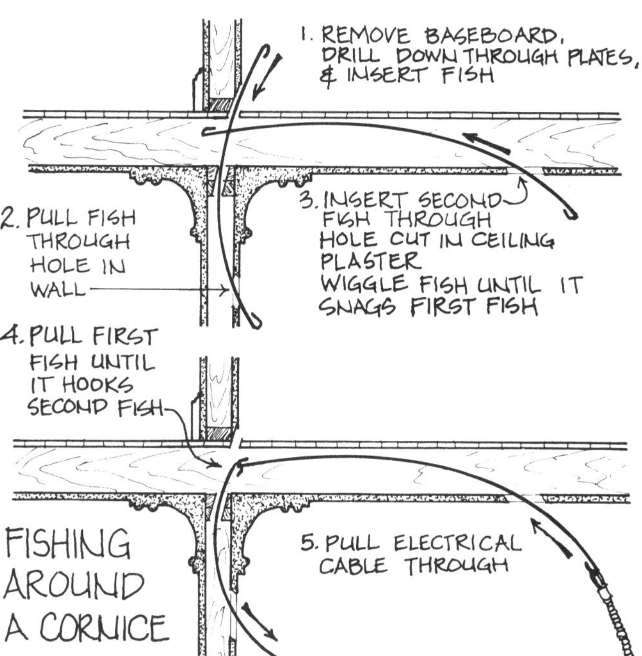

Wall-To-Ceiling Connection

IF YOU'RE RUNNING wire from a wall switch to a ceiling fixture, there are two ways to round the corner at the ceiling wall connection. If there is no ornamental plaster work to go around, you can simply cut a hole in the wall and ceiling at the corner. Pull the wire through, cut notch in plate and staple wire in place, and patch the plaster.

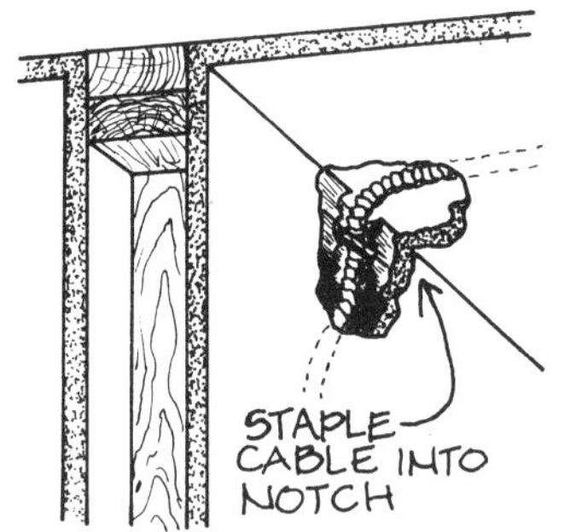

IF YOU HAVE TO AVOID cutting holes at the corners because of an ornamental plaster cornice, you can use the two-fish method to round the corner. It takes time and patience, but not as much as repairing ornate plasterwork. The procedure is as follows:

1. CUT holes in plaster on flat parts of wall and ceiling.
2. REMOVE baseboard on floor above ceiling and drill through plate with spade bit on an extender.
3. PUSH a long fish down through hole in plate and work through the hole in plaster wall.
4. INSERT a second fish through the hole in ceiling and push it through until it contacts first fish.
5. WORK fish #2 back and forth until it snags fish #1. This step will require some patience.
6. WITHDRAW ceiling fish until wall fish appears at ceiling opening.
7. ATTACH wire to fish and pull through as usual.

. . . And A Few Fishing Tips

* FISH have a pronounced curve in them because they are stored rolled up. You can use this to your advantage. If the fish gets stuck on an obstacle, just withdraw it a bit, turn it over, and press on. The end of the fish will now rest against the opposite surface and bypass the obstruction.

* HELPERS are perhaps your most useful resource when fishing wire. It's definitely a two-person job, especially when you're going between floors.

* SOMETIMES, try as you may, you won't be able to get the fish around an obstacle. After you've spent a reasonable amount of time struggling with the fish, open a small hole in the plaster at the point where the fish is hung up. There's no point in getting frustrated and angry for two hours, just to save an hour's worth of plaster repair.

* WHEN you're notching studs or joists, you should try to avoid breaking any lath. Careful work with a key-hole saw and chisel will allow you to remove two half-sections of lath; allowing plenty of room to pass cable, while maintaining the integrity of the lath framework.

Supporting Your Old-House Obsession *Owning An Inn Or B&B*

by Shirley Maxwell

THERE WAS A TIME, before the advent of the plastic highway palace, when front yards in America's towns and cities blossomed with helpful signs directed at passers-through. "Tourist Home," they said in large and welcoming, sometimes neon, letters. Or "Guest House." Or, with admirable abruptness, "Vacancy." Behind each sign, more often than not, was a commodious old house and a landlady with more roof than people to put under it or money to fix it with. She gave road-weary travelers a clean bed and a warm breakfast; they gave her a small but agreeable income and a bit of company.

THE SIGNS are mostly gone now, but the bed-and-breakfast concept is as deeply entrenched as ever -- with important differences. For one thing, the "landlady" these days may well be a young professional couple in search of an alternate lifestyle (or a tax shelter). The commodious old house, helped on by the income from paying guests, has probably never looked spiffier. And the service? Well, it's not for nothing that B&B hosts read all those gourmet magazines.

VISITORS, far from having just popped in off the road, are likely to have made reservations weeks in advance, through one of nearly 200 local, regional, and national reservation services. They may have selected their lodgings on the basis of a host/house profile in one of the dozens of recently published bed-and-breakfast directories, or they may have followed a lead in the "Country Inns" or "Bed & Breakfast" section of a favorite periodical (like The Old-House Journal).

AND ALTHOUGH B&B rates generally run 30% to 40% less than those at good motels in the same area, they aren't always cheap. Prices for deluxe accommodations may outstrip those at nearby motels.

MONEY STILL MATTERS, according to Patricia Wilson, president of the American Bed & Breakfast Association, but it may be overshadowed by the desire for personalized hospitality and travel options tailored to specific interests. B&Bs appeal to senior citizens, singles, couples (married and unmarried and not necessarily of opposite sexes), business travelers, pleasure seekers, the well-to-do, and the short-of-the-ready. Even with the current U.S. supply standing at close to 11,000 B&Bs --

mostly small, at-home operations -- there appears little danger of a glut in the market. All across the country the demand is growing for the blend of comfort, economy, and bonhomie which only a flesh-and-blood host in an honest-to-goodness home can deliver.

AS TRAVELERS THEMSELVES, old-house owners find B&Bs a great way to avoid orange-plastic burn-out, to stay in (and learn from) thoughtfully restored, vintage houses, to share restoration war stories with kindred spirits, and, sometimes, to save a little money.

MORE AND MORE, they're also learning to turn their own expensive habits into part-time wage earners by sharing them with strangers. Opening a one- or two-room B&B in your own house, the experts say, is almost as easy as putting up an out-of-town cousin for the weekend. It demands a relatively low level of time commitment, virtually no capital, and very little inconvenience. It requires only a clean, comfortable spare room or two, an attractive house in a suitable location, and enough of your own time, energy, and good will to greet and care for guests enthusiastically.

OPENING a bed-and-breakfast inn, however, is quite another story -- one that many old-house owners find too intriguing to ignore. Innkeeping is a full-time business, calling for a heavy dose of capitalization, an addiction to hard labor, and, for an estimated 75% of those

Gibson Hall, built in 1832, was acquired by a group of Washington, D.C., investors in 1983. In the heart of Virginia's hunt country, the heavily renovated inn provides such up-scale amenities as queen-size beds, skylights, and private baths with sunken tubs and jacuzzis — a far cry from the down-the-hall facilities of most home-style bed-and-breakfasts. A small mortgage, relatively low interest rates, and many investors put the inn in a better position than most to withstand high renovation costs and inevitable seasonal lags in rental income.

who succumb to its allure, a large and steady source of outside income.

WHETHER it's a small inn or a private home, "bed and breakfast" implies a comfortable bed and a memorable breakfast, both for a single price. A private bath is a bonus, not a necessity. A gregarious, well-informed host (or more frequently, hostess) who takes pains to make guests feel right at home -- only better -- is the final fillip.

THERE ARE BASIC DISTINCTIONS between a simple "bed and breakfast" and a "bed-and-breakfast inn." Generally, a B&B is in a private home with fewer than four guest rooms, which are rented only occasionally. An inn usually has more rooms to rent, and the aim is to keep them constantly filled, at least during a defined rental season. An inn may include a restaurant. B&Bs have "hosts"; inns have "innkeepers." Innkeepers are professionals, committed to making a living, or at least a reasonable profit, from their rentals. Most private-home bed-and-breakfast hosts cherish their amateur standing and hope, at most, to pay the property taxes or part of the kid's college expenses from their B&B income.

Hosting

IF YOUR HOUSE is nice enough for the fussier members of your family, our sources say, hosting costs should be minimal. ("Don't spend a penny!" insists Eleanor Chastain, creator of Washington, D.C.'s Sweet Dreams & Toast Reservation Service.) You don't have to add bathrooms, renovate the kitchen, or wallpaper the bedrooms. You don't even have to buy new sheets. You do, however, have to provide a high level of old-fashioned, spit-and-polish cleanliness and order, and you should be prepared to offer -- in person -- a tasty, nicely served, home-cooked breakfast.

UNLIKE A MOTEL, a B&B doesn't have to be open for business every day of the year, nor does it have to take in every traveler who happens by. It can be "full up" when the hosts need a rest or when the family comes home for the holidays. Many hosts even manage full-time jobs away from home. But the more often you say yes to guests, the more likely you are to be called again -- and the more profitable your hosting is likely to be.

SALLY REGER of Charlottesville, Virginia's Guesthouses, Inc., confesses that although she lists about a hundred hosts, she relies mostly on 20 to 30 regulars, "homebodies" she has learned to count on. Similarly, Ellie Chastain recites the virtues of one of her favorite hostesses, 75-year-old Camille Bullock, who owns a Victorian rowhouse in a popular uptown neighborhood:

"She's a delightful person with a wonderful house, she's in a perfect location, and she's always willing to take guests."

CAMILLE BULLOCK thrives on the hustle-bustle of hosting and obviously enjoys her guests, many of whom are business travelers. But what really sold her on opening her house and her collection of Oriental bibelots and antiques to overnight visitors was the chance to defray some of the costs of owning property in one of America's most expensive cities.

DEPENDING on what you bring to it, the financial returns of hosting can range from pin money to a genuine second income. AB&BA's Patricia Wilson estimates that 95% of all private-home B&Bs bring in less than $1500 a year. But, she notes, there is nothing to stop an energetic host in a prime location from grossing several times that amount.

ASIDE FROM AVAILABILITY, accessibility is the key to profitable bed-and-breakfasting. Like a successful restaurant, a successful B&B requires a good location -- in this case a safe, convenient neighborhood in an area with a real need for transient rooms. That might be a college town, a restored village, a big city, a beach or ski resort, near a major hospital or a corporate or industrial site, or on a working farm or dude ranch.

Getting Going

THE IMPACT of home-operated B&Bs on their neighborhoods is usually so slight that communities have only recently begun to regulate them. Most small B&Bs fall into a category called "customary home operations," according to Hostkit, a treasure trove of information and advice prepared for prospective hosts by AB&BA. Local officials may think of

Mrs. Camille Bullock, shown here with some of her prize Oriental memorabilia, followed a neighbor's lead into bed-and-breakfast hosting in Washington, D.C., and now has only one regret about her venture: 'Why didn't she tell me about it sooner?'

B&Bs as restaurants, hotels, boarding houses -- almost anything but the quiet, occasional activity you are contemplating. So it's important to make sure that they understand what you have in mind.

TALK WITH your local zoning authorities. You may need a business license or a zoning variance, and you should expect regular, if infrequent, visits from state or local health inspectors. Although most B&Bs are paragons of cleanliness compared to the hygienic nightmares inspectors face in their daily restaurant rounds, you may have to meet special kitchen requirements. Serving complimentary cocktails should present no problems; selling alcoholic beverages in any form certainly would. Thoughtful parking provisions for your guests can help ward off complaints in crowded urban neighborhoods. Ask your lawyer or tax consultant about the tax implications of income and expenses.

The living room of John and Rosemary Garton's Black River Inn — "In order to maintain the original patina of the floors, we make all guests remove their shoes at the door (winter and bad weather only!).''

The Role Of The RSO

ALTHOUGH BOTH inns and B&Bs use reservation-service organizations, the benefits of membership are probably more critical for the latter. RSOs are clearinghouses that, for a modest annual fee and 15% to 30% of room receipts, screen hosts and guests, thereby assuring a measure of quality and safety on both sides. They also foster compatibility in expectations about rates and accommodations, and in attitudes toward children, pets, smoking, and shared baths. They can explain general guidelines for guest behavior, so that your visitors know in advance, for example, just when, how, and how much you expect to be paid, as well as when they should arrive and when it's time to go. RSOs often handle part or all of the financial arrangements, and supply guests with accurate directions to your house.

ONE OF THE MOST USEFUL SERVICES of a good RSO is to coordinate marketing and publicity for its members. This is of particular value to beginning hosts and innkeepers, who have no track record to encourage word-of-mouth advertising, no budget for paid ads, and no time for promoting in person. RSOs can even protect the privacy of the host while publicizing the B&B through their listings. And although they should never be substituted for your own lawyer, accountant, or tax consultant, RSOs often can help with general information about zoning, health, and tax considerations.

SHOP AROUND before you choose an RSO. Check RSO lists in some of the publications noted here, and look under the Bed-And-Breakfast heading in your local yellow pages. Call as many as possible. The level of professionalism varies widely, and one of the first clues to how effectively an organization will represent you lies in the way it answers (or, depressingly often, fails to answer) its phone.

HOW MANY member hosts does it have? What is the nature of its clientele? Does it offer ongoing support activities (such as host meetings, which encourage the exchange of information and support on common problems)? How large is the geographical area served? A small, local organization works well for some people, whereas others benefit from exposure

Mrs. Bullock's sun porch is a favorite breakfast spot for guests.

The 1835 Black River Inn is Federal on the outside and Victorian on the inside — the result of a mid-19th-century modernization (which also gave the house the first indoor plumbing in Ludlow, Vermont). In their restoration of the interior, owners Rosemary and John Garton chose to retain most of the 1860s changes. "To most of our guests, being able to spend a little time in an earlier era makes their stay at Black River Inn special for them as well as for us."

to a larger market. You may want to join one of each type. Above all, ask for references from hosts and guests, and check them out. A comprehensive, regularly updated list of RSOs nationwide can be obtained from Sweet Dreams & Toast, Inc., P.O. Box 4835-0035, Washington, DC 20008 ($3.00).

TWO EXCELLENT SOURCES of guidance in setting up a B&B operation are: Hostkit, available from the American Bed And Breakfast Association, P.O. Box 23294, Washington, DC 20026 ($15.00); and the preface to Bed And Breakfast USA by Betty Rundbeck and Nancy Kramer, available from the Tourist House Association of America, R.D. 2, Box 355A, Greentown, PA 18426 ($7.95, plus $1 fourth-class postage). Both organizations publish newsletters and directories in which members are listed for free but only by specific request. They also serve as clearinghouses for information as well as advocates for the B&B industry.

Innkeeping

JUST A COUPLE OF YEARS AGO, Amy and Craig DeRemer moved with their daughter Kate to an old brick house in the Virginia hunt-country town of Leesburg, where they started a bed-and-breakfast inn they call the Norris House. Last year, Warren Topelius left his job as a government economist to work full-time on the renovation of Gibson Hall, a six-room inn he and seven friends have since opened in Upperville, Virginia, a horsey village an hour from Washington. About the same time, California physician John Shaw set up his Shaw House Inn in the Pacific coastal town of Cambria near Hearst Castle. And in Ludlow, Vermont, Rosemary Krimbel and John Garton began welcoming skiers to their Black River Inn.

ALL OF THESE NEW INNKEEPERS are confident, energetic souls willing to invest heavily in time, money, and personality to get their dreams on the road. None of them admits to any regrets about doing it, although most of them say they could write a book about their experiences. (A couple of them might actually do that.) Here's a recap of their advice:

● LOCATION COMES FIRST. Find the right place, then the right house at the right price. Don't be put off by a reasonable amount of competition. Remember that often "one inn feeds another."

● DON'T UNDERESTIMATE THE JOB AT HAND. Inns are complex business ventures with implications that reach deep and wide into your personal and financial resources. To succeed, you'll need an abundance of:

1) start-up capital (much more than your highest early estimates).
2) income from a reliable source apart from the inn, to see you through seasonal lags and unexpected financial crises.
3) time for pre-opening preparations (far more than you now believe).
4) help, both before and after you open, from friends, family, paid and unpaid workers.
5) persistence, especially during the shake-down period while your market is becoming established.

● EARLY IN YOUR PLANNING, round up the best advisors you can find. Look for people who have some experience in old houses and/or inns. You'll need:
1) a good lawyer
2) a good accountant
3) a good general contractor
4) a successful fellow innkeeper, whom you'll <u>pay</u> to serve as a consultant.

● SLEEP AROUND. Visit other inns as a paying guest. It can be the best way to savor a sightseeing vacation, try out a potential home town, and test your will to acquire and live in an old house (or to renew your commitment to the one you already own). Many a renovation-torn marriage might have perished under the weight of its own plaster dust but for a timely escape

Amy and Craig DeRemer's Norris House, in Leesburg, Virginia, was built in 1806 and Victorianized late in the 19th century. Although the DeRemers have full-time jobs an hour's commute away, they still manage to prepare breakfast for their guests. On weekends, they can join their visitors for quiche and conversation. In this photo, Amy is at the far end of the table; Craig (back to camera) sits opposite her.

to the sanity -- and the sanitation -- of a well-restored inn. This is your chance to see first-hand how others handle the exigencies of maintenance, rehabilitation, restoration, and decoration. And it's far and away the best means for gathering ideas for your own bed-and-breakfast inn.

The DeRemers' daughter Kate is a willing partner in the Norris House operation. (Kate's move to the Leesburg hostelry was considerably eased when she and twelve friends were allowed to take over the house for a memorable Halloween slumber-party celebration of her thirteenth birthday.)

UPDATE ON THE OHJ GUIDE TO INNS AND B&BS

In the January-February 1985 OHJ we asked readers to write us about your favorite inns and B&Bs. We've since sent detailed questionnaires to the places you've recommended, as well as to our own in-house list of about 1,000 inns. The response has been amazing! There are over 400 inns and B&Bs that qualify for listing in our book: Their owners are subscribers who'd welcome other members of the OHJ family — and who'd love to share restoration tales.

Unlike other guides, ours will focus on the history and architecture of the houses (and will also include the basic guidebook information). Watch for our publication announcement next spring!

Long–Bed Wood Lathe

Finally! Someone — Conover Woodcraft Specialties, to be precise — has developed an AFFORDABLE, heavy-duty, long-bed wood lathe. If you've ever tried to get wooden porch columns turned to match your old ones, you know just how important this is. Very few millworks have wood lathes with beds long enough to turn porch columns, especially 6-x-6-in. ones (and if they do, chances are the company is so big they're not interested in turning just a few).

Conover supplies beautifully designed cast-iron lathe parts; you supply the timber for the bed. (Wooden beds have a springiness that takes some of the shock out of woodturning.) All you need are two straight timbers, free of cup and wind (1-3/4 to 2 in. thick and 5-3/4 to 6-1/4 in. wide). They find that Baltic Birch, a 3/4-in. thick, 13-ply plywood that comes from the Soviet Union in 5-foot square sheets, can be laminated together to produce a very good bed. Lumberyard 2x6s can be used to put the lathe up on the job site, and then discarded after the project.

Backyard business opportunity? We know of several fellows in Utah who got together and built a backyard wood-turning shop (with two old long-bed lathes). For four or five years they've been snowed under with business, turning porch columns, balusters, and spindles for restoration projects – without even advertising! They're able to match old columns, working from drawings or even old photos to turn items more economically than larger commercial shops can. There's a need across the country for this type of service, and a few jobs could pay for the lathe.

The 16-in. lathe can turn porch columns or small bowls; you can even drill through the head stock via a special cup center. The lathe comes with head-stock, tailstock, 6-in. and 12-in. tool rest, spur and cup centers, knock-out bar, a manual (including plans for bed construction), and Yellow Poplar bed planks to make a 45-in. lathe bed. The price is $895, shipped freight collect. To get a copy of their latest catalog send $1 to **Conover Woodcraft Specialties, Dept. OHJ, 18125 Madison Rd., Parkman, Ohio 44080. (216) 548-3481.**

Finish–Repair Kit

Our friends at Woodcraft Supply are constantly coming up with new tools and products to help old-house owners. Their latest boon is a handy kit for repairing scratches, nicks, and burn marks on wooden furniture. Developed by professional refinishers, the kit includes illustrated instructions, five basic dye powders (for matching oak, walnut, pine, teak, and mahogany), which are mixed to any desired color, neutral filler stick, mixer finish and tray, camel hair brush, brush cleaner, steel wool, sandpaper, and cleaning cloth. You get all the tools and information you need to make professional-quality repairs on wood or formica. The Wood Repair and Touch-up Kit sells for $14.95 ppd. from **Woodcraft Supply Corp., Dept. OHJ., 41 Atlantic Ave., P.O. Box 4000, Woburn, MA 01888. (617) 935-5860.** And be sure to get their main catalog ($3 refundable with order) or the free supplement.

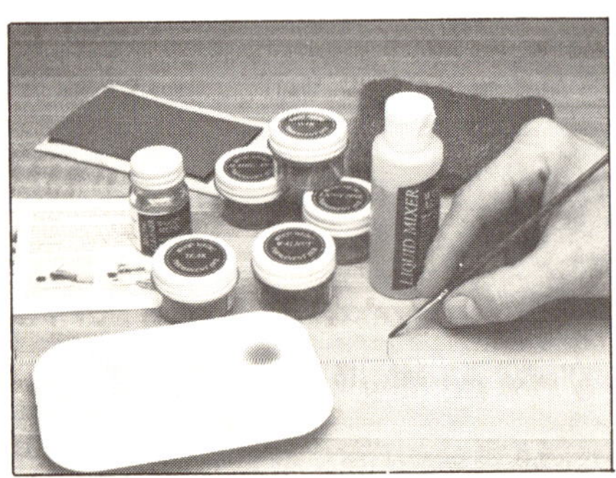

Wide–Pine Flooring

Seasoned wide-pine flooring or panelling are available from Carlisle Restoration Lumber in widths from 14 to 21 in., for $2.25 per sq. ft. Their floorboards can be milled to 7/8- or 1-in. thickness, or they can custom mill to match your floor. Carlisle also offers wide oak boards in widths from 5 to 10 in. at $3.50 per sq. ft.; ship-lapped pine clapboards for $1.25 per sq. ft.

Each shipment includes a handy brochure that explains how to install and maintain the flooring and panelling. They prefer Minwax Flooring Stains (either Early American or Puritan Pine) diluted 50% with turpentine, followed by two coats of semigloss polyurethane. Tremont 10-penny cut- or wrought-head flooring nails are recommended for securely anchoring the floor boards. For more information and a free brochure contact: **Carlisle Restoration Lumber, Dept. OHJ, Rt. 123, Stoddard, NH 03464. (603) 446-3937.**

Fumed–Oak Flooring

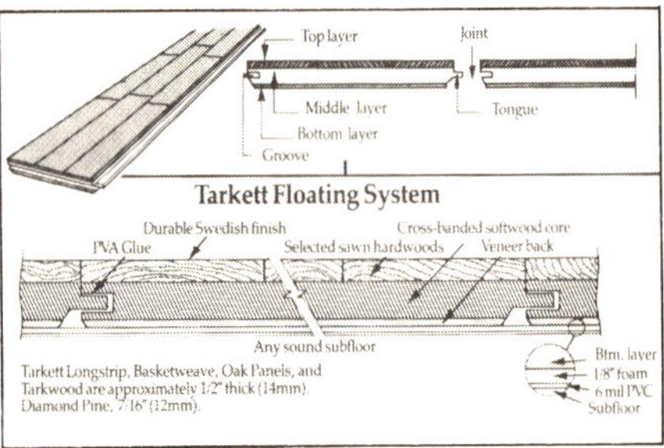

Harris-Tarkett offers a Swedish wood-flooring system, designed for do-it-yourself installation. We especially like their fumed-oak flooring (a finish common to Craftsman-style furniture & Bungalows), as well as the availability of wide-plank pine flooring.

An unusual feature of the ½-in.-thick, Longstrip Plank flooring system is that it's free floating. The flooring isn't glued or nailed down; it simply rests on the subfloor. The floorboards fit snugly together, using tongue-&-groove joints and woodworking glue. Unlike conventional wood flooring, Tarkett's comes with a 1/8-in. rigid-foam insulation laminated to it. This reduces noise between floors (often a problem in old houses) & makes it more resilient. There's a ¼- to ½-in. space allowed around the perimeter of the floor at the walls, which is covered with baseboard trim.

About the only potential drawback we could see for old houses is that the substrate must be level to within 1/16th of an inch within a 10-ft. radius.

The Longstrip Plank flooring ranges in cost from $4 to $5.50 per square foot, depending on the type of wood. For a free brochure on this and other flooring systems, contact **Harris-Tarkett, Dept. OHJ, 333 East Maple St., Johnson City, TN 37605. (615) 928-3122.**

Moravian Tile & Pottery

The Moravian Pottery and Tile Works produces tiles almost exactly as they did in 1900. The company's founder, Harry C. Mercer, wanted to preserve the American handicrafts which he saw being lost to machines. Today, Moravian's decorative tiles, mosaics, sconces, borders, and quarry tiles are produced by a reproduction system that matches Mercer's originals right down to the glaze color.

Just about everything in the Moravian catalog is appropriate for a Craftsman house or Bungalow. Especially noteworthy are the tile designs available for fireplace surrounds and hearths. Other low-relief tiles & mosaics depict nature, history, or the world of Arts & Crafts. The

Ceramic Tile Catalog

Hand-painted, decorative, solid-color, and terra-cotta floor and wall tiles are available from Portugal, France, Italy, Spain, England, Holland, Finland, Mexico, Peru, and the U.S.A. There are even antique tiles from Portugal, England, and Holland. Country Floors has made a special effort to get many of their tiles produced in selected color-ways, designs, or as exact reproductions of antique tiles. These include the Chelsea, a Victorian English wall tile with floral designs. The Giralda is a Spanish wall tile matching the tiles found around the openings of turn-of-the-century fireplaces; it has matching

Moravian staff frequently assists buyers in working out designs, so the tiles can be used to their best advantage.

They also have an excellent selection of quarry-tile patterns for counter tops, floors, & hearths, as well as a collection of decorative borders. Decorative tiles (4x4) sell for about $5.20 each; quarry-field tiles, about $6. Larger pictorial mosaics, originally designed for use in floors (but ideal for placement in walls), sell for around $60.

Quarry tiles sometimes had their exposed surfaces wiped with dirty, black motor oil before they were laid, to give

half- and full-border tiles which somewhat resemble Lincrusta wallcovering.

Norman Karlson was a professional photographer back in the '60s. His photos for a home magazine caught some European tiles in the background, which triggered a tremendous nationwide response from people who wanted the tiles. Thus began Country Floors, which has grown from his New York basement to a firm with four branches, representatives across the country, and one of the finest selections of decorative ceramic tiles we've ever seen. To illustrate them, they've just released a beautiful full-color catalog.

For bathroom and kitchen wainscotting, there's Amathyste, which has a white glaze over a dark clay body; it has matching ogee and bead tiles for borders top and bottom. The Coloratura is a handmade American tile, one of the first to offer Art Deco borders in a wide variety of colors, trim tiles, and even matching sink basins. You can also order personalized tile name plaques and house numbers.

Tiles range in price from $1.40 to $20 or more per square foot. For more information, send for a free color brochure, $2 for a 16-page color accessories catalog, or $10 for the full-color, 96-page catalog. Also ask for the address of the nearest showroom. Country Floors, Inc., Dept. OHJ, 300 E. 61 Street, New York, NY 10021. (212) 758-7414.

them an aged 'patina.' Once laid & fully cured, the tiles were sealed with a mixture of 3 parts turpentine to 1 part boiled linseed oil. This was allowed to soak in, and then the excess was wiped off.

Moravian is open to the public seven days a week, from 10 AM to 5 PM, with tours given on the half hour. For their color catalog, send $6 to Moravian Pottery and Tile Works, Dept. OHJ, Swamp Road, Doylestown, PA 18901. (215) 345-6722.

Wiring & Lighting History

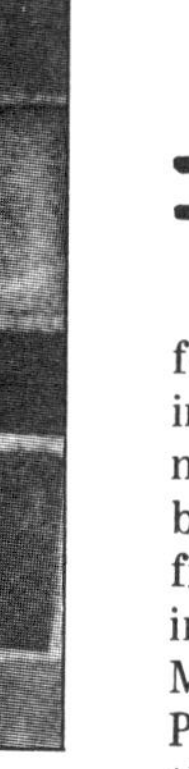

If you've ever searched for information on early electric lighting fixtures or the wiring techniques commonly used in old buildings, you probably didn't find very much; practically nothing exists in print. Max Ferro and Melissa Cook of the Preservation Partnership in conjunction with the AFC/A Nortek Co. (makers of armored electrical cable), have produced a new publication that's been sorely needed for years. *Electric Wiring and Lighting in Historic American Buildings, Guidelines for Restoration and Rehabilitation Projects* has 102 pages of useful (if somewhat dry), well illustrated information on wiring and lighting.

The book examines wire, insulation, and wiring systems from 1880 up to the present, pinpointing some of the problems of re-wiring historic buildings. It also covers lighting, including a chronology of lighting fixtures from the 1880s to the present. Preservationists will read this book from cover to cover, but homeowners will also find it interesting and useful (especially its illustrated section of the styles and dates of electric lighting fixtures).

For your copy send $5 plus $1.50 for shipping to AFC/A Nortek Co., Dept. OHJ, 55 Samuel Barnet Blvd., New Bedford, MA 02745. (617) 998-1131. also ask for their free brochure on Nortek Armored cable.

Ask OHJ

Alas, Poor Slate

TWENTY-FIVE YEARS ago, when my slate roof needed patching, the roofers I hired recommended installing asphalt shingles nailed directly over the slate. I went with this recommendation, as it was the least expensive alternative at the time.

NOW THE ASPHALT shingles need to be replaced. My roofer tells me that the asphalt shingles and the slate must be removed, and plywood installed as a base for new asphalt shingles.

THIS SOUNDS EXPENSIVE. Is there any way to install a second layer of asphalt shingles without removing the old shingles or slate?

--Leonard Golding Cranbury, N.J.

YOU SHOULD NEVER apply a third layer of roofing. It doesn't provide a sound nailing surface, untraceable leaks often develop, the roof might not take the weight, and the finished product will look messy. You'll have to have the present roofing removed.

IF YOU'D HAD the slate roof repaired before, it might have cost you a little more, but your roof wouldn't be troubling you now. Most often, a slate roof leaks because of missing slates or bad flashing. These problems usually can be repaired by a roofing contractor familiar with slate roofs.

Old-House Wall Insulation

I WANT TO insulate the walls of my 1870s farm house, but I don't want to destroy the walls in the process. I've heard that insulating the walls of an old house causes the paint on the outside of the house to peel. What's the best way to insulate my walls?

--Josephine Elsen Wheaton, Ill.

THERE'S NO good way to do it. If you insulate the exterior walls of your house, you'll have to have a continous vapor barrier on the inside of the walls; otherwise, the paint on the outside of the house will peel, as you mentioned. (Your wall framing could rot, too.) If you don't want to rip out all your plaster and install a plastic or foil vapor barrier, you'll have to paint your interior walls with a vapor barrier paint. If this paint fails, your vapor barrier fails with it.

YOU COULD INSTALL insulating foam panels on the inside of the walls. They're highly flammable, though, so you'd have to cover them with wallboard. Do this, and your walls get about an inch thicker -- you'd have a terrible time trimming around windows, doors and electrical outlets.

CONCENTRATE on tightening, not insulating the walls of the house. Caulk open joints on the inside of your exterior walls (around baseboards, window and door frames, outlets, etc.), and weatherstrip all your windows and doors. These low-tech, inexpensive, resource-efficient measures are the best way to hold down heating costs in an old house.

Stained Bathroom Fixtures

WHAT CAN I DO about stains and worn spots in my old clawfoot tub and pedestal sink? I've tried (unsuccessfully) an array of bathroom cleaners on the stains; also, water pools in worn-down areas around the drains of both fixtures. Are there products I can use to (a) build up the worn-down areas, and (b) refinish the stained areas?

--Dorothy Kann Alameda, Cal.

YOU CAN BUY products, or hire contractors, that claim to do both things. The bad news: To our knowledge, even the best jobs don't last. Porcelain "refinishing" is nothing more than a patch-and-paint job; it looks fine for a while, then starts to chip, bubble, and pop off. These repairs generally don't last over two years, and neither the products nor the contractors come cheap. If you can't live with the fixtures the way they are, buy reproduction fixtures -- they'll be cheaper (and look better) in the long run.

Green Goo And You

MY 1905 HOUSE was carpeted wall-to-wall in the '40s, and a green foam was used for padding. This padding has since become a green goo that's stuck all over the beautiful parquet floor. It isn't hard enough to sand off or soft enough to scrape off without damaging the floor. Is there some type of solvent that will remove the goo without damaging the floor?

--Jolene Orr Asbury Park, N.J.

IF YOU WORK CAREFULLY, you can remove the bulk of the goo by getting a putty knife under it and scraping; it'll peel away in big chunks. The sticky leftovers can be removed with mineral spirits and 0000 steel wool. (On stubborn areas, use lacquer thinner instead.) Make sure the room is well ventilated when you work with these flammable liquids.

General interest questions from subscribers will be answered in print. The Editors can't promise to reply to all questions personally—but we try. Send your questions with sketches or photos to Questions Editor, The Old-House Journal, 69A Seventh Avenue, Brooklyn, NY 11217.

Peeling Ceiling Got You Reeling?

HAVE YOU ever faced: (1) A ceiling that keeps peeling down to bare plaster, no matter how many times you scrape and paint it; (2) A surface that causes freshly applied latex paint to peel off in ribbons; (3) A ceiling or wall paint that resists stripping by either heat or chemicals? The culprit is usually <u>calcimine paint.</u>

CALCIMINE WAS POPULAR for ceilings (and walls) in the 19th and early 20th centuries. Made from whiting (chalk), glue size, tinting color, and water, it created a beautiful silky finish. Calcimine was water washable so the old coat could be removed before a fresh coat was applied. The lines of the decorative plaster never became blurred under paint buildup.

AS READY-MIXED oil paints took the place of older preparations, it sometimes happened that a coat of oil paint was applied over unwashed calcimine. Not good, because calcimine forms a relatively weak bond with the plaster. As paint layers build up over the years, the calcimine will pull away, peeling all the paint layers with it.

WATER -- not heat or chemicals -- is what removes calcimine. If the calcimine isn't covered with oil paint, you can scrub it off with sponges and hot water. (A half cup of TSP speeds the cleaning.) If the calcimine is covered by a moisture-proof layer of paint, you've got a tougher problem. Try steam. Using a rented wallpaper steamer, start at the edges of a peeled spot. As the calcimine loosens, scrape with a putty knife. Continue working at the edges until stripping is completed.

THEN WASH the surface thoroughly with hot water to remove all traces of calcimine. Just to be safe, your first coat should be an alkyd primer, rather than latex.

It Pays To Use Industrial-Quality Tools When You Have A Lot Of Stripping To Do

HEAT TOOLS soften paint so you can scrape it off with a putty knife. With a little practice, you can lift long strips of paint in one continuous motion. The stripped paint solidifies into crispy flakes, which can be easily swept or vacuumed up — unlike the messy slime you get from chemical strippers.

Heat stripping works best for thick layers of paint on top of varnish; the varnish acts like a releasing agent. Heat is NOT recommended for removing shellac or varnish — use chemical strippers instead. Heat tools will remove about 98% of the paint; a one-coat clean-up with chemical stripper takes off paint residue plus any underlying shellac or varnish.

There's a big difference in heat tools. Most hardware stores only carry plastic "homeowner-grade" heat guns. The two heat tools below have proved best in tests conducted by the OHJ editors.

THE HG-501 HEAT GUN
Most rugged heat gun anywhere!

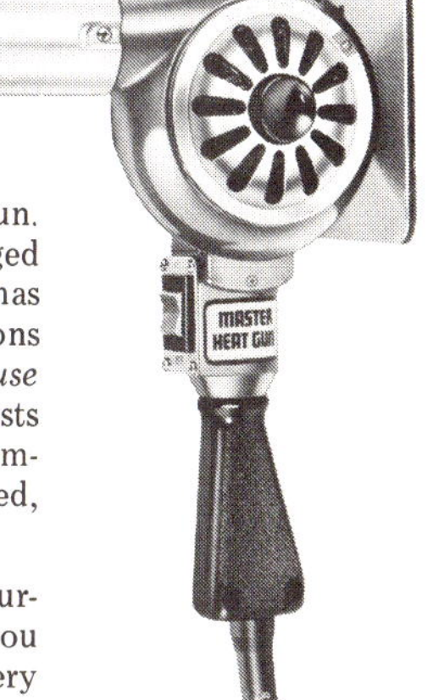

The red, all-metal Master HG-501 is the original paint stripping heat gun. Over 10,000 have been purchased by OHJ readers since 1976; it's a rugged industrial tool with a *proven track record!* The success of the HG-501 has led several manufacturers to come out with "homeowner-grade" versions in hardware stores. But based on independent tests by *The Old-House Journal* and *Family Handyman*, the HG-501 does the best job and lasts the longest. The all-metal HG-501 operates at 500-750 F. (higher temperatures can possibly volatilize the lead in old paints). It has a rugged, die-cast aluminum body, and draws 15 amps at 120 volts.

The HG-501 is the most flexible heat tool; it'll strip paint from any surface. It's especially valuable on mouldings and carved work, where you want to push heat down into recesses. The HG-501 pays for itself very quickly; its price ($77.95) is about the same as 3½ gallons of good chemical paint remover. So if you have a lot of stripping to do, and you want the most rugged, long-lasting tool, choose the heat gun that has been stripping paint in old houses since 1976: The original, all-metal Master HG-501.

THE HEAT PLATE
Ideal for broad, flat surfaces

The Heat Plate is the best tool for stripping broad flat surfaces, such as clapboards, door panels, baseboards, etc. It has a wide-area electric heating coil that heats about 12 sq. in. at a time by radiation. (The heat gun, by contrast, has a blower that pushes hot air against the paint.) The Heat Plate is light (only 1½ lb.), making it easier to hold for long periods than the heat gun.

The Heat Plate has sturdy all-metal construction and no moving parts, so it's virtually maintenance-free. The Heat Plate is safer than a propane torch or heat gun to use around hollow partitions, such as cornices, walls, etc. (Hollow spaces often contain insulation, animal nests, and other combustible trash that could be ignited by a flame or hot-air stream.) The Heat Plate draws 7 amps at 120 volts, and heats paint to 550-800 F. It costs about half as much as the heat gun, so if you have a lot of flat surfaces to strip, the Heat Plate is the most economical tool. Of course, having *both* tools on hand makes most jobs go faster.

Both heat tools come with 4 pages of operating instructions and 2 pages of safety data compiled by the OHJ editors. *The Old-House Journal is the only stripping tool supplier that provides full details on how to avoid lead poisoning and other hazards of paint stripping.* See Order Form at the back of this book for details on ordering both tools.

THEY SAY TWO WRONGS don't make a right. But two rights <u>can</u> make a wrong! This pair of post-Victorian houses have been grafted together into an office building. In old neighborhoods, adaptive reuse is sometimes an economic necessity. But there are tried-and-true architectural guidelines for successful conversions -- standards this job ignored.

IT'S AN "OFF-THE-SHELF" remodelling, wherein standardized modern elements are used to create a pre-packaged facade. No thought was given to the original houses; the new windows and substitute siding are slap-in, slap-on solutions. So is the ever-popular phoney Colonial symbolism: the oversized "carriage lamp," the undersized balustrade, the odd lit-tle door with its broken pediment. All proportion has gone awry. The relationship of the new to the old is downright bizarre! Look at those massive hipped roofs hovering over the characterless united facade.

SHOULDN'T A PLACE OF BUSINESS seek to impress? In our opinion, this building invites either ridicule or a sad sigh. That such a remodelling is acceptable is a disturbing reminder of America's unfortunate ignorance about architecture. This isn't a one-of-a-kind remodelling; subscriber William B. Lees of Topeka, Kansas, wrote that "there are several like this in Topeka. I wish I could send these buildings rather than just sending pictures, because I sure am tired of looking at them."

The Old-House Journal®

69A Seventh Avenue,
Brooklyn, New York 11217

Postmaster: Address Correction Requested

Restoration and Maintenance Techniques
For The Pre-1939 House

November 1985 / Vol. XIII No. 9 / $2.

The Old-House Journal

The Queen Anne Parlor

by John Crosby Freeman

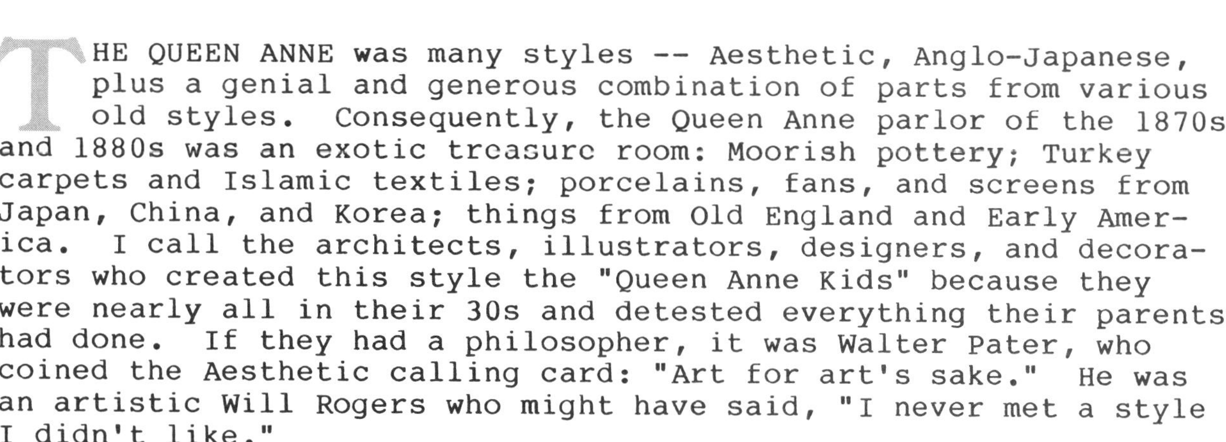

THE QUEEN ANNE was many styles -- Aesthetic, Anglo-Japanese, plus a genial and generous combination of parts from various old styles. Consequently, the Queen Anne parlor of the 1870s and 1880s was an exotic treasure room: Moorish pottery; Turkey carpets and Islamic textiles; porcelains, fans, and screens from Japan, China, and Korea; things from Old England and Early America. I call the architects, illustrators, designers, and decorators who created this style the "Queen Anne Kids" because they were nearly all in their 30s and detested everything their parents had done. If they had a philosopher, it was Walter Pater, who coined the Aesthetic calling card: "Art for art's sake." He was an artistic Will Rogers who might have said, "I never met a style I didn't like."

cont'd on p. 195

In the next issue...
RECONDITIONING YOUR FLOORS

The Old-House Journal®

WE'VE MADE our decision: Instead of launching a new publication for owners of post-Victorian houses, we're going to expand the OHJ to be sure that all readers get all we have to offer.

AS OF THE Jan-Feb 1986 issue, OHJ will be bigger, OHJ will have a color cover, and (in part to pay for all this) OHJ will accept paid advertising for the first time.

THERE'S A LOT of excitement around here! We've long wanted to run more detailed articles, and more illustrations, and more features, and more of your letters -- but our format was limiting. Our new plans call for not only new advertising pages but also extra editorial pages. We can use some of the great material that we just haven't had room for -- and we can continue our leadership as "the restoration bible."

HERE ARE some highlights: Advertising on the inside covers will pay for editorial on the outside. On the back, we're planning a new feature on vernacular houses. (Remuddling moves inside to the last page.)

INSIDE, some pages will be regularly reserved for articles about restoring and decorating early 20th-century houses such as Bungalows, American Foursquares, Tudor Revival houses, and Colonial Revival styles. Not much else will change inside the issues -- except that more pages will be available. We'll continue to produce our own copy and print on warm ivory paper. Ads for appropriate restoration products and services will run in the front and back (but won't interrupt feature articles).

IS DEAR OLD OHJ finally going glitzy? Most decidedly not. Our reputation, which lives in the preservation field more than in the publishing business, is based on the practical techniques and we've-been-there feeling that you've always found in OHJ. It's what we do best; we won't change that.

Patricia Poore

Editor
Patricia Poore

Production Editor
Cole Gagne

Senior Technical Advisor
Larry Jones

Assistant Editors
Sarah J. McNamara
William J. O'Donnell

Contributing Editors
Walter Jowers
John Mark Garrison
Roland A. Labine Sr.

Architectural Consultant
Jonathan Poore

Circulation Supervisor
Barbara Bugg

Circulation Assistants
Jeanne Baldwin
Elaine Lynch

Office Manager
Tricia A. Martin

Catalog Editor
Sarah J. McNamara

Publishing Consultant
Paul T. McLoughlin

Publisher
Clem Labine

THE OLD-HOUSE JOURNAL *(ISSN 0094-0178) is published ten times annually for $18 per year by The Old-House Journal Corporation, 69A Seventh Avenue, Brooklyn, NY 11217. Telephone (718) 636-4514. Application to mail at second-class postage rates is pending at Brooklyn, New York, and additional mailing offices. POSTMASTER: Send address changes to* **THE OLD-HOUSE JOURNAL,** *69A Seventh Avenue, Brooklyn, NY 11217.*

Subscriptions in Canada are $36 per year, payable in Canadian funds. Contents are fully protected by copyright and must not be reproduced in any manner whatsoever without specific permission in writing from the Editor.

We are happy to accept editorial contributions to The Old-House Journal. Query letters that include an outline of the proposed article are preferred. All manuscripts will be reviewed, and returned if unacceptable. However, we cannot be responsible for non-receipt or loss — please keep copies of all materials sent.

Printed at Photo Comp Press, New York City

---

a rare opportunity . . .
Lace Panels Available

VICTORIANA expert John Burrows of J.R. Burrows & Co., Boston, and formerly of Bradbury & Bradbury Wallpapers, hopes to offer imported lace panels to OHJ readers by prior subscription. Here's his letter to us:

"I have just located a lace mill that makes Victorian lace panels of exquisite design and quality, and they are willing to run them in 12-foot and 15-foot lengths for me! The panels are 60" wide and 95% cotton/5% polyester.

"To run the longer lengths, I will need to order the panels in quantity, and the aid of the OHJ would be greatly appreciated. Many of your subscribers across the country have high ceilings and large windows; I am sure there is great interest in availability of long (and affordable) lace panels."

For more information about this opportunity, please send $1 (for mailing cost) to J.R. Burrows & Co., 25 Huntington Ave., Room 220, Boston, MA 02116.

by Steve Conlon

Old House Dreams and Mysteries
AD 1790 ~ 1985

WE WERE IDLY reading the Sunday papers in bed when we found it. "10 room farmhouse, built 1790, 2 barns, 2-1/2 acres." It was located in our small New England town, Guilford, Connecticut. The asking price was almost affordable. To us, lovers of old houses, dreamers, and veterans of many a real-estate spiel ending with price quotations in the stratosphere, the tiny ad sounded fake. Three weeks later, one week before Christmas, we were the proud owners of an unheated, 18th-century farmhouse with peeling paint, a couple of post-and-beam barns, a few rotted chicken coops, and 2-1/2 acres of underbrush. Thus started our old-house adventure -- one that has taken all of our time and most of our money, but given us in return what we had long dreamed of: a beauty of an old house, restored by our own hands.

OUR SEARCH HAD been a long one, though of varying intensity. Over the dozen years we lived in our first home, we looked at old houses now and again. As we learned to identify architectural styles, we became more and more intrigued with the idea of renovating a neglected old beauty.

I PASSED IT OFF as a pipe dream. But when our babies turned into teenagers, we found ourselves sorely in need of more rooms. We started looking for a bigger house. In earnest. The newly intensified search was disappointing. Everything was so expensive or needed too much work. Occasionally, we would find something, but our low offers were rejected out of hand.

SO, IT WAS with some pessimism that we answered the ad one grey December day. The owner, Eleanor, was waiting for us as we turned into the drive. Behind her loomed a weathered, two-storey, white clapboard farmhouse with a bad roof. Attached to one side were a one-storey ell, a carriage barn, and a shed. The front yard was ankle-deep in leaves from three ancient maples; out back, a hodgepodge of out-buildings led to the woods.

WHEN WE STEPPED into the cold entryway, we were greeted by the dank smell of a house unoccupied for many years. The paint was flaking off and the wallpaper tattered. Floors sagged and the plaster ceilings were cracked. Trapped squirrels had gnawed away a number of window mullions. Detritus covered the window sills and floors.

STILL, BY THE TIME Eleanor had shown us the second or third room, it was obvious that be- neath the grime and decay was the real thing: an elegant old house in all its faded glory. We were already falling in love with it.

EACH OF THE FIVE DOWNSTAIRS ROOMS had its own fireplace. The brickwork looked sound and the hearths were solid slabs of granite. The biggest fireplace, the one in the keeping room, incorporated a beehive bake oven. The smallest, a tiny shallow affair, was in a corner of the borning room. The plain beauty of the mantels shone through the caked-on layers of paint. Above some of the mantels were built-in parson's cabinets.

UPSTAIRS, THERE WERE sunny bedrooms, their original floor planks still handsome after decades of wear. The bathrooms had old-fashioned marble sinks and plumbing that looked serviceable enough. There was a big clawfoot bathtub. Despite the damage done to the windows, much of the original wavy and bubbled glass was still intact.

WHEN WE WERE finally shown the enormous, high-peaked attic, we saw that the massive post-and-beam framework of the house was in remarkably good shape. Handmade pegs held them together as tightly as the day they were pounded into place.

IT DAWNED ON US what a wonderful find we had! A tour of the outside encouraged us further. The 2-1/2-acre lot had a fine 19th-century post-and-beam barn in excellent shape, and the foundation of another old barn that had blown

By summer 1983, the house gleamed under its new coat of white paint.

The Conlons' dream house as they found it, one grey day in 1983.

down in the hurricane of 1938. There were also a newer barn, a post-and-beam corn crib, a potting shed, chicken coops, tool sheds, and a stone smokehouse, all of which had been used by generations of farmers.

IT LOOKED LIKE the opportunity we'd searched for and dreamed of for so long. I quickly figured that the land value would be worth the asking price in a few short, inflationary years. Still we agonized. Our resources were limited and there were serious problems. The house had no heat, save the undampered fireplaces, and no insulation. There was no kitchen except for a leaky shed with a mold-blackened refrigerator and grease-encrusted stove. We worried about rotted sills and faulty wiring. The plumbing looked OK, but who knew for sure? Some of the clapboards were rotted and the shingles curled up like big, black potato chips. Small wonder the house had long been on the market!

WHAT WOULD IT TAKE to make this place livable? Did we have the right stuff to carry off a project like this and not end up bankrupt, crazy, or divorced? Finally, we looked at each other and made an offer. Eleanor accepted our low price and agreed to provide bridge financing while we sold our other house. We gulped and signed the papers.

WE SPENT CHRISTMAS week in our parkas, scraping off layers of gluey paper with a steamer. It seems laughable now that we bothered with wallpaper when the place was falling down, but we had to do something. Anything. Just to get started was essential.

WE BEGAN WITH the interior renovation, but it will probably be the last finished. After all, almost anyone can strip old wallpaper, scrape paint, patch plaster, and repaint. But for the real carpentry, you have to know what you are doing. We were fortunate to have a good friend and excellent carpenter, Fred Kroll, working for us. We worked only nights and weekends, but he worked every day and the renovation really began to move along. We were also lucky to have my father helping us. He had the experience and patience to do such things as rebuild our squirrel-gnawed windows using parts scavenged from other old windows.

THIS PAIR must have saved us thousands of dollars. They expertly shored up, scarfed, and replaced a number of the old posts and beams

that had rotted out. The sills were the major problem. When we realized that many of them were partially deteriorated, my heart sank. Visions of a jacked-up house and huge expenditures flashed before me. Fortunately, they still had enough integrity to support the house, so Fred devised a simpler method to repair them. After supporting the floor joists with posts, he removed the damaged sections. Then, using lap-jointed 2x6s, tripled or quadrupled so their combined thickness equalled that of the old sills, he replaced the damaged parts, working along about ten feet at a time. Thus he avoided jacking up the whole structure and finished the job in only a few days.

THEN WE TACKLED the roofs of the ell and the carriage shed. We believe that this two-room structure actually isn't an ell, but the first house on the property. The kind of lath used in this part is of the older, split-in-place type. The ell also has its own center chimney. A post-and-beam carriage barn had been added at a right angle to the ell. We decided to make it into a kitchen. But the roof leaked.

WE TORE OFF the old layers of roof. Most of the nailers, random planks, were fine. We decided to re-roof with cedar, reproducing the original roof. The difference in cost between cedar and asphalt was not as great as many people seem to believe. Aesthetically, there is no comparison. With the new roof in place, we started work inside the kitchen.

BY THEN, it was spring, especially welcome that year. Our first house finally sold. We paid off the bridge loan and moved in. Spring rushed into summer and as any New Englander knows, summers are short. We knew it was time to install a heating system.

HEATING AN OLD HOUSE must be one of the easiest ways to destroy antiquity and go broke at the same time. We finally decided that an oil-fired, recirculating hot-water system with baseboard radiators would be the least destructive and provide the best heat. We found a local heating company with a good reputation that agreed to do the job on a materials-plus-labor basis. The job was done efficiently and professionally in a couple of weeks and came to a couple of thousand dollars less than the cheapest estimate from a big-time contractor.

The bake oven in the ell as it appeared before the Conlons restored it.

The split lath in the ell predates the sawn lath in the rest of the house. The boards were cracked along the grain after they were nailed in place.

The exposed post was rotted and had to be repaired. Note the tripled 2x6s used to replace a rotted section of the sill.

The carriage house was turned into a spacious kitchen. The Conlons made kitchen cabinets from the original oak-plank flooring.

WITH CARPENTRY and heating work underway, we turned to the monumental-looking job of painting the outside while the warm weather held. Here our maxim was that a paint job is only as good as its preparation. Any paint that had not peeled off was alligatored. To eliminate subcoat failure and to restore the crisp lines of the clapboards, we took the old paint off, down to the bare wood. In the process, we must have experimented with every known method of paint removal. We came to the conclusion that scraping and sanding, the old standbys, were the best solution.

WE USED A GOOD QUALITY oil-base flat paint over a thorough coat of well-dried oil primer. The results were spectacular. People would stop their cars to look at the farmhouse. We were very proud. Of course, what they could not tell from the road was that, like an old western movie set, it was a false front. Behind the gleaming facade were twelve rooms of peeled paint and cracked plaster.

AS FALL SLIPPED into winter, we started inside work again. By now, we had become experts at plaster repair. We found that patching plaster was easier to work with; regular plaster set up too fast for us amateurs. We soon had a number of walls and ceilings repaired and painted. It was beginning to look like home.

BY JANUARY, we had figured out how to heat a twelve-room, uninsulated, drafty New England farmhouse for less than $600 worth of oil: Buy a coal stove, close eleven rooms and live in the one with the stove. We moved the TV into that room and let the wind howl its worst. The bedrooms were a different story. We slept with parkas piled on the blankets and didn't get up to let the cat out.

BY OUR SECOND WINTER, we were more prepared. Over the summer, we installed fiberglass-roll insulation in the attic bays. We decided against blowing insulation between the walls because, in the absence of a vapor barrier, we were afraid the material would trap water and cause the framework to rot. Part of living in a home like ours, I'm convinced, is accepting that we will never win awards for energy efficiency. We are content if on cold days the water in the sink doesn't ice over.

MEMORIAL DAY, 1985, marked our second year in our now beautiful old house. While we wonder if we will ever actually finish (we have three rooms and two bathrooms left to do), the end is in sight. It's so near that this summer we have finally been able to do fun things like gardening.

IN FACT, it was while doing yard work that we made one of our most exciting finds. My son and I were digging out fill behind the corn crib on a sweaty July afternoon when my shovel hit yet another rock. When I tried to lever it out, I realized that it was an old gravestone! Excitedly, we brushed the dirt away and read the carved inscription: "In memory of Mr. Joseph Post who died of smallpox in the 48th year of his age, June 10th AD 1788." Who was this man? Was he the builder of the ell? Is he buried here behind the corn crib or down by the river in the old smallpox cemetery?

THE DIRT FLOOR of the cellar yielded another mystery: a badly-rusted gun that an expert identified as a standard issue Civil War Navy revolver. Why was the gun buried in the cellar? We do know of a violent death, documented in old newspaper accounts, that took place on the property. A former owner shot and killed an escapee he found prowling in the barnyard. We aren't especially superstitious, but we keep the barn locked at night.

WE WONDER what stories the house has to tell. We do know from a State of Connecticut Historical Commission survey that our house was owned in the early 1800s by a local shipwright, Eber S. Hotchkiss, who built his first vessel here. He may have been the builder, at least of the two-storey part. In any event, we're looking forward to tracing the history of our home. This may prove to be the most exciting part of our old-house adventure yet.

Casting Decorative Plaster

by John Mark Garrison

RNAMENTAL PLASTER was practically mandatory for homes of the 19th and early-20th centuries. No house with any pretension to style lacked a decorative accent to its central chandelier, or stylish embellishments to its cornices and other linear mouldings. Unfortunately, tastes change, electricians and plumbers wreak havoc, and plaster itself fatigues. Much of the cast ornament in your old house may be damaged or lost. If you want to replace them, they'll have to be recast.

IN PREVIOUS ARTICLES (Aug.-Sept. and Dec. 1984) we discussed how to make cornices and linear mouldings from plaster. Compared to those techniques, casting plaster is relatively simple. This article will take you through a specific plaster-casting project, but the procedures we'll describe can be used to make any kind of plaster ornament in any style.

CASTING IS A PROCESS for reproducing an original piece of ornament. The original is called the model, and may be either a cast element itself (for example, a leaf ornament, or a section of egg-and-dart moulding), or it may be sculpted from clay or carved in wood.

A RUBBER MOULD is poured over the model. The rubber is liquid when applied, but when it sets, it becomes a flexible reverse image of the original piece. After the model is removed, the mould gets new plaster poured into it. When the plaster has set, it's removed from the mould, and you have an exact copy of the original piece. Any number of castings can be taken from one mould, and combined together to form repeating decorative elements.

SOUNDS EASY, doesn't it? Well, it really is. There are just a few things to watch out for, and we'll try to point these out by taking you step-by-step through an actual project.

THE SUPPLIES YOU'LL NEED are few: plaster, water, materials for making the rubber mould, and a few other odds and ends that we'll mention as we go along. One of these is a "separator," or "parting agent": a slippery brush-on liquid that's usually required to keep the mould material from sticking to the model. There are several commercially available parting agents made specifically for this kind of work. Silicone in spray cans also works quite well, or, in a pinch, a little Ivory soap and water.

THERE ARE SEVERAL kinds of rubber moulding materials available; most commonly used are either urethane or polysulfide rubbers, which come in a two-part formulation. They set into a flexible rubber when the parts are mixed. (See the list of suppliers on page 188 for more detailed information about these products.) Some mould materials are formulated in either a trowellable or brush-on consistency, so you can take moulds of an existing element that's in place on a wall or ceiling.

AS FOR THE PLASTER, it should be "moulding" or "casting" plaster, so called because of the fineness of its particles and the resultant fineness of detail it will reproduce. As we said back in the August '84 article, plaster of Paris, or gypsum, is capable of reproducing incredibly fine detail in casting. It's essential therefore that both the model and the mould be kept free from dirt and bits of dried plaster.

A Case Study

FOR OUR EXAMPLE, we've chosen a ceiling medallion in the Greek Revival Style. This ornament appears complicated, but it's actually made up of many smaller, repeating elements. These elements are cast separately and then assembled into the completed ornament.

Left: Parting agent is thoroughly applied to the model. Note the marble slab — the model must rest on a smooth, level surface. Any warps or twists in the surface can result in an imperfect cast piece, which won't lie flat against the ceiling. *Right:* The next step is to pour liquid rubber over the model. The bottom edge of the tin strips has been sealed with plaster to keep the rubber from leaking out.

THE MEDALLION is pictured at the top of page 186. You can see how the circular pieces at the center form a sort of abstracted seed pod of the flower. There are also two sizes of leaf radiating out from the center. The design is finalized with a flower or leaf ornament (proper name: "anthemion," derived from classical Greek ornament), and a small flower that fills the space between these outer pieces, completing the outer ring. To show the steps in casting, we'll concentrate on the larger, outer anthemion. This element has a long, stemlike piece that fits in between the large leaves.

How To Cast

THE FIRST STEP is to obtain the model, or original piece. Any plastering shop has a large number of such elements on hand in a variety of styles and sizes. Different ornaments can be composed by recombining or slightly modifying these elements. If you already have some pieces from an existing ornament, then you're way ahead of the game. If not, the model can be shaped in clay.

APPLY PARTING AGENT to the model and the background surface, so the rubber won't stick to them. Brush it on with a soft brush, working it up into a lather that reaches all the surfaces and recesses of the model. Once the piece has been thoroughly coated, remove the excess foam and soap with a dry brush. Examine the model to make sure that no bubbles or specks of dirt have adhered to it.

BEFORE POURING THE RUBBER, you'll have to build a wall around the model, to hold the liquid rubber until it cures. Master ornamental plasterer David Flaharty -- that's him in the photos -- uses strips of tin held together with small clamps. These handy devices can be expanded, contracted, or bent to any shape, depending on the size of the model; they're reusable, too. (Clay or small slats of wood can also be used for the wall.) If you use wood or sheet metal, you must seal the bottom edge of the wall with clay or plaster to keep the rubber from leaking out.

MIX ENOUGH RUBBER to cover the model completely -- about 1/8" to 1/4" above the model is sufficient. More than that, and the mould will only become stiffer, making the pieces more difficult to remove. David uses a urethane rubber that's mixed in equal parts by weight, but you should follow the directions for the product you have.

POUR THE RUBBER in a small, steady stream, so that any bubbles formed during the mixing will break on the way down. Applied this way, the rubber will also flow smoothly over the model, without trapping air in any of the crevices.

AFTER THE RUBBER has cured, remove the retaining wall and the plaster or clay around it. Lift the mould and model off the surface in one piece and flip it over. Then remove the model by gently peeling back the rubber mould.

NOW YOU CAN CAST as many pieces as you want with the mould -- you won't even need to use a parting agent when casting new pieces from

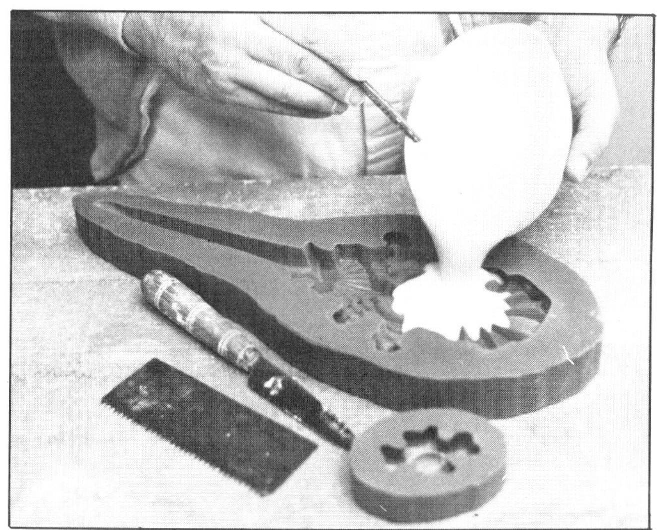

After the rubber hardens, you have a flexible mould which is an exact reverse image of the model. The plaster poured into this mould will become an exact duplicate of the original piece.

Before the plaster sets, the back of the cast piece must be leveled, or else it won't lie flat against the ceiling.

fresh plaster. Simply mix the plaster in a small bowl (a flexible plastic bowl is good because old batches of plaster can be left to dry and then just popped out); then pour it into the mould, making sure it reaches all surfaces. Pieces with long narrow parts, such as this one, can be reinforced by placing a small stick of wood in the wet plaster.

TO ENSURE that the plaster completely fills the mould, jiggle it and slap it gently on the table top; this also brings any air bubbles up to the surface. Before the plaster dries, level the back surface by scraping off the excess. Scrape small gouges into the surface to provide a keying action when the piece is applied to the ceiling.

ONCE THE PLASTER has set (after 15 minutes or so), remove it from the mould just as you did with the model. There's your finished piece, ready to be used in the medallion. Any ornaments in low relief can be made with this process.

FOR DEEPER PIECES, an additional back-up mould may be necessary. This extra, or "mother," mould is used around the rubber mould to keep it from bending out of shape when the plaster is poured into it. The mother mould is usually made of plaster itself. The photo at right shows the mould used to cast the deep central

the finished anthemion

Sources For Materials

THE THREE most commonly used rubber casting materials are polysulfides, polyurethanes, and silicones. Of these, polyurethanes are the most tear-resistant and the easiest to use. They come in a two-part formulation, mixed either 2:1 or 1:1 by weight. Working time ranges from 12 to 30 minutes, and the material sets in about 16 hours. Some polysulfides are useful when you must work on a model that is in place. Some of these products are formulated to be brushed on or, with additional thickeners, trowelled on.

IF YOU CAN'T FIND these materials locally, call or write one of the following companies:

MANUFACTURERS

Abatron, Inc.
141 Center Street
Gilberts, IL 60136

Adhesive Products Corp.
1660 Boone Avenue
Bronx, NY 10460

Industrial Plastic Supply
309 Canal Street
New York, NY 10013

Perma-Flex Mold Company
1919 Livingston Avenue
Columbus, OH 43209

Polytek Development Corp.
P.O. Box 384
Lebanon, NJ 08833

Smooth-On, Inc.
1000 Valley Road
Gillette, NJ 07933

SUPPLIERS

Baker & Collinson, Inc.
12000 Mt. Elliot Avenue
Detroit, MI 48212

D & B Moldmakers
5851 Southwest 23rd Street
Hollywood, FL 33023

Lance Gypsum & Lime Products
4225 West Ogden Avenue
Chicago, IL 60623

Read Plastics
12331 Wilkins Avenue
Rockville, MD 20852

Sculpture Associates
40 East 19th Street
New York, NY 10003

Sculpture House
38 East 30th Street
New York, NY 10016

Westwood Ceramic Supply
14400 Lomitas Avenue
City Of Industry, CA 91746

element of the flower, together with its mother mould. Notice the "undercuts," or flaring parts at the top of the cast piece. When casting such pieces, remove them from the mould _carefully_, or else they'll break.

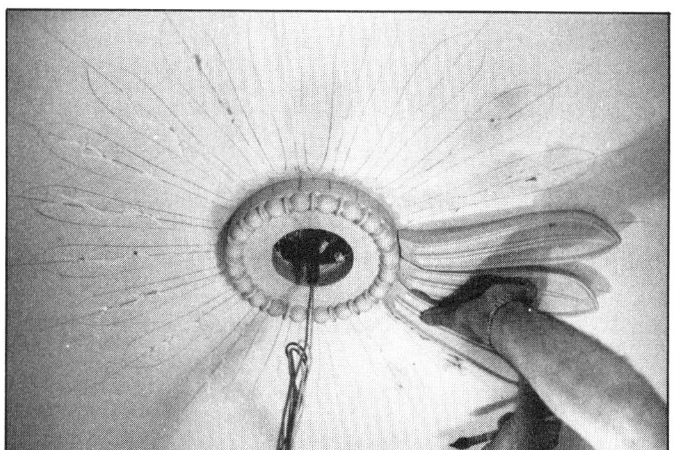 

Top Left: David Flaharty transfers the layout of the medallion to the ceiling. This medallion is designed for an electrical chandelier, and an electrician has already pulled wires for it.

Top Right: To the back of the first piece, David applies plaster that will serve as a glue, holding it fast to the ceiling. (Only very large pieces would need the extra support of nails or screws.) Note the scratches on the back of the piece; they'll make for a stronger bond once the piece is set in place.

Bottom Left: With the piece attached to the ceiling, David can begin applying the large leaves of the ornament. You can see that the ceiling has been marked for the placement of the leaves, and its surface scratched for tight bonding. As David works, he has to be sure to clean up excess plaster after each piece is applied. With that little brush, he keeps both the ceiling and the pieces damp throughout the installation. (If the surfaces are too dry, they'll absorb too much water from the plaster 'glue,' weakening the strength of the adhesion.)

Bottom Right: After the leaves are in place, David can insert each anthemion.

Left: The piece is now 75% complete; it lacks only the inner leaves and a few of the outer flowers.

The centerpiece used in this article was made for the Greek Revival Room of New York's Metropolitan Museum of Art. Our thanks to the Museum for allowing us to photograph the installation, and to David Flaharty for his generous help in the preparation of this article.

YOU SHOULD NOW have a pretty good idea of how it's done. Imagine the possibilities! Just one word of warning: If you want to try this in your own home, by all means have fun when you do it -- exuberant ornament like this should be a joy. But it's also a cultivated taste, and so you should educate your eye by looking around at good examples before you plunge ahead with your own design. And remember our motto: "To thine own style be true." Not only period style, but also ceiling height, room proportions, and degree of formality all play an important role in the design of ornament in general -- and a ceiling centerpiece in particular. A Georgian centerpiece in a Bungalow dining room would probably make both the room and the centerpiece look ridiculous.

WE DISCUSSED THE TECHNIQUES for repairing a deteriorated or damaged cornice in the August/September 1985 OHJ. In this article, we'll assume that you want to replace a wooden cornice that's either missing or so deteriorated that it can't be repaired -- which means building a cornice from scratch. Of course no two cornices are exactly alike, but, when building any cornice, you'll have to duplicate the details and proportions of the original design; build up a decorative bracket; and weatherproof the cornice.

MOST MISSING CORNICES were removed because previous owners of the house didn't want to invest in having them fixed. Yours may have been removed for structural reasons, however, so don't just assume you can hang a several-hundred-pound cornice -- your facade may not be able to support it. (In an upcoming issue we'll examine the methods -- and special precautions -- of cornice installation.)

IN THE LATE 1800s and early 1900s, wooden cornices were built in place. Today, cornice specialists like Mike Pangia often prefer to build a cornice in the shop, and then attach it to the building. There are several advantages to building a wood cornice in a shop:

• EASIER & FASTER ASSEMBLY -- In the shop, you have access to all sides of a cornice, so you can drive screws from the back. Production and test fitting of pieces proceeds quickly and orderly with shop tools nearby. Gluing and clamping a cornice is also easier.

• LESS TIME SPENT ON SCAFFOLD -- Not only is it safer to build the cornice in a shop, but scaffold rental costs are greatly reduced, too. No time is wasted climbing up and down the scaffold.

• CLIMATE CONTROL -- A shop project won't be delayed by rain; unprimed pieces won't get wet. There will be no drastic changes in temperature and humidity to interfere with the curing of glued joints.

• GREATER STRUCTURAL INTEGRITY -- In a shop the cornice is built as a single unit, so every piece can add to its overall strength and stability. For example, decorative brackets and consoles used to be toe-nailed onto a cornice; they did nothing but look good and add weight. When a cornice is built in a shop, the bracket can be screwed tight to the frame above it, and to the backboard behind

it. The brackets of this cornice will act as trusses supporting the cornice framework.

ALBEIT EASIER TO CONSTRUCT, a shop-built cornice must withstand the stresses of being hoisted into place, and so it has to be sturdier (and heavier) than a site-built cornice. The original spike board and the wall on which the cornice is to be mounted might not be strong enough to hold the new cornice (more on this in a future article).

Planning The Design

BUILDING AND INSTALLING a large wooden cornice is an expensive and time-consuming project, so you'd better be sure you'll be happy with the design, decoration, and proportions of the finished cornice before you buy any materials. Do your homework; planning the design and developing working drawings are the most critical aspects of cornice construction.

HERE ARE SOME WAYS to figure out what your original cornice looked like:

• TRY TO FIND old photographs of your building. The building records department in town hall or your local historical society are good places to check.

• LOOK AT CORNICES on nearby buildings that are similar to yours. If you see the same cornice on several buildings (a common occurrence), chances are your cornice looked like the "standard" model in your area. This is especially true with row houses; the row was built with identical cornices. Even if the buildings adjacent to yours no longer have their cornices, it's most appropriate to match the original row.

• LOOK FOR PAINT (or dirt) lines on your building, which outline the edges of the missing cornice -- "ghosts" can provide valuable clues about the shape of the original cornice.

• IS THERE anything left of the old cornice? You can often figure out what the cornice looked like by examining the skeletal remains.

ONCE YOU KNOW what your old cornice looked like, you'll need to develop a set of working drawings for the new cornice. Working drawings show the dimensions, profiles, locations, and spacings of all the pieces of the cornice. Drawings reassure you when you think you're building the cornice too big -- it's easy to be fooled by the <u>seemingly</u> gigantic proportions of a cornice, because it looks much larger in a workshop than when it's crowning a building. Designs laid out in working drawings can be carefully studied, permitting modifications to produce assemblies that are more efficient: stronger, lighter, more weather resistant, and less expensive. A good set of drawings will avoid costly errors and provide a valuable record for future repairs.

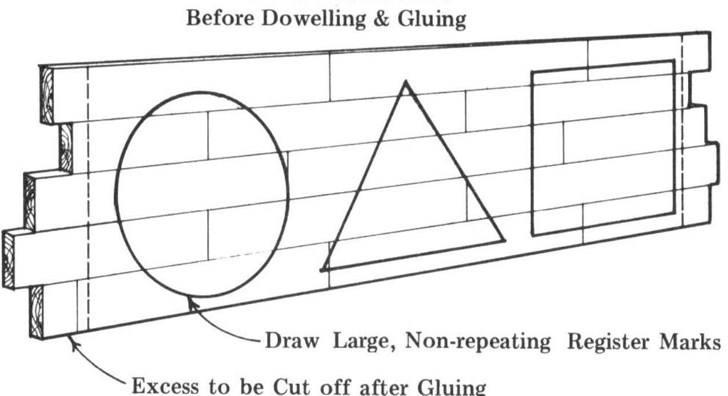

UNLESS YOU'RE EXTREMELY confident in your ability, you should have an architect, master carpenter, or cornice specialist develop the working drawings -- you'll get a better set of drawings from a design professional than you could do yourself as a novice. Realize that even experienced restoration architects will have to do some homework and field analysis to arrive at an appropriate design. If a cornice specialist is involved, he or she should work closely with the architect to insure that the talent and experience of both are reflected in the final design.

Building The Backboard

THE BACKBOARD is the rigid foundation onto which all the other parts of the cornice are fastened. The backboard spans the width of the cornice. It must be straight, true, and strong.

THE BEST LUMBER for a backboard is 5/4"-x-6" fir floor decking. This material is less prone to warping than lighter stock; it's also available in longer lengths, reducing the number of joints. If it's unavailable, 1"-x-6" common fir with factory-milled tongue-and-groove joints can be used. For smaller cornices, 1"-x-8" boards with edge-to-edge joints may be adequate. Avoid boards that have loose knots, knots along the edges, splits, checks, or warps. The backboard is an important part of the cornice, and these defects will reduce its strength.

DON'T USE PLYWOOD for a backboard. Even the best grade of plywood will "jag" over a period of time. The backboard will require more vertical joints with the standard 8-ft. lengths of plywood, reducing overall strength. And if some future owner of the house doesn't properly maintain a plywood cornice, the eventual repairs will be more difficult. Solid lumber can be patched, consolidated, and filled, but

once plywood starts to separate, there is little hope for in-place repairs.

LAY THE BOARDS out in the "cup-up/cup-down" pattern and stagger the joints. Clamp the boards together and test for fit, then rearrange or replace the boards as necessary to get a straight, true surface. Keep in mind that while alternating grain, you also want the best side of the boards facing out. Mark the faces of the boards (as illustrated at left) so you can duplicate the layout when you glue up the boards. Don't put any vertical joints within about 18 inches of the end of the backboard: You're going to square off the ends of the backboard after you've glued it up, and you don't want very short pieces at the ends.

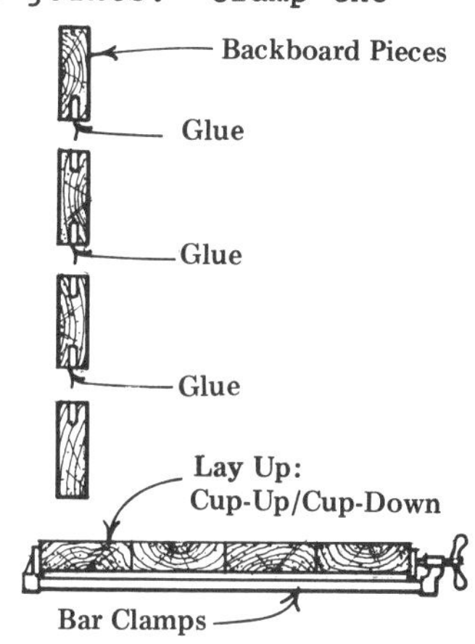

ONCE YOU'RE SATISFIED with the fit and layout, it's time to dowel and glue-up the boards. With the boards temporarily clamped together, mark the positions where the dowels will go. The dowels should be placed 12" on center and about 2" from the ends of the boards. Drill the holes just a little deeper than half the length of the dowel, so the dowels can extend almost equally into each board and the boards can come flush together. A dowel jig and a drill stop are a great help at this stage.

WITH DOWEL HOLES drilled, you're ready to glue. Check to be certain you drilled each dowel hole. You can apply all the glue at once if you lay the boards up as illustrated, but beware: The glue sets up quickly, so be sure you're completely prepared before mixing. Use a waterproof adhesive such as Weldwood Phenol Resorcinol. Apply the glue, insert the dowels, and clamp the boards together. Be certain to place the clamps on alternate sides of the boards to prevent warping. Leave the backboard lying flat in a warm (70 degrees F.) room for 24 hours.

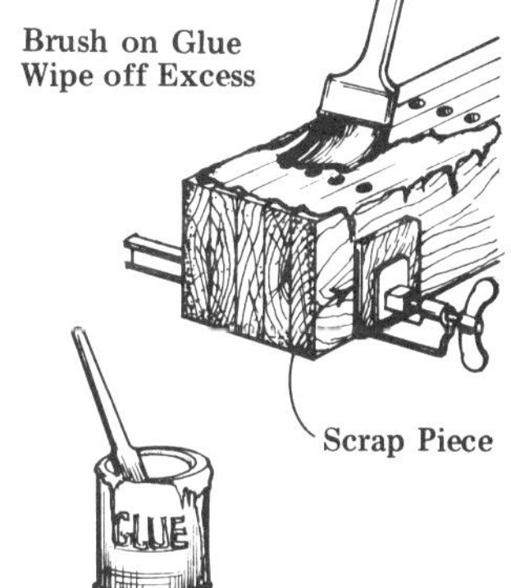

AFTER THE GLUE has dried, cut the excess length off the glued-up backboard. Be especially careful to get a square cut, so the endboards will be plumb when you attach them. Keep in mind the thickness of the endboards when making your final cut (i.e., your backboard length will be slightly shorter than the final cornice).

THE ENDBOARDS should be made of the same material as the rest of the backboard. They are attached to the rest of the backboard with dowels and waterproof glue. The endboards can

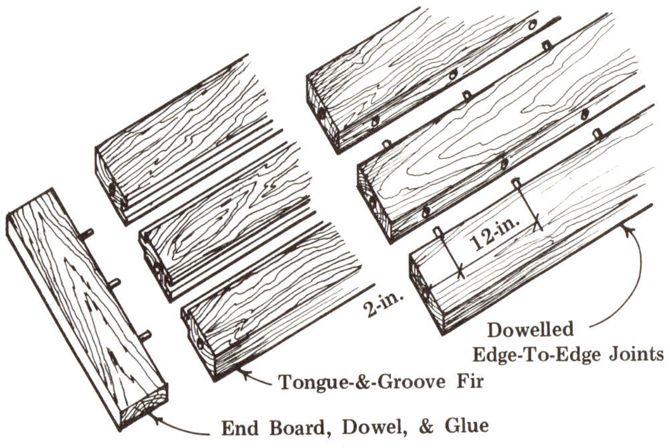

be clamped into place with pipe clamps linked together with couplers, or a single long piece of pipe. Leave the endboards clamped in place for 24 hours, then trim the backboard to its finished length.

These two workmen are gluing up a backboard in Mike Pangia's shop. Note the identifying figures drawn across the boards — they're the real-life versions of the triangle and circle shown in the illustration on page 191.

Lookout Frame

SOME CORNICES consist only of a decorated backboard and a small roof with no soffit or enclosed overhang. For larger cornices with an enclosed overhang, an internal framework is needed.

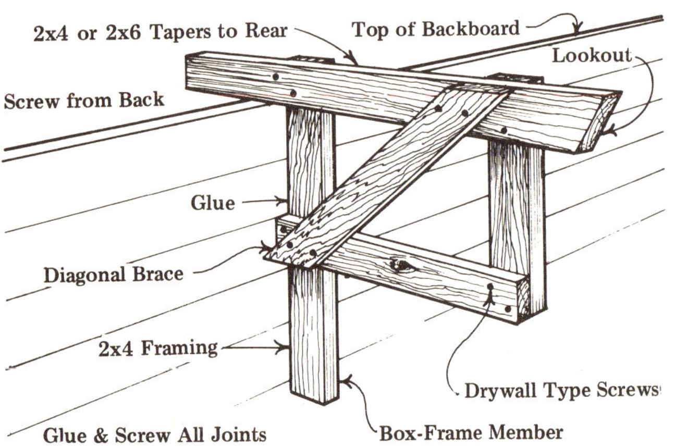

THE INTERIOR FRAMING of the cornice is made up of a series of box frames. Box frames are simply 2x3s or 2x4s, glued and screwed together using an overlap joint. The boxes have a 2"-thick diagonal brace glued and screwed in place. The upper horizontal member of each box is sometimes made from a 2x6 to allow a taper cut at the top of the frame. This cut lets the cornice roof slant back to the roof of the building.

THE BOX FRAMES are fastened to the backboard from the back with long screws and water-resistant glue. The box frames must be placed so that the low end of the diagonal brace is toward the backboard. This makes the frame more resistant to a downward load (like snow, swing-stage scaffolding, or years of plain old gravity). Also, be sure that the box frames at the ends of the cornice have the diagonal brace attached toward the inside of the cornice -- otherwise, you won't be able to cover the ends of the frame.

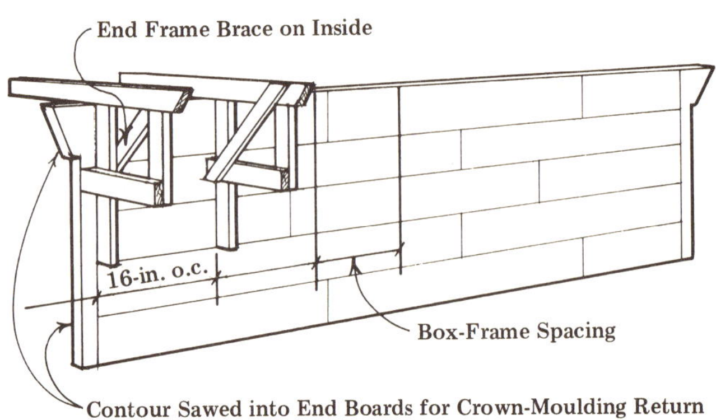

Frames Glued & Screwed to Backboard

SPACING OF THE FRAMES should be sixteen inches on center. Consider where the "decorative" brackets will be located when spacing the box frames. The bracket will play a more important structural role, giving firmer support to the lookout assembly, if you planned ahead so that one of the box frames is above it. (This may require a slightly altered spacing of the box frames.)

ALL THIS FRAMING goes a lot faster if you use drywall screws driven by an electric screw gun or an industrial-strength drill. Don't leave any drywall screws exposed to the weather, or they'll eventually rust.

WITH THE BOX FRAMES in place, sheathe the lookout frame with 1" lumber. Be careful to keep the frames aligned when you apply the first boards. If you cut the bottom sheathing to a width about 1/8 inch short of the front piece, you'll be leaving a small gap under the lip, allowing for ventilation. Screen this gap from the inside with brass screening.

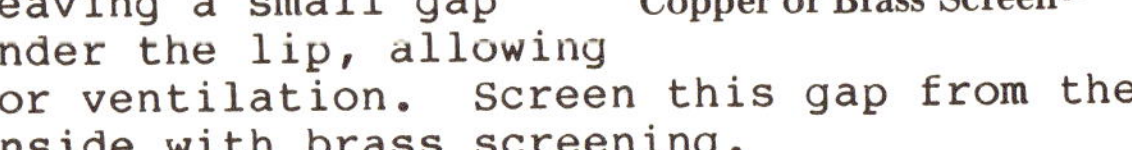

Building Brackets

DESIGNING and building decorative brackets is a craft in itself. Some brackets are simple, undecorated diagonal supports. Others can be highly complex, and loaded with carved, sawn, and turned ornamental details. A cornice console or bracket may contain carved sections, but the entire piece usually isn't carved. Most brackets are simply built-up from multiple layers of wood, a process that involves simple carpentry and produces a long-wearing piece. Built-up brackets aren't as prone to splitting as brackets carved from a single piece of wood.

THE FIRST STEP is to find a bracket to copy, which fits the style and size you need. (It's more appropriate to duplicate a design than to create your own.) When you find a bracket appropriate for your cornice, you can duplicate its details in one of two ways:

1. CAREFULLY MEASURE the height and width of the piece you want to duplicate, then take a slide photograph of the piece, making certain the lens is exactly perpendicular to the object. Project the slide onto a sheet of white poster board, making sure the image is the same size as the actual object (check it against your earlier measurements). Trace the details onto the poster board, and there's your pattern.

2. TAPE A PIECE of paper (a brown paper bag works well) against the side of the bracket. Burnish the design onto the paper by forcefully rubbing a small piece of wood against the scrollwork. A crayon or piece of chalk may also be used to burnish the design onto the paper. Remove the paper and touch up the details. Measure the bracket to double check your tracings.

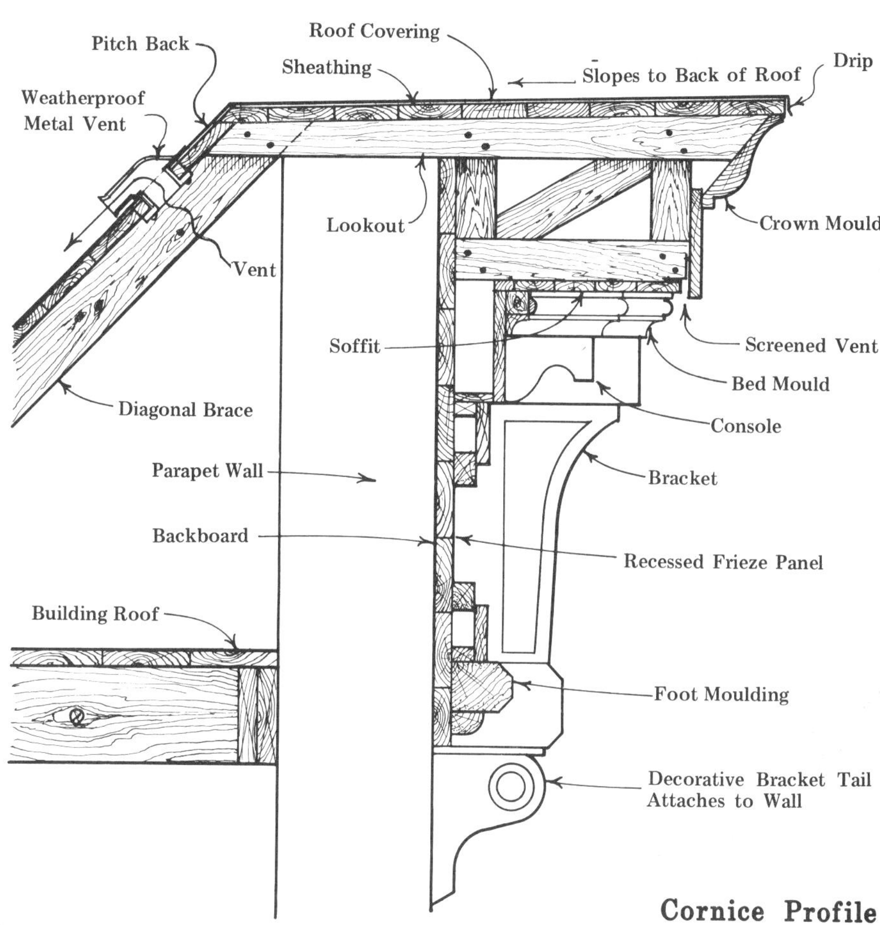

This masonite template of scrollwork was copied from the old bracket shown alongside it.

EITHER WAY, once you have a drawing of the side of the bracket, trace it onto a piece of masonite or 1/4" plywood. Cut the pattern out and clean up the edges. Now you have a template from which you can duplicate numerous bracket ends. The scrollwork may have to be up to 1-1/2" thick on some cornices.

THE DECORATIVE SCROLLWORK will be applied with adhesive to the inner layers, or "side plates" of the bracket. Construction of the side plates varies depending on the size and style of the bracket. Generally, though, they can be fashioned from two pieces of 5/4" stock separated by a couple of spacer blocks made from 2x3 or 2x4 scrap. The front of these boards are cut to match the forward edge of the decorative scrollwork. Again, if you make a template, you'll greatly hasten the process of reproducing numerous pieces.

COVE OR OTHER appropriate mouldings can be used to crown the top of the bracket. Combining quarter round and cove moulding makes a nice classical design. The face of a bracket can be built in a number of different ways. It may have a ribbed appearance if built from many small overlapping pieces of lumber; it may have intricate detail if it's a synthetic cast of a salvaged bracket or a single hand-carved bracket; it may be a simple kerfed piece of lumber. Wherever possible, the face of the bracket should either be removable or applied after installation, so that the backboard can be screwed into the facade without marring the surface of the finished cornice. A large hollow bracket should be ventilated.

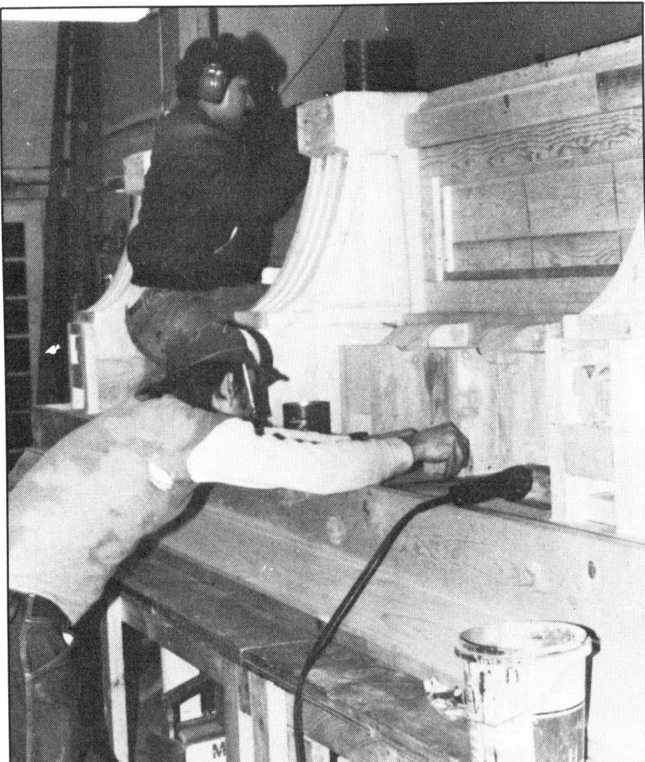

Two workmen are attaching decorative brackets and modillions to a cornice being built in Michael Pangia's shop.

INCISED CARVINGS and other decorative work can now be added. Many brackets have decorative turnings like pendants hanging down from the scrollwork. These can be reproduced on a lathe after you've carefully measured and traced them onto paper with a contour gauge.

BRACKETS and other projecting pieces should be treated with a water repellent before install-ation. All parts of a cornice should be back primed prior to assembly.

Mouldings

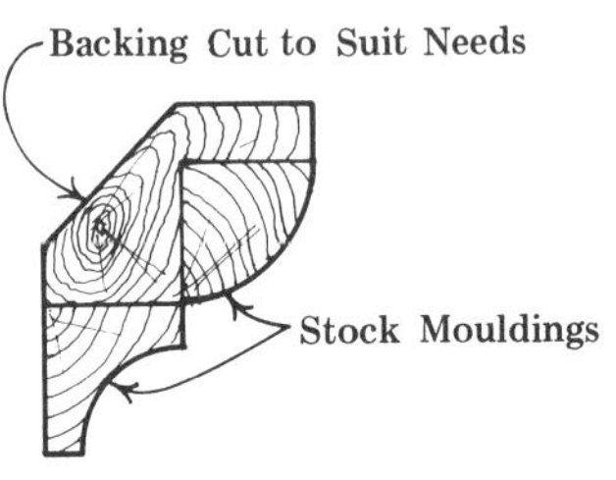

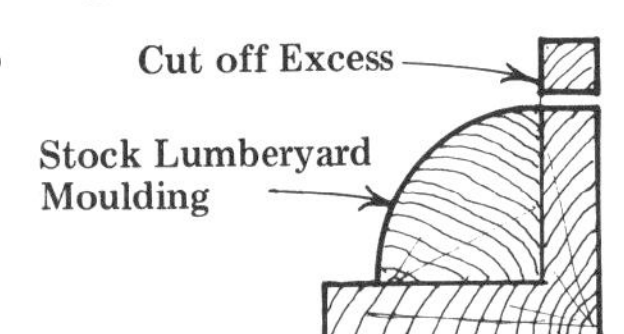

THE LARGE MOULDINGS for a large new cor-nice (crown mould-ing, foot moulding) will probably have to be custom-cut or built up from smaller stock mouldings; there are no modern companies churn-ing out quantities of large stock mouldings. Having large mouldings custom-milled can get fairly expensive. Start-up costs are the problem -- you'll have to pay for producing the knives. Before you call the lumber mill, check with the millwork suppliers listed in the OHJ Catalog. New reproduction mouldings are being introduced all the time.

SMALLER CORNICES can be crowned with available stock, however. You may be able to find mouldings up to 8" wide in 16' lengths. Make up longer lengths by gluing and dowelling the shorter lengths together with a scarf joint.

Finishing

ALL SCREW HOLES, nail holes, and cracks or checks in the wood should be filled with a quality wood filler. Latex fillers will fail within a few years, but epoxy fillers will last longer and are easier to tool. Marine sealants are also good for this appli-cation. Narrow joints between elements should be sealed with a suitable exterior caulk. Do not leave fillers and caulks in globs around holes and joints; they should be tooled so they'll shed water.

A proper paint job is essential for cornice longevity. If it's well designed and maintained, a shop-built cornice should outlast the building to which it's attached.

AFTER THE FILLERS and sealants have cured, the cornice can be painted with an alkyd-based ex-terior wood primer from a major manufacturer, then topcoated with two coats of a compatible paint. (Use primer and topcoat from the same manufacturer.) High-gloss paints -- either alkyd or latex -- weather slightly better than semi-gloss or flat paints, and give the cor-nice a well-maintained look.

Some Cornice-Building Tips

- Plan your project so that you build the smallest parts and as-semblies first. There's no point in having a 20-ft.-long backboard cluttering your shop months before you're ready to assemble the cornice. For the same reason, order only the lumber you'll need for the next two or three work sessions.
- Wipe off excess glue immediately after clamping. The glue is water soluble while still wet, but once it sets, it's nearly impos-sible to remove.

Article illustrated by Larry Jones.

JOSEPH J. CECERE is Assistant Professor of Civil Engineering Technology at The Pennsylvania State University.

We wish to thank Michael D. Pangia for his technical assistance. Mr. Pangia, a cornice specialist in Brooklyn, N.Y., developed many of the procedures described in this article. Readers inter-ested in further information are invited to write or call Mike at:

Michael D. Pangia & Co., Inc.
63 Wyckoff Street, Dept. OHJ
Brooklyn, NY 11201
(718) 875-0800

Queen Anne Parlors

continued from page 181

IT IS PROBABLY easier to decorate a parlor in Queen Anne than any other style. Although museums are paying outrageous prices for the best Aesthetic pieces, there is enough good, but common, Queen Anne left. Prices are reasonable because dealers don't like it.* But you don't need original Queen Anne antiques. You can opt for the oriental version of Queen Anne. A visit to your local import shop will yield bamboo and rattan furniture, plus Japanese fans and ceramics. New oriental textiles for floors, doors, windows, and cushions complete your picture. Or start with some Colonial Revival things or some Windsor chairs or other antiques -- as long as they are not Greek or Gothic Revival or French. Let circumstance, your own taste, and the design principles that follow be your guide. In describing the Queen Anne parlor, I have tried to let the Queen Anne Kids speak for themselves.

PROPER VICTORIAN PARLORS (the overstuffed type of the 1860s) were ridiculed in the writings of the Queen Anne Kids. Rhoda & Agnes Garrett -- the first professional women interior decorators -- called mid-Victorian floral carpets things "whereupon the whole contents of a conservatory have been upset." Constance Harrison in her <u>Woman's Handiwork in Modern Houses</u> (1881) shuddered at "florid mirror frames, rosewood furniture with marble tops, and fern-leaf wallpaper."

TO HAVE A MODERN Queen Anne parlor, according to Clarence Cook's <u>The House Beautiful</u> (1878), you should avoid "large pieces of furniture and large spaces of wall or drapery; nothing should dominate a room; accents should be small."

THE BASIC DECORATION for late Victorian parlors was Queen Anne works of art, e.g., art pottery, art embroidery, art tiles, art furniture, artistic wallpaper, etc. As decorators, the Queen Anne Kids thought and talked like painters -- especially when it came to colors. For example, Constance Harrison enthused about the colors used by Louis Comfort Tiffany, both in his glass and in complete interiors. She admired fabrics "dyed in tone of color to delight the eye of an impressionist"; stamped leathers of "fiery copper, the golden luster of Moorish pottery, and melting pomegranate blended to produce the effect of clouds at sunset."

FURNITURE FOR THE QUEEN ANNE PARLOR, said Harrison, is "successor to the more ponderous 'Eastlake' and is made of mahogany, cherry,

Quintessential Queen Anne: this Anglo-Japanese parlor corner from *The House Beautiful* (1878). Oriental porcelain and china are everywhere: stuck to the wall, on the hanging cabinet, and lurking on the shelf beneath the sculpture of "Minerva Disrobed." There's a hanging oriental scroll painting, and a large oriental rug on the parquet floor. Other Queen Anne touches: curtained, bookshelved desk. . .paisley shawl slung on the ottoman. . .light, ebonized furniture. . . wainscotted wall topped with a tile-like surface decoration. . .artful plant and floral arrangements on the floor, desk, and in the hanging basket.

walnut, or ebonized cherry." It is "elegant shapes, with many panels, carved balustrades to finish tops and edges, and bevelled glass abeam in doors." <u>Get rid of upholstery and stuffing</u>, thundered Clarence Cook. Substitute bolsters, cushions, and pillows. Seating with rush or cane was also admired, as was wicker and rattan, oriental bamboo furniture, or an orientalizing stick style in ebonized wood. That was the new stuff.

AS FOR THE OLD, the Queen Anne era begins what we now call "flea market" decorating. Some of the Queen Anne parlors look like the junk shops and curiosity shops from which much of the furniture, pottery, and textiles came. Not only were they looking for "donkey-bags of the East" to convert into luxurious drawing-room easy chairs, but also "Old Colony" and "Revolutionary" American furniture of the 17th and 18th centuries. "There was <u>style</u> in those days," sighed Cook. During this first Colonial Revival bull market, grandparents with old American furniture in their attics became very popular!

---

*Victorian Queen Anne furniture should not be confused with the Queen Anne furniture of the early 1700s, which collectors covet. Avant-garde Victorian designers of the 1870s greatly admired the architecture and furniture of the reign of Queen Anne (1702-1714), and so gave her name to the design revolution they were carrying out.

This elegant 1882 parlor, with its sumptuous combination of textures, patterns, and materials, is a visual guide to decorating in the Queen Anne style. On the walls, a rich sunflower-and-pomegranate frieze is placed over a restrained geometric wallpaper. The massive yet delicate mantel has art tiles surrounding the firebox, which contains Aesthetic Movement sunflower andirons. Oriental ceramics embellish the mantel top, niches, and the panelled-door mantel cabinets. Window drapes with horizontal banding hang from rings held on stout brass poles. Behind the drape on the right, the viewer gets a tantalizing glimpse of an Adamesque fanlight surmounted by a picturesque sunburst art-glass panel. The fan motif is echoed in the panel over the mantel mirror. A Japanese print hangs on the wall, and in the window bay, an oriental vase sits atop a delicate Japanese-style stand. Candles adorn the mantel shelf and wall sconce — proclaiming that this modern style has its roots firmly in the past.

The term "parlor" was used by late Victorian traditionalists who preferred the old French-derived term meaning a place to parley. Others favored the Anglo term "drawing room" — a place to withdraw after dinner. Still others with literary inclinations scattered a few books on the shelves and called it a "library." Advanced thinkers referred to the chamber as a "living room."

ON FLOORS, oriental carpets were preferred. Harrison liked "small, blended geometrical patterns" in blue & crimson or green & brown. Cook advised against several small rugs because they gave the floor a patchy look, destroyed the room's unity, and tended to trip children and old folks. He preferred a large rug covering the floor up to the large furniture at the wall.

VOLUMINOUS CURTAINS AND DRAPES, province of the enemy upholsterers, were despised as much as floral carpets for many of the same reasons: too important, too expensive, too tough to remove for cleaning. In addition, heavy window drapery blocked the window mouldings and view. "The only sensible way to support curtains is by rings running on a brass rod,"

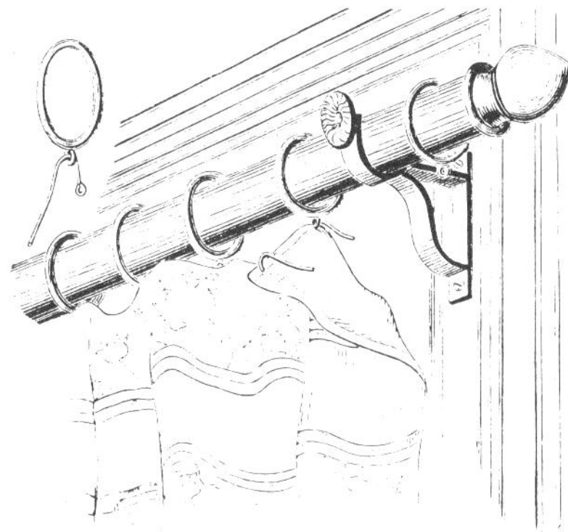

said Cook. Do away with the old cornices, valance or lambrequin, fringes, borders and tie-backs. Because vertical stripes get lost in the folds, curtains were designed in horizontal bands and hung straight to emphasize the flow of the fabric.

DOORS WERE DEADLY because they were dull, ate up floor area, and broke spatial flows. When stuck with a working door, decorate its panels, said the Queen Anne Kids. Otherwise, take it off, drape stuff on a rod with rings, and call it a portiere. (Curtain design principles also applied to portieres -- but a portiere should not be a copy of the curtains.) Bits of old oriental rugs, carpets, or shawls were often adapted to portieres, bringing "to the senses a waft from far Cathay." Portiere rods were placed a few inches from the top of the door frame to let in light and provide a magic glimpse beyond. The rod should not only be strong enough but also <u>look</u> strong enough.

WOODEN MANTELS with mantel cabinets or chimney mirrors echoing Chippendale or the Brothers Adam were specified by the Queen Anne Kids. In addition to mantel shelving, there were hanging cabinets on the walls and rows of shelves above doors and windows. "Chinamania" filled these shelves with exotic pottery and porcelain, along with oriental fans and other curious bric-a-brac. If you were stuck with an old-

This 1878 illustration shows the Queen Anne style at its most nostalgic: antiques mingling cheerfully with new furnishings. In front of the art-tiled fireplace, our hostess pours from an old Adamesque tea service. On the floor, an oriental rug overlays a larger, geometric-patterned rug; the furniture is light and ebonized. Queen Anne candlepower has banished gaslights. The wall is wainscotted, covered with oriental porcelains and fans, and features three old mirrors from a curiosity shop.

fashioned marbleized slate or white mantel, you'd have to cover it up as best you could. Harrison advised putting a board on the mantel shelf and attaching a valance of "maroon cotton velvet edged with crewel fringe."

SCREENS were the primary means by which parlor space was organized. Screens, as well as furniture, were often thrown across corners. "Corners are a mistake," Cook declared, "seldom any good is gotten out of them."

LONGING TO MAKE your own Queen Anne parlor? Decorative freedom is heady stuff. You can be timid or bold. Make a stage set, or artist's studio, or bohemian den; make a tea-room fit for Prince Edward or a Lily Langtry salon. Most of all, have fun: The Queen Anne style is delightful entertainment.

Restoration Products  *by Larry Jones*

GUESS WHAT'S JUST AROUND THE CORNER?

Victorian Rocking Horse

Nathan Lanni of Sacramento produces the kind of holiday gift you'll want to keep long after your children outgrow it: handmade wooden rocking horses that are exact reproductions of an 1830s model. Nathan builds them in his home shop, using the construction techniques traditionally employed for 19th-century rocking horses and carousel horses. He takes no shortcuts in the quality of his materials: red-oak rockers, solid-pine body, natural horse-hair mane and tail, glass eyes — there's even a real leather saddle & bridle. The horses are painted with 4 coats of (antiqued) baltic blue, carriage red, white, buckskin tan, brown, or black. (Clear finishes or other colors are available on request.) The rockers come stained a deep mahogany or painted in red, yellow, or blue, with a clear finish (either glossy or satin).

A smaller rocking horse is designed for children ages 1 through 6; it's 48 in. long and 30 in. high, and sells for $425 ppd. The larger horse, for children 5 and up, is 66 in. long and 40 in. high, and costs $525 ppd. For Christmas delivery, contact Nathan early at **Victorian Rocking Horse Works, Dept. OHJ, 4316 Vulcan Drive, Sacramento, CA 95825. (916) 483-9313.**

Great Screwdriver

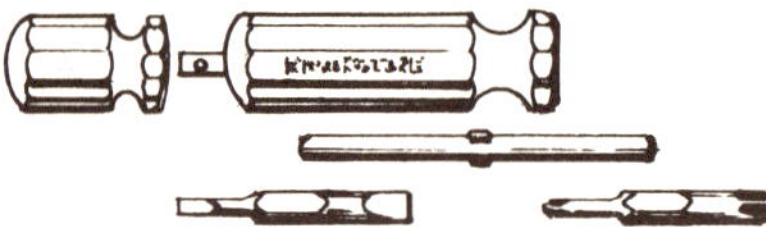

Once this screwdriver is in your toolbox, you'll probably never want to use anything else. It has a reversible tip giving two sizes of slot blades. Remove the shaft, and on the other end is another reversible tip with two Phillips blades. At the opposite end of the Tenite handle is a stubby handle that pulls off, allowing you to get into tight spots. You can buy it for $16.95 plus $3.45 shipping (and remember to ask for a free catalog) from **Brookstone Company, Dept. OHJ, 757 Vose Farm Rd., Petersborough, NH 03458. (603) 924-7181.**

The Christmas Store

Gerlachs of Lecha has the most extensive collection of reproduction Victorian Christmas decorations we've ever seen; what follows is just a sampling.

Fifty different shapes of glass figural light covers, from animals to houses to Santa himself; they come with rubber grommets so you can slip them over the miniature light bulbs that adorn your tree or home ($3 ppd.).

A dazzling array of blown-glass ornaments, including a Victorian lady with roses, Cherub on balloon, and a Green Pickle — a good luck symbol in Germany & a big seller! (Prices from $2 to $7.50.)

Cardboard cornucopias for nuts & candies — a must for every 1890s Christmas tree (approx. $1.75).

Christbaumshmuck, a hardcover book with over 500 illustrations and 30 color pages, will delight everyone who collects Christmas decorations. ($28 ppd. — in German with an English translation.)

Plan on spending a week just reading their catalog: There are recipes, histories, how-to information, and more — a bargain at only $1.25. Contact **Gerlachs of Lecha, Dept. OHJ, P.O. Box 213, Emmaus, PA 18049. (215) 965-9181.**

This hand-painted, museum quality, iron Christmas-tree stand, made from original 1908 moulds, is available in limited numbers from Gerlachs of Lecha.

Window Candles

These window-sill lights, hand-crafted in iron and tin, can add a warm, festive look to the windows of your old house. Fifteen different farm-animal designs are available; there's also one shaped like an angel. Each light has a 4-watt electric candle and a beeswax or white sleeve. They sell for $27 each plus $4 shipping from **Hurley Patentee Lighting, Dept. OHJ, R.D. 7, Box 98A, Kingston, NY 12401. (914) 331-5414.**

Cast-Iron Firebacks

The Halley's Comet Fireback is the ultimate fireplace accessory as well as a most unusual gift. This limited-edition, extra-heavy casting commemorates the comet's crossing of the celestial equator (which will be on New Year's Eve 1985). The fireback protects firebrick and radiates additional heat out into the room; it weighs 56 lbs., measures 19½ in. x 21½ in., and sells for $168 ppd. For a free brochure (or the $2 catalog) write **Pennsylvania Firebacks, Dept. OHJ, 1011 E. Washington Lane, Philadelphia, PA 19138. (215) 843-6162.**

Lilliputian Stoves

Here's a wonderful line of period-style, cast-iron stoves, tiny but highly functional, which would be equally at home in your restored wooden boat or camp cottage. The rugged little Fisherman stoves are available in the following models: Gift (burns wood, oil, or coal); Little Cod (wood or oil); and Sardine (wood only). The handsome Sardine measures 12 in. x 11 in., weighs 28 lbs., and costs $82 (Canadian) plus shipping.

You can also get the Atlantic, an especially popular and useful single-oven stove. It has tightly securing doors; a large, heavily lined, cast-iron firebox; & a protective rail around the top. It burns wood, oil, or coal, and comes in 4 sizes: The smallest is 20 in. x 15 in. x 21 in. high; the largest is 35 in. x 30 in. x 32 in. high. Prices range from $302 to $992 (Canadian) plus shipping. For more information, send for a free brochure from **Lunenburg Foundry & Engineering Ltd., Dept. OHJ, Lunenburg, Nova Scotia, Canada B0J 2C0. (902) 634-8827.**

Christmas Tree Stand

Want your Christmas tree to have a real period touch — at a reasonable price? Here's a German, antique-style, cast-iron or cast-aluminum tree stand that'll have you singing "O Tannenbaum" this holiday season! You can also get an Art Deco stand, another design that holds a gallon of water — 6 models in all, priced from $10.90 to $29.85 (plus shipping). Send for a free color flyer from **Black Forest Imports Corp., Dept. OHJ, 325 Redmond Rd., S. Orange, NJ 07079. (201) 762-4634.**

Owl Andirons

Made in 19th-century moulds, these cast-iron owl andirons have glass eyes that will reflect the glow of a cozy fire. A 13-in.-high pair sells for $37.95 ppd.; a heavier, 14-in. pair costs $49.94 ppd.

Also there are cat andirons (with green glass eyes), Hessian Soldier andirons, andirons suitable for bungalows, Dutch oven doors, and loads of other fireplace equipment. For a catalog, send $1 to **Lemee's Fireplace Equipment, Dept. OHJ, 815 Bedford Street, Bridgewater, MA 02324. (617) 697-2672.**

Goose Feather Tree

The tradition of brightening the house with handmade, goose-feather Christmas trees dates back to the 1870s — Sears catalogs of the early 1900s listed a variety of them. They're still available, now larger and stronger with wire limbs and a wooden dowel trunk (and their feathers are treated with fire-retardent dye). Like the originals, these trees have tiers of limbs for displaying candles, ornaments, and other decorations; they come with 3, 4, or 5 tiers, and range in height from 2 to 3 feet. Prices run from $37.50 to $110 (plus shipping).

Send $2 for a Christmas catalog from **Christmas Treasures, Dept. OHJ, P.O. Box 53 HJ, Dewitt, NY 13214.**

Homestead Hints

Does Mother Nature undo all your restoration work on your house & garden? Rejoice! *Homestead Hints for the Home, Garden, & Household* probably has the answers to your problems. Don Berg, a New York architect (& owner of a rapidly deteriorating homestead), scoured hundreds of late-19th-century volumes for long-lost hints that can help today's old-house owners. This 112-page, softcover book has 192 of the best hints, illustrated with old woodcuts. It's $5.50 plus $1.50 postage. (You get a money-back guarantee plus a free copy of their latest catalog.) Contact **Antiquity Reprints, Dept. OHJ, P.O. Box 370, Rockville Center, NY 11571. (516) 766-5585.**

Check the brand new 1986 Old-House Journal Catalog for more Christmas gift ideas ... it's also a terrific gift in itself!

After-Holiday Cleanup

It looks like a Super Chief Locomotive but it's a fully restored Electrolux vacuum cleaner. This slide-along cruiser, common about twenty years ago, has been equipped with new bearings, cord, gaskets, handle, hose, and whatever else was needed to make it function like new. And with all its outside parts rechromed, this classic even looks new. The cleaning head has been reconditioned, with its original, flip-over, rug-and-floor brush. A dusting brush, crevice tool, & upholstery tool give you all the attachments you need to battle the most insidious dirt in your home or shop. Send for information and a free catalog from **Vermont Country Store, Dept. OHJ, 531 Main Street, Weston, VT 05161. (802) 362-2400.**

opinion...

Remuddling of the month

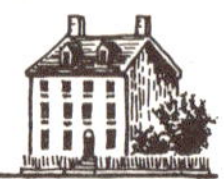

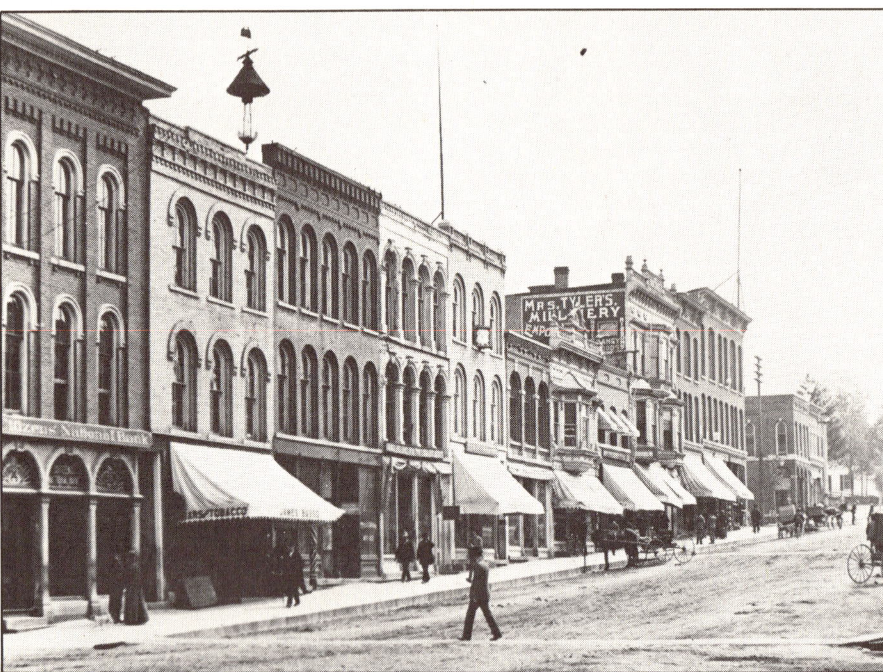

AT LEFT is Main Street in Niles, Michigan; the photo was taken in 1900. Below is the same street as it looked two years ago. "Here is a case of remuddling on a grand scale," says subscriber Roger E. Lorenzen, who sent us these pictures. "This town was rated second in the state of Michigan for its architectural beauty, but in the name of progress many historic homes and other buildings have been destroyed." Projecting cornices and bays were undoubtedly lopped off long ago, but experience in other towns suggests that most of the facades are still intact underneath their aluminum shroud. But that's cold comfort for anyone who's walking down a street dwarfed by those faceless walls. Come on, Niles, do yourself a favor and bring Main Street back to life.

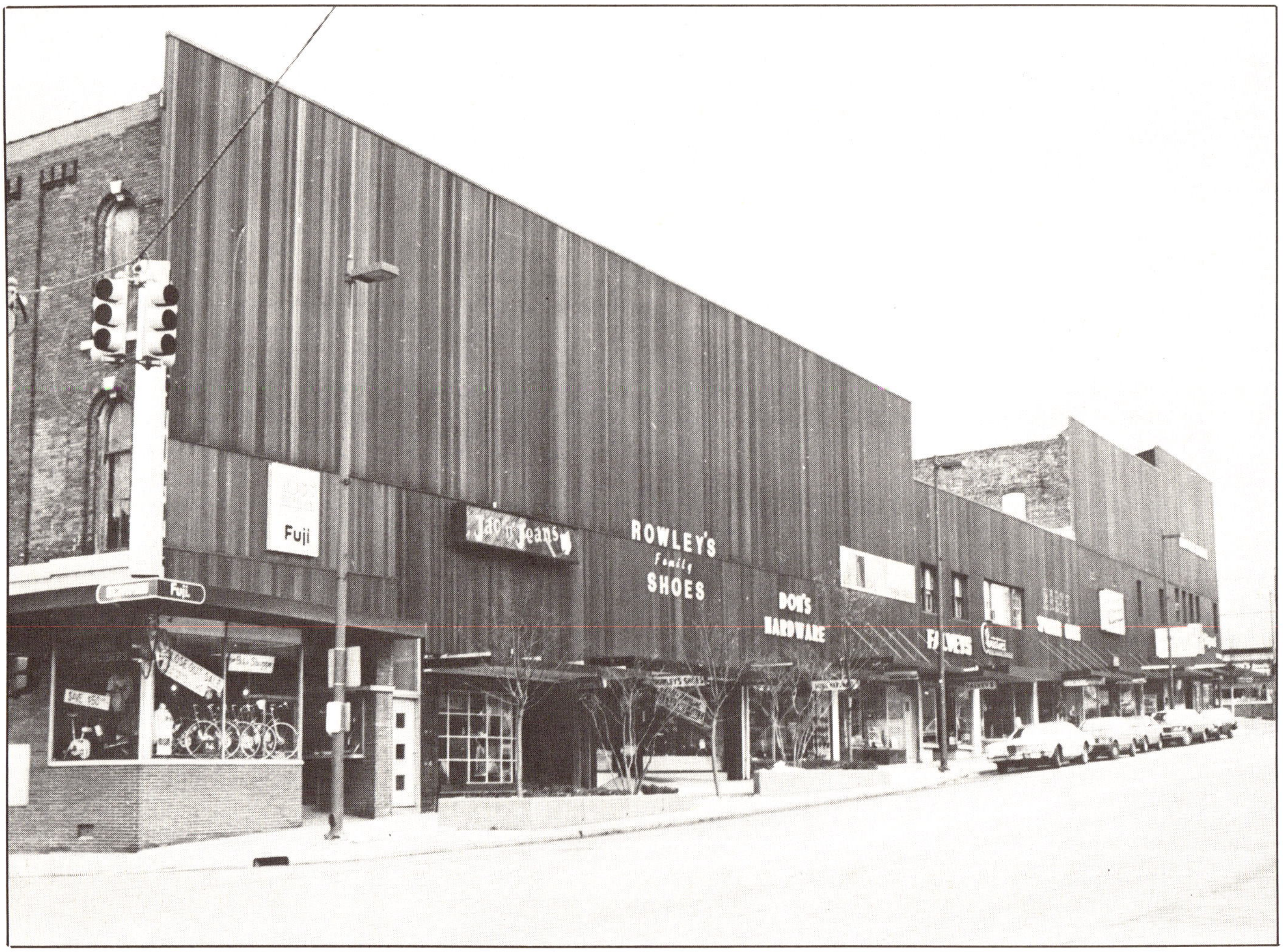

Restoration and Maintenance Techniques
For The Pre-1939 House

December 1985 / Vol. XIII No. 10 / $2.

The Old-House Journal

Annual Index Inside

Reconditioning Floors

by Bill O'Donnell

MY LATEST RESTORATION PROJECT involved reviving the finish of a parquet floor. At the time, I thought the fastest method would be to power sand and completely refinish the entire floor. I chose not to for practical rather than aesthetic reasons: I hadn't the time to sand the floor, and I didn't want to deal with the noise and dust generated by a drum sander. Also, I knew from past experience that I didn't possess the deft touch necessary for using a power sander without damaging the floor.

INSTEAD, I DECIDED to simply clean the floor and add a new finish right over what was left of the existing one. With the job now completed, it's clear that my practical solution was also correct aesthetically: Rather than appearing new and out-of-place, the floor is full of patina and warmth. It now graces an old house as only fine old woodwork can. Equally important (to me anyway), I spent less time cleaning the floor than I would have had I power sanded.

FOLLOWING are the procedures to use when you want to <u>gently</u> revive your floor's finish.

cont'd on p. 218

In the next issue...
AN EXPANDED OHJ!

Imagine Walking Barefoot!

Sharing Temporary Burnout with a Sympathetic Audience

I LONG FOR a normal family life. I want to live in the kind of house where you can get on with the day-to-day stuff of living, a house that's a backdrop for all the usual activities (you know, like cooking and watching television).

TAKE LAST WEEKEND. Jonathan and I went down to see Mom and Dad's new house. (It's nice: a shingled ranch with lots of windows looking out at the woods that practically come right up to the house.) Mom kept apologizing, "Sorry the place is so disorganized, kids; we just moved in on Wednesday." This was Saturday -- of the same week -- and would you believe you could get out of bed and sleepily pad around barefoot?! Wall-to-wall carpeting! A clean tile floor in the bathroom! I thought I'd die of cozies.

(I'VE BEEN LIVING in my aquamarine cave for 15 months and you _still_ can't go barefoot.)

THEIR HOUSE didn't demand to be the center of attention all weekend. The double-glazed Anderson windows kept us warm, the kitchen functioned, there was no dust. There were no holes in the walls, no slop-buckets of paint stripper.

MOM AND DAD had just moved all their belongings into this six-year-old house, and already it was a home.

BACK IN Brooklyn, it all came clear: what's been nagging me is not having a home. True, I own a house. But I live on a job site.

SINCE THAT REALIZATION, I've become obsessed with home-less thoughts. The other day I was on the phone, holding for someone, and I glanced at a mail-order catalog on my desk. Hey, LOOK AT THAT: The people on the cover are _sitting_ on the _floor_, wearing silk pajamas, playing Trivial Pursuit! Imagine sitting on the floor! (Imagine having nothing else to do at night!)

MAYBE YOU'RE WONDERING about the state of our floors. They're going to be great some day, even better than wall-to-wall, but for months the parquet has been covered with kraft paper, onto which have fallen plaster chunks and all sorts of toxic dust. The kitchen floor is a total gross-out: multiple layers of old linoleum and vinyl, cracked and peeling and dulled to a medium grey-olive. The layers are so porous that if we spill milk on the floor and go get a paper towel, when we turn back the milk is gone.

SOMETIMES I don't know whether to be proud of our fortitude or ashamed of our lifestyle. Last week, for instance, a photographer came to get some shots of Clem and me in a "before" setting -- my house, naturally. The photographer showed genuine interest in the evidence being uncovered by our scraping. The more fascinated he seemed, the more excited I got about showing him all the neat stuff. I opened up to a non-initiate, who just maybe didn't think this was a disgusting way to live.

THEN CAME his killer question: "So where are you living while all this is going on?"

THIS LIMBO LIFESTYLE -- stacked furniture, eating pizza because you can't face the kitchen -- isn't as much of a hoot as it was the first time around.

IF MY ONLY WISH were for a home, plain and simple (and clean), there certainly would be easier ways to go about it. But for me, it just had to be an old house -- and once the adventure has begun, you can't escape. During the adventure, the house isn't a backdrop for the other activities in your life, it _is_ the activity in your life.

IN THE MEANTIME, we've decided to finish one room (the bedroom). _Really_ finish it, right down to a three-color paint job and, yes, a carpet. It's like playing tag: The bedroom'll be a safe "home base," where the rest of the house can't get me.

Patricia Poore

The Old-House Journal®

Editor
Patricia Poore

Production Editor
Cole Gagne

Senior Technical Advisor
Larry Jones

Assistant Editors
Sarah J. McNamara
William J. O'Donnell

Contributing Editors
Walter Jowers
John Mark Garrison
Roland A. Labine Sr.

Architectural Consultant
Jonathan Poore

Circulation Supervisor
Barbara Bugg

Circulation Assistants
Jeanne Baldwin
Elaine Lynch

Office Manager
Tricia A. Martin

Catalog Editor
Sarah J. McNamara

Publishing Consultant
Paul T. McLoughlin

Publisher
Clem Labine

THE OLD-HOUSE JOURNAL *(ISSN 0094-0178) is published ten times annually for $18 per year by The Old-House Journal Corporation, 69A Seventh Avenue, Brooklyn, NY 11217. Telephone (718) 636-4514. Application to mail at second-class postage rates is pending at Brooklyn, New York, and additional mailing offices. POSTMASTER: Send address changes to* **THE OLD-HOUSE JOURNAL,** *69A Seventh Avenue, Brooklyn, NY 11217.*

Subscriptions in Canada are $36 per year, payable in Canadian funds. Contents are fully protected by copyright and must not be reproduced in any manner whatsoever without specific permission in writing from the Editor.

We are happy to accept editorial contributions to The Old-House Journal. Query letters that include an outline of the proposed article are preferred. All manuscripts will be reviewed, and returned if unacceptable. However, we cannot be responsible for non-receipt or loss — please keep copies of all materials sent.

Printed at Photo Comp Press, New York City

CAVEAT EMPTOR

The Pitfalls of Restoration in the Big City

by Greg Jackson, Boston

SO, YOU'VE DECIDED to buy an old house and fix it up. You and your mate have been doing very well in your respective careers; you're hopscotching into higher tax brackets and need a good tax shelter. You both have IRAs and some safe stocks. But what you really want is something you can enjoy as it escalates in value, something into which you can channel your creative energies.

YOU TRY NEVER to miss <u>This</u> <u>Old</u> <u>House</u>. But what your own friends are doing with their old houses makes the work you see on television pale by comparison. Just last week, for example, you went to Sue and Alan's . . . what they've done in just a few years is unbelievable. They've created an elegance in living you thought no longer existed.

BUT WHAT <u>REALLY</u> impressed you is the fond way in which Sue and Alan spoke of their house. They acted as if it were a living, breathing member of the family rather than a heap of bricks and mortar. Their feelings were evident from the way they stroked the wainscotting in the dining room and explained the long process by which Alan had removed layers of paint from the walnut. And from the way Sue reverently showed you where the original owner had scratched her initials and the date -- 1/29/95 -- with her diamond on the windowpane in the master bedroom. And the way they displayed the scrapbook of before and after pictures of each room in the house.

TO RETURN TO the white walls and exposed bricks of your small apartment leaves you depressed and claustrophobic for days. You're green with envy every time you remember the 12-foot ceilings, the ornate mantels, and the rich wallcoverings. You read the real estate section of the Sunday paper even before you read "Parade." You begin to suggest to your partner that "fixing up our own place" would be just the thing to restore some of the magic that has gone out of your relationship. You make a few calls and find several realtors who have "just the thing for you."

IF, DURING A TIME of diminished mental capacity, your spouse agrees to buy an old house, make sure he thinks he made the decision for himself. The first rule of restoration is to convince your mate that it was his idea in the first place. The ability to scream, "It was your idea to buy this stupid house!" will see you through many difficult times.

THIS RULE IS particularly helpful when a neighbor calls to say that he has just seen the 100-pound hatch go sailing off the roof in high wind. It also comes in handy when the plumber doesn't show up to reconnect the heating pipes by Labor Day, or by Columbus Day, or by Thanksgiving. And when the city threatens to shut off the hot water because the previous owner didn't pay the bill. You get the point. Being able to blame someone else when something dreadful happens is very therapeutic.

Greg Jackson's corner rowhouse in Boston, Massachusetts.

Top left: The work begins. Top right: Dental pick in hand, Greg removes paint from ornate plaster instead of cooking dinner. Bottom left: Atop makeshift scaffolding, Greg applies a new coat of paint.

AND DREADFUL THINGS do happen. If you think nothing could be more frightening than the shower scene in "Psycho," you haven't gotten a phone call from a tenant, informing you that firemen are removing your tenants from the house with a cherrypicker. And if you think nothing can be more frustrating than dealing with an amoral landlord, you've never stood in housing court and heard the judge dismiss your case against a tenant who refuses to move out of your house so you can move in, and who refuses to pay his rent in the meantime. This tenant has told the judge, through an inter- preter, that he is virtually destitute and unable to speak or understand English. This same tenant operates a business, owns an apartment building, and drives an El Dorado. He also displays an amazing ability to speak English outside the courtroom, calling you every vile name in the language. To add insult to injury, his octogenarian mother spits at you when you meet in the hallway.

IT WOULD BE IMPRUDENT to tell the judge what you think of his idea of justice and you most certainly cannot trade spit for spit with an 85-year-old woman. However, being able to shout, "Why did you ever suggest we buy this house in the first place?" at your partner provides no small comfort.

THE SATISFACTION of pointing a finger is only one of the many things you must be aware of before you buy a "neglected Victorian queen" or that "diamond in the rough," euphe- misms employed by realtors to describe inner- city wrecks. One very important rule to remember is never to believe anyone who says, "Restoring an old house is fun." Restoring an old house is not fun unless the only active role you're required to play is to write checks from a very fat bank account. If you are financially able to become the primary source of income for a dozen or so skilled craftsmen for the next two or three years, then, by all means, buy a house that has "great potential." If, however, your bank account barely enables you to be the primary source of income for yourself, buy a condo.

A MEAGER BANK ACCOUNT requires that you do the
work of a dozen or so skilled craftsmen for
the next nine or ten years. Learning plastering, roofing, and electrical work is <u>not</u>
fun . . . particularly if you avoided shop
class like the plague in high school. Learning to route waste pipes and lay electrical
systems will be no more appealing to you as an
adult than it was when you were a teenager.

IF, IN THE PAST, you enjoyed spending a weekend painting your apartment, good for you.
But spending months removing other people's
paint from fireplaces, oak staircases, and
parquet floors will not provide you with the
same sense of satisfaction. It's true that
Michelangelo lay flat on his back for years,
paintbrush in hand, working on a ceiling.
But, in the end, he had the Sistine Chapel to
show for his efforts. After you've lain on
your back for months, using dental tools to
remove lead paint from an ornately-plastered
ceiling, you will have a damned nice ceiling
under which to recuperate from lead poisoning.
However, it is doubtful that busloads of tour-
ists from all over the world will descend upon
your house to see your ceiling.

L IVING IN A RESTORED house <u>is</u> fun. Therefore arrange to live in someone else's restored house while you're working on your own.
It would be very difficult to overemphasize
the despair generated by living in a house
which has a fine layer of plaster dust over
everything. Few people enjoy shaking fine
powder from their pillows each night or
blowing dust out of the bristles of their
toothbrushes in the morning. Sitting down to
dinner among saws, ladders, and paint brushes
soaking in turpentine is unappetizing and
demoralizing. To be able to leave the chaos
of construction behind you at the end of the
work day is invaluable to mental well-being.

At long last — a bedroom free of plaster dust!

Although it took many hours of hard work to remove paint from this
carved mantel, the result was worth the effort.

B EFORE YOU BUY that house with all the detail, you must understand the formula for
determining how much time each task will take
and how much it will cost. The arithmetic is
quite simple. After you decide the absolute
maximum amount of time a job <u>should</u> take,
multiply this number by two <u>and add</u> three
months. This new figure will be fairly
accurate if all goes well. To determine how
much a project will cost, multiply the absolute maximum you think it should cost by
three. This amount will be close if you cut
out all extras and allow for inflation.

YOU MUST DETERMINE exactly what standards of
workmanship your partner demands in advance,
because, after you buy, it will be too late.
A good test is to gauge his or her reaction to
<u>The</u> <u>Old-House</u> <u>Journal</u>. If he or she scoffs at
the techniques of the OHJ editors and accuses
them of being hacks and renovators, then, for
the sake of your sanity, put your foot down
and insist on buying that maintenance-free
condo. Otherwise, you'll be a slave to a
master of perfection. If your partner also
harbors a secret desire to have your house
profiled in <u>Architectural</u> <u>Digest</u> magazine
someday, beware, beware.

I F NOTHING I'VE SAID thus far has deterred
  you from your dream of restoring an old
house in the city, let's talk about the
neighborhoods in which old houses are most
often found. There's a very good reason why
so many inner-city houses are in disrepair.
Poor people have owned these houses ever since
the affluent fled to the suburbs decades ago.
They've struggled to keep the houses from
collapsing, but few have been successful.

Though it's not the Sistine Chapel, Greg is very proud of his parlor and the ceiling he painted himself.

THE FEW FRIENDS who do visit will leave firmly convinced you've gone off the deep end. They will never be able to understand why you have hours to devote to scraping paint from egg-and-dart moulding, but no time at all to tighten the windows to keep out the cold air. They'll be equally puzzled that you bought new chandeliers but you're not concerned at all that your stove has only one working burner. How can they understand that you're too busy stripping paint-encrusted plaster to cook?

COOKING WILL BE only one of many activities that you no longer have time for. Reading will be limited to the backs of paint cans. Your gym membership need not be renewed -- who needs aerobics after wrestling with scaffold-ing? There will be no winter trips to Jamaica; the cost of eight days in Negril will almost pay for a new roof.

WHY, IN THE LIGHT of such harsh realities, do people buy and restore houses in tran-sitional neighborhoods? Several reasons come to mind. Some of us are masochists who enjoy the pain of it all. Many of us are martyrs: We present our friends only with the finished product, never relating the blood, sweat, and tears we've put into the restoration.

ALSO, RESTORING an old house tests your per-sonal mettle as well as the mettle of your relationship. If your relationship can withstand the rigors of restoration, then it is truly made in heaven. And someday, at long last, the house will be completely restored, right down to the last walnut baluster and brass hinge. Then, if you don't hit your mate over the head with an andiron when he or she says, "Okay, now let's sell it and buy another one," you'll be nominated for canonization.

ANYONE WHO WOULD BUY a house in one of these neighborhoods by choice, not necessity, is not poor -- at least not in the beginning. You need not feel guilty about being middle-class among the poor. Once you've bought your house and take on the struggle to keep it from col-lapsing, you'll soon become a poor person yourself. Being a poor person among other poor people will probably be the only way you'll feel at home in your new neighborhood. It's not unlikely that you will be the only person of your race, ethnicity, educational background, and possibly sexual preference on your block. This can be culturally enriching if you enjoy new experiences.

IF YOU FEEL the slightest reluctance to insist politely but firmly that your stoop can no longer be used for drug trafficking, you should look elsewhere for a home. You must also be able to turn a deaf ear to the lady who tearfully explains that removing an old mattress from your backyard will deprive her of her livelihood. I won't suggest you should be heartless enough to kick the homeless from your foyer on nights when the temperature is sub-zero, but you must insist they leave long enough to answer nature's call.

YOUR NEIGHBORS have been trying to get the hell out of the area for years, so don't be surprised that they think you're crazy to move in. This attitude will also be prevalent among your friends and family. However, they will show less tact in expressing their opin-ions. Be prepared to hear, over and over again, "You moved WHERE!?!" Don't be offended when no one comes to visit you. Your parents will never set foot in your neighborhood, much less your house. Your home will be inacces-sible to friends who don't own cars. How can you let them walk alone from the subway?

If you're working on an old wood house, you're eventually going to have to do some stripping outside. Maybe it's just a door or a few porch balusters that need the paint taken off. But if every clapboard is thick with alligatored paint, how would you proceed? Here we explain *when* to strip and *how* to do it.

by Patricia Poore

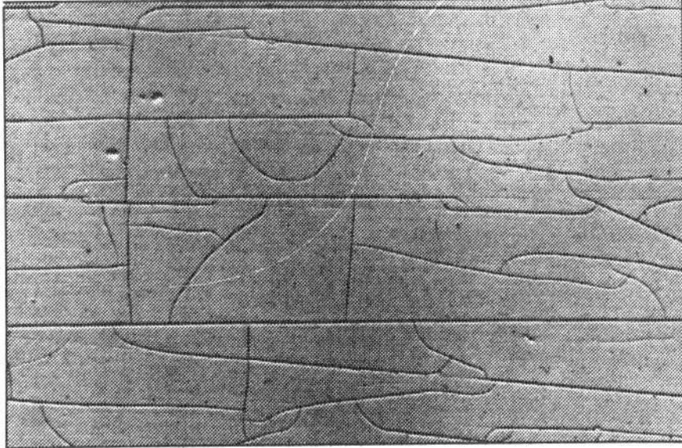

Crazed, alligatored, and blistering paint.

Stripping Paint from Exterior Wood

TAKING PAINT off exterior masonry is an all-or-nothing proposition -- you strip all the paint off to expose the masonry. Not so with exterior wood. Even when you intend to repaint, old paint may have to be stripped off in some areas. And the methods and materials for stripping wood are somewhat different from those used to strip masonry.

BEFORE YOU PICK a stripping method, take a good look at all the parts of the building. What's the problem, and what is the extent of paint failure? Inspect to determine:

● What is the underlying material? If you own a simple clapboarded farmhouse, it isn't hard to tell which parts are made of wood. But complex late Victorian or early 20th century buildings can fool you. Some elements may actually be made of stucco, metal, or terra cotta. These would require different stripping methods.

● What kinds of paint failure exist in various areas? Many places won't require stripping. The siding may be fine (just dirty). Yet the eaves may be peeling and the balusters on the porch caked with alligatored paint. An essentially sound but worn painted surface needs only washing and a topcoat. Failure of the top layers calls for limited paint removal before repainting. Only substantial failure throughout paint layers or down to the wood calls for total paint removal.

Limited Removal

A COMMON KIND of paint failure is intercoat peeling, where layers on top are peeling away from paint underneath. This condition is usually caused by bad preparation in the past coming back to haunt you: Maybe paint was laid on a dirty surface and now the bond is failing. It can also be caused by incompatibility of paint types. You don't necessarily have to strip to bare wood in these cases. Just scrape the surface to sound paint; wash it thoroughly to remove dirt and paint chalking; wipe it dry; and sand it lightly. Prime the area with an oil or alkyd exterior primer.

CRAZING OR CRACKING of the upper layers of paint should be taken care of now, as it will worsen to alligatoring: deep cracking down to bare wood. And that condition would call for complete removal. Sand the surface by hand or mechanically, just down to sound paint.

Down to Bare Wood

HOW DO YOU KNOW if you need to totally strip the paint? Don't count paint layers; look for obvious signs of failure and "ugliness." Is the paint peeling, splitting, alligatoring, flaking, chipping, blistering, and loose? Are all the edges and details blurred and fat?

WHERE PAINT IS PEELING down to bare wood, a moisture problem is probably to blame. Find the cause and correct it or the wall will peel again. Moisture may be coming from a humid interior if you've tightened the house but the walls have no vapor barrier. It may be coming from outside because of rain splashback, inadequate or clogged gutters, or a roof leak.

EVEN IF paint problems -- here and there or all over -- require stripping the paint down to bare wood, you may not have to strip the whole house. That's a job to avoid if you can.

IF DOORS, shutters, or windows are inoperable because of a thick paint buildup, strip only those areas down to bare wood. If new wood is

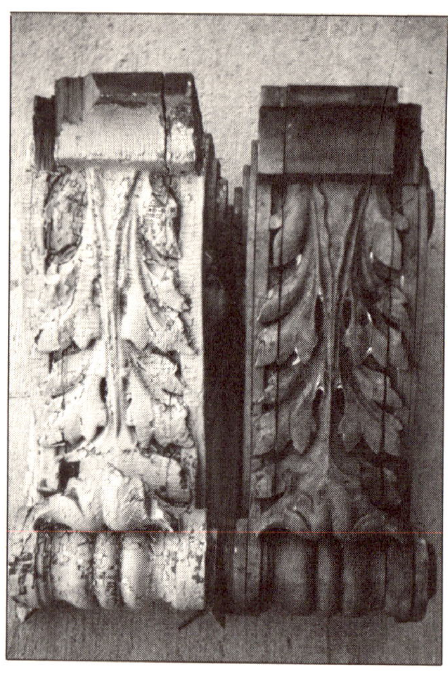

Thick, alligatored paint build-up on these porch balusters must be removed before repainting.

Stripping with chemicals removed the paint without damage.

Stripping the bracket not only uncovered crisp detail, but lets you see better for repairs.

being pieced in and will be painted, the area surrounding the patch has to be stripped so that there will be a smooth transition between the old and the new.

HINT: Most exterior trim should be stripped in place. Shutters are usually an exception, because they're easy to remove and a pain to strip -- dip them. Doors and other trim pieces may be an exception, but think twice: Will you really save time? You have to dis-assemble or detach the pieces, transport them, pick them up, and re-install.

Biting the Bullet

IF THE PAINT BUILD-UP is extreme and the problems past simple scraping, don't deny the inevitable. Painting over problems is doomed to failure and will cost extra in the long run. At this point, you'll just have to realize that it's not a paint job you have on your hands. You have a major exterior resto-ration coming up. That happens every 75 or 100 years, and you pulled the short straw. It will be time-consuming and expensive, but once it's done, the house will look a lot better and the next paint job will be a breeze.

IF IT TURNS OUT that you do have to totally strip most of the exterior, there is an al-ternative to the mess and expense of doing it all at once. As paint fails, it will "self-strip" a little at a time. Why not scrape, prime, and paint only the bad areas each spring? Or, starting with the worst side, strip (then prime and paint) just one side of the house each year for the next four years. As long as you prime and paint bare spots, nothing bad will happen if you don't do the whole job at once.

IN THE MEANTIME, will the house look like hell? Only up close. Remember: It's an old house and maintenance is a process. Do the worst side or the worst patches; next paint job, do others. Whenever you can get away with it, do only the problem areas. But wherever you <u>do</u> strip, do it right. Take it down to a <u>sound</u> substrate, then sand it, prime it, and paint it.

IF EXTREME PAINT FAILURE exists all over the exterior, you may prefer to strip it all at once. Stripping a large house in one sea-son is going to require a crew; you'll proba-bly hire a contractor. Various stripping methods are described in the following pages.

REMOVING <u>ALL</u> THE PAINT from an old house is not well regarded these days. Technologists are wary of techniques such as chemical strip-ping and sandblasting because of the irrever-sible damage they can cause. Preservation-ists, including many decision-makers in the SHPO and National Register offices, condemn the like-new appearance of a stripped house as well as the removal of historic coatings.

WHEN YOU STRIP an old house clean, you're making it impossible for anyone in the future to investigate original paint colors or any-thing else about the decorative history of the exterior. Always leave inconspicuous areas unstripped for future reference -- on the siding, on the porch ceiling, on the window trim. Mark each sample off or cover it with a metal plate. Don't add any more paint to it.

The D-I-Y Decision

A CAUTION for do-it-yourselfers: Exterior stripping can become unmanageable. It's a different animal from interior strip-ping. Factor in the greater expanses to cover, the heights, the changing weather and seasons. You can get hurt, too: The tools are heavy and sharp, the old paint contains lead, and much of the work is done two or three storeys above the ground.

STRIPPING SAFETY

Always wear goggles. Experience has probably taught you that flying paint chips are very sharp. And it's hard to describe the panic you feel as you run to a sink, stripper in your eye.

Have fire extinguishers and plenty of water near each worker. The water can be used for chemical spills as well as to put out fires.

Wear rubber gloves with chemicals, heavy work gloves with heat.

Tidy up often. Know where things are. Don't track sludge around. Watch for slippery drips, especially on ladders and scaffolds.

Contrast the picture at left with the charring committed by a blow-torch, above.

Bix exterior stripping formula was used to strip paint from wood columns on a 1794 Vermont house.

IF YOU'RE FUSSY, doing it yourself may be the only way to get it done right. But keep in mind that contractors already have experience, skill, materials, equipment, scaffolding -- and they can better estimate the time needed. The right contractors will even know about restrictions and waste disposal.

HINT: If you're doing the whole job without a big crew, do just one side of the house at a time. Strip, prime, and paint before going on to the next side. Two good reasons: (1) You don't have to move the scaffold back and forth; (2) You get the psychological reward of seeing something finished before proceeding with still more grunt work.

Tried-and-True Stripping Methods

THE MOST COMMON METHODS for exterior-paint removal aren't too different from those you use to strip interior woodwork. But the tools are bigger, heavier, and faster. The familiar methods described below are what most homeowners use. In fact, the simple, common techniques are used even by painting contractors.

ABRASIVE METHODS: These can be manual (scraping and sanding) or mechanical. Sometimes a very sharp, wide scraper can be used to remove paint to bare wood, but most often abrasive methods are used to remove only the loose paint. Use an orbital sander for finishing or smoothing. (It's good for feathering the edges between stripped wood and surrounding paint layers.) A belt sander works fast, so it can cause damage fast. It should be used by a skilled operator.

SAFETY HAZARDS associated with abrasive methods are eye damage and inhalation or ingestion of dust that contains lead and other toxins. You should always wear a dust mask and goggles when sanding.

HINT: When hand-sanding to remove paint, don't tear at it with lots of muscle. Instead, get three or four sandpaper grits, from open-coat 50 up to medium-fine 180 or so. Take a few swipes with the 50, then move through the grits to the finer papers. It'll go faster, you won't clog the medium and fine papers as often, and you don't need any muscle.

HEAT METHODS: Torches or any kind of open flame are out of the question. Even if you don't burn the house down (a distinct possibility with plenty of precedents), an open flame will char the wood. The heat gun works, but has several disadvantages outdoors. It's too heavy to hold at a vertical surface all day, especially if you're on a ladder. It heats up only a few square inches at a time, which gives you commendable control on interior woodwork but will drive you crazy when you've got a whole side of the house to cover. Also, it blows hot air, so there is a small possibility that it could heat combustibles (like a bird's nest) hidden in hollow spaces. Save the heat gun for solid wood on porches.

ALL IN ALL, the most practical heat tool to use outdoors is a heat plate. It doesn't blow hot air, it isn't heavy, it heats up the width of a clapboard all at once, and it works quite effectively on thick paint build-up. Use it with a scraper for total paint removal, followed by a quick sanding before priming.

CHEMICAL METHODS: When used outdoors, hardware-store chemical strippers are generally

Here's the wholesale approach in progress. A workman rinses effluent from clapboards that had been coated with chemical stripper.

NOW TELL US HOW TO DO IT!

Researching this article was difficult — no one claims any expertise. We came upon a chemicals-manufacturer who's being sued for a job that went sour (he claims it was the applicator's error); an independent contractor who purposely "forgets" to neutralize caustic-stripped wood if the homeowner's payments are not current (thus dooming the next paint job); and companies that talk clients out of the job, or bid it so high that nobody can afford it. Wood just isn't as predictable as masonry.

We're looking for case histories — successful *and* unsuccessful. We'll pay for information we publish. Please include photos, specifications on materials and how they were used, and notes on the outcome of the job.

less controllable than heat, and the sludge makes a mess for the do-it-yourselfer. But chemical stripping comes in handy for a final cleanup, for very ornamental surfaces that heat might scorch, and for window muntins (heat will break glass). Chemicals have to be used for removing varnish and urethane, as heat is ineffective. And you can use chemicals to create a cold dip-tank for removable items such as shutters and fluted posts.

USE methylene-chloride-based stripper for outdoor items, not lye; lye residues interfere with the adhesion of new paint. Allow the wood to dry thoroughly before priming.

DON'T USE water-rinsable chemical paint strippers outdoors. All that watery sludge is hard to contain. Also, those removers sometimes leave a gummy residue on the wood that you'll have to remove with a solvent. Water-rinsed removers raise the grain more than others, requiring more sanding.

AS YOU STRIP, scrape the sludge into an empty paint can. When the can is full, cap it and dispose of it according to local regulations. The toxic waste in there contains concentrated lead, among other things.

Wholesale Stripping

WITH STRIPPED MASONRY getting more common, readers ask if a similar process can be used to remove all the paint on wooden buildings. Yes; there are contractors willing to completely strip the exterior of a wood building -- using much the same methods that have been used on masonry. Sandblasting, waterblasting, and application of special chemical strippers have all been used to strip clapboards, shingles, and trim down to bare wood.

Bix Process Systems
PO Box 3091, Dept. OHJ
Bethel, CT 06801

Contact: John Schmuecker
(203) 743-3263

Mr. Schmuecker says that caustic (alkaline) strippers are trouble. Even reputable, experienced contractors can follow neutralization procedure only to see paint fail during a humid period years later. Bix recommends solvent-based stripper. Theirs is *Power-Off*, a methylene-chloride formula that needs no neutralizing; can be rinsed with a hose. Won't work in direct sunlight, in wind, or under 50 degrees. It is 25-35% more expensive than caustics.

American Building Restoration
9720 South 6th St., Dept. OHJ
Franklin, WI 53132

Contact: Jack Tadych
(414) 761-2440

800s line of caustics (2-80% solution); average price $8.60/gal. (to contractor). 700s series are methylene-chloride-based, $9-$14/gal. ABR recommends "the old 700F" for wood. Recommend using caustics on thick build-up, then switching to 700 line for last layers of paint. No. 800 — 2% lye stripper recommended for d-i-y homeowners: Alcohol-based and with only 2% caustic, it's relatively safe. Dwell time longer than average.

Diedrich Chemicals
300 A East Oak St., Dept. OHJC
Oak Creek, WI 53154

Contact: Larry Kotke
(414) 764-0058

For wood buildings: 606 and thicker 606X products. Potassium-hydroxide-based, so proper rinsing, neutralization, drying must be carried out. (Stripper releases natural tannic acid content in cedar, redwood, and cypress — can be overcome with special neutralization and extra-long drying time.) Diedrich 505 Special Coating Stripper is methylene-chloride-based; because of expense, recommended only for enamels, epoxies, etc.

ProSoCo
PO Box 1578, Dept. OHJ
Kansas City, KS 66117

Homeowner inquiries discouraged

For wood, their Heavy-Duty Paint Stripper (a caustic) works for thick build-up. Company recommends using the caustic only until wood starts to be visible, then switching to solvent-based 509. Neutralization still needed, but less chance that caustic will have soaked into wood. Caustic, $22-25/gal.; no. 509, $28-31/gal., and gives less coverage.

This South Carolina church looks pretty good after stripping . . .

. . . until you get close. Sandblasting left behind wood that has in effect undergone accelerated weathering. Experts believe that pitted, roughened wood like this will deteriorate much more rapidly than normal.

SANDBLASTING does not destroy wood in the same way it can destroy masonry. Still, it is not generally recommended. Old wooden houses are "loose" and the sand is often forced through walls and into the interior. Dry sandblasting creates dust that obscures the surface being blasted, which can leave pitted wood. (Wet-blasting wood has its own obvious drawbacks.) Wood is not a homogeneous material: It has harder and softer fibers in the grain. Blasting leaves an unevenly eroded surface reminiscent of the fake wood grain in vinyl siding. Blasting leaves some woods with a fuzzy surface. And, of course, it blurs edges and details. We <u>have</u> seen acceptable sandblasting jobs, usually the result of a hand-picked contractor who took his time. In one notable case, an acceptable outcome was produced when the homeowners hand-sanded every first-storey clapboard after blasting.

SOME CONTRACTORS now accomplish all-over stripping with chemicals specifically formulated for use outdoors. This is a developing technology, worth exploring though even the chemical manufacturers seem hesitant to recommend this method for wood. The problem is neutralization: Wood absorbs the chemicals and that can lead to subsequent paint failure. In particular, caustic formulations (lye, etc.) are very tricky to neutralize. If they are not completely neutralized and rinsed, the wood will continue to self-strip any new paint.

METHYLENE-CHLORIDE-BASED formulations are available, but they're expensive. The material itself is costly to use on such a large job as the exterior of a house. Also, these chemicals are quite volatile; the stuff evaporates quickly outdoors, so it has to be reapplied frequently.

RINSING OFF the chemical sludge creates problems of its own. If the water pressure is too high, the damage is similar to that of sand-blasting. Also, it's always risky to throw that much water at a wood building. It may get inside, causing water damage to plaster and interior finishes. If there's any side-wall insulation, it'll probably get wet. That much water in walls and wood creates swelling and, if it's trapped, could even lead to wood rot, mildew, and failure of the new paint.

ALL OF THESE scary scenarios should convince you that whole-house stripping is not an easy proposition. Avoid it if you can. If you must remove all the paint quickly, you need to pick an experienced contractor who will:

● inspect the building first, taking precautions to mask and caulk where necessary;
● use specially formulated, tested chemicals;
● neutralize and rinse properly without high water pressures/volumes; and,
● contain the effluent. Local authorities are becoming stricter about what goes into town sewers -- you may be slapped with a $500 (or higher) fine if your contractor hasn't made arrangements to contain and haul the runoff.

IT'S A MORAL ISSUE, too. In my article on masonry stripping back in January, I stated that the effluent was a toxic waste and should be contained. Letters in response showed that my comments weren't popular with contractors, who claim that "nobody contains the runoff" and "it's too expensive to haul away" and "it's an insignificant amount of waste."

THE DECISION IS YOURS, but here are some facts to help you make it: (1) The effluent that comes off a stripped building contains lead, as well as various solvents from both the paint itself and the heavy-duty stripping chemicals. (2) The amount of sludge that comes off a big, thickly-painted two- or three-storey house is hardly insignificant. (3) The homeowner and/or the architect can be held responsible for fines, damage, and suits.

What Goes Up, Should Stay There!

HOW MANY TIMES HAVE YOU been working on a roof and had a tool slide down and over the edge? It took me many trips up and down the ladder before I finally decided to solve this problem. After a bit of experimentation, I finally devised a platform that holds tools level regardless of roof pitch.

CUT TWO PIECES of 1/2-in. plywood, 3 feet long and 1 foot wider than the width of your extension ladder. Drill a series of 1/2-in. holes six inches in from each side along the length of one of the pieces. Attach a 2x4 cut to the length of a ladder rung to the back of the top edge of this piece. Notch the underside of the 2x4 so the ladder rung will fit into it.

NEXT, ATTACH THE TWO PIECES of plywood together at their top edges with a piano hinge. Then, hinge two pieces of 2x4 to the bottom of the undrilled piece of plywood, and attach a 1-in. dowel between them.

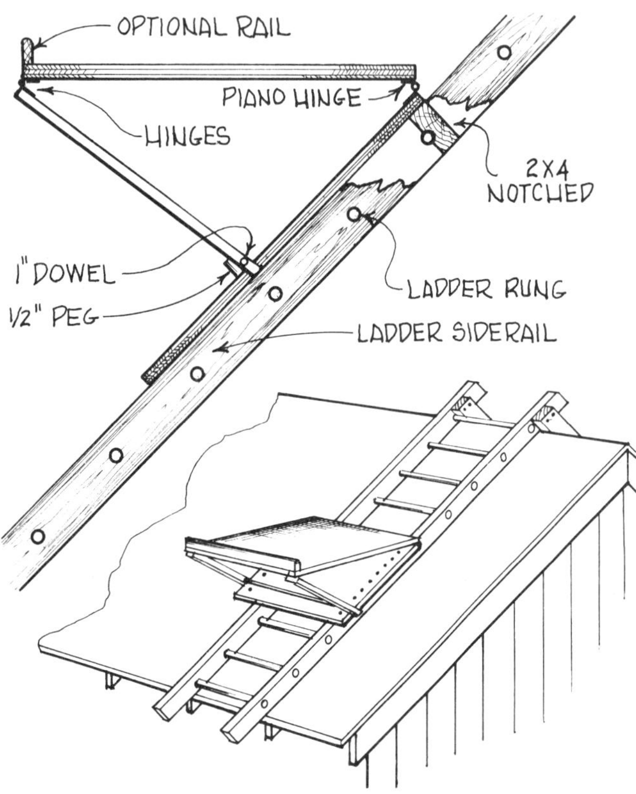

TO USE THE PLATFORM, hook the extension ladder over the peak of the roof and rest the notched 2x4 over a rung. Lift the top piece of plywood until it's level. Hold the piece in place by inserting a couple of 2-in.-long dowels into the predrilled holes in the bottom piece of plywood. The 1-in. dowel will rest against the small pegs, holding the platform in place.

W.A. Rolke
Columbus, Ind.

Pesti-Strip

I RECENTLY HAD TO REMOVE many layers of shellac from every piece of woodwork in my house. I scrubbed the gummy mess off with steel wool dipped in denatured alcohol. This was a terribly messy process; the steel wool dripped alcohol all over the floor, and the dry weather caused rapid evaporation of the solvent.

I SOLVED THESE PROBLEMS by putting the alcohol in a plastic spray bottle (the kind you might use to mist your house plants). Now I can apply just as much alcohol as I need without drips, spills, or excessive fumes. I still use the bottle to mist plants, too! I've found that a gentle mist of denatured alcohol kills the mealy bugs that feed on my porch plants.

Donna Presnell
New Haven, Conn.

Candle Controversy Continues

YOUR AUGUST/SEPTEMBER 1985 issue included a reader tip concerning the vexing problem of cleaning wax-encrusted candlesticks. I've found that this annoyance can be largely avoided by storing your candles in a freezer. The candles seem to burn slower and drip less wax.

Lucille A. Cook
Gilmanton, N.H.

THE IDEA OF USING A HEAT GUN to remove wax from candlesticks (Aug./Sept. '85) is indeed ingenious. However, there is an equally simple way for those of us who do not possess a heat gun.

BOIL WATER IN A LARGE POT, immerse the candlesticks, and remove the pot from the stove. Allow to soak until the water has completely cooled and a film of solidified wax has formed on the surface. Skim off the wax, remove the candlesticks, and clean and polish as usual. This works especially well on really ornate candlesticks where wax works its way deep into crevices. Large candelabras can be done in sections.

Susan Parrott
Philadelphia, Penn.

Tips To Share? Do you have any hints or short cuts that might help other old-house owners? We'll pay $15 for any short how-to items that are used in this "Restorer's Notebook" column. Write to Notebook Editor, The Old-House Journal, 69A Seventh Avenue, Brooklyn, NY 11217.

MAKING PHOTOS LAST

... and bringing back the old ones

by Walter Jowers

WE OLD-HOUSE DWELLERS have a strong attraction to images of the past: Our houses are images of the past, carefully rescued and given life in the present. And much of the attraction is visual; when we speak of the scale, warmth, charm, and detail of an old house, we're talking about visual impressions. We fuss over colors, shop for antiques -- mostly to please our eyes. So it makes sense that a lot of us enjoy looking at or taking photographs. Old-house owners have been known to go to great lengths to find an original-condition picture of their house. And most of us have a photo album full of before-and-after pictures which we can't wait to show off.

BUT, PROUD AS WE ARE of the care we've taken with our old house, as much as we covet that original-condition picture, as much as we enjoy the before-and-after shots, most of us have little or no idea how to take care of the old -- or the new -- pictures.

WHERE DO YOU KEEP your special photographs? Are they stuffed into a box in the attic? Or in the basement? Are they in a desk drawer, or framed and displayed in a nice sunny room? If you have photographs stored in any of these places, the images are fading away faster than they have to.

PHOTOGRAPHIC MATERIALS are remarkably stable; with a little care, they will last for generations. A properly processed and stored black-and-white negative or print could last for hundreds of years.

IF YOU WANT the images that are important to you to survive as long as your house -- if you want them to survive as long as you -- here are some things you should know....

What Not To Do

MOST PHOTOGRAPHIC MATERIALS consist of a support material (film base* for negatives; paper for prints) and an emulsion layer of gelatin in which the photographic image is suspended. Film base, paper, and gelatin are all water-permeable;

---

*Some pre-1950 negatives can have a cellulose-nitrate film base. This film base deteriorates quickly; in advanced stages of decomposition, it can be extremely flammable. Many experts believe that nitrate-base negatives should be copied and then destroyed. (Deteriorating nitrate negatives can also damage other negatives that are stored with them.) A decomposed nitrate-base film is recognizable by its acrid odor — any film labeled 'safety film' is not nitrate-base film.

this makes the photographic material susceptible to attack by moisture. High temperatures are also a problem: Detrimental chemical reactions, caused by residual processing chemicals in the photograph, are accelerated by heat. If a photo gets sufficiently hot and damp, fungus can grow in the gelatin emulsion, destroying the image.

THAT'S WHY hot attics are bad places to store photos -- and damp basements are even worse. But it isn't difficult to arrange proper storage conditions for your photos. The

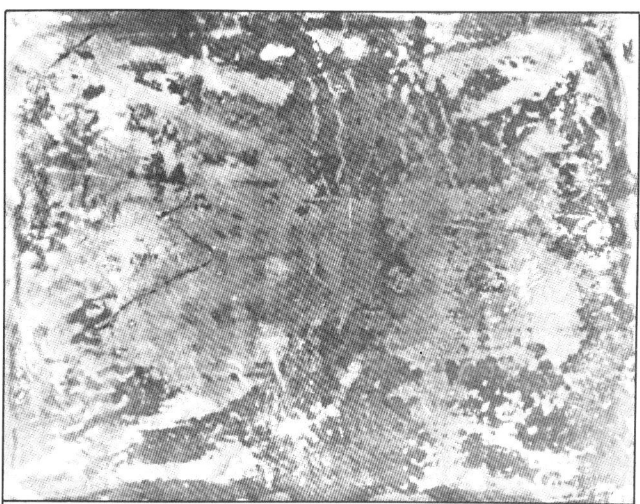

Above: Lost under the layers of tarnish on this early daguerrotype is a view of Providence, Rhode Island.
Below: A careful cleaning has removed all the tarnish. (Unfortunately, you can't clean away the scratches.)

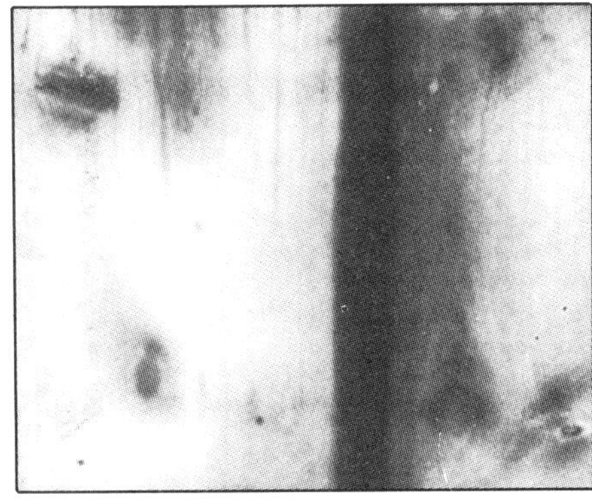

Above: This is the back of a cardboard mount which has been touching a sheet of plywood for years. Materials from the wood migrated to the cardboard, producing this stain pattern.
Right: There's no way to repair the havoc fungus has wrought on the negative of this print.

temperature should be 75 degrees Fahrenheit or less; the relative humidity, 20% to 60%. Keep your negatives and prints in the living area of your house -- if you're comfortable, they will be, too.

Above: Even a print as badly faded as this one can be saved ...
Below: ... by copying it with a high-contrast, continuous-tone film and developing the negative.

BOXES OF WOOD OR CARDBOARD are poor containers for photo materials. Wood and wood products, such as plywood and chipboard, contain volatile substances that stain and fade photos. Drawers with plywood bottoms are particularly bad places for storing photographs. Cardboard boxes put together with glue and tape also give off damaging chemical compounds. (Specially made cardboard boxes are available for photo storage, and these are okay.) The best storage boxes are enameled steel, stainless steel, or anodized aluminum.

ALUMINUM FRAMES ARE BETTER for your photographs than wood frames. But this presents a particular problem for many old-house owners: Aluminum picture frames in a room full of antiques? Solution: Don't put rare, one-of-a-kind photographs in a wood frame. Have a duplicate made of the rare photo, and put _it_ in the wood frame. (There'll be more on duplicating later in the article.) You should also replace a plywood frame backing with a sheet of high-quality photo mounting board. And use a matte -- if the photo is pressed up against glass, the gelatin could stick to it under humid conditions.

PHOTOGRAPHIC MATERIALS should not be stacked and then placed under pressure. Residual processing chemicals in one negative or print could migrate to adjacent photos and damage them. So even if you're using a box that can safely contain photos, don't stuff them all in as if you were packing an undersized suitcase.

FEW THINGS ARE WORSE for a photograph than to be sandwiched between glue and plastic, and yet this is precisely what many modern photo albums do. Old-style photo albums, with paper pages and corner tabs to hold the photos in place, aren't perfect, but they are decidedly better than the glue-and-plastic types. A nearly perfect photo album can be made up from acid-free, pre-punched binder pages available from Technical Library Association (TALAS).

IDEALLY, prints should be stored interleaved with acid-free paper, cellulose acetate, or polyethylene dividers. These materials are available from custom photo shops or shops that cater to professional photographers. Negatives should _always_ be stored in sleeves or bags made of one of these materials.

PRINTS, especially color prints, should not be displayed in areas where they will suffer prolonged exposure to direct sunlight or fluorescent light. Black-and-white photographs will yellow under these conditions; color prints left in bright sun will fade to nothingness in a very short time. As a general rule of thumb, don't display your prints anywhere that you wouldn't display an antique floral sofa.

What About Color?

BLACK-AND-WHITE photographic images are made up of particles of pure metallic silver, and so black-and-white negatives and prints, properly processed and properly stored, can last indefinitely. Color negatives, prints, and slides contain unstable dyes, and fade noticeably in just a few years. It doesn't matter if it's your wedding picture and you paid $300 for it -- if it's color, most of the detail will be gone within a few dozen years. If you want to make permanent photographic records of an important event, shoot the photos in black and white. If you want color prints to show your friends and relatives, shoot those too, but don't consider them a permanent record. (NOTE: Color materials can be kept indefinitely under certain tightly controlled conditions; consult Kodak's <u>Storage</u> <u>And</u> <u>Care</u> <u>Of</u> <u>Color</u> <u>Photographs</u>, Kodak publication #E-30.)

FINALLY, what can be done with old, deteriorated negatives or prints? More than you might think. Old, stained prints can be rephotographed through an optical filter, eliminating the stain from the new print. Faded prints can be reshot on very high contrast paper, and the new print can be remarkably

Above: This print was made from a stained negative. The damage is most clearly visible in the sky at the top center, and in the extreme right-hand side of the photo.
Below: After its stains were chemically removed, the negative yielded this quality print.

clear. Scratched photographs can be retouched to restore lost detail. And badly deteriorated negatives or prints can sometimes be restored by cleaning or retouching. Restoration work (especially of negatives) is sometimes risky, usually complicated, and almost always expensive; it should be done only by a competent professional. Check local custom photo labs (and their references) to find someone who can do this type of work.

Getting The Full Picture

Two books used as sources for this article deal specifically with the care of photographic materials. Kodak's *Preservation of Photographs* discusses the physical make-up of negatives and prints; what causes them to deteriorate; and what can be done to slow the deterioration. One chapter explains how to process new photos for maximum stability. A two-page section on how to identify old materials (daguerrotypes, tintypes, etc.) is helpful for answering the question: What *is* this thing in the funky old frame?

AASLH's *Collection, Use, and Care of Historical Photographs* is divided into two parts. The first deals with the problems of collecting and cataloging historic photos — information useful to museum curators. The second half of the book discusses the care of photographic materials. An appendix gives sources for hard-to-find items: acid-free mounting boards; storage sleeves.

The Kodak book is a paperback; the AASLH book, hardbound. Both are well illustrated. For their current prices (and a list of other publications), write:

Eastman Kodak Company
Rochester, NY 14650

American Association for State and Local History
1400 Eighth Avenue South
Nashville, TN 37203

TALAS (213 West 35 Street, New York, NY 10001) handles Hollinger 'Permalife' negative envelopes, acid-free mounting boards, and storage boxes. Pre-punched acid-free pages for 3-ring binders, which make a fine, safe photo album, are also available. Minimum order, $3.

Well, winter is here again. Still don't have the old house tightened up to seal out the cold north wind? We've found a way to temporarily weather-seal loose windows, glass, and other cracks: UGL Removable Caulk. The clear caulk seals out moisture, drafts, and dust until you can make permanent repairs. Best of all, you can remove it without damaging the surface it's applied to, which means you can use it indoors (instead of sealing from a tall ladder outdoors). We don't advise applying the caulk to delicate old wallpapers, but we've applied and removed it from painted wood and found that it doesn't pull off the paint or leave stains.

The caulk comes in tubes and is applied with a caulking gun. It's easier to remove when left in a bead rather than smoothed out. One tube will do four average windows and sells for about $3.95 at building-supply stores nationwide. For more information contact **United Gilsonite Laboratories, Dept. OHJ, P.O. Box 70, Scranton, PA 18501.**

Seasons Greetings

Have a big list of hard-to-find old-house parts? You need the new 1986 Old-House Journal Catalog.

Iron Snowguards

We are happy to announce a source for hard-to-find snowguards. Ray Zeleny of Windy Hill Forge hand casts these reproductions for use along roof edges and above entry ways. The cast-iron guards come in several shapes: fan, $8; acorn, $6; eagle, $6; rose, $2.80; and the pipe rail, $5.50. The guards vary in height from 2 in. to about 4 in. The ornament is mounted onto a steel, L-shaped bracket designed to be nailed or better still, screwed, into the roof sheathing. The shingles are relaid over the top of the bracket to prevent leaks.

If you're installing snowguards, we suggest you consider putting down a waterproofing course such as the Ice & Water Shield by W.R. Grace as well (see RP Aug./Sept. 84). When reroofing, the waterproofing is laid along the roof edge, before the snowguards are installed. This reduces the chances of ice dams causing roof leaks. Often, the guards are attached in two or more rows in a staggered pattern. The pipe rail forms a continuous fence along the roof edge. Ray supplied the cast brackets — you supply two lengths of 1/2-in. pipe (copper pipe works well).

All of the guards come primed, but we suggest that you apply two more coats of gloss enamel before installation. For a free brochure that also shows decorative cast-iron tie rod ends and shutter hold-backs write to **Windy Hill Forge, Dept. OHJ, 3824 Schroeder Ave., Perry Hall, MD 21118. (301) 256-5890.**

Kitchen Hardware

The Woodworkers' Store has a fine collection of hard-to-find kitchen remodeling supplies nestled into their new woodworking catalog. It's loaded with specialized drawer and cabinet hardware, such as swing-out shelves and racks found only in custom-built kitchens. We were particularly impressed with a fold-out ironing board in a drawer. Previously, this hardware was pretty much unavailable to home owners doing their own kitchen remodeling.

Galvanized

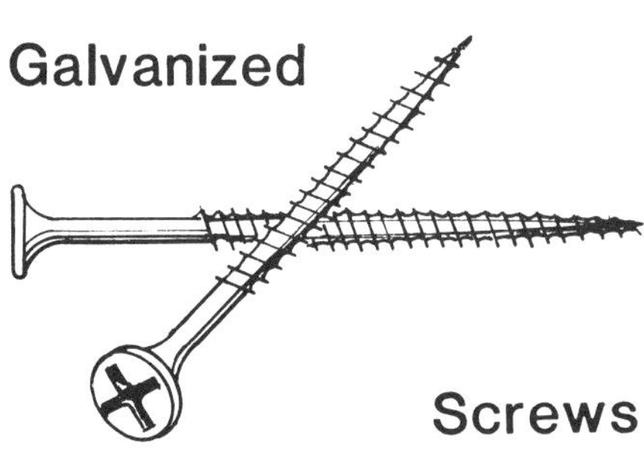

Screws

Weather Challenger is a new type of machine-driven, hardened steel, all-purpose exterior screw made by the Philstone Nail Corp. The screws look like standard, screw-gun driven, drywall screws, but they're galvanized so they can be used outdoors without rusting. The screws were designed for use with pressure-treated lumber and deck building, where fasteners have to resist weathering and the corrosive effects of wood preservatives.

Formerly such galvanized screws were not available because no one could figure out how to coat the extra sharp screws without getting a zinc buildup that either made them hard to drive or that came off when driving. These screws have a mechanically galvanized finish that is very smooth. We tried them out and they drove very well with no predrilling or head stripping.

They have coarse threads for better holding and reduced popping. (Always wear safety goggles when driving them.) They come in 8 sizes (1 in.-4 in.) in bulk cartons or smaller packages. The 8-x-3-in. size we tried comes in 250 count boxes for $16.40 ppd. For more information write **DJ Inc., Dept. OHJ, P.O. Box 825, Brattleboro, VT 05301. (802) 254-6023.**

The Woodworkers' Store also offers a wide variety of unusual books, tools, veneers, pulls, laminates, and finishing supplies — in short everything for building a comfortable, functional kitchen (or anything made of wood). What's more, it's tested and guaranteed. The catalog sells for $1 ($2 for 1st-class mail) from **The Woodworkers' Store, Dept. OHJ, 21801 Industrial Blvd., Rogers, MN 55374. (612) 428-4101.**

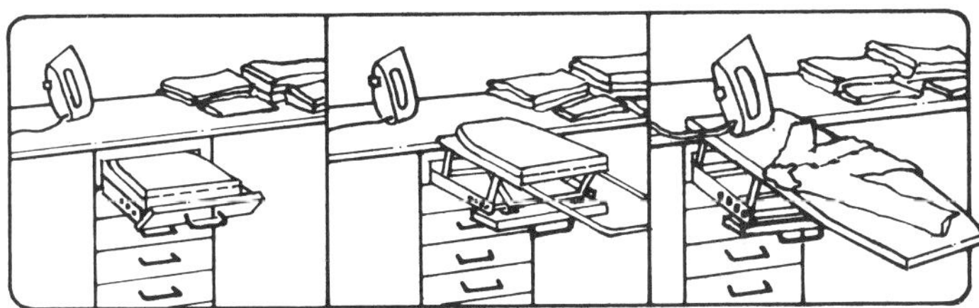

Space Lighter

If you're tired of bumping your head in the dark or having to use a flashlight every time you go into a closet, Black and Decker's Space Light is for you. It's great for old houses because it's designed for use in places where wiring doesn't exist: closets, stairway enclosures, basements, under sinks, in sheds.

The cordless Space Light uses rechargeable storage batteries that hold a charge for up to six months and allow the light to burn for up to two hours.

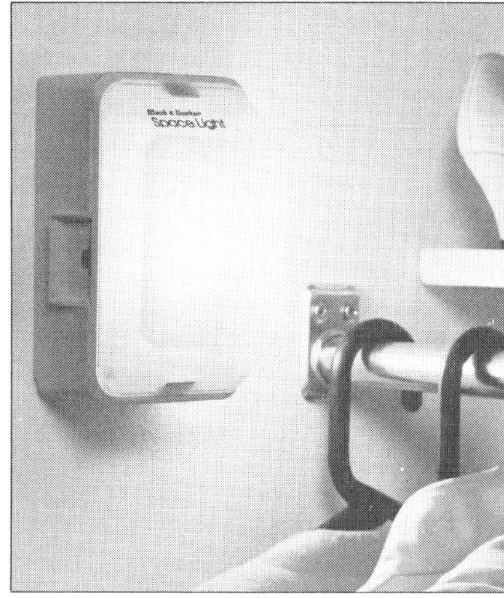

The charger is self-contained in the light case. A bracket allows you to mount the light horizontally or vertically and remove it for portable use. The Space Light is an excellent old-house gift and sells for about $21.99 at local hardware and home-improvement centers.

Cane Supplies

If you're considering any type of caning, rushing, or basketry project, you need Bill Fimpler's new Cane & Basket Supply Catalog. I've never come across such an extensive array of caning supplies, tools, and books for the professional or hobbyist. Best of all those of us who have unknowingly purchased inferior and short-lived cane in the past will appreciate the fact that all of the items sold by this firm have been tried and tested by them.

If you haven't done any recaning, rush seating, or basketry, you will find the catalog full of good tips and suggestions to make your project easier and more enjoyable. They have cane-webbing styles I didn't even know were still available and some I never knew existed.

Copies of the firm's 50th Anniversary Catalog are available for $1 each from Cane & Basket Supply Co., Dept. OHJ, 1283 S. Cochran Ave., Los Angeles, CA 90019. (213) 939-9644.

At a show hosted by the Art Deco Society of New York we came across a firm that sells antique telephones. For over 20 years, the Chicago Old Telephone Co. has been collecting and restoring just about every type of old telephone imaginable. Each one has been carefully and completely restored to work on modern service. Unlike most reproduction phones available today, these instruments were built with great care and the best materials available. You probably can't break or wear one out, but each phone comes with a 1-year warranty. All the parts are authentic from the dial right down to the cord. They come with a 14-ft. modular service cord (fabric or rubber) that plugs into existing outlets.

We were impressed with the rich sculptural quality of these robust old phones. The oldest phone in the brochure is a 1919 Erickson Upright, $279. The rarest is an Art Deco cradle phone, the 1922 Kellogg, $239-$269. The best value is the solid brass 1930 Elite, $119-$149. Our favorite was the Western Electric no. 202, $189, which was the classic Bell Telephone of the Roaring '20s. There's a $5 shipping and insurance charge for each phone.

Send an SASE for a free color brochure. There are lots of options. If you don't see the phone you want, contact them; they have many types not listed in the brochure. They also have publications on the history of telephones showing all the styles. Write to **Chicago Old Telephone Co., Dept. OHJ, P.O. Box 189, Lemon Springs, NC 28355.** (919) 774-6625.

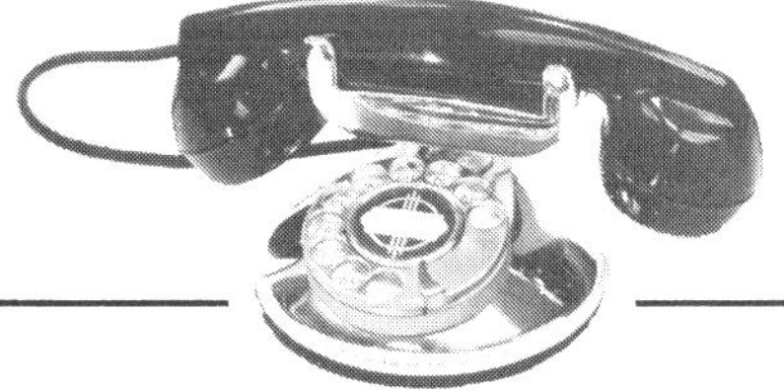

Wood Rack

Vermont Castings offers an attractive and rugged wood box that would look great by the fireplace or stove in any old house. The wood box has a black cast-iron frame with a stained wooden back and bottom. The front is open for easy access. The hand-sculpted frame features shell motifs, latticed fanlight, raised panels, and mouldings finished in glossy black. The box holds 3-1/4 cubic feet of wood and measures 26 in. wide x 16 in. deep x 19-1/2 in. tall. It sells for $140 plus shipping.

If you're considering a wood-burning stove installation, send $4 for the new Vermont Castings Design Portfolio. There's a decorating guide, a techbook for installation planning, a stove clearance template, plus a copy of their owner newsletter. Vermont Castings stands behind their customers — they'll even answer installation questions over the phone. Be sure to send $1 for their catalog of stoves and accessories and a listing of dealers near you. **Vermont Castings, Inc., Dept. OHJ, Prince St., Randolph, VT 05060.** (802) 728-9561.

Gas-Light Parts

In restoring his 1886 brick duplex, OHJ reader Eric W. Jack needed to replace the missing ceramic candles and bobeches on several of the gas chandeliers. He discovered that matching replacement parts for antique gas-lighting fixtures are darn hard to find, so he decided to make his own. Eric developed a technique for producing white ceramic, heat-resistant pieces in several styles, and they look and function just like the originals. If you need similar parts for your gas lights, Eric would like to try making them for you. Write **Eric W. Jack, Dept. OHJ, 2409 Madison Ave., Baltimore, MD 21217.** (301) 669-3992.

Floors *continued from p. 201*

Clean It First!

YOUR FLOORS may simply have "Dirty Wax Buildup." You can remove wax, and all the dirt in the wax, with mineral spirits. Apply it, scrub the floors with a bristle scrub brush or fine steel wool, and wipe with rags. A quick hands-and-knees scrubbing removes all surface grime and gooey deposits. Mineral spirits are quite flammable, so use caution.

YOU CAN ALSO CLEAN your floors with commercially available floor cleaners. The Bruce Company*, for example, makes a good one. Wood-floor cleaner is sold at well-stocked hardware stores. Don't use caustic cleaners; they're essentially weak lye solutions, and may change the color and texture of the wood.

PROPRIETARY CLEANERS like Mex or Spic'n'Span will also clean floors, but they do so by removing some of the floor's finish. If you've tried mineral spirits and a commercial floor cleaner without good results, try giving the floors a good scrubbing with one of these products -- providing they still have a good finish left on them. Never let water stand on your floor; wipe it dry immediately after using any aqueous cleaning solution, or else you'll permanently stain it.

The right side of this photo shows scratches and nicks where traffic passed through a doorway. Some sanding will be necessary here, but the rest of the floor can simply be cleaned.

ONCE THE FLOOR is fairly clean, go back to really troublesome spots with mineral spirits and coarse (#3) steel wool. Scrubbing will lift all but the most stubborn stains.

YOU MAY FIND darkened areas under the old finish. If the offensive spot is localized, try making it less conspicuous by blending the blemish into the surrounding wood with an oil stain. You can adjust the color of a stain by thinning it or varying the amount of time you let it sit on the wood.

---

* Bruce Hardwood Floors, 16803 Dallas Pkwy.
  Dallas, TX 75248. (214) 931-3000.

A thorough scrubbing with steel wool and mineral spirits removes all traces of wax and grease. Return to stubborn stains with coarse steel wool and more mineral spirits.

A LARGE STAIN (around a once-leaking radiator, for example) will have to be bleached out. Brush full-strength bleach onto the darkened area and allow it to work for two minutes. Rinse with a damp terrycloth until you are sure all the bleach is removed. If the bleach changed the color too drastically, choose an appropriate shade of oil stain to blend the area into the surrounding woodwork. Bleaching may raise the grain of some woods, requiring sanding. As always, test this method in an inconspicuous location first.

IF YOUR FLOOR looks pretty good after a thorough cleaning, but still has a few scratches and maybe some dark water spots... so what? The water spots may never come out, and removing all scratches on floors is nearly impossible. Remember that this large expanse of floor will look a lot better with some finish or wax and some furniture on it. Besides, scratches and spots help you decide where to put your rugs.

Selective Sanding

SOME SANDING IS INEVITABLE when restoring a badly worn old floor. Deep scratches, raised grain, and areas where the finish has worn all the way through (allowing staining) need more than cleaning for restoration.

SAND THESE AREAS by hand with a sanding block. Use a belt sander for large areas and especially deep gouges. Don't use rotary sanders on parquet flooring -- they'll leave swirl marks, and they'll dish-out softer woods.

START WITH a medium-grade paper and work your way down to finer papers. Feather out the edges of the area you're working on. That is, don't leave an abrupt line between the area that was sanded and the rest of the floor. Sand with the grain, especially with the coarser papers.

CABINET SCRAPERS ALSO come in handy for re-moving a small amount of material from your floor. Don't use a regular paint scraper, though; you'll end up gouging your floor.

DON'T GET CARRIED AWAY with sanding. Some nicks and stains pene-trate deep into the wood and you'd have to remove a lot of material to get them out. Seek to restore the severely damaged or worn areas up to the level of the adjacent areas, and not beyond. That way you'll be creating an even patina without removing all evidence of age and use. When you think you've done a good enough job, wipe some mineral spirits over the area; that will show you how the wood will look when varnished.

Spruce Up The Finish

AT THIS POINT your floors may look worse than they did when you started. The sanded areas, as well as the spots where you scrubbed out stubborn stains, will appear faded and lusterless. All this can be reme-died with one quick application of varnish.

PREPARATION IS THE KEY to varnishing. Be cer-tain the floor is free of all traces of wax and grease. Then thoroughly vacuum the area. Even a tiny bit of dust and grit would mar the appearance of your floor. After you've vacuum-ed, go over the whole floor with a tack rag.

DON'T USE POLYURETHANE finishes here; they often don't bond well over an existing finish. Use an oil-based varnish. One coat will work wonders, especially if you follow it with a renewable coat of wax.

As you sand, wipe some mineral spirits on the floor now and then to see how it will look after you apply the finish.

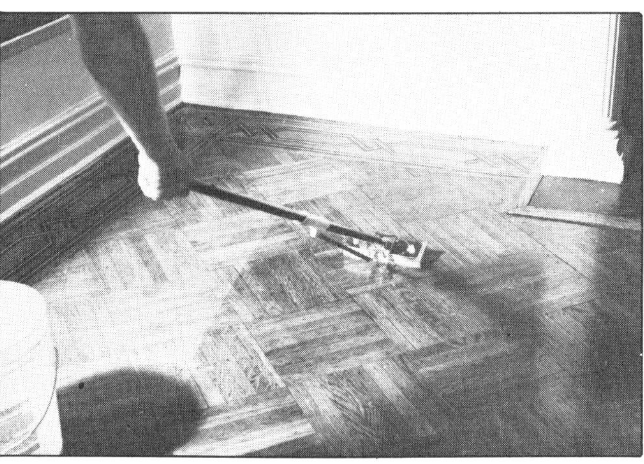

Above: Careful work with a belt sander removes deep scratches. *Below:* New finish is applied over existing one with a sponge mop. The floor retains its patina while gaining luster.

SPOT-PRIME BARE WOOD before varnishing the whole floor, and wait the recommended between-coats time before varnishing the entire floor. You can apply the varnish with a natural-bristle brush. If you're tired of being on your hands and knees, though, a perfectly good alternative is to apply the varnish with a clean, new sponge mop. Remember, you're just trying to add a bit of luster to your antique floors, not finish a mirror-smooth surface. Work methodically to ensure uniform coverage. <u>Pull</u> the mop along gently and steadily to avoid creating bubbles in the varnish.

AFTER YOU CLEAN and varnish your floor, apply a coat of paste wax. Paste wax will protect the varnish from scuffs and spills -- it's a lot easier to renew a layer of wax than a coat of varnish. Trewax is a good brand.

USE A TACK RAG to be sure the surface is free of grit and dust. Put a few tablespoons of wax in a cloth towel, fold the towel over it, and rub the floor until wax comes through the towel. Let the wax dry for five minutes, then polish it with an electric floor polish-er. The wax should fill in the minor imperfections in the fin-ish, <u>not</u> sit as a slippery layer on top of the floor, col-lecting scuff marks.

Beyond Remuddling

ONCE A MID-CENTURY Italianate with Gothic details, this house has now entered a twilight zone that exists beyond remuddling. In fact, for once we can applaud the decision to apply substitute siding; it's the only unifying feature for this agglomeration of architectural shapes. What perplexes us is that big round addition -- a skating rink? ... storage for circus carousels? ... the world's biggest jacuzzi? (Thanks to Cathy Anderson of Shokan, New York, for the photos.) -- CG

The Old-House Journal®

69A Seventh Avenue,
Brooklyn, New York 11217

Postmaster: Address Correction Requested

The Old-House Journal

INDEX

References are to
Month and Page of issue

(B) = Book Review or Literature
    Listing
(L) = Letter
(P) = Product Listing
(RN) = Short Item (Restorer's
    Notebook, Ask OHJ, etc.)

It's finally here — the long-awaited **OHJ Cumulative Index,** providing access to all issues of The Old-House Journal published from October 1973 (Vol. 1, No. 1) through December 1984. This brand-new, 48-page book is your key to over 2,000 pages of restoration know-how. It's available for only $9.95 — or you can receive it FREE if you order the full set of OHJ Yearbooks. See the Order Form in the back to get your copy of **The OHJ Cumulative Index.**

Index To Restoration Products And Companies

IF YOU LOVE
YOUR OLD HOUSE,
YOU SHOULD SUBSCRIBE
TO THE OLD-HOUSE JOURNAL!

THE OLD-HOUSE JOURNAL is the only publication devoted exclusively to the restoration, maintenance, and decoration of old houses. Our plainly-written articles show you practical and economical ways to turn that old house 'with a lot of potential' into the house of your dreams.

The Journal is written and edited by people who have restored old houses themselves. We've learned how to balance history with convenience, lasting quality with a budget. Our first-hand articles concentrate on do-it-yourself procedures that assure good workmanship, yet save you money in the long run. And even if you hire contractors to do the work, you'll know what they're up to — and you'll learn to avoid costly mistakes. The OHJ will teach you to look at your house with an expert's eye.

The Journal is about *sensitive rehabilitation*. It's not about gut-and-strip remodelling — we call it remuddling — that destroys forever the house's antique charm . . . and its tangible evidence of the past.

In each of our no-nonsense issues, you get solid, usable information. Instead of glitzy photos and dopey picture captions, we show step-by-step diagrams, photos that get to the point, and original drawings.

But The Journal isn't *all* nuts and bolts. We feature articles about period interiors, landscaping, and the history of various house styles, too. For example, our ground-breaking series on post-Victorian, early 20th century house styles has received attention nationwide and spawned a soon-to-be-published book. Our 1982 article about Lincrusta-Walton wallcovering — a Victorian imitation of leather — received so much attention among excited readers that the English manufacturer decided to reissue three of the discontinued Victorian patterns. And there's more: free classified ads for current subscribers; *Ask OHJ* — our Q & A column; *Restorer's Notebook* — time-saving and money-saving hints from readers who learned it the hard way.

Whether you're fixing up the old house you love, or simply like reading about old-fashioned quality, we think you'll be delighted by our unique Journal. See the back of this page for more information.

The Old-House Journal

69A Seventh Avenue, Brooklyn, New York 11217
(718) 636-4514

ORDER FORM

The Old-House Journal

Our magazine — published ten times per year — is the only how-to-do-it periodical in America for old-house people. Filled with money-saving, mistake-saving ideas and techniques, *The Old-House Journal* will help you restore, maintain, and decorate your pre-1939 house. Every issue is packed with practical advice, and generously illustrated with drawings, photos, and step-by-step diagrams.

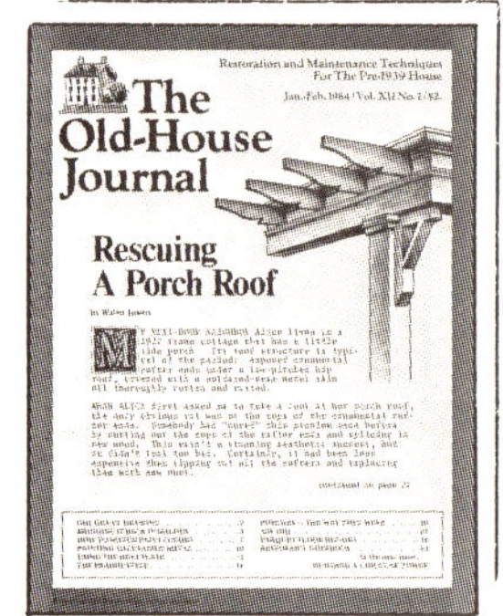

[ ] New Subscription   [ ] Renewal (Enclose Current Mailing Label)

[ ] 1 Year — $18   [ ] 2 Years — $32   [ ] 3 Years — $39

Bound Back Issues
The OHJ Yearbooks

We keep back issues in print, bound in sturdy, softcover books. Our set of 'Yearbooks' is like a Restoration Encyclopedia: the biggest, most complete, most authoritative reference on old-house restoration available anywhere. Over 2,000 pages in all!

700 [ ] **The 1970s Set — $39.00**
1976-1979 at 77% the price. You save $17!

801 [ ] **The 1980s Set — $69.00**
1980-1985 at 64% the price. You save $39!

700-801 INDEX [ ] **The Full Set — $108.00**
All 10 Yearbooks at 66% the price — plus a FREE Cumulative Index. You save $66!

Individual Yearbooks are also available:

76 [ ] 1976 — $14 79 [ ] 1979 — $14 82 [ ] 1982 — $18 85 [ ] 1985 — $18

77 [ ] 1977 — $14 80 [ ] 1980 — $18 83 [ ] 1983 — $18

78 [ ] 1978 — $14 81 [ ] 1981 — $18 84 [ ] 1984 — $18

INDEX [ ] **OHJ Cumulative Index — $9.95**
Your key to all the information that has appeared in OHJ since 1973!

Paint-Stripping Tools

OHJ's staff has tried just about every paint-stripping method known, and these tools are the best at their respective tasks. *The Master Heavy-Duty Heat Gun* is the finest tool around for stripping paint from interior woodwork — mouldings, corners, recesses, turned wood. *The HYDElectric Heat Plate* is the best tool for large jobs such as exterior clapboards, shingles, and flush doors. Both are backed with the OHJ Guarantee: If the tool fails for any reason within 60 days, we'll take it back and replace it.

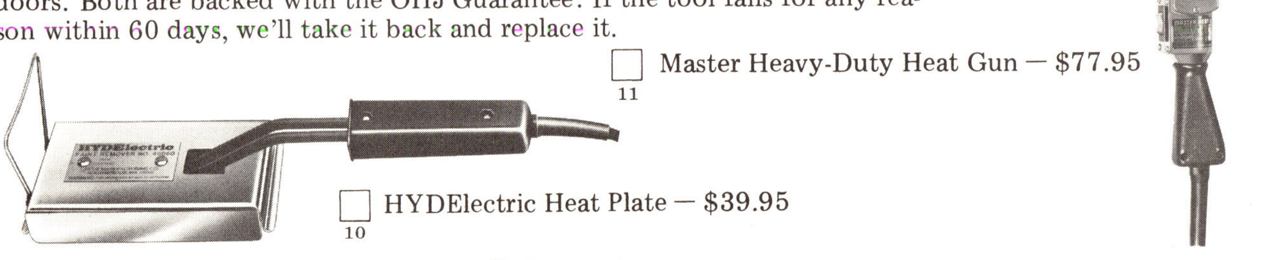

[ ] 11 Master Heavy-Duty Heat Gun — $77.95

[ ] 10 HYDElectric Heat Plate — $39.95

All prices postpaid, and include fast UPS shipping.

Send My Order To:

Name _______________________________________

Address ____________________________________

City _______________ State _______ Zip _______

Amount enclosed: $ _________________________
YBK85   *NY State residents please add applicable sales tax.*

NOTE: If your order includes books or merchandise, you must give us a STREET ADDRESS — not a P.O. Box number. We ship via United Parcel Service (UPS), and they will not deliver to a P.O. Box.

Please clip this page and mail together with check payable to The Old-House Journal to THE OLD-HOUSE JOURNAL, 69A Seventh Avenue, Brooklyn, NY 11217.

Prices valid until Sept. 1, 1986

The OHJ Catalog

[ ] 12 Please send me _______ copies of this invaluable sourcebook, which lists companies supplying almost 10,000 products & services for pre-1939 houses. *The OHJ Buyer's Guide Catalog* is fully cross-referenced & indexed for easy use, so I can find whatever I need to repair, restore, or decorate my old house. ($10.95 ppd. for current OHJ subscribers; $13.95 ppd. for non-subscribers.)